Group Survival in the Ancient Mediterranean

Group Survival in the Ancient Mediterranean

Rethinking Material Conditions in the Landscape of Jews and Christians

Richard Last and Philip A. Harland

LONDON • NEW YORK • OXFORD • NEW DELHI • SYDNEY

T&T CLARK
Bloomsbury Publishing Plc
50 Bedford Square, London, WC1B 3DP, UK
1385 Broadway, New York, NY 10018, USA
29 Earlsfort Terrace, Dublin 2, Ireland

BLOOMSBURY, T&T CLARK and the T&T Clark logo are trademarks of Bloomsbury Publishing Plc

First published in Great Britain 2020
This paperback edition published in 2021

Copyright © Richard Last and Philip A. Harland, 2020

Richard Last and Philip A. Harland have asserted their right under the Copyright, Designs and Patents Act, 1988, to be identified as the Authors of this work.

For legal purposes the Acknowledgements on pp. viii–ix constitute an extension of this copyright page.

Cover design: Charlotte James
Cover image: Portion of fresco from House of the Triclinium (V.2.4), Museo Archeologico Nazionale di Napoli, inv. 120029. Original photo © Roger Viollet.

All rights reserved. No part of this publication may be reproduced or transmitted in any form or by any means, electronic or mechanical, including photocopying, recording, or any information storage or retrieval system, without prior permission in writing from the publishers.

Bloomsbury Publishing Plc does not have any control over, or responsibility for, any third-party websites referred to or in this book. All internet addresses given in this book were correct at the time of going to press. The author and publisher regret any inconvenience caused if addresses have changed or sites have ceased to exist, but can accept no responsibility for any such changes.

A catalogue record for this book is available from the British Library.

Library of Congress Control Number: 2019956620.

ISBN: HB: 978-0-5676-5748-0
      PB: 978-0-5677-0413-9
      ePDF: 978-0-5676-5749-7
      eBook: 978-0-5676-5750-3

Typeset by RefineCatch Limited, Bungay, Suffolk

To find out more about our authors and books visit www.bloomsbury.com and sign up for our newsletters

Contents

List of Figures and Tables		vi
Acknowledgements		viii
Epigraphic and Papyrological Abbreviations		x
	Introduction	1
1	Who Belonged to Associations?	15
2	Scenarios of Success, Survival and Decline	33
3	Starting an Association: Collective and Individual Agency	51
4	Counting the Costs of Communal Life	75
5	Acquiring Resources	99
6	Communal Collections, Part 1: Fund-Raising and Group Values	119
7	Communal Collections, Part 2: Associations Devoted to the Israelite God	135
8	Mutual Assistance and Group Cohesion	151
	Conclusion	187
	Appendix: Women Participating in Associations, 1st Century BCE–2nd Century CE	189
Bibliography		193
Index of Inscriptions and Papyri		215
Index of Ancient Literary Sources		223
Index of Modern Scholars		227
Subject Index		229

Figures and Tables

Figures

1.1 Monument depicting the priestess Stratonike approaching the deities Cybele and Apollo with banqueting members, musicians, servers and souvlaki below. Courtesy of the National Archaeological Museum, Athens. 24

1.2 Banqueting records from Tebtynis (*PTebt* I 118). Courtesy of the Center for the Tebtunis Papyri, University of California, Berkeley. 28

1.3 Bronze coin from the reign of Ptolemy V Epiphanes (203–181 BCE), with head of Zeus Ammon and eagle with thunderbolt. Courtesy of Ancient Coin Collectors, used under a Creative Commons licence, via Wikimedia. 29

2.1 Bronze Membership List (Album) of a Mithras association from Virunum, now in the Landesmuseum Kärnten, Klagenfurt, Austria. Courtesy of John S. Kloppenborg, used with permission. 38

2.2 Painting from Pompeii, depicting the riot in and around the amphitheatre. Photo by Harland. 42

3.1 Pillar from Sarapis sanctuary A (*RICIS* 202/0101). Courtesy of Laurent Bricault, Université Toulouse II and l'École française d'Athènes. 57

3.2 Plan of Sarapis sanctuary A at Delos. From Roussel (1916: 21). Public domain. 61

3.3 Sketch of the Epikteta monument. Courtesy of Wittenburg (1990, plate 2). 69

4.1 The so-called 'Terrace of the Foreign Gods' on Delos, showing various sanctuaries used by ethnic associations. Courtesy of l'École française d'Athènes / Brigitte Sagnier. Used with permission. 87

4.2 Banqueting rooms of the cowherds at Pergamon. Photo by Harland. 89

5.1 Epiodoros' letter (*PMich* IX 575, front [r.]). Courtesy of the University of Michigan Papyrology Collection, used under a Creative Commons licence. 111

5.2 Pottery fragment from Maresha reused as a 'ticket' stating a member's fine amount. Courtesy of Ian Stern, Director of the Maresha Excavation Project. 115

6.1 Collection receptacle from Sarapis sanctuary A (*IG* XI,4 1247 = *RICIS* 202/0124). Courtesy of Laurent Bricault, Université Toulouse II. 120

Figures and Tables   vii

6.2 Fishermen and fish-dealers' monument, now in the Selçuk Archaeological
     Museum. Photo by Harland.   130
7.1 Tyrian shekel dated 31/30 BCE, with bust of the god Melqart and eagle.
     Courtesy of the Art Institute of Chicago, used under a Creative Commons
     Zero licence.   137
8.1 Regulation of the sheep-raisers' (?) guild (*PMich* V 243, APIS inv. 720,
     front [r.]). Courtesy of the Papyrology Collection, Graduate Library,
     University of Michigan, used under a Creative Commons licence.   164
8.2 Loan agreement involving Josepos and Agathokles (*PTebt* III 818).
     Courtesy of the Center for the Tebtunis Papyri, University of California,
     Berkeley.   177

Tables

1.1 Demographic categories for the Roman empire in Friesen (2004) and
     Longenecker (2010)   21
1.2 Income categories with estimated percentages of population, excluding
     military households. Adapted from Scheidel and Friesen (2009)   27
1.3 Bronze to silver drachma ratios in Ptolemaic Egypt, based on Reden (2010:
     145–6)   30

Acknowledgements

We would especially like to thank John M. G. Barclay at Durham University, Markus Öhler at the University of Vienna, Onno van Nijf at the University of Groningen and Maia Kotrosits at Denison University, who generously read and provided helpful feedback on drafts of this book. For Chapter 8, Ryan Schellenberg at the Methodist Theological School, Ohio, made useful suggestions and Andrew Monson at New York University gave feedback on the Demotic regulations. For the same chapter, Ben Kelly at York University provided advice on the distribution of Egyptian papyri and on the record offices.

Richard would like to thank Brigidda Bell, Thomas Blanton IV, Ian Brown and John S. Kloppenborg for insights and ideas that came up in recent discussions about association finances. Richard's research assistant, Alec Mullender at York University, helped to organize data that appears throughout the book. Richard is grateful for generous research funding (2015–17) from a Banting Postdoctoral Fellowship, Social Sciences and Humanities Research Council of Canada, from York University and from Trent University.

Phil would especially like to thank Maia for all of her support in life and work. Ongoing discussions with Maia about research have been pivotal. As usual, Phil's sons, Justin and Nathaniel, were a much welcomed escape from the ancient world. As research assistant, Victoria Muccilli of York University helped in various ways with the final preparation of the manuscript and with the indices.

Preliminary research that initiated work on this book was presented by Phil in 2012 at the Society of New Testament Studies, Social History of Early Christianity section, and in 2013 at the University of Uppsala, Jewish and Christian Groups in the Greco-Roman World Conference. Special thanks go to Anders Runesson, Markus Öhler and Hermut Löhr for the invitation to the former and Cecilia Wassen for the invitation to the latter. Benedikt Eckhardt and Clemens Leonhard also invited Phil to participate in the Exzellenzcluster at the Westfälische Wilhelms-Universität in Münster, where these ideas were further discussed and developed. The paper then appeared in English as Harland (2015), and in German as Harland (2018) thanks to Benedikt's translation. Although further transformed, an earlier version of Chapter 6 first appeared in the honorary volume for John S. Kloppenborg (Arnal et al., 2016), whose guidance in years past has been instrumental in both Phil's and Rick's scholarship. The writing of this book was supported, in part, by grants from York University and (in the final stages) by a grant from the Social Sciences and Humanities Research Council of Canada.

Portions of this book were developed out of an article by Harland, 'Associations and the Economics of Group Life: A Preliminary Case Study of Asia Minor and the Aegean Islands', *Svensk exegetisk årsbok* [*Swedish Exegetical Yearbook*], 80 (2015): 1–37. We would like to thank the journal for permission to reemploy some material in heavily revised form.

The discussion of Symmasis' foundation in chapter three is based, in part, on GRA II 149. This is adapted here with permission from De Gruyter.

Portions of Chapter 6 overlap with a previous article by Harland, 'Fund-Raising and Group Values in the Associations', in William E. Arnal et al. (eds), *Scribal Practices and Social Structures among Jesus Adherents: Essays in Honour of John S. Kloppenborg*, BETL, 285 (Leuven: Peeters, 2016), pp. 465–82. We would like to thank Peeters Publishing for permission to reemploy some material from that article.

Epigraphic and Papyrological Abbreviations

Epigraphic and papyrological abbreviations follow those listed on the Associations in the Greco-Roman World website, under the tab 'How to use this site', available at http://www.philipharland.com/greco-roman-associations/?p=12/#abbrev.

Introduction

This study asks a simple, yet largely unanswered, question regarding collective life in the Hellenistic and Roman eras: how did associations of various kinds, including gatherings devoted to the Israelite god, *survive* as groups? These diverse collectivities, positioned between the family and structures of the city, had no consistent flow of resources from official institutions. They possessed no blueprint for using funds effectively. Each association had to figure out how best to raise, manage and invest available resources in order to cover benefits and fulfil expectations of participants. Some associations could dissolve because they did not do this well. Rather than contemplating such issues, scholars tend to look past the question of group survival and to focus instead on what associations offered members. This has led to interesting findings concerning the benefits these groups offered. But in this study, we argue that the rush to understand why individuals joined associations results in significant blind spots with respect to how ancient associations of various types survived and functioned. In particular, this has often obscured things like differentiation in material circumstances from one group to the next and the central role of collective agency in group sustainability.

We engage in this social historical and comparative enterprise while spanning disciplines that examine groups in the ancient Mediterranean. Our commitment to studying associations without excluding groups devoted to the Israelite god has helped us to better understand both Judean (Jewish) and non-Judean associations. Advantages arise from exploring local, collective life from such a comparative perspective without concern for sometimes artificially drawn disciplinary boundaries. For informal associations, immigrant groups and guilds that dotted the social landscape of the ancient world provide a fresh vantage point on how associations devoted to the Israelite god, including Jesus followers, gained necessary resources to pursue their aims and to meet expectations of participants. Likewise, literature produced by Judeans (Jews) and Jesus adherents (Christians) can occasionally attest to circumstances and practices only hinted at in papyri or inscriptions. Rather than considering such collectivities in isolation, then, this study places gatherings of Judeans and Jesus adherents alongside others within wider social, cultural and economic milieux. However, we do not give a privileged position to these particular minority groups, which appear alongside many other groups in these pages and are only part of a puzzle we hope to solve.[1]

---

[1] On Judeans and Jesus followers as cultural minority groups, see Harland (2009).

The point of this work is not just to add to the growing body of scholarship on associations or on economic conditions, but rather to use these issues as an opportunity to approach ancient social history from a fresh angle. Our focus on nitty-gritty aspects of material interactions at the local level serves as a means to cut through ideological, mythological, legal and religion-encoded pictures of ancient social life, pictures evoked by scholars but also in some cases by our ancient subjects. Nothing like ostensibly humdrum matters of managing drachmas and parcelling out beer or wine to bring our lofty imaginations of social life back down to earth. From this vantage point, we demonstrate how to thoroughly diffuse into a larger world – rather than merely 'contextualize' – groups devoted to the Israelite god, including Jesus adherents. This helps to decentre and differentiate them in ways that do not play into their own hyperbolic, romanticized or otherwise partial rhetoric. We show how these groups, like other associations, were in many respects interwoven into the fabric of daily life in the ancient Mediterranean.

This book also illustrates complexities in generating historical reconstructions of group life. In the process, we provide one possible model for how to deal with inscriptional, papyrological, archaeological and literary forms of evidence together in capturing daily lived realities and relationships. Our attention to material contingencies and seemingly trivial matters of everyday communal life both mitigates scholarly generalizations propagated about social constituencies and reveals a more colourful and varied social landscape.

Overall, we hope this study will resonate with scholars, students and others interested in social, cultural and economic history in the ancient Mediterranean, as we range across a variety of fields that are too often kept separate. Our focus is on Greek-speaking areas of the eastern Mediterranean from the third century BCE to the third century CE, particularly in Greece, Turkey (Asia Minor) and Egypt, although we also have things to say about associations in other regions as well.

Progression

A brief clarification of the progression of our argument is in order. Beginning with the question of what socioeconomic levels of the population were most represented within many associations, we challenge recent scholarly proposals that those of middling wealth predominated while also rejecting the older view that only the most poor were highly represented (Chapter 1). We argue here that participation within associations was open to many people between the level of subsistence (those living with a minimum level of food, shelter and clothing) and the wealthier segments of the non-elite population in cities and villages. Of course, each group might differ from another, but there are some generalizations that can be made regarding overall trends. We then go on to argue that the survival of associations had less to do with socioeconomic status and more to do with how well groups both adapted to available material means and managed resources, with three scenarios arising from these circumstances: decline, survival and success (Chapter 2).

This sets the stage for considering material circumstances of associations at the point of foundation (Chapter 3). Challenging common scholarly assumptions, we emphasize the critical importance of collective agency and social interaction in the formation of many such groups more so than individual wealthy founders. And this focus on group cohesion and collective action forms the basis for many other points we establish in subsequent chapters (especially Chapters 6, 7 and 8). The book as a whole proposes that this collective element is the key to understanding group survival in many cases.

A few foundation narratives that have survived emphasize the inevitability of success, which has sometimes misled scholars. Still, a careful reading of some origin narratives reveals hints of financial struggles that many associations would likely have faced from the outset. The moment of establishment was crucial for many groups as it set the stage for sustainability or precarity. Consideration of expenses at start-up then segues into our survey of a range of communal costs faced by groups as they continued beyond the first days and months. These costs included things like arranging a meeting place, honouring local notables and covering the costs of honouring the gods and feasting with friends (Chapter 4).

The question of how associations of various kinds acquired necessary resources for survival then occupies us in several chapters. While contributions from outsiders could be more or less important depending on the group in question, internal sources of income were essential to the sustainability of the majority of groups (Chapter 5). Beyond regular contributions and fines paid by participants, special communal collections were essential in many situations (Chapter 6). Expanding out from a case study of Delos island, we show that communal fund-raising both expressed and reinforced group cohesion in relation to shared aims. Principal among these collective aims for many groups was the maintenance of ancestral customs for deities, who were thought to protect the group and ensure its success. But a concern for economic efficiency is also notable in some instances involving guilds, as with the fishermen at Ephesos.

Both the aims and procedures of fund-raising in associations find counterparts in the practices of at least some gatherings of Judeans and Jesus adherents (Chapter 7). Before its destruction in 70 CE, communal collections in support of the temple in Jerusalem were an important factor in how Judean gatherings, like other associations based on ethnicity, maintained contacts with the homeland and its ancestral customs while expressing a sense of belonging together with others from the same geographical origin. While Paul's collection for the 'poor' in Jerusalem may have owed something to the Israelite practice of regularly sending funds to the homeland, it had a particular purpose for Paul. He sought to ameliorate tensions between his Greek-speaking and primarily non-Judean assemblies and the Judean leadership of the Jesus movement in the homeland. Some of the procedures his assemblies instituted make better sense within the framework of mechanisms within other associations. For many groups, it seems that collective action in raising resources served to express participants' sense of commitment to the group, reinforcing cohesion and ensuring the continuation of customs in honour of the group's patron deity.

Another important sign, and contributing cause, of group cohesion and, therefore, survival were practices related to mutual support (Chapter 8). While some scholars in Jewish Studies and Christian Origins tend to stress the prime importance of mutual aid among Judeans and Jesus devotees, framing this in culturally specific terms as 'charity' or 'almsgiving', the practical ways in which members in other associations assisted one another has not been given sufficient attention. There is considerable evidence from Egypt and elsewhere that individual members and the collective as a whole assisted other participants in tough situations and by various means, including material help at crucial moments in life and at death.

Scholarly context

While we will delve into specific scholarship at relevant points in this study, we need to briefly situate the present work on group survival in the broad sweep of scholarship. Scholarly work in fields which we cover tends either to neglect the subject of group survival or to underestimate the evidence for material conditions that is available, and it is important to ask why. Jonathan Perry, for instance, states that one 'remarkable, and often-noted, feature of [association] inscriptions ... is how little economic detail is contained in them'.[2] On closer examination, however, much more is to be gained by carefully evaluating material circumstances of associations from different angles.

Interest in ancient associations first arose in earnest in the mid- to late nineteenth century, at a time when voluntary organizations were on the rise within European and Western societies.[3] Certain scholars, such as Franz Poland (1909), did give considerable attention to the financial basis of Greek associations and even contemplated financial failure due to lack of resources, but few other scholars followed through on these reflections.[4] Instead, much scholarly attention since the pioneering work of Theodor Mommsen (1843) was on the *legal standing* of existing associations within the Roman empire.[5] Mommsen and Jean-Pierre Waltzing (1895–1900) and those who follow them were at least indirectly concerned with the economic status of members, but primarily in order to characterize associations as 'associations of the poor' (*collegia tenuiorum*) or 'funerary associations' (*collegia funeraticia*), categories that have since proven problematic.[6] This was due, in large part, to a focus on a particular interpretation of a passage in the sixth-century legal collection known as the *Digest* (47.22.1) and on a Roman senatorial decree cited by groups such as the one at Lanuvium (*CIL* XIV 2112). So the evidence for associations was often interpreted from the imperial perspective rather than from below – that is, from the perspective of participants in such associations as reflected in inscriptions.[7] These scholars argued that Roman authorities attempted to stifle the formation of groups generally but allowed the poor specifically

---

[2] Perry (2011: 503).
[3] For the historiographical context of these early works, see Perry (2006).
[4] Poland (1909: 453–98, especially 495, 498).
[5] E.g. Mommsen (1843), Radin (1910), Carolsfeld (1969 [1933]), De Robertis (1938, 1955, 1971). See the similar observations of Ausbüttel (1982: 11–15).
[6] Cf. Schiess (1888). For a detailed historiographical look at Mommsen's work in this period, see Perry (2006: 23–60).
[7] An exception to this is Liebenam's work (1890), which was expressly concerned with the perspective of the lower classes to some degree.

to form associations so long as this was aimed at 'religious' purposes and at addressing the economic deprivation that such individual members faced.[8] In particular, from this scholarly perspective, the main purpose of such groups was to offer burial to the most poor who could not otherwise afford it. So there was a focus on the dire economic circumstances of individual members that joined these associations. But little attention was given to the question of how groups maintained themselves materially, or to potential socioeconomic diversity from one group to the next or diversity in the composition of particular associations.

Beyond the focus on legal issues, few substantial studies of associations in the eastern Mediterranean appeared from the 1920s to the 1970s.[9] Then a new interest in social history began to emerge within various historically oriented disciplines, including ancient history and Christian origins. It is in the wake of contributions on 'social relations' by the likes of Ramsay MacMullen (1974) and Géza Alföldy (1985) and on associations in the West specifically by Frank M. Ausbüttel (1982) that scholars are increasingly turning their attention to social dimensions of associative life within ancient society.[10] MacMullen in particular emphasizes that a range of people gathered in guilds not to secure economic protection or leverage in labour disputes, but rather for the purpose of socializing, eating and drinking – with a thin 'religious' or 'funerary' veneer.[11] As Keith Hopkins (1983) puts it, 'perhaps commemoration of the dead was merely an excuse for a good party'.[12] Or, as MacMullen expresses it, 'if piety counted for much, conviviality counted for more'.[13] This is a welcomed turn to the social with a shift away from the supposed destitution of most members. But the emphasis on 'social' dimensions of group life – narrowly conceived – sometimes results in an imbalanced view of the various intertwined purposes that such groups served for their members, including the importance of honours for gods or goddesses.[14] Despite this turn to the social, however, material conditions or economic functions of the associations remained under-explored.

Beginning in the 1990s, the turn to social history did start to lead certain ancient historians to economic matters in important ways, a point we return to in Chapter 6. Particularly significant in this respect is Onno van Nijf's study of guilds in the Greek East, which was published in 1997. Since then, scholars such as Philip F. Venticinque, Matthew Gibbs and Koenraad Verboven have given considerable attention to occupational associations specifically, including their importance for economic relations and socioeconomic status issues.[15] Regionally focused studies also address the importance of associations for local economies, including contributions by Nicholas K.

---

[8] Cf. Bendlin (2011: 232).
[9] Detailed studies such as Ferguson (1944) are an exception to this generalization. Cf. Tod (1932), Boak (1937), Schulz-Falkenthal (1965, 1966).
[10] For more on this, see Perry (2011: 499–515).
[11] MacMullen (1966: 173–8), ibid. (1974: 71–87).
[12] Hopkins (1983: 214). Also quoted in Perry (2011: 507). Cf. MacMullen (1974: 71–87, especially 19).
[13] MacMullen (1974: 77, 80). Cf. Nilsson (1957: 64, 147).
[14] See Harland (2013: 47–69) = ibid. (2003: 55–88).
[15] Cf. Pleket (1983), ibid. (1984), van Nijf (1997): 11–23), ibid. (2002), Venticinque (2009: 11–16), ibid. (2010), Verboven (2011a, and the other essays in that journal issue).

Rauh on Delos and Vincent Gabrielsen on Rhodian societies.[16] Numerous works by Andrew Monson and by Venticinque delve into some socioeconomic dimensions of associations in Hellenistic and Roman Egypt as well.[17] Other studies look at how associations functioned to connect people to broader networks, particularly through patronage or benefaction, as in John Patterson's work on Italy, van Nijf's on the Greek East and Harland's on Asia Minor.[18] Yet group survival itself and the mechanics of how associations managed resources still remain sidelined in many respects. The sustainability of associations is still taken for granted as it was in earlier research that concentrated on legal questions. An exception to this is Jinyu Liu's very recent article which looks at scholarly efforts to employ sociological approaches concerning social capital and trust networks in the study of associations. In the process, she does begin to raise important questions regarding group survival along the lines of what we explore from different angles in this book.[19]

Gatherings devoted to the Israelite god or to both the Israelite god and Jesus are notably absent in most scholarship by classicists or ancient historians reviewed above.[20] As we will soon see, some scholars in Jewish Studies and Christian Origins, like Justin J. Meggitt, Judith Lieu and Pieter van der Horst, continue to discount the relevance of associations to the study of Judeans or Jesus followers altogether, apparently without looking at epigraphic and papyrological evidence for themselves (see Chapter 8). In particular, such scholars put an emphasis on groups of Judeans and Jesus adherents as unique from all others in their concern for members within the group in the form of 'charity' or mutual material aid, a view that we will soon deconstruct. Our own previous interdisciplinary research diverges by placing these groups located at similar levels of society alongside one another in order to better understand different groups and to illuminate the cultural, social and, now, economic landscape of the ancient Mediterranean.[21] Furthermore, particularly since 1996, many other scholars of ancient Judean culture and Christian origins mentioned in footnote 22 and discussed in our previous works likewise recognize and, more importantly, demonstrate the value in comparison for understanding diverse social groupings, including those devoted to the Israelite god.[22] Associations as well as gatherings devoted to the Israelite god coexisted in the same social space between the household and the city and needed to find ways to finance themselves within that context. A study about how groups formed and

---

[16] Rauh (1993), Gabrielsen (1997), ibid. (2001).
[17] E.g. Monson (2006), Venticinque (2009, 2010).
[18] Patterson (1992, 1994), van Nijf (1997: 73–128), Harland (2013: 119–40). Cf. Terpstra (2013).
[19] Liu (2016).
[20] An exception would be an ancient historian who thinks that Judeans and Christians are 'something entirely different' (and other associations presumably 'the same' as one another) and who is concerned that any comparison will result in 'denying any special traits to' Judeans (Eckhardt, 2017a: 260; ibid., 2016a: 662; cf. Gruen, 2016). On these misunderstandings of the nature and purpose of comparison, see Smith (1990).
[21] See Last and Harland entries in the Bibliography.
[22] E.g. Kloppenborg and Wilson (1996), Richardson (1996), Harland (1999) later published as ibid. (2003) = ibid. (2013, 2nd edn), Runesson (2001), Ascough (2003), Harland (2009), Hanges (2012), Gillihan (2012), Harland (2014), Kotrosits (2015), Last (2016a).

survived in that social space is enriched by including in its purview gatherings that honoured the Israelite god or both the Israelite god and Jesus.

So rather than hesitating from the comparative enterprise as a few others have, we engage in comparison of contemporaneous and geographically proximate social formations in a sociologically minded way in order to find out what happens, find out what new things we might begin to notice that would have otherwise remained more obscure.[23] The heuristic value of comparison does not rest on our ancient subjects necessarily recognizing the precise sociological or other similarities that draw our attention as scholars and social historians, even though, in fact, certain ancient people do notice overlaps. Nor does analogical comparison amount to an identification of distinctive groups or the obliteration of variety. The historian's concern with specificity need not exclude sociologically informed explorations of other dimensions of ancient economic, social and cultural life. We can explore both the general and the specific. No association was exactly the same as any other. Each and every group was 'distinctive' or 'special' in some way, not just those that happened to devote themselves to the Israelite god, which were, in fact, diverse as well. But comparison of sociologically similar phenomena can still provide new vantage points on numerous distinctive groups. Sometimes a bird's eye view can provide new perspectives.

Despite scholarly advances in the area of comparison since 1996, seldom have economic or material issues been the focus. There are very recent exceptions in contributions by John M. G. Barclay, Bruce W. Longenecker and, more extensively, John S. Kloppenborg, where such issues begin to be addressed, although in an incipient and piecemeal fashion in some respects. So, for instance, Barclay raises the prospects of placing associations alongside groups of Judeans and Jesus followers precisely with respect to better understanding money matters, but space does not allow him to go beyond introducing the issue.[24] Engaging with recent studies by Steve Friesen and others on the socioeconomic level of Jesus adherents, Longenecker's extensive study of Paul and poverty gives some attention to economic dimensions of associative life more generally, and he sometimes looks at important inscriptions pertaining to associations.[25]

In several more detailed comparative studies, Kloppenborg discusses regular membership contributions and rotating funding arrangements for communal meals; he considers attendance and absenteeism as they relate to financing such groups; and he delves into financial mechanisms within associations to shed light on Paul's collection, topics that occupy us in more detail in this study.[26] In this way, work by Kloppenborg and others is beginning to show how inclusion of material from Jesus adherents in the study of associations can help raise new questions about associations and lead to advancements in our knowledge of group life.

Together with a survey article which Harland presented in 2012, Last's own previous book on the Corinthian assembly (a revision of his thesis of 2013) set the stage for the

[23] Cf. Smith (1982, 1990).
[24] Barclay (2006).
[25] Friesen (2004), Barclay (2004), Oakes (2004), Longenecker (2009a, 2010). Cf. Longenecker and Liebengood (2009).
[26] Kloppenborg (2016, on financing meals), ibid. (2013, on membership practices), ibid. (2017, on collection).

present study in its emphasis on financial matters and the socioeconomic status of membership in Pauline assemblies and associations.[27] That work highlights problems with neglecting economically modest associations, an issue that we explore in more depth now.

More will be said about scholarship on associations at key points as we progress. For now, this will suffice to show that, although some advancements have been made, a wide-ranging, comparative study of material conditions and group sustainability remains to be done.

Our current study is by no means an attempt to explain the ancient economy as a whole, then, but rather to look at material issues as they impact everyday group life and survival. Yet it is still important to say something about scholarly approaches to the 'economy' and 'economics' before we proceed. These are categories that our historical subjects in the ancient world would not necessarily recognize or separate out from other facets of life, as the compartmentalization of life into the 'social', 'cultural', 'religious', 'economic' and 'political' is a modern development. This is why Peter Oakes' recent survey rightly emphasizes Karl Polanyi's point that all ancient economies were 'embedded economies'.[28] Focusing on the ancient context, T. F. Carney explains the scholarly concept of 'economy' as: 'that complex of activities and institutions through which a society manages the production and allocating of goods and services, and organizes and maintains its workers ... "The economy" is not just an aggregate of individuals' actions. Groups, and overall societal interests, are involved.'[29] This is helpful, and economists and economic historians sometimes pare this down, with 'economics' referring to the 'study of the allocation of scarce resources', and we adopt this economical explanation.[30]

In investigating the flow of scarce resources within particular societies or subgroups within societies, economists often distinguish between macroeconomics and microeconomics. Macroeconomics have to do with the overall structure and performance of the economy as a whole. So, for instance, scholars such as Walter Scheidel, Ian Morris, Richard Saller, Peter Temin and others explore the overall performance of the ancient Roman economy and attempt to make comparisons with other historical economies.[31] In this book, there are times when we need to draw on the findings of such macroeconomic studies: for instance, we employ Scheidel and Steve Friesen's model of the Roman economy in order to understand the socioeconomic levels of people who belonged to associations (Chapter 1). One might also explore macroeconomic questions regarding the roles that guilds and associations may have played within the overall performance of the ancient economy, but that is not our focus here.

---

[27] Last (2016a). The 2012 presentation at the Society of New Testament Studies in Leuven, Belgium, was later published as Harland (2015), now translated by Benedikt Eckhardt into German as Harland (2018).
[28] Oakes (2009a: 11–12). Cf. Polanyi (1968).
[29] Carney (1975: 140).
[30] Oakes (2009a: 11–12). Cf. Burkett (2006: 1–16).
[31] Scheidel, Morris and Saller (2007), Scheidel (2012), Temin (2013).

Microeconomics concern the flow of produce and resources within markets at the local level among individuals, groups and organizations.[32] The so-called 'New Institutional Economics' approach often makes contributions in this area by focusing on the role of both formal and informal institutions in the functioning of the economy.[33] While this book does not attempt to engage in an analysis of either macroeconomics or microeconomics in a strict sense, it is true that our study would more readily feed into microeconomic questions. After all, we do focus on material issues and the flow of resources within unofficial groups at a local level and on socioeconomic interactions both among members and between members and outsiders.

While on the topic of economics, it should also be clarified that, despite valuable attempts at quantifying ancient economies (as in Alan Bowman and Andrew Wilson's volume), any study of ancient material conditions is faced with a dearth of data, and this restricts statistical analysis of economic relations, whether at the micro or macro levels.[34] So, although we do deal with numbers when we have them and we also draw on economic models concerned with quantification, we must still face the fact that any study in this area will need to be more qualitative than quantitative. There is a sense in which we are engaged more fully in social history than economic history specifically, although we would not draw sharp lines between the two. Besides, economic questions and the allocation of scarce resources specifically have been at the centre of social history itself since its inception as a subfield of History.[35]

Defining associations

It is important to clarify what groups will and will not occupy us in this study. We use the term 'unofficial associations' as an etic, analytic and sociological category in reference to certain groupings located socially between the structures of the family and the official structures of the city or village in the eastern Mediterranean. By 'unofficial', we simply mean that such associations were not consistently sustained by resources from civic or imperial institutions and that their membership was not defined primarily in terms of citizenship or in terms of belonging within civic subdivisions. Unofficial associations in this scholarly sense were small, relatively informal and non-compulsory groups with memberships usually ranging between ten and fifty members, but some were larger. Such associations were collectivities whose members met together on a *regular basis* to socialize with one another and to honour both earthly and divine benefactors. These ongoing groups varied in the nature and extent of their organization, so there is no one model regarding leadership or other internal structures. The definition and nature of these groups and their activities have occupied us at length in

[32] Burkett (2006). Cf. Temin (2013: 95–192, regarding microeconomics of markets in the Roman empire).
[33] See the summary discussion by Verboven (2015).
[34] Bowman and Wilson (2009).
[35] Early works by Marxist social historians illustrate this point well: Hobsbawm (1959), Thompson (1964), Hill (1972).

previous studies, where you can read more about associations – and comparison of them – beyond the focus of the present study.[36] We also maintain a website devoted to collecting together and translating relevant ancient sources based on the definition here, where you can read and assess the ancient materials for yourself: http://www.philipharland.com/greco-roman-associations.

This category of the unofficial association is a modern scholarly or sociological one aimed at understanding important dimensions of ancient social, cultural and economic landscapes. Sometimes, though not always, groups that scholars have considered under the rubric of 'associations' or 'guilds' or 'clubs' happen to be recognized as analogous collectivities by people in the ancient context, whether participants or civic or imperial authorities.[37] So this etic (outsider or scholarly) category has significant overlaps with ancient, emic (insider) categorizations, even though the value of comparative study does not necessarily depend on ancient observers consistently categorizing groups in a particular way. There are a variety of ancient terms for 'groups' that are enveloped within this category, with the more common ones being Greek terms like *koinon, synodos, thiasos, synagōgē, politeuma* and *synergasia,* and Latin ones like *collegium* and *corpus.*

Our previous research shows that associations in this sense served a similar set of social and cultural purposes.[38] So it is problematic to categorize them based on some ostensible primary purpose, as some typologies do in speaking of (1) burial associations, (2) religious associations and (3) occupational associations. Rather, it is more appropriate and productive to consider associations in terms of the ancient social networks that help to explain their existence. For decades, sociologists have recognized the importance of pre-existing social ties for understanding the formation and expansion of social groups of various kinds in the modern context, and so it is no surprise that ancient groups would reflect similar social processes.[39] The unofficial groups discussed in this study drew participants from intersecting webs of connections associated with (1) the household, (2) the neighbourhood, (3) the workplace, (4) the sanctuary or temple and (5) common geographical origins or shared ethnic identifications. Groups could, of course, draw membership from several of these overlapping networks, but often a certain set of connections seems more prevalent than others as a source of participants.

Our definition and approach here seeks to set aside certain scholarly approaches of the past, some of which Vaia Touna recently reiterates and critiques.[40] Many of the groups included under this rubric of unofficial associations were in some sense what modern observers working with modern categories might be tempted to label 'religious'

---

[36] See, especially, the bibliographies in Last (2013, 2016b and 2016a), Harland (2003) = ibid. (2013), ibid. (2009, 2014).
[37] The collection of legal perspectives regarding *collegia* and similar collected in the *Digest* (see *AGRW* 43–54) seem to presume the authorities' development of a broader category under which many types of groups were gathered.
[38] Harland (2013: 45–70) = ibid. (2003: 55–88).
[39] Lofland and Stark (1965), Gerlach and Hine (1970), Stark and Bainbridge (1985: 307–24), Welch (1981), Cavendish, Welch and Leege (1998).
[40] Touna (2017).

or 'cultic'. Yet it is problematic to speak of particular groups as 'religious associations' and others as something else (implied 'secular') simply because patron deities or rituals happen to be mentioned in one inscription or document but not in another.[41]

Furthermore, research since the 2000s within the disciplines of Cultural Studies and Religious Studies (which has yet to fully impact study of the ancient Mediterranean, unfortunately) show how tied to modernity the concept of 'religion' is. Such studies underline how the categories and discourses of 'religion' and the 'religious' (expressly or implicitly juxtaposed with the 'secular') are themselves characteristic of cultural developments since the early modern period, particularly in the wake of the so-called Enlightenment in the 1700s and of nineteenth century colonialism.[42] Our ancient subjects, on the other hand, had no category approaching what a modern means by 'religion', and employment of this particular modern concept can, more often than not, lead us further away from understanding human behaviours in ancient societies, in our view. In fact, the tendency to make a hard distinction between 'religious' associations and other (implied 'secular' or non-religious) associations seems to underlie some objections (discussed earlier) to comparative study. In this book, we therefore choose not to employ the category of 'religion' and the 'religious', since many other less problematic and more appropriate modern descriptive options are available to the scholar interested in explaining individual and group practices and behaviours.[43] There is no need to defend *not* employing a particular modern scholarly category, even if there is a strong scholarly tradition that continues to result in its rampant use with respect to the ancient context in the face of problems (sometimes, although not always, acknowledged) with the category.[44] Employing other carefully chosen scholarly categories may provide a new vantage point on the evidence rather than reproducing anachronisms or missing important dimensions of social or cultural life because of an attachment to particular discourses. The broader concept of 'culture' is itself another modern scholarly category, but one with far less problematic baggage and with continued value in the study of various historical periods, in our view, as William H. Sewell and others also show.[45]

While there are certain affinities between our definition of associations here and the quite broad concept of '*voluntary* associations' as it is used in modern studies in sociology and anthropology and in some previous studies of ancient associations,

---

[41] On scholarly discourses surrounding philosophical groups as 'secular' schools and not 'religious' societies, now see Harland (2019).
[42] Asad (2003), Jakobsen and Pellegrini (2008), Arnal and McCutcheon (2013), Nongbri (2013).
[43] This was also Harland's approach in *Dynamics of Identity in the World of the Early Christians* (2009).
[44] The frequent employment of the notion of '*embedded* religion' is an example of an attempt to recognise problems while still employing the category in the ancient context, for instance (e.g. as in the otherwise helpful book by Beard, North and Price, 1998; see Nongbri, 2008). Unfortunately, many works by Jörg Rüpke, while valuable in giving attention to social dimensions of life in the Roman empire, take the category of 'religion' as self-evident, do not actively engage theoretical issues surrounding use of the category, and seem unaware of recent work within the disciplines of Religious Studies and Cultural Studies regarding the modern origins of the concept. E.g. Rüpke (2007, 2014, 2016), works that are nonetheless helpful in some other respects.
[45] On 'culture' as a useful category in the study of history, see Sewell (1997, 1999) and Bonnell and Hunt (1999).

certain distinctions are important to note.[46] In particular, we need to qualify the 'voluntary' or 'elective' nature of the groups under examination in this study. There is some truth in the statement that, for many associations in antiquity, people might join or leave of their own volition; still, there were certain factors at work in limiting the 'voluntary' nature of participation in associations of particular types, in part because of the social networks that supplied membership. Does it make much sense to speak of a purple-dyer *voluntarily* joining with other purple-dyers, or to imagine that a Judean, Idumean or Phoenician could easily have nothing to do with the local group formed around that common sense of ethnicity, or to assume that an enslaved person within an extended household had a choice in whether she belonged to a group that met within the enslaver's home? Nonetheless, the groups we are most interested in here were certainly less *in*voluntary than the more official civic subdivisions at Athens, or age-based educational organizations of the gymnasia, for instance.

The commonly employed categories of 'private' (or related concepts of 'individualistic' or 'personal religion') vs 'public' have often been misleading in the study of social life in the ancient Mediterranean, and these will be avoided in this study of groups that have traditionally been categorized as 'private'.[47] Nevertheless, the unofficial associations that occupy us in this study should be distinguished from other collectivities that, for instance, were consistently and substantially supported by village or civic institutions (e.g. the *polis*, with its Council and People) or imperial authorities. It should be noted that these official civic or imperial frameworks are what certain recent scholars do mean when they employ the term 'public' in contrast to 'private'. Certain groups that began as unofficial associations could, over time, come to be more fully involved in civic-run activities or come to be more or less financially supported by civic institutions, and it is not always easy to distinguish between groups that were transitioning in this way.

Our definition of unofficial associations consciously distinguishes these rather informal groups from official institutions or subdivisions of cities and provinces (e.g. demes, civic tribes, regional or provincial leagues), from boards of civic functionaries, from boards of priests or priestesses connected with temples and from age-based educational organizations connected with the gymnasia (e.g. boys, youths, young men, elders). It is true that these more official collectivities may have sometimes served similar purposes for their participants as unofficial associations did for theirs. Nicholas F. Jones' study of 'public organization' in southern Greece during the classical era, in which he speaks of *official* civic subdivisions (e.g. demes and phratries) in terms of 'associations', demonstrates this point.[48] The present study is not focused on these more official groups and organizations, despite comparable dimensions of some of their

---

[46] On voluntary associations, see Mishnun (1950), Little (1957), Geertz (1962), Anderson (1971), Kerri (1976), Thomson (1980), Krysan and d'Antonio (1992), Moya (2005). A recent resurgence in the study of ancient groups since the mid-1990s began by using the term '*voluntary* associations' without much reflection. Cf. Kloppenborg and Wilson (1996), Ascough (1998).

[47] See Harland (2013: 71–94) = ibid. (2003: 90–7). Cf. Ustinova (2005). Benedikt Eckhardt (e.g. Eckhardt, 2016b, 2017b, 2018) continues to employ the terminology of 'private' associations without much explanation, although I suspect that by this he simply means not 'state' run or financed. Similarly, see Gabrielsen and Thomsen (2015).

[48] Jones (1987).

activities. Now that we have a sense of the sorts of groups under investigation, we can turn to material circumstances of associations in the ancient world. For those interested in reading the ancient sources for themselves, which we would encourage, a final note is in order.

A note on reading ancient sources on the AGRW website and on course usage

The vast majority of ancient sources discussed in this book are now readily available in English translation in the sourcebook *Associations in the Greco-Roman World* (*AGRW*, Baylor University Press),[49] in the multi-volume and multilingual scholarly work *Greco-Roman Associations* (*GRA*, De Gruyter),[50] and, even more comprehensively in terms of coverage but not detail, on the 'Associations in the Greco-Roman World' website at: http://www.philipharland.com/greco-roman-associations/.

We hope that readers will see this as an opportunity to read the sources for themselves and that professors and students will integrate this book within courses as they read, analyse and discuss the ancient sources together and test proposals made in this book or in other scholarship. Readers will easily find an inscription or papyrus on the website by using the site's search box to type (in quotation marks) the number using the abbreviated form that is cited in this book, e.g.: 'AGRW 231', 'GRA II 121', 'IEph 20', 'PTebt I 118'. The book *Associations, Synagogues and Congregations* (by Harland), which also contains embedded links to sources on the website, is also freely available for download in a second, electronic edition of 2013 at: http://philipharland.com/publications/Harland 2013 Associations-Synagogues-Congregations.pdf

---

[49] Ascough, Harland and Kloppenborg (2012).
[50] Kloppenborg and Ascough (2011) (*GRA* I), Harland (2014) (*GRA* II), Kloppenborg (2019) (*GRA* III).

1

Who Belonged to Associations?

Much more numerous, nearly innumerable, ... were the funeral guilds, proper. Composed of poor people ... they chiefly aimed to furnish decent burial ...
Waltzing, 1895: 347

The Christian communities grew up ... in the midst of poverty. They had a special message to the poor, and the poor naturally flowed into them.
Hatch, 1881: 42

In general, the members of the associations seem to have been drawn from the upper echelons of the urban plebs and can best be characterized as 'employers' rather than 'employees'.
Patterson, 2006: 255

Paul's undisputed letters ... [lead] ... to the conclusion that the vast majority of the people in his assemblies lived just above or just below the level of subsistence.
Friesen, 2004: 357

Introduction

The question in the title is asked, to some extent, with tongue in cheek. An answer would be: many types of people from all walks of life belonged to unofficial associations, and it depends which specific group you are talking about. Yet, as the citations above show, the question of how we can *generalize* about the overall socioeconomic profile of participants in associations from a bird's eye view has occupied scholarship in the past. This subject must be broached for us to address important questions regarding group survival: what segments of society were most well represented within associations overall and what implications would this have for the ability of members to support an association and contribute towards its survival?

Recent scholarship generally affirms that most associations drew members from non-elite segments of society (primarily, although not solely, in the cities), and we agree. After all, the imperial elites at the top of society – those senators and equestrians who had exorbitant wealth and held official Roman positions – amounted to an extremely small percentage of the overall population of the Roman empire, probably less than 2 per cent. And the relatively wealthy civic elites who took on important official positions in cities and sat on various boards in the provinces probably made up less than 10 per cent of the urban population.[1] So it is not a surprise to find non-elite strata prevalent within most associations, since those below the imperial and civic elites made up the vast majority of the total population (probably more than 95 per cent). However, in recent decades, it is recognized that non-elite portions of the population were, themselves, considerably varied in terms of wealth, occupation, ethnicity and other status variables, rather than being socially or economically monolithic.

Scholarly debates are, therefore, centred more on the question of what segments of 'the masses' or non-elite populations ('plebs' or 'plebeians', in Roman imperial terminology) were more fully represented than others in associations of various types. Of course, the answer is, it depends which group is under investigation. Associations were constituted from social network connections pertaining to the household, neighbourhood, occupation and ethnicity.[2] Certain groups, such as those formed through occupational contacts, may have had a more homogeneous composition than others, with at least some other specific groups reflecting a cross section of status levels in local society. In this chapter, we are less concerned with re-exploring specific cases of the socioeconomic status of those who belonged to this or that association.

Rather, like some recent scholars, we are concerned with broader patterns that are discernible regarding the profiles of membership across many groups and in what demographic generalizations may or may not be reasonable. In particular, while some recent studies propose that associates, especially those in guilds, predominantly came from wealthier segments of non-elite strata, and that membership would be relatively expensive or unaffordable for people living at lower levels, this chapter proposes a more complicated scenario. We argue that, instead, it is more reasonable to suggest that the majority of groups likely drew their members from those living between subsistence (those living with the minimum level of food, shelter and clothing) and those of middling wealth.

In this context, there was not necessarily a direct correlation between the socioeconomic standing of members in a particular group, on the one hand, and group material survival, on the other. Rather, as we will see in the next chapter, associations that survived were ones that were cognizant of their members' situations and functioned with available, if limited, means. Often, associations that were unable to weather financial storms would be those that, regardless of associates' socioeconomic level, mismanaged funds or overburdened participants and so lived beyond the means of their constituencies, failing to meet established communal goals.

Two scholarly models: Relatively wealthy, or poor?

It is common for scholars to generalize about the socioeconomic profiles of associations in one of two ways. On the one hand is a more recent proposal since the 1990s, which

---

[1] See Harland (2013: 20–3).
[2] Harland (2013: 23–43) = ibid. (2003: 25–54).

pertains primarily to occupational associations but is sometimes generalized beyond that. In a study of Italy, John Patterson (2006) suggests that, in general, members of associations 'seem to have been drawn from the upper echelons of the urban plebs and can best be characterized as "employers" rather than "employees"'.[3] Patterson's assessment is concentrated on Italy during the early imperial age, but some others draw similar conclusions about the overall picture for other parts of the Mediterranean. And so van Nijf (1997) finds that members of associations in Greece and Asia Minor 'came from a level of society intermediate between the rich and the poor .... [T]hey constituted the group which Aristotle describes as the *mesoi* ["those in the middle"], and of which the Romans used the specific term *plebs media*.'[4] Similarly, Nicolas Tran's (2016) study of guilds in second- and third-century Arles (in Gaul) finds that most participants of occupational associations there 'seem to have belonged to the highest echelons of the world of work – they were part of a "plebeian" elite that was well integrated into the city'.[5] Tran acknowledges that epigraphy tends to give us access mainly to the wealthier segments of the plebeian population, however.[6] A significant corollary of this emphasis on middling wealth is the notion that the cost of association membership may have been too expensive for those of lower economic strata.[7]

There have been both positive and negative outcomes of this scholarly trend. These recent assessments are often accompanied by a relatively new and valuable realization that the functions of associations went well beyond the material: membership in such groups was something of symbolic value to people, rather than something they necessarily required, as had been implied by the old notion of 'burial associations' of the poor.[8] Yet the primary focus on those of middling wealth to the neglect of other demographic cohorts means that such scholars often take the financial stability of associations and their members for granted rather than exploring other scenarios.

In some ways, the focus on these middling groups represents a pendulum swing away from a second, older but problematic proposal regarding the constituency of associations. Since the time of Theodor Mommsen and Jean-Pierre Waltzing (in the mid- to late-nineteenth century),[9] it was common for many scholars to assume that associates were primarily drawn from the poorest segments of society. This view is closely linked with the notion that there were 'burial associations' (*collegia funeraticia*) that were 'associations of the poor' (*collegia tenuiorum*).[10] From this perspective, these groups were providing services that many underprivileged individuals living in urban conditions and financial destitution could not otherwise access or afford.[11] It is noteworthy that, early on, scholars such as E. G. Hardy (1906) argued that groups

---

[3] Patterson (2006: 255) and, earlier, ibid. (1992: 21). Cf. Verboven (2007: 882).
[4] Van Nijf (1997: 22).
[5] Tran (2016: 267–68). Cf. Verboven (2009).
[6] Tran (2016: 258).
[7] E.g. Verboven (2007: 882).
[8] Royden (1988), van Nijf (1997: 33, 109–11), Tran (2006), Verboven (2007, 2009).
[9] Mommsen (1843), Waltzing (1895–1900).
[10] See Perry (2006: 23–60).
[11] See Waltzing (1898, 1899), Finley (1973), Alföldy (1985: 134). On theories of decline, see Harland (2013: 71–94) = ibid. (2003: 89–114).

devoted to Jesus were, by default, assumed to be such 'funerary associations' of the poor, since Hardy, like many others at the time, also assumed that these groups consisted principally of the poorest strata.[12]

Both of these scholarly approaches to association membership – whether the middling wealth model or poorest cohort model – tend to miss what we hope to sketch here: various elements of the non-elites belonged to associations, including a substantial portion of those below the middling economic register. The recent notion that those of middling wealth (e.g. the employers rather than the employees) dominated membership is made on the basis of certain associations that are attested on monumental inscriptions, which include most of the wealthier on record, in our view. On the other hand, some less noticed papyri from Egypt, some of which we discuss further below, show that associations could adjust the cost of membership to fit the income levels of individuals living in lower economic registers.[13] Such groups may not have left many traces in stone.

Furthermore, there are other demographic factors that, we argue below, make it very unlikely that associations consisted principally of those of middling wealth. Most now realize that there is a need for careful attention to stratification with respect to non-elite populations, rather than an oversimplified picture of an extremely small elite and the undifferentiated masses, and the existence of a cohort of 'middling wealth' is part of this picture.[14] A recently developed economic scale by Scheidel and Friesen provides a new approach to this question. If it can be shown plausibly that a higher percentage of people would likely have joined associations than the percentage of those with middling wealth, this would provide further leverage for considering the significant presence of other demographic cohorts, particularly those at lower socioeconomic levels at or above subsistence.

Implications for debates on Jesus adherents

Before turning to those demographic factors, a few words are in order regarding how the two perspectives outlined above relate to scholarly debates on the constituency of groups devoted to both the Israelite god and Jesus. In some cases, there are important overlaps in these debates that remain unnoticed, and it is worth briefly mentioning these. Yet scholars from either discipline (ancient history or Christian origins) do not really bring the discussion in both fields together with attention to primary evidence for group composition. Moreover, while 'pagan' associations sometimes get brief mention in the debate, we believe that there needs to be far more careful attention to epigraphic and papyrological evidence regarding the material conditions of these other associations, something we begin to remedy in this study. In addition, study of these primary sources needs to be done in a way that recognizes regional differences and

---

[12] Hardy (1906: 149, and 129–50 generally). Cf. Hatch (1881: 26–42, although he does not directly mention *collegia funeraticia*). Contrast Harnack (1905: 206 n. 2), who completely dismisses any comparison.

[13] Cf. Verboven (2007: 881).

[14] See Last (2016a: 99–106), Liu (2016), Tran (2016).

variety in unofficial associations more broadly when considering general questions regarding a comparative study of socioeconomic levels. Such careful work would best precede, rather than follow, sweeping generalizations or stark contrasts between 'associations', on the one hand, and congregations devoted to Jesus, on the other.

Friesen's (2004) return to the ongoing question of economic status rightly clarifies that Gerd Theissen (1982 [1974]), Abraham Malherbe (1983 [1977]) and Wayne Meeks (1983), whose works were instrumental in directing the debate, had misrepresented the view of Adolf Deissmann (1922 [1909]) specifically.[15] Meeks and others suggest that Deissmann characterized the earliest Jesus movement as a proletarian movement of the marginalized, drawing its constituents from 'the poor and the dispossessed of the Roman provinces'.[16] If this had been the case, then Deissmann's view would approximate the view of Mommsen and Waltzing concerning the composition of associations. But Friesen shows that Deissmann's view actually matches quite closely what scholars since the early 1980s began calling the 'new consensus' regarding Pauline assemblies. That 'new consensus' was that groups devoted to Jesus in the mid-first century represented a 'fair cross-section' of the non-elite urban population or a 'mixture of social levels'. But artisans and tradespeople were particularly important in Meeks' view.[17]

While Deissmann may not be to blame, then, it is still true that Mommsen's (1843) and Waltzing's (1895–1900) view that associations consisted primarily of the most poor, who could not necessarily afford burial, find echoes in some portrayals of the socioeconomic level of those devoted to Jesus – both before and after the so-called 'new consensus'. Yet there does not seem to be a direct dependence on those early works about associations. Rather, these scholars of the Jesus movements reflect general assumptions among scholars of the Roman empire in an earlier era (whose expertise was not, in fact, on the Jesus movements) regarding the supposed social level of those who joined. And so John G. Gager, for instance, cites as factual Arthur D. Nock, A. H. M. Jones and E. R. Dodds' assumptions regarding the lower class or underprivileged status of those who followed Jesus generally.[18]

Gager (1975), John H. Elliott (1990 [1981]) and Meggitt (1998), who do not cite either Mommsen or Waltzing, put an emphasis on economic insecurities and societal exclusion in proposing a very low social level for most Jesus adherents.[19] Elliott's study of 1 Peter asserts that the 'vast majority' of its addressees were literally 'aliens' from the 'working proletariat of the urban and rural areas' of Asia Minor.[20] Subsequently, he characterizes the overall economic situation of this 'proletariat' or 'the ignorant and exploited masses' in harsh terms.[21] Directly challenging the so-called 'new consensus',

---

[15] Friesen (2004), also see the responses by Barclay (2004) and Oakes (2004). Theissen (1982 [1974]), Malherbe (1983 [1977]), Meeks (1983).
[16] Meeks (1983: 51–2), as also cited by Friesen (2004: 324–5).
[17] Friesen (2004: 324–6). Malherbe (1983 [1977]: 31), on the 'new consensus'. Meeks (1983: 51–73, especially 73, mixture quote).
[18] Gager (1975: 96, 107–8, referring to Nock, 1933: 187–211, and to Dodds, 1965: 102–38).
[19] Ibid., 96, Elliott (1990 [1981]: 59–100, especially 70–2), Meggitt (1998: 99). Cf. Holmberg (1990: 28).
[20] Elliott (1990 [1981]: 59–100, especially 70–2). For critique, see Harland (2013: 9–10, 161–240) = ibid. (2003: 177–264).
[21] He cites Dickey (1928).

which proposed a cross section of society belonged to such groups, Meggitt's entire work is heavily indebted to an exaggeration of the binary model of Alföldy: 'The Pauline Christians *en masse* shared fully the bleak material existence which was the lot of more than 99% of the inhabitants of the Empire, and also . . . of Paul himself.'[22] There is little room for nuance in socioeconomic levels and conditions in such scholarly generalizations.

Furthermore, the recent shift in studies on associations outlined in the previous section, where the stress is on the presence of those of middling wealth, contrasts somewhat to research since 2004 on groups of Jesus adherents, where (in partial reaction to the 'new consensus' / 'mixture of social levels' view) there is a return to an emphasis on the lowest socioeconomic strata. Even though these scholars are more careful than Meggitt in approaching the question of stratification, they give a similar final conclusion, as Barclay also highlights in his response to Friesen's paper.[23] So we need to recognize the inadequacy of employing a simple binary approach to stratification in the Roman world. It will no longer do to simplify things by sketching a picture of an extremely small percentage of the population (1 per cent) that were very wealthy elites to be distinguished from the undifferentiated 'masses' or 'poor', as in Alföldy's study of the *Social History of Rome* (1985).[24] In some respects, such a bifurcated approach results in scholars replicating the categories of the wealthiest elites in antiquity, who themselves thought in terms of 'us' and 'them', the few honourable ones (*honestiores*) and the insignificant masses (*humiliores*), as Bruce W. Longenecker and Liu also note.[25]

Friesen therefore first made an attempt at developing a more differentiated economic scale for the Roman empire, mapping out seven economic categories. We will see below that, together with Scheidel (an expert on the Roman economy), Friesen considerably refined the percentages assigned to each category in the model compared to his earlier work, which is why we do not supply the percentages at this point. Yet, in 2004, one of Friesen's overall conclusions with respect to those devoted to Jesus is as follows: 'careful examination of explicit references to financial issues in Paul's undisputed letters leads to the conclusion that the vast majority of the people in his assemblies lived *just above or just below the level of subsistence*'.[26] These were the lowest two categories of the seven categories in Friesen's scale at the time, as can be seen in Table 1.1. Longenecker appreciates Friesen's scale and revises the percentages somewhat (e.g. enlarging those of 'middling wealth' in the empire generally), but Longenecker's assessment of Jesus adherents is quite similar to Friesen's.[27] So there is a sense in which both the supposed 'old consensus' and these recent, post-'new consensus' descriptions of the composition of groups devoted to Jesus sound very much like older generalizations about the so-called burial associations composed of the most needy in society.

[22] Meggitt (1998: 99). See also p. 13, where he cites Alföldy (1985: 127).
[23] Compare the observations of Barclay (2004: 363).
[24] Cf. Oakes (2009b: 46–7).
[25] Longenecker (2009a: 247), Liu (2017: 26–7).
[26] Friesen (2004: 357, our italics).
[27] Longenecker (2009b) = ibid. (2010: 22–59). Cf. ibid. (2009a).

Table 1.1 Demographic categories for the Roman empire in Friesen (2004) and Longenecker (2010)

Number	Demographic category
1	Imperial elites (e.g. senators)
2	Regional or provincial elites (e.g. equestrians and rising civic elites)
3	Municipal or civic elites
4	Those with moderate surplus
5	Those stable but near subsistence level
6	Those at subsistence level (and in danger of moving lower)
7	Those below subsistence level

More than others who discuss the social level of Jesus followers, Longenecker pays at least some attention to associations and makes some helpful points in the process. Longenecker gives centre stage to the very work by Patterson (2006) that we discussed above regarding the socioeconomic composition of associations in Italy. However, Longenecker generalizes Patterson's view as applicable to associations in the empire generally and then uses this as a foil for the characterization of groups devoted to Jesus. Longenecker does not seem familiar with the older discussion arising from the work of Mommsen and Waltzing. Longenecker then poses a contrast between groups devoted to Jesus and other associations in his citation of Patterson, stating that, while 'there were *collegia* whose membership included rather poor sectors of society (e.g. funerary associations), *collegia* members generally were "drawn from the upper echelons of the urban *plebs*".[28] Once again, such very recent characterizations of groups devoted to Jesus sound a lot like the older view concerning the so-called burial associations.

In Longenecker's work, the proposal that *other* associations drew mostly from those of middling wealth, from employers rather than employees (categories 4–5), then serves as a contrast with groups devoted to Jesus.[29] The latter are thought to derive from the bottom three economic categories of his scale, significantly including those *below* subsistence (categories 5–7). Longenecker does see some overlap between the segments of society that joined both associations and groups devoted to Jesus. However, the overlap is very minimal, consisting only of a portion of those near subsistence but stable (category 5), which did not make up the bulk of members in groups devoted to Jesus, in his view. Associations also tend towards the category above, those with 'moderate surplus' (category 4) who are just below the wealthy civic elites. As we argue below, the scholarly focus on monumental evidence for associations skews – towards the higher echelons of the non-elites – our picture when, in fact, there are clear signs that those precisely in Friesen's or Longenecker's categories 5 and 6, namely those near or at subsistence level, were likely to be participants within associations generally. So the supposed contrast between groups devoted to Jesus and other associations needs to be further investigated as it seems founded on problematic assumptions and a lack of attention to primary evidence.

---

[28] Longenecker (2009b: 53–4, cf. ibid., 2010: 264–5). Longenecker cites an early article by Kloppenborg (1996), but seems to miss the problem relating to the view of Mommsen, who developed the category of 'burial associations' based on a simplification of the social level of those involved.

[29] Longenecker (2009b). Cf. ibid. (2010: 220–78).

There is a need for future studies in Christian origins to carefully integrate information regarding economic conditions in unofficial associations of various kinds. By 'carefully integrate' we do not mean that such future studies merely refer to articles by scholars of associations dealing with particular locales and generalize from that, but that scholars take the time to examine inscriptions and papyri regarding unofficial associations of various kinds with attention to regional and local variations (if they wish to make comparisons). Advances may be made if scholars of Christian origins and ancient historians both examine the primary sources they tend to neglect due to ostensible disciplinary boundaries or a problematic notion that some groups are 'religious' or 'distinctive' and others are not. After all, those who joined associations and those who joined groups devoted to Jesus were living in the same Mediterranean world and, potentially, interacting within common social networks, so there is some disjoint involved in imagining that primary evidence for these people should not be considered together. The present study begins to make a contribution in this regard, but it is only a starting point and much remains to be done.

Soon we will see that both of the more common approaches to generalizing the socioeconomic composition of associations by focusing on one economic register to the exclusion of others are problematic in some important respects, and this may also be true of similar generalizing tendencies reflected in the recent study of groups devoted to Jesus. It may well be that 'pagan' associations represented a 'cross-section of society' (to reuse Meeks' phrase in a different way) in either of two senses. First, in the sense that certain groups, although not necessarily the majority, were more heterogeneous in membership than others and a single group could draw members from different socioeconomic strata of the non-elites.[30] This is similar to what scholars such as Meeks and Malherbe mean in reference to groups devoted to Jesus. And, second, associations reflect a cross section of society in the sense that, if we were to generalize about where *associations on the whole* found their members, it seems that they found them not only in the higher segments of the non-elites (those of middling wealth), but also in other lower strata beneath that, all the way down to subsistence levels. It is hoped that this discussion may nudge scholars in different disciplines towards a more comprehensive perspective on the issue of socioeconomic conditions and composition of unofficial groups of various kinds in the ancient Mediterranean.

How many belonged to associations?

Before expanding on our view of socieconomic levels and associations, it is important for our argument to consider scholars' attempts to gauge what percentage of the population even belonged to such groups and to determine whether this was mostly limited to men, as is often assumed. Estimates of *how many people* belonged to associations would have direct implications regarding what strata supplied members and what members could offer to their own groups. With a focus on the western part

---

[30] Harland (2013: 19–44) = ibid. (2003: 25–54).

of the Roman empire, Ramsay MacMullen proposes that one-third (i.e., about 33 per cent) of all free males residing in urban areas would have been members of associations (*collegia*) by the second century, and many scholars agree with this estimate.[31] Rather than oversimplifying members' socioeconomic status, however, MacMullen appropriately suggests that 'the urge to congregate and incorporate ... inspired ... every conceivable ... social class'.[32]

MacMullen proposes a figure of one-third from two angles. On the one hand, he bases his assessment on problematic assumptions that the Roman imperial era, more so than other eras, was a time of loneliness and social dislocation. And so the banqueting and other social functions of associations met urgent social needs peculiar to that time.[33] On the other hand, MacMullen is on more solid ground when he gathers epigraphic data from two cities, counting fourteen associations at ancient Vienna (in Gallia Narbonensis) and seventeen at nearby Lugdunum (in Gallia Lugdunensis), although with data from different periods.[34] Using membership lists (*alba*) from these sites, MacMullen calculates an average membership size of between 100 and 200 in associations from these two towns which, with his estimate of the civic populations, gives a figure of one-third.[35]

Other scholars offer similar, reasonable estimates with a focus on information from other locales. Dealing with rates in Pompeii, for instance, Jörg Rüpke arrives at a figure of about one-quarter to one-third of the population: if Pompeii's adult population is estimated at 8,000–10,000 and there were at least forty-five associations (*collegia*) with about fifty members each, then there would be about 2,250 total male members, a rate of between 22.5 and 28 per cent.[36] Turning to Egypt, Micela Langellotti estimates the population of the village of Tebtynis at 3,500 people, and shows that there were eighteen occupational guilds in the first century, with an average membership size of 20–30 adult men, for a total of 360–540. This generates a membership rate of 10–15 per cent among the adult male population in the village, but this lower estimate includes only occupational groups rather than unofficial associations of all types.[37]

While such estimates are valuable in giving us some orientation, the focus on free adult males leaves out other demographic cohorts that were also present within some associations, including women, enslaved persons and children.[38] For example, documentation of free or freed women in associations often contains references to

---

[31] MacMullen (1966: 174). Cf. Ausbüttel (1982: 36–7), Patterson (2006: 260), ibid. (1992: 21). Similarly Peter van Minnen (1987: 37–8) estimates that 36–40 per cent of inhabitants in Byzantine Oxyrhynchos would have been craftsmen.
[32] MacMullen (1966: 196).
[33] Ibid., 174. For critique, see Harland (2013: 71–94) = ibid. (2003: 90–7).
[34] Vienne: *CIL* XII 1898, 1917, 1911, 1877, 2462, 2438, 2331, 1929, 1815, 1869, 1814, 2459 (cf. 2560, 5874), 1914. Lugdunum: see Waltzing (1895–1900: 3.558–64). Now also see Bérard (2012).
[35] MacMullen (1966) seems to assume that 9,380–18,760 free adult men lived in Vindobona (cf. 20,000–25,000 in Pelletier, 1982: 226–7) and that 11,390–22,780 free adult men inhabited Lugdunum (cf. 25,000–30,000 in Audin, 1986: 10–11).
[36] Rüpke (2007: 207).
[37] Langellotti (2016: 118).
[38] On enslaved people in associations, see Poland (1909: 328–9), Zoumbaki (2005), Waltzing (1895–1900: 4.251–429), Ausbüttel (1982: 39–42), Tran (2006: 49–53) and Liu (2009: 171–8). On children in groups devoted to Dionysos, for instance, see Nilsson (1957: 106–15), Harland (2013: 39–40).

24   *Group Survival in the Ancient Mediterranean*

Figure 1.1 Monument depicting the priestess Stratonike approaching the deities Cybele and Apollo with banqueting members, musicians, servers and souvlaki below. Courtesy of the National Archaeological Museum, Athens.

women as sources of contributions and so these women may be important for any evaluation of material conditions and group survival. This picture of women sometimes playing a key role in the life of associations is illustrated in the monument from Triglia in Bithynia, pictured in Figure 1.1 (*IApamBith* 35; 119 or 104 BCE). This monument was set up by a mixed society of both men and women in honour of a woman, Stratonike, who had served as priestess in a way that benefited the group. Stratonike is prominently featured offering sacrifice under the watchful eyes of Cybele and Apollo, and members of the society are depicted banqueting while musicians and servers engage in their duties beneath.

Unlike those scholars who tend to assert the general absence of women without much investigation, Emily Hemelrijk does re-examine evidence for women's involvement in the western part of the empire.[39] However, she concludes that, while 'some women actually

---

[39] On the supposed absence of women: see Waltzing (1895–1900: 1.348), Poland (1909: 289–98), Pomeroy (1975: 201, on guilds), Ebel (2004: 198), Rüpke (2007: 207, on guilds). For guilds with women, see *CIL* VI 10109 (mimes) and *CIL* VI 37826 (neighbourhood association of textile workers). Cf. Saavedra Guerrero (1991).

were members or even officials', the total number of women within these associations was 'negligible when compared to the numbers of male members and officials'.[40] Hemelrijk further proposes that the majority of women participants had informal connections to associations as external donors or patrons, rather than participants or members.

Setting aside Hemelrijk's argument for the moment, however, the actual data she collects in several tables may well indicate that it was more common for women to appear as members or functionaries rather than as external supporters. For there are ninety regular members (her table 4.2) and only forty-two patrons and persons designated 'mothers' in materials she gathers (her tables 5.2 and 5.4).[41] Furthermore, at another point, Hemelrijk does rightly recognize that those called 'mothers' were likely holding functional roles within a group rather than merely honorific titles for an external supporter.[42] So the traditional position on women's relative absence requires closer scrutiny, not only for the western part of the empire but also for the Greek-speaking eastern Mediterranean.[43] At the same time, with the exception of actual membership lists, we need to recognize that sometimes our evidence does not make it possible to distinguish confidently between external supporters, on the one hand, and members or functionaries, on the other.

To begin to address the issue of male-to-female ratios of participation in associations from another angle, we have gathered a substantial sample of sixty lists of contributors or lists of members relating to associations from various regions, ranging from the first century BCE to the third century CE and spanning the Mediterranean (see Appendix 1).[44] Rather than limiting ourselves to membership, we are interested in women's participation or affiliation in a broader sense. For this reason, we include lists of contributors (who may or may not be members), particularly since our interests are in how associations achieved financial survival and not merely in who belonged to them as full members. Our necessarily anecdotal sample of sixty lists is not selective in a way that would favour an overestimation of women's participation, and men do outnumber women by a significant margin in this sample.[45] Many associations that consisted solely or partially of women are known from other types of inscriptions beyond such lists,

---

[40] Hemelrijk (2015: 181).
[41] Ibid., 532–35. Liu (2008: 179 n. 63) highlights a number of Roman groups with women, and these are missed in Hemelrijk's Table: *CIL* VI 9398 (undated), *CIL* VI 30983 = *ILS* 3840 (101–150 CE); *CIL* VI 34004 = *ILS* 7342 (9 CE); *CIL* XIV 2120.
[42] Hemelrijk (2008). Cf. Harland (2007).
[43] For women members in the Greek East, see, for example, *IG* II² 2354 (Athens; late-3rd BCE); *IG* V,2 266 (Mantineia, Greece; mid-1st BCE); *GRA* II 143 = *IMagnMai* 215 (c. 278–250 CE); *IStrat* 149, 174, 352 (Panamara); *IStrat* 666 (Lagina); *GRA* II 99 = *IApamBith* 35 (119 or 104 BCE); *IG* XI,4 1216–1222 (Delos; 3rd or 2nd BCE); *IG* II² 1292 (Athens; 215/14 BCE); *IG* VII 687 (Boiotia; c. 200 BCE); *GRA* II 117 = *TAM* V 1539 (Philadelphia, Lydia; 1st BCE); *GRA* I 71 = *Philippi* II 340/L58 9 (1st–2nd CE). On Egypt, see also Monson (2007a: 192–3, on *PLilleDemotic* 98). Cf. Poland (1909: 289–98) and Hirschmann (2004).
[44] Thirteen of these available lists are from the first century BCE, twelve from the first century CE and thirty-five from the second and early third centuries CE.
[45] Thirty-eight of the sixty lists include all men and two lists consist of all women. The remaining twenty lists are mixed. Ten of them consist of at least 90 per cent men, and twelve of the twenty-four lists that were produced by mixed associations consist of at least 90 per cent men, whereas only one consists of more than 50 per cent women.

but that is not our focus since here we are interested in male–female ratios and the importance of women's resources.

The sixty lists name a total of 3,087 association members or participants, with 2,771 men and 316 women (excluding 'mothers' and patrons). So 10.2 per cent of those affiliated with associations are women in this sample. The table in Appendix 1 can be used to compare regional patterns within the overall picture. For example, 764 names come from Attica and Asia Minor – of which 95 are women (12.4 per cent).

But this overall figure of 10.2 per cent more than doubles the numbers proposed in other studies of women's involvement in association activities, including Sarah Pomeroy's estimate of less than 5 per cent and Hemelrijk's estimate of less than 3.5 per cent.[46] Most importantly for present purposes, the lists in Appendix 1 show that women's participation often included financing the associations' activities, whether as external contributors, as leaders or as members. These sources clarify that studies of financial dimensions of group life must account for more than adult male members, regardless of what socioeconomic level participants came from.

Socioeconomic levels and the improbability of the 'middling wealth' model

A recently developed model of the Roman economy with a focus on socioeconomic stratification of the population can help us to evaluate issues surrounding what segments of the population were active within associations. This will also clarify the range of material resources available from participants, whether men or women. In particular, since many now argue that association membership was drawn predominantly from urban populations of middling wealth, we need to consider whether that scenario is realistic. Employing a modified version of an economic model developed by Scheidel and Friesen, we demonstrate that it is not realistic to propose that those of middling wealth were predominant within associations generally. We then demonstrate the plausibility of lower socioeconomic cohorts (closer to subsistence level) playing a significant role within associations.

Any model of the ancient economy and stratification needs to remain theoretical due to the fragmentary nature of the evidence and a lack of comprehensive statistical data. Nonetheless, Scheidel and Friesen's model remains one of the most carefully constructed and heuristically helpful economic models to date, in our opinion.[47] We need not go into all the details and justifications of calculations (based on wheat as income) here, which can be consulted in Scheidel and Friesen's article. But our Table 1.2 illustrates the more important results of their calculations, particularly the total percentage of the population

---

[46] Pomeroy (1975: 200), drawing on the collections of Clemente (1972, 300 inscriptions) and Waltzing (1895–1900: 4.388–406), Hemelrijk (2008: 118, 148–50). Hemelrijk, in fact, estimates that 3.5 per cent of association patrons for the western part of the empire were women, and maintains that women patrons would have outnumbered women members.

[47] For scholarly assessments of the model in Scheidel and Friesen (2009), see Longenecker (2009a, 2010: 49–51), Liu (2017). Cf. Oakes (2004).

that Scheidel and Friesen place in elite wealth categories, 'middling wealth' categories, and below 'middling wealth' but above subsistence categories.

Even on Scheidel and Friesen's optimistic reading, those of middling wealth would amount to a small segment of the population which would not reach the numbers necessary for recent scholarly proposals regarding how many belonged to associations. Even MacMullen's figure of 33 per cent of the male population belonging to associations considerably exceeds that figure, particularly if one takes the lower (pessimistic) figure of 12.5 per cent of urban populations in Table 1.2, but even if one chooses the higher (optimistic) figure of 25 per cent of urban populations. This brings us to those large segments of the population who lived somewhere between subsistence and middling wealth (our 'below middling wealth' bracket). To what extent was association membership feasible in those economic categories?

Before approaching that question, we must stress that the difference between 12.5 per cent and 25 per cent ('middling wealth' category in the urban population) and 44.5 per cent and 54 per cent ('below middling' category in the population overall) is so large that even a significant adjustment of Scheidel and Friesen's figures would fail to overturn the simple logic that many more members would likely come from the level between subsistence and middling if membership was plausible all through those subcategories in our 'below middling' bracket.[48]

Table 1.2 Income categories with estimated percentages of population, excluding military households. Adapted from Scheidel and Friesen (2009)

Income level	Population % Pessimistic	Population % Optimistic
Elites with high levels of wealth	1.6578	1.2446
'Middling wealth'	5.5 (or 12.5 urban)	10.2 (or 25 urban)
5	0.4	0.8
4	0.6	1.2
3	1	1.8
2	1.5	2.7
1.44–1.9	2	3.7
Below 'middling wealth'	44.5	54
1.43–1.0	1.5	2.8
0.99–0.75	8	19
0.74–0.60	35	32
Below subsistence (<300 kg wheat)	47+	33+
0.59–0.50	25	23
0.49–0.25	22	10
< 0.25	Remaining %	Remaining %

Note: We place in parentheses possible higher middling figures in urban contexts. For a discussion, see Scheidel and Friesen (2009: 90).

[48] In the urban context (although associations were not exclusively urban), the logic stands even when pressured as heavily as possible by Scheidel and Friesen's model. Namely, if we imagine a 14.8 per cent increase in the optimistic urban middling figure coming exclusively at the expense of the 'below middling wealth' categories, we would still be dealing with the difference between 25 per cent (middling) and 39.2 per cent (below middling wealth but above subsistence). So, if involvement in associations can be well-documented in these lowest strata, then it is not likely that most members were drawn from the middling wealth cohort.

Lower socioeconomic levels: A case from Tebtynis

In order to think through the issue of how accessible association membership might have been to those individuals living in the lowest subcategory of our 'below middling wealth' bracket, we will present a case study of association membership fees from Tebtynis. To what extent would this association have been affordable to those living just above subsistence?

The papyrus in question (*GRA* III 195 = *PTebt* I 118), which is pictured in Figure 1.2, comes from the village of Tebtynis, or possibly Kerkeosiris, in the Arsinoites district of Egypt and dates to about 112 or 111 BCE. This financial account of fellow banqueters (*syndeipnoi*) is short, as the document records only three meetings that were scheduled over the course of three months (from 17 Hathyr to 25 Tybi). Expenses for the first funerary feast in the month of Hathyr pertain to wine and bread. At the next banquet, participants purchased an honorary crown and wine, but no bread. They evidently used the money that would otherwise go to bread for this crown, and there is no record of any of the eighteen members taking it upon themselves to procure bread from their own resources for the meeting. At another banquet in the month of Tybi, there was wine and a crown but, again, no bread, and the association recorded a 20 bronze

Figure 1.2 Banqueting records from Tebtynis (*PTebt* I 118). Courtesy of the Center for the Tebtunis Papyri, University of California, Berkeley.

Figure 1.3 Bronze coin from the reign of Ptolemy V Epiphanes (203–181 BCE), with head of Zeus Ammon and eagle with thunderbolt. Courtesy of Ancient Coin Collectors, used under a Creative Commons licence, via Wikimedia.

drachma deficit. Despite very limited resources, the association still continued. In one interpretation of this papyrus, individual members could not afford to spend any more resources on participating than what they had spent, which is why they went without the staple of bread: they were at their maximum.[49]

The cost of participating in this group, 100 *bronze* drachmas per meeting, is important to examine more closely, since we are concerned with questions of socioeconomic level. Some monetary issues in the Ptolemaic period are necessary to explain here, since they have implications for amounts mentioned in any Egyptian documents after 220 BCE (and before the Roman imperial period), including our papyrus and others we discuss in subsequent chapters. Our main point here has to do with repeated devaluations of bronze drachmas (such as the one pictured in figure 1.3) used in Ptolemaic Egypt (in comparison with *silver* drachmas) beginning in 220 BCE, something that Sitta von Reden explains.[50] See Reden's carefully constructed model of currency ratio variations in Egypt (based on amounts mentioned in papyri and on coins) summarized in Table 1.3.[51] By the era of our Tebtynis papyrus (c. 112 BCE), numerous papyri reveal a value of 600 bronze drachmas to 1 silver drachma (as in *PTebt* I 112, line 113). So our Tebtynis association was active in the period of the highest bronze to silver ratio – 600 bronze drachmas to 1 silver drachma – and there are many examples of this 600:1 ratio from Tebtynis itself.[52] In Reden's analysis, only

---

[49] Last (2016a: 131–3).
[50] Reden (2016), cf. ibid. (2007, 2010), Faucher and Lorber (2010), Maresch (1996: 181–7).
[51] Reden (2010: 145–6). Cf. Reekmans (1948: especially 17, 33–43).
[52] 600:1: *PTebt* I 112, lines 58, 113, 118 (112 BCE); *PTebt* I 224 back [v.] (108 BCE); *PTebt* I 116, lines 2, 32 (late II BCE); *PTebt* I 117, lines 10, 47, etc. (99 BCE); *PTebt* I 120, line 72 (97/64 BCE); *PTebt* I 208 (94/61 BCE); *PTebt* I 121, line 140 (96/61 BCE); *PTebt* I 109, line 15 (93 BCE); *PTebt* I 110, line 9 (92 or 59 BCE).

Table 1.3 Bronze to silver drachma ratios in Ptolemaic Egypt, based on Reden (2010: 145–6)

Date range	Ratio
	Bronze drachmas ≈ 1 silver drachma
220–200 BCE	2
200–180 BCE or later	60
180–164 BCE	120
164–130 BCE	240
130–30 BCE	600

five out of fifty-one documents in the period from 130 BCE to the end of the first century indicate a smaller ratio of 300 bronze drachmas to 1 silver drachma, but none of these are from Tebtynis.

So the regular dues in our Tebtynis association, which were 100 bronze drachmas, represent one-third (0.33) of a silver drachma with a 300:1 ratio, and one-sixth or 0.167 of a silver drachma with the far more commonly attested 600:1 ratio. This group of about twenty people paid, on any reckoning, very minimal regular contributions (often called 'fees' in scholarship) to participate.[53] In relation to the cost of living in this period, how little was this amount? Reden compiles data showing that 1 artaba (about 29.5 kilogrammes) of wheat sold at an official rate of 2 silver drachmas during the Ptolemaic era.[54] If 13 artabas (= 383.5 kilogrammes)[55] of wheat represents annual subsistence for a moderately active adult, then individuals in this association would pay 26 silver drachmas per year or about 2.17 silver drachmas per month for their own subsistence-level food costs.[56] In this case, contributions of 0.33 silver drachmas per month would amount to just over 15 per cent above the cost of food for an individual's subsistence, if using the less likely 300:1 ratio.[57] Using the far more likely 600:1 ratio (0.167 silver drachmas per month) would bring down the cost of membership to just under 8 per cent above individual subsistence costs.[58]

---

[53] We quite consciously avoid the term 'fees' since the English word can have negative connotations and might presume a payment that people would avoid. The phrase 'regular contributions' avoids such an assumption.

[54] Reden (2007: 123 n. 27), ibid. (2010: 200–5). On subsistence, see Liu (2017: 32–44).

[55] This estimate of bare subsistence is slightly less than the 390 kg minimum adopted by Friesen and Scheidel. We do this here to be conservative, since this makes our estimate of percentages err on the higher side rather than underestimating the ratio of subsistence to membership cost.

[56] The estimates here are based on Scheidel and Friesen (2009: 68–9) and Scheidel (2010), together with Allen (2009), where the focus is on the imperial era. On subsistence and caloric intake, see Jongman (2007). For a summary of recent discussions of subsistence, see Liu (2017: 33–6).

[57] No Tebtynis papyri attest to the 300:1 ratio, and there are only a few attestations from elsewhere: e.g. *P. Chicago Field Mus. dem.* 31321, line 14 (Thebes; 109 BCE); *P. Turin dem. Suppl.* 6086, line 16 (Thebes; 108 BCE); *P. L. Bat.* XXII 5 *dem*, line 20 (106 BCE); *POxy* XIV 1639, line 13 (73 or 44 BCE).

[58] All papyri from Tebtynis in this period attest to the 600:1 ratio, e.g. *PTebt* I 112, lines 58, 113, 118 (112 BCE); *PTebt* I 224 back [v.] (108 BCE); *PTebt* I 116, lines 2, 32 (late II BCE); *PTebt* I 117, lines 10, 47, etc. (99 BCE); *PTebt* I 120, line 72 (97/64 BCE); *PTebt* I 208 (94/61 BCE); *PTebt* I 121, line 140 (96/61 BCE); *PTebt* I 109, line 15 (93 BCE); *PTebt* I 110, line 9 (92 or 59 BCE).

With the 600:1 ratio, membership in our Tebtynis association was just about 8 per cent above the cost of subsistence. Such an expense was readily accessible to 70 per cent of people in the lowest subcategory of our 'below middling wealth' bracket (using Scheidel and Friesen's calculations). When you add this figure to the rest of the population percentages in the 'below middling wealth' bracket, the total percentage of individuals below middling wealth for whom membership was affordable comes to 34–44.2 per cent.[59] In addition, membership in this Tebtynis group was, of course, affordable to all people in the *middling wealth* bracket, which amounts to 22.4–24.5 per cent of the *total population*. So, this case study illustrates that there was a greater number of people below the middling category who had the ability to make good on the contributions recorded in this Tebtynis account than the number of people living within the middling category. In Chapter 2, we will present further examples of association members coming from these lower economic registers, but this case study can suffice for now.

Conclusion

When we look at our information about associations in light of recent approaches to economic stratification, the current majority opinion that association members were primarily composed of those with middling wealth starts to break down. Scheidel and Friesen's model of economic stratification in the Roman empire helps to establish that it is unlikely that those of middling wealth were the principal source of membership. Our application of this model suggests that even lower economic segments of the population right down to subsistence would very likely be well represented in some groups. At the same time, it would be problematic to suggest that association membership was entirely free or that those below subsistence level would be very common in these groups, as scholars like Meggitt, Friesen and Longenecker suggest with respect to Pauline assemblies.[60]

One might be tempted to further categorize association members or even associations themselves – assuming homogeneous membership in at least certain groups – using Scheidel and Friesen's scale, but such a project of plotting out associations on an economic scale would be problematic for several reasons. The most obvious difficulties are the fragmentary nature of our evidence and the imbalance in what types of groups we encounter most when economic arrangements are mentioned. Longenecker's attempt to categorize groups devoted to Jesus using Scheidel and Friesen's scale illustrates problems with doing this, in that his approach reifies the common opinion that association members, but not members of Pauline groups, came exclusively or mostly from those of middling wealth, even though there is not nearly enough data to generalize about economic conditions in Paul's assemblies.[61]

---

[59] Since we are following Scheidel and Friesen's figures above, we follow them here as well in calculating the mean income level as the midway point within an income bracket (2009: 83).
[60] Meggitt (1998), Friesen (2004: 357), Longenecker (2010: 295).
[61] Longenecker (2010: 267).

Focusing on the island of Rhodes, Vincent Gabrielsen recognizes difficulties in ranking associations according to wealth. Gabrielsen notes that: 'a distinction, however crude, needs to be made between two kinds of brotherhoods: on the one hand, those with just enough liquid assets and realty to sustain a decent level of corporate activity; and, on the other hand, the much more interesting cases ... of those capable of rising to distinctly higher levels of financial performance'. However, he realizes, no 'means are available with which to quantify the relationship between the two, other than the indirect – and hardly foolproof – one provided by the scale of expenditure on attested honorific activity, which gives a clear numerical preponderance (at any given time) to the second kind'.[62] As Gabrielsen articulates here, our information about the material conditions of individual groups is partial and we are faced with the problem that much of the epigraphic evidence that survives would, by its very honorary nature, give us a view of the more materially successful groups that could afford to purchase and inscribe such monuments in stone.

The consolation here is that, in some ways, an attempt to scale associations from the less well off to the most well off would, in many instances, be somewhat irrelevant to the issue of survival, we argue. For as our Tebtynis group shows, even associations financially accessible to members living near subsistence level could sometimes survive if they functioned within limited means and adapted to changing circumstances. In other words, groups at either end of the scale, whether relatively wealthy or relatively poor, could disband, survive or thrive, depending on how they adapted to their own material conditions, as we explain in more detail now.

[62] Gabrielsen (2001: 234).

2

Scenarios of Success, Survival and Decline

Now our number has dwindled to a few ... and we do not have the means to pay for rent ...

IG XIV 830

They went out from us, but they were not of us.

1 John 2:19

Introduction

These two excerpts, one from a letter by Tyrian merchants (settled in Puteoli, Italy) and the other from an 'elder' in a group devoted to Jesus (perhaps in western Asia Minor) highlight experiences of struggle for group survival, one more directly relating to costs and the other with resource implications. Episodes such as these raise basic questions concerning the circumstances faced by unofficial associations at different times in their histories and regarding participants' efforts to make collective life feasible.

Our discussion of the Tebtynis association that functioned just barely above the very limited means of its members in the previous chapter illustrates that some groups could survive or thrive regardless of the socioeconomic composition of membership, so long as they paid attention to available resources from internal and external sources. Due to the nature of our evidence, many associations discussed in this study were among the more successful ones which could afford to erect a stone altar, statue, inscription or even building. Before we engage that material, it is important to theorize a range of possibilities in the resource situations of different groups. This will help us to be attentive to what might otherwise be missed about the struggle for survival and the various material situations that an association could face at particular moments.

Based on our necessarily anecdotal evidence, we argue that it is helpful to think in terms of three main scenarios regarding the resource situation of a given group at particular moments in its history. First, some associations could at some point go beyond the means of the group or its members, or could fail to function in some other way that could lead to decline and, potentially, insolvency and dispersal. Second, there were times when a group functioned near or slightly above the means available from members, supporters or the group's common fund, as with our Tebtynis group in the previous chapter. At these points, there was potential to last and meet at least the minimal material and non-material benefits of group membership. Third, still other associations could function with less resources than what members or supporters could actually provide. These associations were, therefore, in a position to call on associates for further resources in difficult times or in connection with special communal collections. Groups experiencing this third scenario could also potentially increase activities, offer further material or non-material benefits to participants or raise the profile of the group within the local context. Towards the end of the chapter, we provide concrete examples of either survival or success where particular associations of various kinds existed for a considerable period of time. Each association could, in theory, fit into only one of the three categories at a particular moment in its history. Throughout the remainder of this book, we will encounter further cases that instantiate these scenarios, especially the second and third ones, which is why it is so important to give special attention to the first scenario of decline and potential dissolution here.

Scenario One: Exceeding material means – Decline or dissolution

This is the most difficult of the three scenarios to illustrate, since the vast majority that faced financial difficulties on a regular basis would simply disappear and leave no further traces, as Jinyu Liu now also notes.[1] Usually, the decline and disappearance of an association would not be recorded for us to see, since further expenses were involved in inscribing the stone monuments that are often our principal evidence outside of Egypt. Only in dry climates like Egypt's do less expensive (and therefore perishable) records on papyrus usually survive. Wooden tablets, like the one from Dacia we soon discuss, were also used to record other aspects of daily interactions such as financial matters, but these, too, rarely survive.[2] Despite these difficulties with our materials, there are examples of associations that seem to be working beyond the means of the group or its individual members to the point of decline and even insolvency and disbandment. Other crises could also lead to struggles, and so associations might disperse for a variety of reasons, as when members of a particular group just could not get along or when there was a lack of attendance for other reasons. Yet even these cases where attendance suffered would have resource implications, as we will see.

The financial collapse of an association in the province of Dacia in 167 CE is perhaps the clearest example of dissolution. When this association (*collegium*), devoted to Jupiter Cernenus in the mining village of Alburnus Major (now Rosia Montana in Romania), publicized its disbandment, the notice (*libellus*) on wax-coated wooden tablets detailed some factors in their decline (*AGRW* 69 = *IDacia* I 31). Absenteeism was rampant, and only seventeen of the fifty-four members remained, perhaps due to the effects of the so-called Antonine plague.[3] Most members were not contributing

---

[1] Liu (2016: 207–8). For scholarly discussions of potential dissolution, see Poland (1909: 271–6), Arnaoutoglou (2003: 95–6), Mikalson (1998: 2–3).
[2] On wood tablets, see Bowman and Thomas (1984: 33–5), Meyer (2004).
[3] Mitrofan (2014: 11). We are grateful to Kloppenborg who drew our attention to this article on the Antonine plague.

what they owed. And there were insufficient funds to pay for funerals. The document inscribed in wax carefully states that, therefore, no member could expect the association to help pay for their funeral any longer. Further details are lacking, but this is a rare glimpse into the end of an association due, in part, to an inability to cover costs. No doubt, similar things could happen to other groups.

Several factors independent of the economic status of participants could contribute to decline or dissolution, including: lack of attendance and, therefore, a shortage of income from members; over-reliance on external supporters such as guests and benefactors, whose contributions would not necessarily be consistent; failure to expel members responsible for financial misappropriation; usage of a foundation instead of interest or income generated from loans, leases or sale of produce; failure to collect dues or fines from members or to collect other funds owed to the group; failure to punish members who did not meet material requirements; and, failure to prioritize expenditures that fulfilled social obligations or expectations of members or supporters (e.g. memorializing members, offering appropriate honours to external supporters).

Ilias Arnaoutoglou discusses the interesting, if fragmentary, record of arbitration in the case of sacrificing associates (*orgeōnes*) at Athens, which indicates problems arising in management of properties.[4] The document reflects a dispute among participants in the group over how communal property was to be utilized. The mutually agreed upon arbitrators ruled that 'the properties are to belong to the goddess and nobody is permitted ... to sell (?) ... or mortgage them; rather, the priest together with the sacrificing associates are to perform the sacrifices according to ancestral custom from the ... income (?)' (*IG* II² 1289, lines 3–7; 255–235 BCE). Although these disagreements over use of assets were solved through informal conciliation here, such disputes over resources could, in theory, lead to decline or the breakdown of the association itself.[5]

There is other information about groups functioning beyond their means and potentially heading for financial failure. As the quote at the beginning of the chapter indicates, Tyrian immigrants settled in Puteoli seem to have come up short on paying their rent.[6] This situation might have led to further economic troubles if Tyre itself had not answered their call for help. In an effort to receive assistance from the homeland, the inscription highlights financial danger and dwindling membership:

> This station has long been cared for by the Tyrian settlement in Puteoli, who were many and wealthy, but now our number has dwindled to a few. In paying for sacrifices and the rites of our ancestral gods that are established for worship here in temples, we do not have the means to pay for rent of the station, 250 denarii per year, especially since the payments for the bull sacrifice at the games at Puteoli are charged to us in addition. We request, therefore, that you provide for the lasting permanence of the station.
>
> *AGRW* 317 = *IG* XIV 830; 174 CE

---

[4] Arnaoutoglou (2003: 57–8). Cf. Ferguson (1944: 84–6).
[5] Arnaoutoglou thinks dissolution was not an option, but he is concerned with formal, legal actions of dissolution.
[6] For discussion, see Harland (2009: 115–16), Sosin (1999), Verboven (2011b), Öhler (2011a).

Moving east, certain papyri from Egypt suggest that an association might fail to fulfil its own contract with a member or might misuse funds in contravention of the group's own rules. Two papyri from Magdola in the Arsinoites district preserve appeals to the king in cases where, it seems, an association failed to follow its own rules in paying for a member's funeral. This failure may have happened due to lack of funds or due to the leadership's refusal for some unknown reason (perhaps simply dislike of the deceased). In one of the cases, a woman named Krateia writes to King Ptolemais in 215 BCE. She requests that the society (*thiasos*) which her brother, Apollodotos, had belonged to be forced by the regional administrator (*stratēgos*) to reimburse the man's funerary contribution (*taphikon*; *AGRW* 293 = *GRA* III 189 = *PEnteuxis* 20). When Apollodotos died, apparently the society had not made adequate provisions for his funeral even though he had paid the amount. We know from at least one other document that such a funerary contribution could be granted to a third party in a will, suggesting the member's co-ownership of that portion of the common fund.[7]

A second person's handwriting on this same papyrus from Magdola is that of an authority figure, perhaps the regional administrator, Diophanes, whom Krateia mentions in her appeal. This authority instructs some subordinate official to review the society's regulation (*nomos*) and to order the parties to resolve the conflict in light of what was specified in that regulation. In the other similar petition, two family members (a sister and a husband) petition the king regarding those in a society of women who had likewise failed to provide the funeral funds for a member named Soeris (*GRA* III 190 = *PEnteuxis* 21). They had done this even though Soeris had been priestess of the group for four years. Our discussion of the Tebtynis group in Chapter 1 shows that other groups might fall short of resources for particular purposes, including food in that case. But the societies that Apollodotos and Soeris belonged to seem to have failed to fulfil important contracts made with their own members, which could threaten members' feelings of attachment to the group and the endurance of the association. Elsewhere in the Mediterranean, there are concerns about funeral funds being properly dispensed.[8]

Beyond financial mismanagement, natural occurrences – or 'acts of god', if you will – could cause financial hardship, potentially leading to struggles or even a group's end. We know that earthquakes were quite common in parts of the Mediterranean and that certain ones, such as the major quake in Lydia in 17 CE, destroyed or heavily damaged many buildings.[9] Although we would not necessarily expect to find evidence of how such incidents impacted associations, there is, in fact, a quite detailed case from Psenemphaia in the Delta region of Egypt (*GRA* III 170 = *IDelta* I 2; 6 BCE). In this case, crisis was averted, but that would not always be the case.

An association of 'fellow farmers' (*syngeōrgous*) who were landowners (*geouchoi*) had been meeting in a building (*oikos*) dedicated to Kleopatra as patron deity, but an

---

[7] *GRA* III 287 = *PRyl* IV 580. Cf. *AGRW* 215 = *IKilikiaBM* II 201.

[8] The treasurer of a society in Athens was praised because, among other things, 'he has paid *immediately* the burial expenses for those who have died' (*GRA* I 31; 194 BCE; cf. *GRA* I 17). This implies that there were occasions when a functionary might fail to act appropriately or quickly enough to act at all.

[9] Strabo, *Geography* 12.8.18; Pliny the Elder, *Natural History* 2.86; Tacitus, *Annals* 2.47.

earthquake almost completely destroyed this meeting place. The decree recounts their difficulties in finding a solution, as they felt that it was impossible for them to afford to rebuild the structure on their own. They therefore searched for a new 'president' (*prostatēs*) from among their members, with the implication being that the candidate would pay a certain amount to hold the office, and that amount would cover the cost of rebuilding. However, the story goes that no one would step up for the position due to the financial burden. That is, until they finally found Apollonios, the son of the previous chief priest, who 'wished to enhance the reputation of the fellow farmers'. Apollonios paid to reconstruct the building from his own resources, also painting it and supplying cushions, presumably for banquets. The group resolved to honour him (and his son) with honorary shields, with a crown and with a double-serving at feasts. Although Apollonios paid for the building itself, the resolution also refers to the membership collecting together 500 drachmas to cover other expenses, presumably much less than what Apollonios paid for the construction work. In other cases, like an earthquake on Rhodes which damaged the communal burial structures of an immigrant association there, the contributing members (rather than any one individual) could pull together a special collection – called simply the 'collapse money' in this inscription – to repair the damage (*IG* XII,1 9). But one could imagine such situations considerably diminishing the material resources available to participants in the period following.

Although outside of our geographical focus, the difficult circumstances faced by Mithras adherents as recorded on a bronze plaque from Virnunum in Noricum (now Zollfeld, Austria), pictured in Figure 2.1, is noteworthy as it involves two different natural disasters in the late second century.[10] In this case, however, the group weathered these storms and survived, unlike our case from Dacia. On the one hand, the members' meeting place had collapsed, due to some natural occurrence such as a storm or earthquake. At least thirty-four members of the association then contributed funds to a special collection to rebuild the structure. The plaque itself, which supplies current members' names, was originally set up at the dedication of the new building (*qui templum vii conlapsum impendio suo restituerunt*), probably between 10 December 182 and 3 January 183 (based on Emperor Commodus' titles). On the other hand, about a year and a half later (in June 184), another disaster impacted the group and the members decided to convene because of 'mortality' (*mortalitatis causa conven(erunt)*), supplementing the original inscription. Also added to the inscription were indications that a significant number of members – five, including two 'fathers', that is leaders in the highest grade of initiation – had, in fact, recently died (marked with a theta for *thanōn*), and so this meeting was a memorial for these members. The original editor of the inscription, Gernot Piccottini, makes the very plausible suggestion that, due to the date and number of deaths, these were likely victims of one wave of the Antonine plague, the same Mediterranean-wide plague that may have impacted the association in Dacia that disbanded.[11] And, as Roger Beck points out, it may have been at this same meeting that eight new names were added to what was now becoming the ongoing membership

---

[10] First publication: Piccottini (1994) = *AE* (1994), no. 1334. Cf. Gordon (1996). Kloppenborg drew our attention to this inscription and supplied the photo.
[11] Piccottini (1994: 22).

Figure 2.1 Bronze Membership List (Album) of a Mithras association from Virunum, now in the Landesmuseum Kärnten, Klagenfurt, Austria. Courtesy of John S. Kloppenborg, used with permission.

list (*album*) for the association.[12] Further names were added to the membership list in the following years, up to 201 CE. So, despite these disasters, it seems that the group was still able to find new members, with eight new ones replacing the five who had passed away and others joining later.

Similar material struggles could arise when a group's buildings were heavily damaged or destroyed in connection with human-made disasters, such as those that could accompany ethnic conflicts. The case of Judeans at Alexandria around 38–41 CE provides an instance of ethnic associations facing such difficulties, even though the extent of negative relations seems exceptionally bad here, and this would not be representative of relations between Judeans and others at most other times and places. The desecration, destruction or damage of numerous prayer-houses of Judeans during ethnic conflicts between Judeans and Alexandrians would, no doubt, have led to considerable financial struggle for the groups involved.[13] There also seem to have been Judean retaliatory actions (see *For Flaccus* 86–91), which could, in theory, have resulted in further injuries and damage to other association buildings. Philo makes it clear that associations ('societies', 'synods' and banqueting groups), such as those linked to the Alexandrian Isidoros, were instrumental in some of these clashes between Judeans and other inhabitants (*For Flaccus* 136–40). Philo speaks of both the destruction and the

---

[12] Beck (1998: 335–6).
[13] See Barclay (1996: 48–59), van der Horst (2003), Gambetti (2009). Cf. *CPJ* II 153 = *PLond* VI 1912 (Claudius' letter).

seizing of Judean prayer-houses, along with ejection of many Judeans from their neighbourhoods (*Embassy to Gaius* 132-4). Philo also highlights the financial toll this took on many Judeans, through both pillaging and an inability to engage in their occupations within local mercantile networks (*For Flaccus* 53-7). So rebuilding would presumably be a major struggle for any gatherings of Judeans that were impacted, and some established gatherings may well have dispersed.

Other issues could contribute to decline, with accompanying material struggles. While we generally lack letters from members or leaders to an association that might shed light on the details of internal problems, we do have such evidence for groups devoted to both the Israelite god and Jesus. Even a cursory glance at the epistles of 'the elder' (1-3 John) or the epistles of Ignatius of Antioch (*c*. 110 CE), for instance, shows that internal struggles over practice and ideology, which may well reflect basic problems with cooperation or personality conflicts, could lead to schisms or the formation of new rival groups (cf. 1 Corinthians 1-4). This, in turn, could result in a considerable decrease in the membership of particular groups as there was competition for allegiances of members or attempts to draw members away from rival associations. This, too, would have material implications as an individual's resources and potential service contributions would travel with them.

In the case addressed by 'the elder', it seems that the author's group (perhaps in western Asia Minor) was struggling with numbers as those who 'left' are seemingly characterized as the majority, as 'the world listens to them' and not to the elder (1 John 4:1-6). Such a loss of participants in an association could, consequently, directly affect the amount of resources that trickled into communal funds. The competitive atmosphere is evident in the elder's concern that the 'many deceivers' who had 'gone out into the world' not be accepted for hospitality or meetings in the houses of those who continued to associate themselves with the elder's favoured association of 'friends' (2 John 7-11). In fact, the author warns that his people should not even say 'hello' to those participating in the other group or groups (2 John 11). A person from another group devoted to Jesus, namely Diotrephes, was clearly adopting a similar strategy: in the elder's terms, Diotrephes 'refuses to admit the brothers and also stops those who want to admit them and throws them out of the assembly' (3 John 9-10). So far, the elder's favoured group was surviving, but he seems concerned about losing people and losing the competition with rival groups.

A similar strategy to that of both the elder and Diotrephes is adopted by Ignatius, a former overseer from an assembly in Syrian Antioch. Addressing assemblies in western Asia Minor, Ignatius attempts to curb the profusion of relatively informal groups of Jesus followers meeting together for meals or other activities as they saw fit. Instead, Ignatius calls for anyone who wants to be considered legitimate to come together in one local group under a particular leadership structure.[14] Like the elder and Diotrephes, Ignatius, too, calls for allegiance to the group he favours and avoidance of other groupings at Smyrna: 'Not only should you not admit them [so-called "wild beasts in human form"], but if possible do not meet with them' (*Smyrneans* 4). So both of these authors show that one gathering or association could become two or more, with each

---

[14] E.g. *Magnesians* 4, 7; *Smyrneans* 8; *Ephesians* 5; *Trallians* 7; *Philadelphians* 4.

new formation having to find means to support commensal and other activities in a competitive atmosphere. Such potential schisms – whether for ideological, practical or personal reasons – are the other side of the coin to the amalgamations we mention in Chapter 3. Limited resources from both wealthier supporters or leaders (as Diotrephes in 3 John may have been) and participants could be won or lost.

Closely related to this situation of schism and pertinent to the issue of competition for financial survival is the evidence for multiple affiliations among associations of various kinds.[15] The practice of belonging in more than one group was so common that, by the third century at least, the Roman imperial authorities felt a need to express their opinion on the matter, attempting to limit the practice at least for occupational guilds for reasons that are not entirely clear (*AGRW* L53 = *Digest* 47.22.1.2). The tendency to participate within multiple unofficial groupings – whether they be neighbourhood collectives, immigrant associations (e.g. of Judeans), groups devoted to Jesus or guilds in places like Hierapolis or Ostia – could be a dilemma for any one association attempting to sustain some degree of loyalty and, therefore, material support from current participants in the group. For, in theory, the base level of resources available to any particular individual would remain the same whether that person belonged to just one group or to many. So, in cases of multiple affiliations, those limited individual resources would need to be spread more thinly, leaving less room for that person to financially contribute and, more importantly here, to step up in cases of communal crises like any of the ones we have just outlined above. A similar issue would hold for substantial donors, particularly those that were participants or leaders in the groups they supported: figures like Dionysodoros (see Chapter 3) and Timapolis on Rhodes and Achilleus in Moesia presumably had to make choices about which of the many associations they affiliated with was, at a particular moment, more deserving of material support than others.[16] The material resources of such special supporters would be limited, too, not just the resources of your average members.

It is worth saying something about how the authorities may relate to the potential dissolution of certain associations or even the confiscation of an association's properties. There is a propensity for certain scholars to stress incidents of controlling intervention by imperial (or royal) authorities, in part because of a strong focus on Roman legal theory (as spelled out in things like the sixth-century collection known as the *Digest*) and in part due to a problematic assumption that legal theory would correspond closely to social circumstances in the provinces.[17] Moreover, studies that heavily emphasize legal sources and, therefore, the perspective of imperial authorities as the key to understanding associations seem to be working with a more traditional top-down approach to history that clashes considerably with doing social history more generally, so this may reflect a more fundamental historiographical difference. In fact, the evidence suggests it was relatively rare for such authorities to encounter local associations in a negative way, particularly in the provinces. Furthermore,

---

[15] Harland (2009: 156–60). Cf. Meiggs (1960: 321–2), Gabrielsen (1994).
[16] See Harland (2009: 157–8).
[17] Harland (2013: 141–60) = ibid. (2003: 162–76). Recent overemphasis on Roman legal theory: Bendlin (2011, 2016), Eckhardt (2016a).

sometimes Roman officials or even emperors could be among benefactors of such associations.[18]

Nonetheless, it is also true that occasionally royal or imperial authorities could encounter and take negative actions against associations when such groups were involved in broader disturbances or negative incidents and when an official happened to be around and aware of the situation (e.g. Pliny the Younger, *Letters* 10.33–4, 10.92–3,10.96–7 = *AGRW* L40). Here, it is important to observe that on such rare occasions, this could have implications for a group's assets and even existence. Imperial rulings collected in the *Digest* suggest that, at least by the second century, a partnership (*corpus*), association (*collegium*) or society (*societas*), like a municipality (*res publica*), was, in theory, entitled to own property, along with having a common fund and being able to hire an advocate in legal cases (*AGRW* L43 = *Digest* 3.4.1).[19] Yet there were also potential precedents for the dissolution of associations (*AGRW* L54 = *Digest* 47.22.3, in a section collected by Marcianus, *c*. 222–235 CE): again, in theory, there were precedents for a Roman proconsul in a province to seize and sell any properties of an association when associates failed to successfully defend the group on some charge (*AGRW* L43 = *Digest* 3.4.1, in the section collected by Gaius, *c*. 130–180 CE). Such incidents of Roman governors interfering in the lives of associations would be extremely rare, however, in part because a single governor would be responsible for hundreds of cities (each potentially with many associations) and would not even be capable (if interested) in controlling local, unofficial groups in any consistent manner.[20]

Two rare examples where an association's existence or properties may have been at risk may suffice. A violent clash such as that at the amphitheatre in Pompeii during Nero's reign, which is recorded by Tacitus and depicted on the wall painting in Figure 2.2, could result in the dissolution of some implicated associations, but nothing is mentioned about seizing meeting places in this account (Tacitus, *Annals* 14.17 = *AGRW* L39). Similarly, an edict by the proconsul of Asia in the late second century refers to disorders perpetrated by bakers 'in the market' of Ephesos and orders 'the bakers not to gather together as a faction (*hetairia*)'. But the focus is on forbidding certain kinds of dissident meetings and there is no explicit reference to either the dissolution of guilds or the seizing of properties used by the bakers, if they did form a guild and did possess any permanent meeting place.[21] On such rare occasions, however, there would presumably be occasions when an association could come to a sudden dissolution, along with any properties it possessed.

While evidence for actual confiscations of association properties is rare, there is a papyrus from Tebtynis in Egypt that preserves an extremely fragmentary decree from

---

[18] An outstanding case would be buildings granted to the guild of athletes devoted to Herakles by the emperor Antoninus Pius (fulfilling a promise of Hadrian) when the guild moved its headquarters from Asia Minor to Rome (*IG* XIV 1054, 1055, 1109, 1110 = *IGUR* 235, 236, 237–8). See West (1990), Pleket (1973), Oliver (1989), *AGRW* 116, 306.

[19] On legal personality, see the different positions of Arnaoutoglou (2003: 120–5, 133–8), Ustinova (2005: 177–90), and Ismard (2010: 141–85).

[20] Burton (1975, 1993).

[21] See, most recently, Venticinque (2009: 172–5), Perry (2015).

Figure 2.2 Painting from Pompeii, depicting the riot in and around the amphitheatre. Photo by Harland.

the Ptolemaic era (*PTebt* III 700). The papyrus fragments relate to two purchases of land (in 124 BCE) by a man named Ammonios. The evidence here suggests that this was land that had likely been owned by associations, had been seized for some reason, and was now being auctioned by the Ptolemaic authorities. This is indicated by an earlier decree by King Ptolemy VIII Euergetes II which is appended to the documents regarding the purchase (lines 22–53). In that decree, pertaining to the city of Alexandria, there is reference to the alienation (*ekdioikein*) of properties owned by gymnasia, several other groups whose names are lost in a missing section (*haireseis* and *thiasoi* are suggestions), 'corporate bodies' of settled foreigners (*politeumata*) and 'synods' (*synodoi*) (see *PTebt* III 700, lines 37–9 and the notes to those lines). The circumstances that led to this unusual action are not preserved. This example still shows that there were occasions when a group's survival, or at least possession of a place to meet, would be dependent on actions by authorities.

Scenario Two: Functioning just within material means – Survival

Often our fragmentary evidence makes it hard to know when we are dealing with an association that was merely functioning within available resources and nonetheless surviving – a scenario we sketch here – rather than working with significant financial leeway, as discussed in the next section. It is only possible to assert confidently that an association functioned close to its means when we have access to barely balanced financial accounts over a significant span, which we lack with few exceptions. Many of the surviving accounts on papyri are so fragmentary or momentary that it makes it difficult to evaluate how often such groups continued to run roughly at their material means without the ominous threat of insolvency.

In Chapter 1, we have already provided an example of a Tebtynis association that, we argued, consisted of people in the lower social registers and near subsistence level. That case would also be a candidate for an association that fits this scenario of functioning barely within members' means. Thankfully, another group from this same locale happens to provide us with one of the lengthiest known financial records produced by any association in the Hellenistic era (*GRA* III 194 = *PTebt* III 894).[22] The local crocodile god Petesouchos, also known as Souchos or Sobek, is mentioned in the documents and may be the patron deity of the association. While with the other Tebtynis group (in *PTebt* I 118) there were only 18 readable lines in the records, this second Tebtynis group's accounting records (in *PTebt* III 894) span 365 lines. These cover nine months during a two-year period, although the months are in no discernible order in surviving fragments. This papyrus dates to 114 or 113 BCE, so like the other Tebtynis papyrus, the references to drachmas in this document would be to the considerably debased bronze drachmas common in Egypt at this time, rather than the silver drachmas used elsewhere.

The financial records of this second Tebtynis association display how meticulously a group might keep track of its finances. The records also suggest this group functioned quite close to its limit. Apparently, this group adjusted the amount of regular contributions for participation according to specific conditions. It is unclear whether this catered to the group's immediate need, the limited means of the specific participant, or both. At one meeting, participants paid 100 bronze drachmas to participate, whereas at another meeting, the amount was 200 drachmas, and there is a range of figures between 100 and 300 at yet another meeting of more than twenty members.[23] It is noteworthy that participants' contribution for a meeting here seems to be around or slightly above similar costs in the other Tebtynis association (in Chapter 1). Yet, in our current group, there were other identified expenses covered by members as well. Some members of this second Tebtynis group paid their regular financial contribution late, came up short, or owed a fair amount of money either in connection with a loan or

---

[22] See also Last and Rollens (2014).
[23] Fragment 1 back [v.], III, line 63; fragment 2 front [r.], I–II; and, fragment 1 front [r.] II. Those listed in the latter fragment include two members who paid 100 drachmas, one who paid 120, one who paid 160, two who paid 190, six who paid 200, one who paid 215 and thirteen who paid 300 drachmas.

overdue regular contributions.[24] These references to delinquencies, small deficits and the very low costs for participation, all indicate that at least some members likely lived near the lower end of the socioeconomic scale, perhaps near subsistence level or at least had minimal monetary capital at the time.[25] Nonetheless, by living within its means, this group seems to have been surviving as well as any association with wealthier members might hope to do, at least during these two years.

We can glean from this account how the group weathered potential financial difficulties in some cases. What is interesting about their sustainability is that their strategies and contingency plans suggest this was not left to chance. First, at one (undatable) banquet, the group spent more money (4,140 bronze drachmas) than their core membership produced in income (3,955 bronze drachmas).[26] The members were precisely 185 bronze drachmas short here, but guests also attended on this occasion. The group frequently invited outsiders as guests (*xenoi* in Greek) to join their feasts. Some contribution was always paid for these attendees, whether coming from the guest's own resources or from another member who invited them. At this banquet, when costs exceeded income from members' regular contributions specifically, there is record of one guest who attended at the rate of 200 bronze drachmas. So, rather than falling into debt as a result of the meal, the group recorded a surplus of 15 bronze drachmas. It does not seem likely that the association realized at the last minute that they would be short at this gathering and somehow pulled someone off the street to pay 200 bronze drachmas to participate – almost precisely the amount of the deficit. Rather, it would seem that they had a social network of friends or acquaintances from which they invited guests when a shortage was anticipated.[27] Guests were also a factor in our other Tebtynis group (Chapter 1). A somewhat comparable situation seems evident in an association at the Piraeus (see also Chapter 8). In that case, there were full members (*thiasōtai*) distinguished from others who participated as 'friends' (*philoi*) – comparable to guests – with some ongoing connection but apparently without full membership (*GRA* I 8 = *IG* II² 1275; 325–275 BCE).[28]

Rather than luck, then, this Tebtynis document suggests thoughtful planning. The practice of drawing guests from an existing network seems to have functioned as a survival strategy to generate extra income beyond what members regularly provided. There are two signs of planning in this case. First, contributing guests are recorded on other occasions when the group met, and so this was not an anomaly for this group. Each time an invited guest attended, however, the guests paid a different contribution amount that was often lower (than 200 bronze drachmas), including 40 bronze drachmas and 60 bronze drachmas.[29] It is plausible to suggest that this group set the entrance amount for guests at a rate determined by current material need in order to

---

[24] Fragment 1 front [r.], II, lines 6–7; fragment 1 front [r.], II, lines 22–4; fragment 4 back [v.], II, lines 19, 24; and, fragment 12 front [r.], II-back [v.] II.
[25] For a small deficit, see fragment 1 back [v.], III; fragment 5 front [r.], II, line 8. There are no references to benefactors in the documents, although see fragment 8 front [r.], II, lines 30–4.
[26] Fragment 2 front [r.] I, lines 6–10, front [r.] II, lines 36–8.
[27] See also Last (2016a: 131–3).
[28] Cf. Tod (1906: 333).
[29] Fragment 4 front [r.], I, lines 8–10; fragment 5 back [v.], II, lines 16–20.

avoid debt, as the regular membership payments were likewise varying. With the other two recorded instances of guest participants, the document names the members who invited them, including Herakleides and Phatreis whose four guests paid 40 drachmas each and Kagos and several other members whose guests paid 60 drachmas each.[30] In such cases, it would be in the association's interest for its own members to go out and 'advertise' banquets so that it would have a sufficient network from which to pull guests when needed to balance the books. Still, these invited guests attended on members' terms. For instance, presumably it would not be in the association's interest to have many more than, say, twenty-five participants at their meals as we discuss below, and so the presence of guests would seem to reveal selectivity in a way that fits current needs rather than having too many or too few such guests.

A second sign of planning is the fact that, despite having twenty-four participants at this banquet, the group ordered their standard, single 9.72 litre jar (*keramion*) of wine and did not increase that amount. It would seem that wine expenses remained relatively stable regardless of the number of members and guests, as when the same amount of wine was available for twenty attendees.[31] Limiting non-member invitees would have been preferable since more attendees meant less wine for each participant.

On a second occasion, the association seems to have recorded a small debt of 10 bronze drachmas in connection with thirteen jars of beer that five members were supposed to purchase.[32] One of the five came up short by 40 drachmas in his contribution, which explains how the association could be caught off guard here.[33] Fortunately, it was at this time that the association collected from a member named Theon 200 bronze drachmas 'for fighting with Hareos', and so this income from the fine would easily cover the group's potential debt for beer.[34] This may seem like a chance occurrence as the group collects a fine precisely when they need additional income to cover an imbalance in the budget. However, this association routinely collected fine payments and pressed members regarding unpaid fines, and the timing of the pressure may relate to immediate need.[35]

In summary, there is no indication that this association of twenty to twenty-five men, who, by all indications lived well below those of middling wealth, experienced any significant financial problems on the dates for which we have records. They never went into serious debt and they were competent in organizing meals and contributing to funerary rituals.[36] Since they recorded small debts here and there, and needed to enact contingency plans to cover them, we can be fairly confident that they squeezed members for just about everything they could. They also brought in other friends or acquaintances when needed. This association and our other Tebtynis group, then, offer

---

[30] Fragment 4 front [r.], I, lines 8–10; fragment 5 back [v.], II, lines 16–21.
[31] Fragment 2 back [v.], II, line 44.
[32] Fragment 5 front [r.], II, line 8.
[33] Fragment 5 front [r.], II, line 1.
[34] Fragment 5 front [r.], II, line 10.
[35] For another paid fine, see fragment 3 back [v.], I.12–13; for a fine owed, see fragment 4 back [v.], II.24.
[36] E.g. fragment 6 front [r.], II, line 4.

instances when we can quite confidently speak of a group living just within its means. Surely there were others in a similar situation about whom we simply know nothing because we do not have their records preserved on papyri or wood tablets.

Scenario Three: Functioning well within material means – Success

In some cases, it seems clear that an association functioned well within the means of its members. It is conceivable that some groups would have settled for less than what members could afford. The benefit of that situation would materialize when things did not go according to plan, and members could then readily fund a new alternative plan that ensured the group continued. There is some irony in the fact that the group most often cited as an instance of a 'burial association' of the poor in early scholarship happens to be, on closer inspection, a very good candidate for a group living well within its means and, therefore, in a position to avoid financial difficulties and to have some degree of success.

We are referring to the association (*collegium*) devoted to both the goddess Diana and the deified Antinous that was founded in January 133 CE, and met in Lanuvium, a town about thirty-five kilometres south-east of Rome and accessible by the Appian Way (*AGRW* 310 = *CIL* XIV 2112; 136 CE). A close examination of the regulation from 136 CE shows that ongoing participation expenses were much higher than they first appear. As a result, the cost of belonging would be considerably more than was the case with both of the Tebtynis associations which seemed to function very close to the means of their members. Nonetheless, *monthly* membership dues themselves at Lanuvium were also quite minimal: they amounted to just 1.25 sesterces per month (x 12 = 15 sesterces = 3.75 denarii total per year, as in lines 12 and 23), which is about the equivalent of 0.3125 silver denarii or silver drachmas per month. This is approximately double the amount of dues for participation in the first Tebtynis association we discussed, where participants paid about 0.167 silver drachmas (at the ratio of 600:1).

Furthermore, at Lanuvium, the relatively modest monthly membership dues were accompanied by other more substantial costs. The entrance payment to belong to this association was not small: one amphora of 'good wine' and 100 sesterces, equivalent to 25 silver denarii ($\approx$ 25 silver drachmas). Although separated by two centuries and inflation may have varied, this entrance amount alone is more than twenty times greater than the single largest contribution any member in our second Tebtynis association (above in this chapter) paid, according to the financial records. That would be a certain Naaros at Tebtynis, who, on one occasion, made a wine contribution of 245 bronze drachmas, plus paid a fine of 400 bronze drachmas, for a total payment of 645 bronze drachmas: 1.075 silver drachmas or denarii (at the 600:1 ratio).[37] The high initiation cost at Lanuvium may be an indication of the higher level of resources available to members. In return for this initiation cost and monthly contributions, a

---

[37] See *GRA* III 194 = *PTebt* III 894, fragment 3 back [v.], I, lines 12–13.

deceased member would receive 300 sesterces (= 75 denarii) for funerary expenses (50 sesterces of which would be given to participating mourners).

There were further significant expenses at Lanuvium as regular members took turns serving as 'magistrates' (*magistri*) of the association, four at a time, and this role meant funding six annual dinners. These magistrates were 'required to provide an amphora of good wine each, and for as many members as the association has, bread costing 2 copper coins (*asses*), four sardines, a table setting, and warm water with service'. Andreas Bendlin estimates the membership size at forty-eight individuals, based on the amount of cash handouts provided by one of its patrons, Lucius Caesennius Rufus. This means that the total annual expenditure for the items above by each of the four current magistrates would be 432 sesterces (= 108 denarii ≈ 108 silver drachmas).[38] Using Bendlin's estimate of membership size, each member would serve as a magistrate once every twelve years, which would require saving, on average, 36 sesterces (= 9 denarii ≈ 9 silver drachmas) per year for twelve years in addition to the monthly dues – for those who planned well ahead, that is.

What is notable about the financial responsibilities of these rotating magistrates is the penalty for members who failed to meet these obligations. There was a fine of 30 sesterces (= 7.5 denarii) if one of the rotating magistrates failed to fulfil responsibilities on a particular occasion. This fine is less than what each person planning to fill the role of magistrate would have needed to save in each of the twelve years they had prepared for the service. When compared with contemporaneous associations, this 30 sesterces fine appears to be a rather weak deterrent.[39] This may be a further indication that these devotees of Diana and Antinous might be understood as living well within available means. Since the delinquent owed a fine of 30 sesterces, and the deliquent's responsibility passed to the next in rotation, that individual next in rotation would need to come up with 36 sesterces when called upon. This is because that person was planning to be the following year's magistrate. If we imagine the delinquent paid his fine immediately and these 30 sesterces were given to the newly selected magistrate, that new magistrate would still be 6 sesterces short. When creating the 30 sesterces fine, therefore, as well as the backup plan of turning to the next in line, the association seems to have assumed that each member would have at least 6 sesterces extra available beyond the normal expected amount. If the Lanuvium group knew its members well, then we can assume that just about all the members would have extra money available to spend on communal activities if called upon to do so.

We have once again chosen a somewhat conservative option in illustrating an association that lived well within its means, rather than using an even wealthier group to illustrate the point. The roughly contemporary associations of hymn-singers at Pergamon and worshippers of Bacchos at Athens, for instance, each had an entrance payment that was twice that of the Lanuvium group – 50 denarii in addition to other costs (see Chapter 4). The idea here is *not* that the Lanuvium group consisted of wealthy

---

[38] See Bendlin (2011).
[39] For instance, the Iobacchoi at Athens expelled members for failing to pay monthly fees for wine (*GRA* I 51, lines 45–9). Those devoted to Herakles charged members twice their membership dues if they paid late, and expelled members who failed to pay at all (*GRA* I 50, lines 42–5).

individuals, then, but rather that the association apparently did not require of members as much as they could afford and therefore they were functioning well within available means.

Because we usually lack such an extensive, inscribed regulation that specifies the costs of participating and we rarely have substantial financial accounts surviving on papyri, we generally lack many other such detailed and well-documented examples. There are notable hints in some other inscriptions that point to groups that may well have been doing even better financially, though. So, for instance, there is the society in Attica which, in commending its yearly treasurer, supervisor, secretary, comptroller and record-keeper, clarifies that these functionaries had managed things in such a way that the society had a surplus of 1,770 silver drachmas, a considerable amount of funds that may also reflect possession of substantial assets such as rental properties and income from loans (*GRA* I 17 = *IG* II² 1278; 272 BCE). So there would be some associations with considerable wealth, so long as they continued to manage it effectively. As we proceed, we will encounter further groups with similar access to substantial funds, assets or properties, alongside more modest groups.

Cases of longevity

We happen to know that the association at Lanuvium had existed for three years by the time it passed its regulation, but we lack information about how long the two Tebtynis groups had been functioning, beyond the two years of records in one case. If we did know how long many associations existed, we would be in a better position to assess which groups may have had longer-term success in managing resources derived from both members and supporters. Even those that disbanded after some time may have had a good run at it before encountering problems, though.

The sparse nature of the evidence does not usually allow us to even witness an association at more than one point in its history. Furthermore, in cases where there are several inscriptions for one group, there can be difficulties in dating them accurately. So often we can say very little concerning relative longevity. While an absence of multiple inscriptions for a particular association tells us nothing about either success or failure, it is still worth noting some clear cases of longevity. We need to realize that other groups for whom we lack such datable evidence may well have been just as enduring as these.

This list is by no means a cross section, geographically speaking, but it is what we have and it does reflect a variety of groups. Here, we leave out the extremely long-lasting and somewhat exceptional associations of performers devoted to Dionysos and athletes devoted to Herakles, where, in some cases, continuity from the Hellenistic to the Roman imperial era might be argued – in other words, centuries of existence.

The fact that one of the longest lasting groups on record below happens to be one that emerged in quite modest material circumstances (see the discussion of the servants of Sarapis in the next chapter) further confirms our point that it was those that functioned within available material means – rather than merely those consisting of

Scenarios of Success, Survival and Decline 49

people from wealthier segments of the population – that could survive or thrive. The following list may suffice in giving a general sense of the possibilities of success for different kinds of unofficial associations:[40]

- Around 192 years: 'Servants' of Sarapis on Delos island begun by the Egyptian Apollonios (see Chapter 2; started around 280, built sanctuary around 200, inscriptions afterwards, sanctuary destroyed in 88 BCE).
- At least 167 years: Devotees of Dionysos Breiseus at Smyrna (see commentary in *GRA* II 137; c. 80–247 CE).[41]
- At least 154 years: Devotees of Demeter at Ephesos (see commentary in *GRA* II 128; c. 23–177 CE).
- At least 150 years: Guild of dyers at Thyatira (see commentary in *GRA* II 123; c. 50–200 CE).[42]
- At least 150 years: Roman settlers at Apameia Kelainai in Phrygia (see commentary in *GRA* II 115; c. 55–200 CE).
- At least 137 years: Dionysiac cowherds at Pergamon (see commentary in *GRA* II 110; excavated meeting place; c. 27 BCE–110 CE).
- At least 97 years: Sacrificing associates of the Mother of the gods at the Piraeus (see commentary in *GRA* I 15; c. 272–175 BCE).
- At least 65 years: Berytian shippers and merchants devoted to Poseidon on Delos (*IDelos* 1772–1796; meeting place destroyed in 88 BCE; ca. 153–88 BCE).
- At least 56 years: Corporate body of Judeans at Berenike (*AGRW* 305–7; late first century BCE–56 CE).
- At least 55 years: Guild of textile-dealers at Rome (*CIL* VI 786; early first century BCE–early first century CE).[43]
- At least 50 years: Sacrificing associates of Amynos and Asklepios at Athens, consisting of citizens (see commentary in *GRA* I 6; excavated sanctuary; c. 313–263 BCE).
- At least 50 years: Judean group at Hierapolis (see commentary in *GRA* II 116; c. 200–250 CE).[44]
- At least 47 years: Association of physicians from the sanctuary of the Muses at Ephesos (see commentary in *GRA* II 129; ca. 114–161 CE or later).
- At least 41 years: Dionysiasts in the Piraeus, consisting of Athenian citizens (see commentary in *GRA* I 33, at death of founder and therefore +30 years, and *GRA* I 36; excavated sanctuary; c. 185–176 BCE + 30 years).
- At least 35 years: Devotees of Helios at Rhodos on the island of Rhodes (*AGRW* 255 = *IG* XII,1 155, section D).

---

[40] Sometimes, there are judgement calls to be made in identifying a particular group in several inscriptions.
[41] Assuming that the use of slightly different self-designations nonetheless entails the same group.
[42] Assuming there was only one guild of dyers at this locale.
[43] Based on the reference to eleven periods of five years (*lustra*) in this group's earliest inscription (Liu, 2009: 38–9).
[44] Assuming that these involved one group despite the use of different self-designations.

Conclusion

So some groups did manage to strike a balance between maintaining members' expectations and keeping the books in the black. Members of the two Tebtynis associations in Egypt (discussed in this and the previous chapter) and the worshippers of Diana in Italy came from non-elite segments of the population, but these segments were considerably varied in terms of participants' resources. It does not seem likely that any of these three groups were drawn from the relatively wealthy upper segments of the non-elites (i.e. the 'middling wealth' cohort). The Tebtynis groups provide likely examples of members from just above subsistence level (if the costs of participation are indicative), whereas the Lanuvium group had members with somewhat more resources. It seems that all three were still surviving and continuing to meet group aims, such as banqueting and honouring deities. Participants at Lanuvium seem to have had more economic leeway, though.

In these cases, survival seems to depend less on the extent of participants' wealth than on adaptation to the means of members and careful management of available resources, regardless of the socioeconomic level of members. Those associations that adapted to the combined resources of participants and supporters would survive or thrive, provided natural or human-made disasters did not strike. Other associations might face the danger of decline, financial insolvency and dissolution.

3

Starting an Association: Collective and Individual Agency

[Diodoros] was partially responsible for the initial gathering and, having also founded the synod himself, he remained head of the contribution-society.

GRA I 48 = *IG* II² 1343

When Poseidonios sent to inquire of Apollo . . . the god answered: 'It is more desirable and better for them to do as their ancestors did and to appease and honour Ancestral Zeus . . .'

GIBM IV 896

For we know, brothers loved by god, that he has chosen you . . .

1 Thess 1:4

Introduction

The scenarios of survival and disbandment we have just outlined were reconstructed from source material produced by associations that had existed for some time. Careful planning with respect to members' means would be a key to sustainability for groups that did get off the ground. In light of the effort that was required to ensure continuation of an existing group, the formation and initial months or years of a group's life could be quite challenging. The Tebtynis associations and the three-year-old Lanuvium group showed that systems of a sort needed to be developed in order to balance internal and external sources of income (see Chapters 5 to 8). It would take some time for such mechanisms – whether consciously constructed or adapted from local custom – to develop in a sustainable way.

The initial period would be especially fragile for several reasons. There would be members without a track record of attending meetings or paying contributions or following regulations. Reliable places to meet would need to be found, rented or built. At the outset, there would only be incipient social forms of organization and leadership. There would be an empty treasury and archived or implied promises of reciprocity and social benefits. Furthermore, stiff competition existed for local benefactors, as there would be many established associations and institutions experienced in navigating exchanges within local social networks.

Even so, the certain success of a new association often comes across as obvious or – as in the opening quote regarding Poseidonios' foundation of a familial association – divinely orchestrated. Certain scholars tend to take the rhetoric of our sources quite literally regarding the inevitability of success rather than digging deeper. So, for instance, Bruce Longenecker, who studies the financial practices of newly formed assemblies devoted to Jesus in light of some recent research on associations, can imagine new Pauline assemblies as essentially indissoluble. Longenecker constructs a scenario where the vast majority of members in these new assemblies 'enjoy the benefits of a benefactor's generosity without being expected either to make membership payments or to be involved in public acclaim of the benefactor'.[1] Practical matters relating to participants' material resources and agonistic cultural practices get left out of this picture, with groups devoted to Jesus seemingly hovering above their cultural and economic contexts.[2] From this perspective, it seems that these new associations were bound to succeed from the very start, precisely as the foundation narratives presupposed by Paul would have it, with the Israelite god bringing the assembly into existence and choosing those who belonged. There are clear dangers in taking rhetoric as a reflection of social realities in these cases, whether it be the rhetoric of Paul or of Poseidonios or of Apollonios the Egyptian as discussed below.

In this chapter, we consider a range of financial circumstances encountered by associations and their founders at the time of their origins while being attentive to the rhetoric and interests of those who produced our sources. There are several types of material that offer insights into group formation, including (1) foundation narratives (written or oral) like the one developed by Apollonios on Delos; (2) honorary inscriptions for individuals, like Diodoros at Athens who played a role in establishing a group, whether alone or together with others; and, (3) financial foundations by wealthy figures like Epikteta on the Aegean island of Thera.

Our assessment of these sources in context leads us to the view that certain commonly adopted scholarly assumptions since the beginning of the twentieth century are problematic. In particular, establishment of an association by an individual wealthy founder that supplied a very large donation was *not* the norm. A number of groups formed from familial networks certainly did start that way, though. Instead, collective action along the lines of what we discuss in Chapters 6 and 7 was behind the formation of many groups, which drew their membership from existing social connections in local neighbourhood, occupational and ethnic networks.

Foundation narratives, we will see, are highly stylized and claim divine favour from the outset. They therefore emphasize the inevitability of success and sometimes obscure signs of difficulties in starting up things. Nonetheless, these narratives and even some honorary inscriptions do cast light on a combination of communal and individual agency that got an association going. There are also important lessons to be learned about the potential for initial struggles in these sources.

---

[1] Longenecker (2010: 271).
[2] Ryan Schellenberg's recent study also highlights several difficulties with Longenecker's approach: Schellenberg (2018).

Challenging a scholarly tradition

Scholars are prone to neglect material conditions at the point of group origins, and this may be due, in part, to a relatively early scholarly tradition. This tradition assumes individual agency by a wealthy founder as the predominant factor without adequately exploring the evidence or sufficiently recognizing collective action. Writing in 1896, Erich Ziebarth's study of ancient Greek associations briefly outlines a threefold typology of origins that, in fact, remains more or less current. First, there were associations that formed from a small collective led by a dominant figure, a 'founder' (*ktistēs*), after whom a group might name itself. Second, there were groups founded by a start-up grant arranged by an individual founder, sometimes deceased. And a third option was the merging together of two or more existing associations into a single new one, a counterpoint to the possibility of schisms (see Chapter 2).[3] Usually our evidence is too partial to witness such amalgamations, but there are relatively clear cases, including those at Ephesos and Smyrna.[4]

For present purposes, it is important to register the prominence of the wealthy, individual founder (*ktistēs*) model – whether a living or deceased individual – within scholarship.[5] This may be a reflection of the primacy of individual agency in historical explanations when scholars were writing, a problem that continues to play a role in some recent scholarship as well.[6] The notion that an association would be established by collective action by a number of individuals together, on the other hand, tends to be set aside too quickly. The epigraphic evidence for this issue is more complicated than often assumed. Some scholars do cite – as an exception to their individual founder rule – an association of Athenian contributors (*eranistai*).[7] The regulation (second century CE) of these contributors refers to the establishment of the group and states that 'the male friends (*philoi*) gathered together a contribution-society (*eranon synagon*) and by communal deliberation (*koinē boulē*) signed an agreement (*thesmos*) of friendship' (*GRA* I 49 = *IG* II² 1369, lines 25–7).

Yet further instances in our very partial sources suggest that it may have been common to explain the initial (or subsequent) convening of an association in terms of collective action. Often there is use of Greek terms for 'bringing together' (especially *pherein* and *synagein*), the same semantic field that gives us the self-designation for a 'gathering' or 'synagogue' (*synagōgē*).[8] In 112 BCE, an Athenian synod describes itself as

---

[3] Ziebarth (1896: 140).
[4] See *IEph* 1595 (Demetriasts joining with initiates of Dionysos Phleos; cf. *IEph* 213, 4337); *ISmyrna* 639 (performers joining with initiates of Dionysos Breiseus; cf. *AGRW* 189–95 and *GRA* II 137). On a possible Piraean amalgamation, see Ferguson (1944: 138–40, on *IG* II² 1316).
[5] E.g. Poland (1909: 271, on Greek associations); San Nicolò (1913: 2.6–8, on Egyptian associations). See also Gibbs (2011: 293).
[6] We do not agree with Jörg Rüpke's (2016) characterisation of scholarship on antiquity as having given too much attention to the collective and not enough to the individual. His consequent attempt to increase attention to the individual is also accompanied by a somewhat uncritical adoption of the category of 'religion', itself bound up in modern notions of individualism (see the definition of associations in our introduction).
[7] E.g. Poland (1909: 271), San Nicolò (1913: 2.6–8).
[8] Deities: e.g. *AGRW* 229 = *RICIS* 202/0194. Individuals: e.g. *IG* XI,4 1227 and *IDelos* 2225; *SEG* 54:794 (from Paros); *OGIS* 325 (from Teos); *GRA* III 163 = *IGR* I 1095 (from Kanopos in Egypt).

'the shippers and merchants who bring together (*tōn pherontōn*) the synod of Zeus Xenios' (*GRA* I 42 = *IG* II² 1012, lines 14–15). When an enslaved person from Lycia in the mining town of Laureion in Attica consecrates a sanctuary for a Phrygian deity around 200 CE (suggesting some individual initiative with respect to the sanctuary), the regulation still presumes the collective formation of contribution-societies: 'Those who wish may gather together a contribution-society (*eranon synagein*) for Men Tyrannos'(*AGRW* 22 = *GRA* I 53 = *IG* II² 1366, line 21). The notion of a group of 'contributors' (*eranistai*) itself, which we discuss at various points in this study, seems to presume collective action as instrumental.

Although not necessarily referring to an initial foundation, communal initiative is also presumed as the norm for gatherings among some Dionysos worshippers at the Piraeus, port city of Athens. Members express their coming together in terms of communal – rather than individual – action as a benefactor is described as having goodwill 'toward all who brought (*pherontas*) the synod together for the god'.[9]

A more complicated relation between apparent individual foundations, on the one hand, and communal agency, on the other, is sometimes evident in the foundation of a building by a group that was already established. Although from a later era (300–350 CE), the case of Theodoros on the island of Aegina illustrates the point well (*IJO* I Ach58–9 = *CIJ* 722–3). The first inscription begins with a seemingly clear case of individual agency in the establishment of a meeting place: 'Theodoros, the head of the synagogue, who has served as supervisor (*phrontistēs*) for four years, built the synagogue from the foundations.' But then things get more complicated in the next sentence. There is a reference to 'receiving' funds for this foundation from two different sources. Depending on how we take the passive construction for receiving, it may be that Theodoros (although not necessarily) was the first source and did, in fact, contribute the amount of 85 gold coins. More importantly here, it is very clear that a larger sum of 105 gold coins had been drawn from 'gifts of god'. This is most likely a reference to either the communal fund or a collection from participants in this Judean group. Theodoros seems to be playing a supervisory role over the construction. This is clear in a second inscription, in which he is mentioned as supervisor over the dedication of the mosaic in this same building, a mosaic whose cost was entirely covered by funds 'from the revenue of the synagogue' (*[ek tēs pr]o[s]odou tēs synag(ōg)ēs*). So it seems that the reference to Theodoros 'building' the structure in the first inscription pertains to his overseeing its construction rather than his constructing it entirely from his own resources. In earlier periods, most dedications of Judean 'prayer-houses' (*proseuchai*) in Egypt, such as the following one from the Delta region, presume collective action: 'For the well-being of king Ptolemaios, queen Berenike his sister and wife, and their children, the Judeans dedicated this prayer-house' (*GRA* III 154 = *IJudEgypt* 22, from 245–222 BCE). Four of the seven sufficiently preserved Judean prayer-house dedications

---

[9] *AGRW* 21 = *GRA* I 36 = *IG* II² 1326, lines 6–7 (176 BCE). So it is somewhat unusual that Jon D. Mikalson (2016: 102) recently takes the list of the deceased honourees' contributions to this same group as an indication that he was 'founder or co-founder' of this association, even though this is not expressed in the inscription itself.

from Egypt are by collective action, one by a combination of individual and collective agency, and two by individuals.[10]

When assessing the relationship between individual and communal agency, it is also important to remember that people in the ancient Mediterranean might speak of a deity causing a gathering or more permanent association to take place, which was a stand-in for either collective or individual action. This is sometimes expressed with reference to an oracle or command from a god that led to the foundation of some group or sanctuary, as with the family of Poseidonios at Halikarnassos, the association of Anthister on Thera, the association in the household of Dionysios at Philadelphia, and Thracians at the Piraeus, who consulted Zeus at Dodona.[11] So, for instance, an inscription from Magnesia on the Maiander relates that the gods caused a storm that made an image of the god Dionysos appear in a tree. On consulting the god Apollo at Delphi, the message was that the gods were calling for the establishment of three different Bacchic societies (*thiasoi*) led by female figures, namely 'maenads'.[12] Supposed divine agency could be a proxy for either communal or individual action, and so a deity might also convene a meeting or make a resolution alongside members.[13] Similar notions are behind invitations from the god Sarapis to attend feasts in Egypt.[14] Followers of Jesus, such as Paul, were also prone to express the formation and ongoing existence of groups as divinely orchestrated.

Beyond these complications for an individualistic approach to group origins, here we show that a scholarly focus on an individual founder is problematic for other reasons relating to survival. After generalizing the presence of a single founder, some scholars then go on to stress the material resources that these figures poured into their new associations, going so far as to assert that such individual founders covered all necessary expenses.[15] This sometimes feeds into a problematic notion that, from the outset, associations were bound to survive relatively free of financial struggle, along the lines of Longenecker's proposal regarding the early assemblies of Jesus adherents. In addition, focus on the individual can lead to neglect of communal agency in fund-raising and reciprocal support among members, an imbalance we correct in subsequent chapters. The ambiguity of some sources and the triumphalist rhetoric of others are liable to skew our understanding of group origins, then, and so it is crucial to evaluate the evidence for the formation of associations carefully.

---

[10] *IJudEgypt* 22, 24, 25, 117 (collective at Schedia, Xenephyris, Nitriai and Krokodilopolis); 13, 126 (individual at Alexandria and unknown); 27 (individual and collective at Athribis). Cf. Levine (2000: 87).

[11] *GIBM* IV 896 (see opening quote), from Halikarnassos; *IG* XII,3 329, from Thera; *AGRW* 121 = *GRA* II 117 = *TAM* V 1539, from Philadelphia in Lydia; *AGRW* 18 = *GRA* I 23 = *IG* II² 1283, from the Piraeus. Cf. *AGRW* 21 = *GRA* I 36 = *IG* II² 1326. On divine legitimacy for founding cults and associations, see Öhler (2015).

[12] *AGRW* 202 = *GRA* II 143 = *IMagnMai* 215.

[13] Convening a meeting: *AGRW* 229 = *RICIS* 202/0194; *IKosPH* 382; *AGRW* 213 = *GRA* II 152. Making a resolution (via lots): *AGRW* 244 = *IG* XII,3 178.

[14] *PKöln* 57 = *NewDocs* I 1; Youtie (1948). See also Aelius Aristides, *Orations* 45.27–8 = *AGRW* L13.

[15] E.g. Ziebarth (1896: 140), San Nicolò (1913: 7), Longenecker (2010: 271). Poland asserts that: 'a single member paid for all the necessities, so that a collection, it seems, was relatively infrequently needed. Even when the requisite sum had been accumulated by a collection, it sometimes happened that a praiseworthy man let the association keep this money, and took the matter completely upon himself' (1909: 497).

Foundation narratives and material struggles

Foundation stories enrich our understanding of how our ancient subjects liked to portray their beginnings, and they can also provide insights into initial struggles.[16] As James Hanges's study shows, Greek and Roman origin stories are often highly formulaic narratives that recount the beginning of an association, cult or community (e.g. city or colony), usually identifying its creator or heroic founder and emphasizing the role of deities in the foundation. In some respects, such origin stories seem designed to curtail even the possibility of precariousness, for there is stress on the divinely ordained success of a founder, whom the commissioning deity selected.[17]

And yet, such narratives frequently have a recurring theme of overcoming obstacles or conflicts before succeeding.[18] Hanges aptly notes that this scenario of struggle offers the narrator or people who share the narrative framework 'the perfect opportunity for the gods to demonstrate their power by rescuing their beleaguered servants'.[19] Often the people who share or relate the narratives attribute their communal existence or success to the commissioning deity's plan. The obstacles that the commissioning deity or deities overcome in such narrative frameworks include illness, political rivalry (e.g. *GRA* I 77), threats to the homeland (e.g. *GRA* II 143), and local opposition to the introduction of honours for a new or foreign deity (e.g. *IG* XI,4 1299; Euripides, *Bacchae*).

So, even though foundation narratives tend to characterize group formation and success as inevitable, they also admit a pattern of resiliency in the face of initial struggles. It is this latter detail of overcoming initial obstacles, including financial ones, that will occupy us more here in looking at the case of a group devoted to Sarapis on Delos as witnessed on a monumental pillar with an inscription. A second, briefly outlined case from a literary source will highlight the ways in which both individual and collective agency in group formation could be overshadowed by divine orchestration in origin narratives. Although, even here, the one telling the story still felt a need to clarify how it was that such a divinely established group supported itself in material terms.

Let us now turn to the first origin story from Delos. This is one of the most extensive origin stories that has survived for an association, and it involves Egyptian immigrants to this Greek island. This story also points to the role of both individual and communal agency in starting an association or sanctuary. A small inscribed pillar that was found in excavations of one of the three Sarapis sanctuaries on Delos (Sarapieion A, described in *AGRW* B7) relates in both prose and poetry the establishment of this sanctuary around 200 BCE (*AGRW* 221 = *IG* XI,4 1299 = *RICIS* 202/0101).[20] The advantage here is that we have both the foundation story concerning the sanctuary and the excavated remains of what archaeologists label Sarapis sanctuary A ('Sarapieion A').

---

[16] On foundation narratives, see Hanges (2012), Öhler (2015). For a review essay on Hanges' work, see Wendt (2014).
[17] Hanges (2012: 70–80).
[18] Cf. Öhler (2015).
[19] Hanges (2012: 210–11).
[20] See also Moyer (2008).

Figure 3.1 Pillar from Sarapis sanctuary A (*RICIS* 202/0101). Courtesy of Laurent Bricault, Université Toulouse II and l'École française d'Athènes.

The narrative preserved on the pillar (pictured in Figure 3.1) tells the story of a priest from Memphis in Egypt named Apollonios I and his son and grandson (Demetrios and Apollonios II) as priestly successors serving Sarapis on the island of Delos. The older Apollonios seemingly migrated to Delos some time during the period of Ptolemaic hegemony on the island (287–245 BCE), bringing a statue of his god with him, as the story goes. A small group of adherents that came to designate itself the god's 'servants' (*therapeutai*) met within rented rooms that may have been Apollonios' own living quarters.

Eighty years later, the story of this association's origins and subsequent construction of a purpose-built sanctuary for Sarapis were inscribed on the pillar by the grandson, Apollonios II. This Apollonios describes the circumstances of the shift from rented quarters to a sanctuary as follows:

> After receiving the sacred things and being appointed to perform the services (*therapeuōn*) in a diligent manner, the god instructed me through a dream that I should dedicate his own temple of Sarapis, and that he was not to be in rented

rooms (*misthōtois*). Furthermore, he would find the place where the temple should be located, indicating this by a sign. And this is what happened. For there was this place full of manure which was advertised for sale on a small notice on a passage to the marketplace. Now since the god willed it, a contract of purchase (*ōnē*) was completed and the temple was quickly built in six months.

There are several indications both in the inscription and in the archaeological data that point to the humble origins and financial struggles that may have characterized the experience of this group devoted to a foreign deity. Nonetheless, this was followed by relative success that led to the building of a sanctuary – although a relatively modest one – decades later. The longevity of the group despite these modest material conditions suggests that this is another collectivity that functioned just within its means, like others highlighted in the second scenario of survival in Chapter 2.

The first possible sign of limited material means relates to the earliest stage and the reference to Apollonios having been a priest in Memphis. Apollonios I (the grandfather), who is claimed to have played a key role in establishing the cult after emigrating from Memphis, may not have been wealthy but rather a lower-class priest, as Helmut Engelmann and M. P. Nilsson also suggest.[21] Recent studies show that as much as 10 per cent of inhabitants in the district of Arsinoites (where Memphis was located) during the Ptolemaic period served as priests, most of whom would, in light of these numbers, function in lower priestly roles.[22] Many of these priests would have farmed or engaged in other occupations for a living, in addition to part-time priestly duties, and some even served in the Ptolemaic army.[23] In addition, Christelle Fischer-Bovet's study explores the evidence for priests in the army, showing that about 18 per cent of priest-soldiers were lower-rank soldiers from districts including Arsinoites.[24] Although neither the dedicatory inscription nor the hymn in praise of Sarapis clearly indicate the elder Apollonios' socioeconomic status or occupation, Engelmann suggests that Apollonios was 'not a wealthy man' and was a 'lower-ranking priest in Egypt'.[25] Engelmann bases this on the fact that Apollonios had to rent quarters upon arrival on Delos, which is a reasonable inference.[26] Engelmann also proposes that the elder Apollonios would not have had access to the fiscal advantages of *full-time* priests in Ptolemaic Memphis, including tax exemptions and high pay for temple services, which may or may not be the case.[27] It seems a good possibility that this was not a wealthy family, which would further explain why it would take eight decades before the worshippers moved out of their rented quarters. Whatever the socioeconomic status of the family and whatever the struggles faced early on, the group was in some respects still working within its (likely) limited means and at least surviving in its first century.

[21] Nilsson (1961: 2.122).
[22] Clarysse and Thompson (2004: 195).
[23] Clarysse (2010: 284, 288–9).
[24] Fischer-Bovet (2014: 303–28, especially 317–19 on lower-level soldiers).
[25] Engelmann (1975: 12).
[26] Ibid. (11–12). See Trümper (2005) on housing options for lower-status inhabitants of Delos.
[27] Clarysse (2010: 288–9). See Thompson (1988: 237–8), on the possibility of lower-level priests sharing these privileges.

A second indication of limited means, then, pertains to the point at which the group could afford to acquire property for a sanctuary. What stands out for our purposes is that the group's financial circumstances required it to initially rent space and to wait the better part of a century after its founding – spanning three generations of leadership – before it secured a stable, purpose-built meeting place. When it did so, the group seems to have constructed the building at a price it could afford, as we shall see below.

The inscription does not specify who paid for the property or construction, although it does emphasize that the grandson, Apollonios, consecrated it. It may be that a communal collection along the lines of those we discuss in Chapter 6 facilitated purchase of the property and construction of the building, rather than a substantial financial donation by Apollonios. In particular, the collective procedure in the purchase of a sanctuary by initiates at Kyme in western Asia Minor may provide a model, even though there, too, a particular individual was chosen by the collective to take the lead in the project (*GRA* II 105 = *IKyme* 37). Back on Delos, a collection receptacle was found within the Sarapis sanctuary itself (*IG* XI,4 1247 = *RICIS* 202/0124). Even more importantly, there is another inscription found within the sanctuary that refers to the priest Apollonios (probably the grandson himself) and 'those who serve the god' (*therapeutai*) contributing or collecting funds in order to make a dedication to Nike (*IG* XI,4 1290 = *RICIS* 202/0121). So communal collections (rather than an individual's sole efforts) may have been instrumental from the beginning, if these patterns are representative of ongoing practices among these Sarapis devotees.

A third sign of the relatively modest means available to the god's 'servants' pertains to the property the group acquired. 'For there was this place full of manure which was advertised for sale on a small notice on a passage to the marketplace.' The inscription emphasizes that the rented rooms they had been using were *less desirable* than the literally shitty (lines 18–21) and 'shameful' (line 53) lot that Apollonios (the grandson) arranged to have purchased to build the sanctuary. To be sure, the description of the new location as apparently undesirable reinforces the idea that Sarapis himself chose unexpected land and miraculously transformed it into a holy place where he could be fittingly honoured (lines 46–59).[28] Still, it seems that the land was indeed undesirable and likely very affordable for that reason. It may be that, in the three generations since its foundation, the association had expanded in membership, required more space and collected the requisite funds to purchase a very affordable property. So humble origins did lead to improvements for the group eighty years later, but even the sanctuary itself may suggest a meagre budget.

A fourth indication of limited means is the excavated sanctuary itself. Although the inscription speaks of the sanctuary being completed quickly because 'the god willed it' (line 21) and describes it as 'famous' (line 59), the actual reason behind its quick completion (if six months is quick, as in lines 20–2) is more likely the overall poor building quality of the project.[29] This is confirmed by examination of the excavated site by Pierre Roussel, who describes some of the erected buildings (the temple and a dining room) as 'petty' and observes that the temple within the sanctuary 'is of

[28] Cf. Hanges (2012: 70–80).
[29] Engelmann (1975: 23), Hanges (2012: 199–200).

detestable construction'.³⁰ Roussel's description seems to miss the point that the association was working within its own material limitations. But these limitations mean that this sanctuary was significantly less impressive architecturally than the other two sanctuaries of Sarapis that were likewise located in the same district – the district labelled the 'Terrace of the Foreign Gods' by archaeologists. Sarapis sanctuary C, in particular, was much larger (120 x 50 metres = 6000 metres squared) and the surviving inventories of valuable objects within that sanctuary suggest very different material circumstances (*IDelos* 1417 = *RICIS* 101/0424). Furthermore, there were at least five different associations that frequented sanctuary B;³¹ and, numerous groups met in sanctuary C, which came to have some formal connections with the civic community itself.³² To put it another way, these other Sarapis sanctuaries seem to have been more popular or desirable among adherents of Sarapis. Although we would refrain from value-loaded descriptions of architectural features or construction quality, the point remains that, compared to other buildings at Delos excavated by Roussel, Sarapis sanctuary A was more basic. It seems that, as Engelmann suggests, Apollonios or, we would suggest, the group as a whole 'lacked the money for speedy and good-quality construction'.³³

The sanctuary itself was to continue in use for more than a century until its destruction, probably in 88 BCE during the assault of Mithridates VI. So the group founded by the grandfather around 280 BCE may well have continued for about two hundred years. Although the structure was somewhat modestly constructed, it was stable enough to be used by adherents of Sarapis for about a century. As illustrated in Figure 3.2, the sanctuary was an extension of an existing complex (insula), which may or may not have been the originally rented domestic quarters mentioned in the inscription. The overall complex, which was entered from the north, measured 19.5 x 15.5 metres (302 metres squared). Within the sanctuary, a small temple measuring slightly more than 13 metres squared (A in the plan, 4.1 x 3.2 metres) was entered from the courtyard, and there was a water basin in the eastern part of the temple. To the south was a separate portico (C) with three niches. The dining room (E, measuring 4.4 x 7 metres) originally belonged to the adjacent house and was entered from a staircase at the main entrance to the north. This dining room was fitted with inscribed benches dedicated to Sarapis, Isis and Anubis by devotees of the god, once again pointing to collective action as central and perhaps indicating the number of participants in that period was around twenty (*RICIS* 202/0114–15, cf. 0116–20).

---

³⁰ Roussel (1916: 19–32, especially 29).
³¹ These include groups of therapeutists, wearers of black and Sarapiasts (*IG* XI,4 1226), and societies of ninth- and tenth-day celebrators (*IG* XI,4 1227–9). The contributors may be another separate group, or simply a subgroup of one of the other associations that raised funds for a particular purpose (*IG* XI,4 1223).
³² See *RICIS* 101/0424 (inventory mentioning therapeutists and Sarapiasts), 202/0161, 0162, (therapeutists), 0165, 0166, 0167 (contributors), 0191 (Sarapiasts), 0206, 0207 (therapeutists), 0257, 0260, 0269 (melanephorians), 0281 (therapeutists), 0282, 0322, 0351, 0352 (melanephorians and therapeutists).
³³ Engelmann (1975: 22).

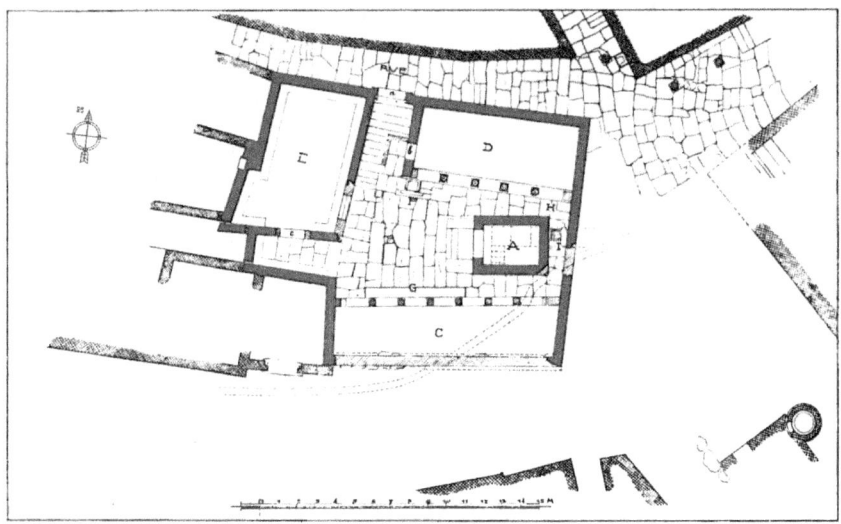

Figure 3.2 Plan of Sarapis sanctuary A at Delos. From Roussel (1916: 21). Public domain.

Before moving on, it is important to recognize that the challenges this particular group faced were not limited to material factors. The inscription highlights a legal case that arose as a result of the construction of the sanctuary:

> Now certain people conspired against us and the god, and sought a judgment against the temple and myself in a public trial, seeking either punishment or a fine. But the god promised me in a dream that we would win the case. Now that the proceedings have ended and we have won, as is worthy of the god, we praise the gods by demonstrating appropriate gratitude.[34]

We simply do not know the reasons for the legal case, but some scholars propose that it arose due to the group's failure to secure formal permission to acquire this land on which to build (see Chapter 4 on foreigners at Athens) or to the sanctuary's potential interference with a source of water (on the case, see lines 23–8, 66–74).[35] In both the prose and poetic sections of the inscription, the emphasis is placed on the god's own intervention in overcoming opposition to this sanctuary for a foreign deity, so ethnic rivalries may have played a role as well.

Overall, foundation narratives like this one stress the divinely ordained success of an association. Yet, in other respects, the narrative reflects the kinds of struggles that one might expect in any other average association's foundation and continuing experience, including a shortage of members or income and a lack of ideal spaces in

---

[34] For another legal case about a meeting place, see the discussion of *IG* XII,1 937 in Chapter 4.
[35] Hanges (2012: 210–48).

which to meet. As this association devoted to Sarapis developed over time, membership may have expanded and so this allowed the group to generate the necessary income to purchase land on which to build. Additional evidence for communal fund-raising practices within this very sanctuary further points towards collective efforts, rather than a single founder's actions. In any case, the inscription expresses success in terms of the agency of the deity, Sarapis, himself. As we turn to the issue of individual founders and substantial starting grants, we will see that some particularly fortunate associations could hit the ground running thanks to very wealthy founders, but these seem exceptional. The Egyptian immigrant family and those who joined together with this family in ancestral customs for Sarapis provide a glimpse into what may have been the more usual and gradual process of development for successful, although materially modest, associations.

Another foundation narrative – although more distanced than Apollonios' narrative from the circumstances it sketches – nonetheless provides insights into how a particular person cast the initial stages of a group's formation. This origin story appears in quite a different literary setting, in a somewhat formal history (in the ancient sense of history-writing) rather than a local inscription. Yet it, too, may have functioned in similar ways to Apollonios' story, in the sense that it seeks to foster a group's sense of belonging together and also presents itself as promoting that group's miraculous success. As with Apollonios' group, this narrative signals a combination of collective and individual agency and does so within the overall plan of a deity. We are speaking of the author of Luke-Acts' story of the initial formation of the Jesus movement in Jerusalem (especially Acts 1–3 here).

The author of Luke-Acts emphasizes divine orchestration in his explanation of the initial stages of this group devoted to the Israelite god and that god's chosen messiah.[36] While the narrative may well share things in common with other literary descriptions of ideal philosophical gatherings, as Gregory E. Sterling emphasizes, this does not exclude the narrative's value for understanding what an ancient author and audience might consider typical of the formation of any unofficial group or association, including philosophers' associations.[37]

The author's first volume (Luke) had outlined the life and execution of Jesus, but ended with the Israelite god's miraculous intervention to raise Jesus from the dead. When the raised Jesus leaves his followers at the beginning of volume two (Acts), he does so with the promise of the holy spirit who will continue to guide any future developments. And, ultimately, this author has the movement extend beyond Judea and Syria as far as Rome, the imperial centre. At Jerusalem, the author sketches a picture of a group of 120 people under the guidance of 11 and then 12 (with the replacement of Judas) figures sent by Jesus himself. While this collective leadership is mentioned, the author still focuses attention on the figure of Peter as instrumental in addressing the crowds, although not in terms of any financial role.

---

[36] For a discussion of Luke's overall portrait of the Jesus movement in Jerusalem in relation to associative life, see Öhler (2005). Cf. ibid. (2011b).
[37] Sterling (1994). On philosophical groups as 'societies' (*thiasoi*) or associations, now see Harland (2019).

When further divine guidance (a holy spirit) comes during the Judean festival of Pentecost in chapter three, other 'god-fearing' Judeans, beyond the 120, marvel at what the god is doing in relation to this special group, implying recognition for, and likely expansion of, the group within this setting. This has similarities with Apollonios' description of the many immigrants to Delos who gathered to watch the trial and marvelled at Sarapis' divine intervention to foil the plaintiffs' case, which may relate to Apollonios' claim that the sanctuary was therefore 'famous'. In the Acts narrative, Peter is once again at the forefront in speaking to the crowd, underlining for god-fearing Judeans gathered there (and the reader) that this new, special group of Judeans following Jesus as the messiah is part of the Israelite god's 'deliberate plan' (Acts 2:23).

It is important to highlight that the author of this story also feels a need to explain how this newly founded and expanding group was to financially support its activities.[38] The author draws a picture of everyone in the group gathering together to eat and pray and to support these activities by collectively pooling resources: 'All the ones who believed were together and held everything in common. They sold properties and possessions, distributing them to everyone insofar as anyone had a need. With a common goal, each day they were gathering persistently in the temple, breaking bread in their homes and sharing food with joyful and simple hearts' (Acts 2:44–7). As the movement expands, the author reiterates the centrality of this collection of a communal fund from the resources of members, with redistribution to any who had need. And the god takes fatal action against any who promised but failed to share their resources, as in the case of Ananias and Sapphira (Acts 4:32–5:11).[39]

So, once again, divine agency is quite central to the ways in which people in antiquity expressed the emergence and continuing stability of a group in an idealized manner. Still, much like other authors of ancient Greek histories or novels who recognized the need to maintain a sense of verisimilitude, the author of Luke-Acts anticipates other down-to-earth expectations of his readers in taking care to reflect common scenarios of group formation, including a role for both collective and individual agency. In this context of literary realism, the author stresses the role of communal action in explaining to his readers how this new group was to sustain itself in material ways and meet members' needs.

Assessing the significance of individual founders

We have begun to see above and in previous chapters that we should not assume that substantial foundations by an individual donor were the most important source of income for most newly established associations.[40] Those that were founded by a

---

[38] While we would not discount the likely role of communal collections for maintaining such a group devoted to Jesus (see Chapter 7), we refrain from assuming that the narrative is an accurate description of the actual material procedures of the early Jesus movement (contrast Bartchy, 1991, on the 'community of goods').

[39] For the view that this is a stock scene building on normal expectations of breaking a vow to a god, now see Harrill (2011).

[40] Correcting Ziebarth (1896: 140), Poland (1909: 272–3), San Nicolò (1913: 8).

benefactor's large endowment would be among the wealthier groups that existed, rather than typical associations.[41] Several chapters in this book are precisely aimed at going beyond such foundations by individuals in order to explore numerous factors in the sustainability of associations, whose resources would vary. It is still important to assess the relative significance of individual founders, rather than neglect them.

Many scholars incline to the view that foundation by an individual wealthy founder was the norm, as we have seen. In a recent study of associations on Rhodes, for instance, Vincent Gabrielsen asserts that there was a 'virtually total correlation ... between, on the one hand, several of [the associations'] attested founders (*ktistai*) and honorands and, on the other hand, the members of an eminently wealthy and politically assertive local elite who had succeeded in securing a monopoly over all higher functions of the state'.[42] There are problems with assuming such a one-to-one correspondence between elite founders and associations, however. Also, we may even be off-track if we assume that those who played a key role in founding an association were necessarily wealthy or primarily remembered for contributing material resources.

There are three types of evidence relating to potential 'founders' that are frequently assumed to suggest that individual founders were most prevalent, and sometimes these are conflated together in a way that does not recognize important uncertainties about this image of association origins.[43] First, while naming practices varied from region to region, in some places, it was common to distinguish one's group from others by reference to a person around whom the group gathered. Associations on Kos regularly distinguished their groups by reference to who they were with (*hoi syn*), particularly in marking communal funerary plots, which were customary on that island: 'Boundaries of the society-members who are with (*tōn syn*) Zopyros son of Zopyros' (*IKosS* EF 460 = *SEG* 57:777).[44] A very similar terminology is widely attested elsewhere, referring to those gathered around (*hoi peri*) someone. This is found in various places in the eastern Mediterranean, as in an inscription from the Greek colony of Kallatis on the western coast of the Black Sea. The group in that inscription is designated the 'society-members who are gathered around (*tois peri*) Philon son of Diokouridas' (*IKallatis* 45; after 15 CE).[45]

Second, in Rhodian territories, groups regularly identified themselves not only by the deities they worshipped but also by some person that may have been a leader or may have been instrumental in bringing the group together in the first place. In this case, the name of the person was built into a group self-designation in the form of an

---

[41] Liu (2008).
[42] Gabrielsen (2001: 223). Contrast Maillot (2015: 164–5), who hesitates from seeing the named figures as original founders.
[43] E.g. Ziebarth (1896: 140–2), Poland (1909: 273), San Nicolò (1915: 6–9), Gabrielsen (2001), Hanges (2012).
[44] Cf. *IKosB* 274, 275, 287. For *hoi syn* on Rhodes, see *IG* XII,1 937 (Lindos); *SEG* 39:737 (Ialysos); *AGRW* 247 = *IKamiros* 84; *IRhodM* 44 (Rhodos).
[45] On 'those around' (*hoi peri*), see also *AGRW* 179 = *IMilet* 935 (in Ionia); *MAMA* IV 230 (in Phrygia); *IBeroia* 371 (in Macedonia); *AGRW* 79 = *IGBulg* I 77(2) (in Moesia); *IBosp* 987 (in the Bosporan kingdom). Performers frequently employed the same terminology in reference to their patron deity to express those 'gathered around Dionysos' (e.g. *CIG* 3082 from Teos).

adjective: for example, 'Alkimedonteian Hermes-devotees' (AGRW 249 = *ILindos* 251), with reference to a man named Alkimedon, and 'the association of Theudoteian devotees of the Dioskouroi', with reference to Theudotos (*IRhodPBlümel* 556). It should be noted that Poland himself was rightly hesitant about assuming that such Rhodian cases were necessarily the names of actual initiators of the groups in question, rather than current or previous leaders.[46]

In all of the above three cases where an individual figure is highlighted, it seems that reference to the person helped to distinguish between the many associations at a particular locale that could choose the same patron deities (e.g. multiple groups of Hermaists) or use the same group designation (e.g. mutiple groups designating themselves a 'society', *thiasos*). Such a person may have been a founder in some sense, namely a person who proposed forming an ongoing group, or a person who was instrumental alone or with others in organizing the group of people in the first place, perhaps acting as initial leader. However, in the vast majority of these cases, there is no indication that such persons were founders in the sense of donors of a large endowment that almost single-handedly established or sustained the association.

A third factor that sometimes comes into such discussions pertains to a Greek term, *ktistēs*, that can sometimes be appropriately translated as 'founder'.[47] Yet here, too, caution is necessary regarding a range of meanings. Because, by the late Hellenistic period and on into the Roman era, this Greek term for 'founder' was also used almost interchangeably with honorary titles such as 'benefactor' (*euergetēs*) and 'saviour' (*sōtēr*). People who were given such titles did not necessarily play an active role in establishing some community or group.[48] These were often figures who stepped in to financially help an existing association or community at a critical moment, like the benefactors we discuss in Chapter 5, but did not start the group and did not necessarily continue to participate within the group.

Moving on to some of the clearest cases where someone designated a 'founder' (*ktistēs*) may have been instrumental in establishing an association, there are the cases of Diodoros son of Sokrates at Athens and Nikasion of Kyzikos on Rhodes.[49] In 36 BCE, sixty worshippers of Artemis the Saviour at Athens passed a decree honouring Diodoros son of Sokrates and, in the process, refer to his role in founding the group (*GRA* I 48 = *IG* II² 1343). Scholars sometimes take this as an example of their model of an individual wealthy founder establishing an association, but the evidence suggests a different scenario, where the foundation itself was a team effort and where there is actually little emphasis on material contributions by this founder.[50]

Based on references to Athenian authorities (archons) in the inscription, we know that this decree in honour of Diodoros was passed by members in the seventh year of

---

[46] Poland (1909: 73–8, especially 74–5).
[47] On this term, see discussion and bibliography in Mortensen (2015). Synonyms include *oikistes* and *archēgetēs* in Greek and *auctor* and *conditor* in Latin.
[48] Cf. Dmitriev (2005: 177 n. 197). See *ILindos* 394 for an association's female benefactor as 'saviour'.
[49] See also the reference to 'the founder of the sacred initiates (*mystai*)' on Melos island, without any further information (*IG* XII,3 1098; 200–250 CE).
[50] E.g. Ziebarth (1896: 140), Poland (1909: 271).

this group's existence (36 BCE).⁵¹ Thankfully, the document also refers to various stages of Diodoros' role, going back to the beginning point of the group in the year 42 BCE. The members of the association acknowledge that Diodoros was part of a team that together arranged the initial gathering (*syllogē*), perhaps a planning meeting, that led to the foundation of the synod: 'he was *partially* responsible for the initial gathering (*paraitios tēs anōthen syllogē*) and, having also founded the synod himself (*tēn synodon autos ktisas*), he remained head of the contribution-society (*archeranistēs*), and having served as treasurer (*tamias*) in the year that Euthydomos was civic leader, he presided over the foundation (*tou themeliōthēnai*) of the synod' (lines 10–11). At this point, there are no references to monetary contributions by Diodoros, it should be noticed, and he was not working alone in planning to establish this group devoted to Artemis. But it does seem he stepped up or was chosen to lead the group, perhaps in the role of organizing a collection by 'contributors' (*eranistai*), if his title as 'head of the contribution-society' is quite literal (on such collections and contributors, see Chapters 6 and 8).

The decree then outlines further services offered by Diodoros. He was treasurer for at least three years (41, 39, 37 BCE). In referring to his first year in this role, the inscription comments that he 'increased the common funds' (*euxēsen ta koina*, line 8) in this role without any further clarification. This may be a reference to financial donations by Diodoros himself but the ambiguity seems more likely to mean that he efficiently managed the communal funds that already existed in his role as treasurer in a way that strengthened the group. The same Greek verb, which means to 'increase', 'strengthen', 'enhance' or 'foster' (here *auxanein*, but elsewhere also *epauxanein* or *synauxanein*), is used in many inscriptions where it does not necessarily entail a specific monetary donation by a benefactor; instead, the term often pertains to a general enhancement of communal well-being or a perceived increase in a group's stability.⁵² A good analogy for usage of the terminology may be the case of the treasurer at the Piraeus who was praised, among other things, for taking 'care in order that they (i.e. the revenues) might increase (*epia[ux]ēthōsan*)' (*GRA* I 33 = *IG* II² 1325, line 36; 185 BCE). Similarly, worshippers of Pan on Rhodes praised Dionysodoros for generally enhancing their material well-being through service without direct reference to any specific large donation: 'Since he has served as head of the contributors (*eranistai*) for eighteen years, he has made the contribution-society (*eranos*) increase' (*AGRW* 255 = *IG* XII,1 155, B, line 83). The contributors belonging to a group at Liopesi use the term to express their overall wish for the group's well-being: 'May the contribution-society be strengthened (*auxanetō de ho eranos*) because of the zealousness of its members!' (*GRA* I 49 = *IG* II² 1369, lines 38–40; second century CE). As treasurer of the Artemis worshippers, Diodoros may also have increased communal revenue through loans

---

⁵¹ See Kloppenborg's notes to *GRA* I 48.
⁵² E.g. *IG* II² 1293 + *SEG* 18 (1962), no. 33, line 8 (Athens, 250 BCE): he 'strengthened ... the Asklepios-devotees'; *IDelos* 1521, line 31 (200–166 BCE): 'they might increase (*epauxōsin*) the importance of the temple (*hieron*)'; *IDelos* 1522 (98–117 CE): he 'increased the revenues (*prosodous*) of the god'; *RICIS* 112/0703 = *IG* IX,2 1107a–b (Demetrias, Thessaly; 2nd century BCE): 'they might increase their honours for the gods even more'; *IHerakleiaPont* 2 (2nd century CE): 'he increases, and honours the reputation of, your city'. Cf. *synauxein* and *epaxanein* in *IAph* 12.27; *CIG* 3082, line 16 (Teos).

like the ones we encounter in Epikteta's testament and in many other groups in Chapters 5 and 8 that designate themselves 'contributors' (*eranistai*). This scenario is also implied for Diodoros' other two years as treasurer, since he is praised for doing what is 'right' or 'zealous' in managing the group's funds without any direct reference to significant material contributions from his own resources.

The only direct reference to Diodoros himself providing any notable help from his own resources comes in the fifth year of his involvement, when he served as priest of Artemis (38 BCE). There, it states that: 'he sacrificed with favourable omens and, not being overly focussed on money, he gave a feast for the contributors (*eranistai*) at his own expense, spending more than a little money (*ouk oligon chrēma*)' (lines 24–7). In light of the tendency to see 'founders' as wealthy contributors of substantial and even group-sustaining endowments, it should be underlined that this final reference is the only clear indication that Diodoros offered any funds, in this case 'more than a little' money to host a particular meal.

The decree for Diodoros closes with the somewhat standard desire that others would see the members honouring someone who had given so much service and at least some funds so that this would inspire others to the same level of effort. In that final statement, he is once again characterized as the 'one who founded' (*ta ktasanta*) the group (line 42), without reference to what was already clarified earlier in the inscription, namely, that he was not alone in this founding role but did likely preside over the foundation in some sense. So being considered a 'founder' and being a substantial financial contributor were not necessarily coincident, and contributing in other non-monetary ways through service was highly valued. Although Diodoros played a role in starting the group, this was alongside others as a team and not single-handedly. Furthermore, there are no direct references to large endowments to establish the group. What we do have are signs that such leaders or co-founders of associations did continue to contribute to the life of the group in various ways, both non-monetary and monetary, and could sometimes be named among those who were central to the group's self-understanding.

Another candidate for a person who started an association and was also given the actual title of 'founder' (using the Greek term *ktistēs*) is Nikasion of Kyzikos on Rhodes (second century BCE), although this has more ambiguities than the case of Diodoros. We know about this mixed group of immigrants that was called the 'association of Nikasioneian devotees of Asklepios and the Olympians' from at least two inscriptions.[53] Unfortunately, the first certain reference to the association named after Nikasion occurs in a very fragmentary honorary inscription for other benefactors, and tells us little regarding his potential role in the group's origins besides the full title of the group cited above.

The second more substantial inscription, which does not mention the title but is likely the same group, is actually a record of victories in contests (*AGRW* 257 = *IG* XII,1 127). This inscription shows us that the group consisted mostly of a mixture of

---

[53] Hiller von Gaertringen and Saridakis (1900: 109, no. 108), *AGRW* 257 = *IG* XII, 127. See also the fragmentary *IRhodPC* 5 (discussed in Chapter 5), which may or may not entail Nikasion.

immigrants, but also about a dozen 'Rhodians', likely sculptors.[54] It also indicates that the association held competitions in which the members were divided into three 'tribes', apparently in imitation of civic organization. One of these tribes is, in fact, labelled the Nikasioneian tribe, again after Nikasion of Kyzikos, and the others are named after what appear to be Nikasion's wife or daughter, Olympias, and another female relative, Basilis.[55] The family is clearly central to the group's self-understanding. The inscription concludes with a list of people, including these family members, who are labelled 'male and female benefactors' (C, lines 55–90). But the list is long (more than 24 names) and seems to include all members or participants as 'benefactors' or 'those who do good' (to be more literal). It is at the beginning of this list that Nikasion appears as 'founder of the association' (C, line 59) without further clarification of whether this refers to his initial role in starting the group or his continuing role as its leader and, therefore, the main person who 'did good things' for the group (in terms of his service in leading the group). So, although it seems that Nikasion played a role in founding the group, we lack details on whether this might have involved a financial endowment and we lack signs that he and his family were alone in bringing the group together.

Founders and family heroes

So we should not assume that all groups were formed by individual wealthy founders who supplied large endowments to ensure group survival. Still, it is important to discuss a few clear cases when this was indeed the case, even though the actual title of 'founder' (*ktistēs*) does not actually happen to be used in these cases. Particularly common in scholarly discussions of substantial monetary foundations are those by Diomedon of Kos island (*IG* XII,4 348; 310–290 BCE), Poseidonios of Halikarnnasos on the western coast of Asia Minor (*LSAM* 72; 300–250 BCE) and Epikteta of Thera island (*AGRW* 243 = *IG* XII,3 330; 210–195 BCE). Kos is just 24 kilometres off the coast of Halikarnassos, and Thera is a bit further into the Aegean, about 257 kilometres from Kos. Although these and other cases are worthy of careful study, they are not broadly representative of the origins of most other associations. In particular, all three happen to pertain to the establishment of an association devoted to deceased relatives as 'heroes' within a domestic setting in the early Hellenistic period in a particular region. There are further familial groups of heroists (*heroistai*) or hero-devotees that have been less noticed, including a group at Koloe in Lydia (second century BCE) who honoured their priestess and daughter of one of their heroes, Stratonike, but the group may include those beyond the family in that case.[56] In all three of the frequently cited cases, we have the head of a household

---

[54] Immigrants from Ephesos, Ilion, Knidos, Chios, Kyzikos, Selge, Soloi in Asia Minor; from Alexandria in Egypt (or in Asia Minor); from Antioch in Syria (or in Asia Minor); and from Amphipolis in Thracia. On 'Rhodians' for sculptors, see Gabrielsen (1993).

[55] See Chaniotis in *EBGR* (2010), no. 113, with corrections to Maillot's views.

[56] *ILydiaHM* 96 = Jones (2008). The foundation of the heroists near Ephesos (at Thyaira) seems to establish an association of 'friends of Peplos', rather than relatives (Jones, 1983 = *IEph* 3214 + *IEph* 3334).

endowing an association of relatives with almost all the necessary funds to participate in specific festivals. These festivals focus on sacrifices and accompanying meals at particular times of year for the family heroes. Here we consider Epikteta's foundation as principal example, with some comparative observations about the others. Then we also discuss another exceptional, although similar, document involving a substantial endowment to a guild of coppersmiths in Lycia.

Epikteta's will or testament, along with the association's acceptance of its arrangements and regulations, is quite long (288 lines total) and appears on marble panels that would have formed the front of the base for several statues of deceased relatives, including Epikteta herself (see the sketch of one possible reconstruction of the monument in Figure 3.3). In her will, which is the foundation itself, Epikteta represents herself as 'bringing together the association of male relatives' (*synagein koinon andreiou tōn syggenōn*, line 22). The foundation and the regulation that accompanied the association's acceptance deals with some very substantial monetary sums but they also present a series of contingency plans to ensure the material stability of the new association. In light of our discussion of the potential for disbandment in the previous chapter, it is worth noting that the regulation that accompanies this foundation anticipates and tries to prevent such a development: 'whatever is decided by a majority of the association shall be binding, except if it concerns dissolution. But in this regard, no one is permitted either to speak or to write anything, to dissolve the association or the above mentioned sacrifices, or to do any harm to anything belonging to the association, or to remove or to use any of the original capital for another purpose' (lines 254–61).

The will relates how Epikteta's husband and her son (Phoenix and Andragoras, respectively) had, when close to death (two years apart) urged Epikteta to establish a new association (*koinon*) comprised of relatives of the extended family. Epikteta completed her husband's construction of the sanctuary of the Muses (*Mouseion*) where the association was to assemble. One of the principal purposes of founding the

Figure 3.3 Sketch of the Epikteta monument. Courtesy of Wittenburg (1990, plate 2).

association was to provide honours and sacrifices to deceased members of the family as heroes (lines 7–9) and to honour goddesses that were closely connected with remembering, the Muses.[57] Epikteta provided for its financial basis after her son's death by arranging a foundation worth 3,000 drachmas in the form of a property she had acquired in an area called Melainai. In comparison, Poseidonios at Halikarnassos pledged a piece of land, along with a courtyard, garden and burial area and rights to half of the agricultural produce from another property to his family association (with anticipated yearly income of 4 gold pieces).[58] Diomedon on Kos granted and dedicated a sanctuary of Herakles, a garden and guest rooms, from which an unspecified amount of income was to be generated, presumably from rentals.

Epikteta's newly founded association consisted of twenty-five men at the time, along with their wives and children. The association was to assemble annually for a three-day festival in the month of Delphinios. Similarly, both Poseidonios and Diomedon arranged, among other things, for a two-day festival with sacrifices each year. The sacrificial activities of Epikteta's association were to be funded from an annual interest of 210 drachmas (7 per cent interest), generated by income (probably from produce) from the plot of land in Melainai and supplied by Epikteta or, when Epikteta passed away, her heir and daughter, Epiteleia (lines 39–41). To provide some perspective on these amounts, Epikteta's donation is a substantially larger source of income than another contemporary association on Thera island: around 200 BCE, a woman named Argea arranged for an endowment of 500 drachmas, which, through loans, was to generate enough interest for an association to have an additional gathering (*synagesthai*) each year, presumably in honour of Argea and her family (*IG* XII,3 329 + *IG* XII,3 Suppl. 1295 on p. 284; *c.* 200 BCE).

There are further specifics regarding usage of the 210 drachmas income from Epikteta's foundation. The regulations that accompany the members' acceptance state that these funds were to be used each year to cover the costs of sacrifices that were to be executed by three members who officiated, each somewhat confusingly (in light of the fact that they did not serve on a monthly basis) called a 'monthly official' (*epimēnios*). One such official sacrificed to the Muses on the first day, a second sacrificed to the heroes Phoinix and Epikteta on the second day and a third sacrificed to the heroes Kratesilochos and Andragoras on the third day (lines 121–5, 158–60). The office of the so-called 'monthly official' was also implemented by Poseidonios and by Diomedon. This once again goes beyond the meaning of 'monthly' in that, for instance, Poseidonios specifies that three such officials were to be chosen to serve *each year*, receiving the 4 gold pieces to cover the costs of sacrifices. These commonalities in terminology also further underline the shared regional (and, in some respects, likely temporally bound) customs that informed all three foundations. All three foundations occurred roughly in the same century, between 310 and 195 BCE.

According to Epikteta's document, members were to take turns (three at a time) officiating in this sacrificial role as 'monthly officials' starting from the oldest to the

---

[57] Carbon and Pirenne-Delforge (2013: 97).
[58] For translation and commentary, see ibid.

youngest. Ten days in advance of the main festival, they were to receive 50 drachmas from the 210 drachmas of income to pay for the sacrificial victims and offerings (or perhaps 50 x 3 = 150 drachmas; lines 158–60). It is important to notice that, when it was a member's turn to officiate, that person was also responsible for covering further costs from his own resources. Each person in this role was to supply 'imported wine, enough for three cups per person, one cup each for the crowning, the music, and the perfume' (lines 138–41). Another official, a financial administrator (*artutēr*), was responsible for managing the 210 drachmas. This included setting aside a further 15 drachmas for the meeting or entertainment. This administrator was also to ensure that any amount not used for the sacrifices and meeting was handed over to those who were chosen to lend the remaining amounts out at interest with proper securities (lines 146–54). The extra amount available for lending may have been about 145 drachmas per year (or just 45 drachmas per year, if the cost of sacrifices was 50 drachmas per day rather than 50 drachmas for all three days).

Unlike the foundations of Poseidonios and Diomedon, Epikteta's arrangements and accompanying regulations (lines 110–288) include several contingency plans. These are important to highlight here since this shows an awareness on the part of Epikteta that potential problems might arise and that there was a need to ensure the new group's sustainability. First, the document anticipates a scenario where Epiteleia (the daughter) failed to provide the stated amount of 210 drachmas in a particular year. In that case, the association was to have the right to the equivalent amount of produce (*karpeia*) from that property (lines 69–75). A second contingency was in place if Epiteleia did responsibly hand over 210 drachmas but a current member in charge of sacrifices for a particular day did not supply the three servings of wine. Such a failure resulted in a service cancellation payment of 150 drachmas (lines 142–3).

A third related contingency was put in place to ensure that there would always be other members to step up in case someone failed to take his turn in officiating over the sacrifices. If no one was officiating, the role would turn to the next oldest person. However, in the event that a person in the sacrificing role did receive in advance the 50 drachmas for the sacrificial costs but failed to actually deliver on the day of the sacrifices, he was to be fined 150 drachmas (again, three times the amount that had been taken). The administrator himself was to step in to cover for the delinquent member in taking on the role of sacrificing official for that day. The delinquent was not to participate again in the association until the fine was paid and he would be seizable for debt according to local law on the island (lines 160–9). It is immediately following this contingency plan that, it seems, the inscription specifies that the overall cost of the banquet might be reduced in cases when a member failed to take his turn in supplying the wine or the offerings and sacrifices (lines 167–9). There is far more to Epikteta's arrangements, including further contingency plans, but this will suffice to make the point that people in antiquity were aware of the potential for failure and careful to make alternate arrangements for endurance. Such careful planning would be important whether the group was more or less dependent on a wealthy donor or on collective resources.

Unlike Apollonios' group on Delos, the associations founded by Poseidonios, Diomedon and Epikteta started off with a meeting place and a significant amount of income-generating resources. All seem to have begun within an extended family context, but Apollonios' group was to expand beyond the family to include others, likely including non-Egyptians. If the three extended family associations limited themselves to the number of gatherings set out by their wealthy founders, there was in theory no need for members to save or to contribute anything further for the costs of sacrifices and meals, beyond taking turns to supply wine in Epikteta's case. In other words, these associations were relatively stable from the outset, even though contingency plans in one case suggest that there was worry about whether that stability would remain. Like our very modest groups at Tebtynis, the resources of even these relatively wealthy groups established by Poseidonios, Diomedon, and Epikteta would need to be carefully managed to ensure continuation of the sacrifices and feasts as planned.

Since we have been arguing that such substantial endowments by individuals were the exception rather than the rule, it is worth touching on another somewhat exceptional document that has recently come to light. In contrast to our familial groups, this one pertains to an occupational guild – in fact, the earliest guild attested in Asia Minor (beyond guilds of performers). It does *not* seem to involve the establishment of the group, but does have some things in common with the arrangements for the familial associations above. The foundation of Symmasis for the coppersmiths at either Tlos or Xanthos in Lycia, which likely dates between 150 and 100 BCE, happens to be the only extensive document of this type that exists for a guild in Asia Minor (*GRA* II 147 = *ITlos* 28 = *SEG* 58:1640).[59] So it stands alone in that respect. Furthermore, this is the lengthiest inscription we possess concerning any one occupational association in Asia Minor (beyond those concerning Dionysiac performers). In addition, there are several signs of Lycian cultural elements.[60] All of this means we should not assume this sort of arrangement was very common as the basis of a guild or association's material stability. This document still helps us to understand the management of financial endowments for particular sacrifices and meals from another perspective.

The aim of Symmasis and his wife was to establish what seems to be two separate sacrifices and accompanying banquets each year, one for Helios on the twenty-fifth of the month of Loios and the other for commemorating Symmasis and his wife, Mamma (side B). Like the foundations by Poseidonios, Diomedon and Epikteta, these activities were meant to remember the family that provided the endowment and some family members were to participate in specific gatherings. We know more about the latter sacrifice and feast than the former, due to damage to the stone on the bottom portion of each of the three inscribed sides.

The surviving portion of side A begins with a reference to the use of interest on the principal of the foundation for a sacrifice and a meal. Towards the end of the same side, there are further references to the funds themselves, which were to be controlled and,

---

[59] See also the commentary by Harland in *GRA* II 147 (which is the basis of the discussion here and is repurposed in keeping with the contract with De Gruyter), Köse and Tekoğlu (2007), Parker (2010) Arnaoutoglou (2012).

[60] Arnaoutoglou (2012: 214–15), Harland in the commentary on *GRA* II 147.

in part, carefully loaned out at interest by a committee of managers (*cheiristai*). Membership of this committee was to be drawn from the coppersmiths, and the beginning of side B names the four members of this committee for the first year. Committee members were to be elected from the coppersmiths each year for a one-year term. The formation of a committee to manage certain financial matters for an association is also attested in the case of the purchase of a sanctuary by initiates at Kyme, as we will see in Chapter 6. Side C of the Symmasis foundation also clarifies that the funds were to be used for no other purpose beyond these sacrifices and feasts.

The use of an association's funds to provide loans was not uncommon, as we saw above and will understand more fully in Chapters 5 and 8. In some cases, the focus was on financially assisting fellow members of an association, in which case an interest-free loan was possible. In other cases, as with Symmasis' foundation, the purpose of loaning the money at interest was to increase communal revenues in a way that ensured the continuation of the sacrifices for years to come. Members of the committee promised to keep the principal safe and to spend the proceeds from the interest during the two yearly sacrifices and feasts.

The yearly sacrifices and feasts described in the opening lines of side A would be initiated while both Symmasis and his wife were alive, and continue after their deaths in their honour. This may be referring to the second, commemorative sacrifice and banquet rather than the sacrifice for Helios at this point, as side B seems to indicate. At the meal, Symmasis would receive the hind leg of the sacrificed animal, the most desirable portion, and his wife would receive the front leg. After their deaths, these desirable portions would go to Symmasis' sons and then to other descendants who served as representatives of the family. The commemorative banquet itself was to be attended by Symmasis' sons and other male relatives up to a total of ten attendees only, and there were arrangements for filling vacancies upon the death of a familial participant. The coppersmiths were designated responsibility for settling any disputes over who would fill a familial vacancy at the feast, and this is where the sanctuary of the goddess Leto is mentioned as the locale for settling any disputes. This may also indicate that Leto was among the patron deities of the guild.

Side B provides further clarification regarding the yearly commemorative gathering on the day named after Symmasis and Mamma. Chosen leaders (*archontes*) from the association of coppersmiths were to do the sacrifice of a goat or a sheep in honour of 'the hero of Symmasis and Mamma' on the altar that was dedicated by Symmasis. Here we now see that at least the managers (from the association), the leaders (from the association) and the ten descendants of Symmasis were to take part in the feast which followed the sacrifice. As Robert Parker notes, the preserved portions of the foundation nowhere state that any other members of the guild beyond the managers and leaders would take part in the commemorative yearly feast, so the arrangements may not have entailed a general invitation for all the coppersmiths.[61] But we need to realize that we only have portions of the document. Unfortunately, it seems that details regarding the second yearly sacrifice are not preserved, beyond the fact that it would be 'a perpetual,

---

[61] Parker (2010: 112).

yearly sacrifice of a three-year-old castrated animal to the god Helios – who has strengthened Symmasis and his wife Mamma – on the twenty-fifth of the month of Loios'.

Finally, side C outlines further prohibitions and gives the managers the authority to seize property from anyone who violated the terms of the foundation. Any misuse of funds for purposes other than sacrifices and feasts would bring punishment from 'Helios and the other gods,' as well as a fine for double the amount taken. No one else (beyond Symmasis and Mamma, presumably) was to be buried in the tomb and a fine of 100 drachmas would be paid by anyone who attempted to do so. Finally, the inscription concludes with a statement regarding agreement by the coppersmiths and a reference to the fact that this was accepted by the vote of members in the guild in the presence of witnesses. This pattern of endowment arrangements followed by acceptance is also characteristic of the inscription of Epikteta.

So this somewhat exceptional document provides an instance where a guild was on the receiving end of an endowment to remember a particular family at specific times of year, but not an endowment to establish the association in the first place. As we will see in Chapter 5, many other much shorter funerary inscriptions from Phrygia, Lydia and Macedonia (in the imperial era), do make special arrangements to have guilds or associations of various kinds gather to take care of a family grave or to have meals in the honour of the deceased, but nothing on the scale of Symmasis' document survives.

Conclusion

As often in the study of ancient history, our evidence for the beginning point of most associations in the eastern Mediterranean is partial and fragmentary at best. We nonetheless gain important insights by exploring available materials. In the third century BCE, there were several cases when familial associations were firmly established by significant endowments from the head of a household, and there was at least one similar endowment to a guild for two yearly sacrifices, but the guild had been previously established. Yet other evidence problematizes common scholarly assumptions regarding the supposed prevalence of individual agency by the wealthy elites for the foundation of many other types of associations. When we witnessed some details of the formation and early history of certain groups, like those devoted to Sarapis on Delos and those devoted to a Saviour-god at Athens, both collective and, less so, individual agency were instrumental. As we further explore the ongoing lives of established associations, we will continue to see both sides of this picture and will begin to understand a variety of factors at play in the relative material success or failure of different groups.

4

Counting the Costs of Communal Life

The god instructed me through a dream that I should dedicate his own temple of Sarapis, and that he was not to be in rented rooms.

IG XI,4 1299

Introduction

This claim by Apollonios, the Egyptian descendant we met in the previous chapter, illustrates well the confidence with which many inscriptions express managing the material needs of a group. In this case, Apollonios attributes the establishment of a purpose-built sanctuary to divine intervention. Yet this was a modest sanctuary and it was built after almost a century of the association meeting in rented quarters, which suggests even less resources early on. Even when divine intervention is not claimed, many other associations tend to present themselves as successful or competent in handling the costs of maintaining meeting places, sacrificing, banqueting, crowning, inscribing and carrying out other collective activities. This presentation may disguise efforts that were required to sustain communal life.

In fact, the range of attested expenses suggests the importance of behind-the-scenes record-keeping, strategizing, and adapting in order to meet collective goals and function at the standard expected by invested participants. There would be times when Sarapis did not come through. Fortunately, some documents offer glimpses into how groups managed their situations, particularly perishable financial accounts on papyri from Egypt but also, occasionally, inscriptions in stone from other parts of the eastern Mediterranean.

Here we provide an overview of expenses while also taking note of sources that hint at anxieties, confirming our point that groups needed to be aware of limited resources and that precarity was a distinct possibility for some associations at certain points in their histories. We approach expenditures from several angles, dealing with things like resources put towards a place to meet; expenses for writing, documenting and inscribing; expenditures for honouring benefactors; outlay for burying or commemorating deceased members or benefactors; and, costs of dedicating, sacrificing and banqueting. The following chapters then explore where groups might get the funds to cover such costs.

Reflections on strains and survival

Before turning to specific types of expenses, it is important to note efforts involved in meeting a group's needs or wants. The burden of necessary expenditures was a topic of reflection for some associations. Around 150 BCE, a synod of fellow sacrificers (*synthytai*) dedicated to Zeus and the local hero Anthas in central Greece honoured their benefactor, Kaphisias. The small monument which they had inscribed thanked Kaphisias for covering 'the costs in advance from his own resources *so that the synod would not fall short of the income it needed*' (SEG 32:453). This decree from Anthedon does not specify exactly what expenses Kaphisias covered. But in another inscription pertaining to the group's dedication of the actual building (*gymnasion*) where they assembled, 102 members are listed as contributors and Kaphisias appears eighth in this list, so this individual benefactor was not alone in contributing to the well-being of the association (*IG* II² 2360 = *SEG* 32:454). It is noteworthy that an association with such a large membership – or financial network at least – would have been in jeopardy of debt if not for the generosity of one particular member. At least that's what the rhetoric of the honorary inscription implies.

Similarly, the first association from Tebtynis in Egypt which we discussed in Chapter 1 likely reflected on how dangerously close to financial insolvency they perpetually were (*GRA* III 195 = *PTebt* I 118). This group required twenty-two participants at their gatherings in order to cover their relatively modest banquet expenses, which consisted of six measures (*choai*) of wine at 2,000 bronze drachmas (3.33 silver drachmas) and six dinner loaves at 190 bronze drachmas (about 0.32 silver drachmas, at 600:1). Sometimes, the Tebtynis synod held gatherings without bread so that they could afford a crown. Perhaps more problematic was that this group did not have enough members to fund a meal by themselves, unless they decreased consumption. This is why guests were invited to help balance the books. Dipping into the common fund to cover occasional debts could only be done so many times before things would become precarious.

These groups from Greece and Egypt, as well as many others whose financial survival was periodically out of their own hands, may have considered the dangers of relying so heavily on voluntary contributions from individuals, whether members, guests or external supporters. There are hints that the fellow sacrificers, who on this occasion seemed to rely so heavily on Kaphisias as benefactor, were already seeking further donors. Like members of many other associations, including Delian groups discussed in the next chapter, they could seek to attract other potential benefactors by communicating clearly how they appropriately honoured those who offered support in the form of service or material contributions.[1]

Meeting places and properties

With these observations concerning insecurity and sustainability in mind, we can now turn to specific types of expenses and assets. Among the most pressing needs, if an

---

[1] Last (2016a: 149–62).

association was to last, was a place for members to meet together regularly.[2] In light of the climate in some parts of the Mediterranean, it is true that some gatherings could take place outside of buildings, which would potentially cut expenses. We know that some groups would gather at the grave of deceased members or, at least in places like Rhodes and Kos, at a communal burial plot. Still other groups, such as many in Lydia, Phrygia, and Macedonia, gathered for rituals or meals at the graves of people who requested a group to take care of their family grave.[3] So picnics in gardens, by a lake or at burial grounds should not be forgotten.[4] Yet here we are more concerned with what sorts of actual buildings some groups might have owned, rented or frequented, since this would potentially entail some expenditure.

Sometimes groups simply met in a room of a member's or leader's domestic dwelling. This was particularly the case if membership was drawn primarily from extended family networks, as seems to be the case with the group founded by Dionysios at Philadelphia in Lydia and with the Dionysiac initiates headed by Agrippinilla in Torre Nova in Italy.[5] But other groups could gather in domestic quarters as well. At Stobi in Macedonia, Claudius Tiberius Polycharmos donated several rooms in his home, including banqueting facilities and a portico, to the Judean gathering (*AGRW* 46 = *IJO* I Mac1; second or third century CE). Polycharmos retained use of the upper rooms for his family only. In these cases, a benefactor or leader offered portions of his or her own home – or some rooms within it – for use by an association.

In other cases, a group needed to rent or acquire appropriate accommodations, with or without the help of a benefactor. The rental of a meeting place, although perhaps common, is only rarely mentioned in inscriptions. We have already detailed the case of Sarapis worshippers on Delos in Chapter 3, a case which may suggest the commonality of renting rooms (perhaps domestic quarters in that case) but also the ideal of constructing or purchasing a building for gatherings. The Tyrian merchants that we have already encountered were finding it difficult to afford rent (*misthos*) on the building they used, likely for both meetings and mercantile activities. We only hear about the rental situation because the association wrote to the civic institutions of their homeland for assistance in paying the rent, and they were successful in gaining Tyre's support (*AGRW* 317 = *IG* XIV 830; 174 CE).[6] In outlining their situation, the Tyrians also mention other expenses aimed at honouring gods that made it difficult to have enough left over for rent: 'Since we pay the expenses for the sacrifices and services to our ancestral gods established here in temples, we do not have the means to pay the station's annual payment of two hundred fifty denarii, especially as the expenses for the bull sacrifice at the games in Puteoli have been imposed on us.'

Some associations, particularly those of lesser means, may not have possessed a stable meeting location, but instead rented this or that location or simply gathered in

---

[2] On association buildings, see Poland (1909: 453–87), Bollmann (1998), Schwarzer (2002). On assemblies of Jesus followers in the context of other groups, see Adams (2013).
[3] E.g. *AGRW* 152 = *GRA* II 116; *AGRW* 42 = *IPhilippiP* II 029/G215; *GRA* I 69 = *IPhilippiP* II 133/G441.
[4] On this, see Adams (2013: 181–97).
[5] *AGRW* 121 = *GRA* II 117 = *TAM* V 1539 (*c.* 100 BCE); *AGRW* 330 = *IGUR* 160 (160–170 CE).
[6] Sosin (1999).

different spots without paying rent. Two Egyptian examples from the second century BCE illustrate this point. A group with less than ten members, likely including enslaved persons, is known from its fairly lengthy records on a papyrus that probably comes from Philadelphia in the district of Arsinoites (*GRA* III 193 = *SB* III 7182). This group records where they met on different occasions, varying between a storehouse, the harness room in a stable and a room in an Isis temple.[7] Likewise, the second association at Tebtynis which we discussed in Chapter 2 records meetings at the house or shop of members (of Menoites and of Harpalos), at a work-related structure, at a storehouse and at altars (*GRA* III 194 = *PTebt* III 894).[8] Since such details would not likely be set in stone (but rather on impermanent materials such as papyri or wood tablets, if at all), it is primarily in Egypt that we have clear evidence for this likely common practice. This mobile approach to meetings may well have been more common for groups whose members' economic means were quite modest. This also shows that a purpose-built sanctuary, although preferable, was not a prerequisite for a group's sustainability.

The case of the Sarapis sanctuary at Thessalonica in Macedonia (built around 315 BCE) provides another instance of multiple groups either renting or simply frequenting the same building.[9] Among the seventy inscriptions found in excavations are three regarding associations that frequented the sanctuary and perhaps met there regularly in the first century CE. In 66 CE, a woman named Herennia Procula dedicated four columns with capitals in the sanctuary, specifying that she did so for the fellow banqueters (*synklitai*) that evidently used that area of the sanctuary (*AGRW* 48 = *IG* X,2.1 70). Another inscription seems to pertain to the same group (either an association or a board), where they also designate themselves 'sacred object-bearers' (*hieraphoroi*; *AGRW* 47 = *IG* X,2.1 58; first century BCE or CE). A bequest made by Gaius Julius to the initiates of Zeus Dionysos Gongylos was found in the sanctuary, suggesting that these initiates likely frequented the sanctuary despite the fact that they were primarily dedicated to another patron deity (*AGRW* 50 = *IG* X,2.1 259). Third, a group of Roman businessmen were at home enough in the sanctuary to dedicate a monument to an emperor as benefactor there (*IG* X,2 33 = *RICIS* 113/0538).

Renting a meeting space brought other ongoing costs. Dining-room lease agreements from Egypt clarify some of these costs, even if these documents do not always pertain to associations.[10] One second-century papyrus from the Apollonopolites Heptakomia district is helpful for illuminating rental situations (*SB* X 10278; 114–119 CE).[11] A certain bath assistant living in Heptakomia, named Horion, writes to the administrator of the district (*stratēgos*), Apollonios, begging to be released from his lease agreement. Horion had rented dining rooms and storerooms (*kellai*) from Apollonios (or Apollonios' representative) for one year. This turned out to be a poor

---

[7] Storehouse (*thēsauros*): fragment 1, II, line 12, fragment 4 front [r.], III, line 62; stable: fragment 4 front [r.], II, line 45–6, fragment 5 front [r.], line 79; Iseion: fragment 3, line 43.
[8] Fragment 2 front [r.], l, line 7; fragment 2 back [v.], II, line 45; fragment 3 front [r.], I, line 3 (*ergeutigō*); fragment 10 front [r.], l, line 4; fragment 6 front [r.], II, line 10; fragment 10 front [r.], line 2; and fragment 11 back [v.], II, line 6.
[9] See Koukouvou (2012), Voutiras (2005).
[10] For such agreements, see Alston (2002: 375, n. 52).
[11] See also Maehler (1966: 342–53).

investment and, the letter indicates, he wants out of the agreement. For some reason, Horion needs Apollonios' consent to do so. Horion claims to have lost 200 drachmas because no one had been subleasing the rooms, 'neither to dwell (*enoikein*) in them nor to dine (*deipnein*) in them'.

Horion's case suggests three noteworthy things for our purposes. First, rooms could be rented for various time frames: a year, a month, a day. An association could make the gamble Horion did by leasing a dining room for a year or more and subletting it to others when the group did not need it. In the next chapter, we will witness sacrificing associates at Athens leasing out their own sanctuaries or properties as a source of income. Second, associations would occasionally deal with entrepreneurial lessors such as Horion when negotiating lease rates. At this particular time, it is hard to imagine that an association from Heptakomia would need to pay much to Horion for using one of his dining rooms given his apparent desperation for clients, but this would not always be the case. Third, when associations leased dining rooms, they would be required to maintain or clean them. Horion himself complained about how much time he spent cleaning the properties.[12]

It is not hard to imagine such rental or leasing situations impacting Judeans and adherents of Jesus, for instance. The author of Acts imagines as realistic a scenario where the Judean Paul rented accommodations in Rome and where people assembled there with him (Acts 28:30). More importantly, the Judeans Priska and Aquila apparently spent some time in several cities (Rom 16:3–5; 1 Cor 16:19; cf. Acts 18:2–3), movement which suggests they perhaps both lived and worked in rented or leased spaces.[13] On more than one occasion, Paul clearly indicates that assemblies met within buildings Priska and Aquila inhabited at Corinth and at either Rome or Ephesos, where Paul refers to 'the assembly in their dwelling' (*hē kat' oikon ekklēsia*; 1 Corinthians 16:19; Romans 16:5; cf. Philemon 2; Colossians 4:15). So this may well be a case similar to the Egyptian family on Delos, where an association assembled within rented domestic accommodations, with the cost of quarters being covered by those who lived in the building. However, as with the Delian case, the hosts need not have been wealthy benefactors, as sometimes assumed. In fact, Priska and Aquila's dwelling may well have been their workshop as well. Buildings used as workshops often simultaneously served as a residence for craftspeople and dealers.[14]

Paul's description of his time teaching those who did come to reject Greek gods and adopt worship of the Israelite deity at Thessalonica suggests that he may have done so in a workshop setting (1 Thess 1:8–10; 2:9; 4:11).[15] So it would not be a far stretch to picture these people continuing to meet together in similar work settings, something we have seen in the case of some Egyptian associations above who met in various locations, including workshops or quarters of members (at Tebtynis). Although we need not accept Celsus' caricature of the typical Jesus follower about a century after Paul, there may still be some truth in his notion that these people were to be found in

---

[12] Cf. *POxy* VIII 128, lines 16–27 (173 CE).
[13] Cf. Oakes (2009b: 69–97), Adams (2013: 5–8, 18–210).
[14] Cf. Adams (2013: 137–45).
[15] Cf. Hock (1979), Hock (1980). On the Thessalonians as a guild, see Ascough (2000, 2003).

the (rented [?]) workshops of wool-workers, shoemakers and clothing-cleaners (in Origen, *Against Celsus* 3.55).

While continuing to recognize the importance of domestic quarters, recent studies of the meeting places used by the earliest groups devoted to Jesus have begun to expand out beyond the typical image of meetings taking place within a large home or villa-like context.[16] David Horrell, Peter Oakes and Bradly S. Billings in different ways challenge the notion that people like Priska and Aquila would be offering a room in a substantial house they owned for the assembly's meetings. Instead, potential domestic quarters for meetings could be more modest and small, including the ancient equivalent of apartments (multistorey tenement housing) which may have been rented rather than owned.[17] Furthermore, Edward Adams explores various other options for assemblies beyond domestic quarters, bringing in evidence for other associations in the process.[18] Many of these overlap with the sorts of places we have just witnessed with associations in Egypt, including workplaces, rented dining rooms, barns, bathhouses and outdoor spaces such as gardens or burial grounds. Adams usefully provides a survey of excavation results that illustrate each of these types of meeting places, so the archaeological evidence need not be repeated here. We should not assume a substantial owned house as the norm for these assemblies of Jesus adherents, then, even though that may have been the case on occasion. Instead, the nature of the meeting locations of Jesus adherents would likely vary from region to region, from group to group and perhaps from one occasion to the next, as with other associations. (See also the discussion of groups connected in some way with 'the elder' and Ignatius in Chapter 2.)

There are indeed associations that did not need to pay rent but rather came to own, or have access to, properties or buildings. Buildings dedicated to deities might also be considered to be owned by the deities in question, it should be noted. Ilias Arnaoutoglou summarizes the evidence from Athens, which may, in some respects, be similar to other sites in the Greek East. There were several ways in which associations came into possession of land (with or without built structures) at Athens, including receipt of donated property; transfer of land put up as security by a debtor who did not reimburse the association for loans; and, for associations of foreigners, grants by the city allowing the group to lease or acquire property (see the discussion of Thracians below).[19] According to Paulin Ismard, collective usage (*chrēsis*) – to be distinguished from collective ownership (*ktēsis*) – was also common, at least in Athens itself.[20] Our evidence about how groups came to have access to properties is somewhat limited but worth exploring. We also need to remember procedures would differ from place to place, and often we know more about Athens than we do about other locales.

---

[16] For earlier studies of the concept of the 'house church', see Filson (1939), Judge (1960), Banks (1980), Klauck (1981), Barton and Horsley (1981), Hellerman (2001), Balch and Osiek (2003), Balch (2004), Gehring (2009), Öhler and Zimmermann (2017).
[17] Horrell (2004), Oakes (2009b), Billings (2011).
[18] Adams (2013).
[19] Arnaoutoglou (2003: 137).
[20] Examples in Ismard (2010: 159). See Kloppenborg (2006: 333–4) on the distinction in Greek and Roman legal frameworks.

For Athens specifically, there are indications of procedures and expenses prior to accessing property and establishing a meeting place or temple, at least for foreigners in a particular era (fifth to second century BCE). It is difficult to know whether the situation here can be extrapolated to other cities, however. In theory, immigrants (whether individual families or groups) in these territories had to gain permission from the civic institutions – the Council and the People – in order to have property on which they could build a meeting place or sanctuary. As early as the fifth century, Thracians at the Piraeus had gained from the citizen body of Athens the right to hold property (*egktēsis*) in order to build a temple for the goddess Bendis (*AGRW* 18 = *IG* II² 1283; 240/239 BCE).[21]

The inscription that documents the Thracians' right to own land claims that this was an exclusive right of Thracian immigrants at first, but other evidence suggests the procedure came to be generalized. Another monument from the Piraeus preserves minutes from the civic assembly about the Kitian merchants' similar request to lease land to build a temple for Aphrodite, and this document makes reference to yet another earlier case involving the Egyptians' temple for Isis (*AGRW* 10 = *IG* II² 337; 333/332 BCE). In the Kitians' case, there are more details regarding procedures: the civic Council first assessed the immigrant group's request for land usage before presenting the request to the assembly of the People. The citizen body then granted the right to lease or hold property where a temple could be built. There could also be diplomatic costs involved in gaining this permission to build a meeting place, particularly if travel to Athens was involved as shown in a later case involving an ambassador for the Tyrians settled on Delos (*AGRW* 223 = *IDelos* 1519; ca. 150 BCE).

Unfortunately, we know very little concerning procedures around purchasing property or buildings in other cities or even for non-immigrant associations building in Attica.[22] There are hints from other places, however. One somewhat extensive, although still ambiguous, document from Rhodes pertains to an association on that island with ownership of properties (*IRhodPC* 18 = *SEG* 3:674; *c*. 169 or 109 BCE).[23] The inscription is a decree in which Zenon, the 'benefactor' of the association devoted to Aphrodite, arranges to have documents (*amphouriasmoi*, a little-attested word) regarding the measurement and purchase of properties belonging to the association inscribed in stone and posted somewhere within the group's communal burial plots (*taphiai*).[24] The emphasis of Zenon's decree is to have these documents fully visible to the contributors (*eranistai*) in perpetuity. This group consisted of a mixture of immigrants to Rhodes, including Zenon of Selge (in Pisidia), Hermogenes of Phaselis (in Lycia), Menogenes the Galatian, Theodotos the Arab and Perdikkas of Argos (in the Peloponnese).[25] There are locals who seem to be members of this Rhodian group as well: Nikasion (not the same Nikasion we discussed in Chapter 3) represented the

---

[21] Cf. Planeaux (2000); Arnaoutoglou (2015).
[22] On Athens, now see some of the hypotheses suggested by Papazarkadas (2011: 191–211).
[23] Cf. Fraser (1977: 60–1).
[24] The phrase is *hoi amphouriasumoi tōn eggaiōn tōn hyparchontōn tō koinō* (lines 3–4).
[25] On associations of foreigners at Rhodes, see Pugliese Carratelli (1939) (= *IRhodPC*) and Maillot (2015).

group in paying for some of the properties, and he was a citizen of Lindos on Rhodes.[26] One of the documents that was eventually inscribed deals with both the communal burial plots and a building (*oikia*) in the city of Rhodos worth 12,000 drachmas that the group seems to have possessed, but there are no references to any requirement to gain special permission from civic institutions.

Another document relating to the acquisition of property comes from Paros, an island about 60 kilometres south of Delos (*SEG* 54:794; *c.* 200 BCE).[27] The inscription details the boundaries of a property in the area of Eles that was bought by adherents of a Saviour god (*Soteriastai*), although this was not necessarily an immigrant group in this case. It also mentions that a deed of sale (*ōnē*) had been inscribed and refers to a payment of 300 drachmas, likely for documentation of land measurement (*periēgētēs*, again a rare word). Unfortunately, the actual amount of the purchase is not preserved. The document concludes with reference to various witnesses and civic functionaries (registrars and an official in charge of commercial dealings) whose responsibility it was to ensure the property sale was properly performed and documented according to local custom on Paros.

Turning to other Aegean islands and to Asia Minor, we do witness associations and guilds dedicating buildings which had already been acquired or constructed, but without much clarification on how this came about. On Delos, the oil-dealers dedicated a temple and statue of Herakles around 100 BCE, referring to the fact that two members had been appointed to oversee construction (*AGRW* 234 = *IDelos* 1713; cf. *IDelos* 1714). In 57 BCE, the Italian worshippers of Hermes there dedicated their temple (*IDelos* 1737). In the Roman imperial period, a group of merchants at Thyatira in Lydia dedicated their workshops to members of the imperial family (*TAM* V 862). Nikomedian shippers in Bithynia dedicated their sanctuary to emperor Vespasian (*TAM* IV 22). And the fishermen and fish-dealers at Ephesos most likely dedicated the toll office to Artemis, that city's patron deity, as we discuss in Chapter 6 (*IEph* 20). A similar picture of associations regularly dedicating buildings is gained by looking at other regions such as the Black Sea area, Syria and Egypt.[28] Still, beyond the case of initiates at Kyme in Asia Minor, whose collections for the purchase of sanctuaries we also discuss in Chapter 6, there is a dearth of detailed information about *plans* to purchase properties or buildings in Asia Minor.

Some of the Egyptian dedications reveal the importance of both collective and individual agency. The dedication of a temple to the deities Thriphis (a little-known goddess), Kolanthes, and Pan at Ptolemais Hermou is suggestive. Here Priskos, a military man, is called out as central, likely in the role of supervisor of the project, but then all twenty-eight participants are considered co-dedicators and, likely, contributors to the funds that were required (*GRA* III 247 = *SB* III 6184; 138 BCE). On the other

---

[26] Cf. Maillot (2015: 161).
[27] For restoration of line 2, see Chaniotis, *EBGR* (2005), no. 85.
[28] Black Sea region: *IKallatis* 46; *IKallatis* 80; *AGRW* 72 = *IHistria* 167; *AGRW* 60 = *GRA* I 83 = *IThraceL* 18. Sidon in Syria: *AGRW* 276 = *SEG* 55:1654; *AGRW* 277 = *SEG* 54:1628. Egypt: *GRA* III 201 = *IFayum* 205; *IFayum* 73; *SB* III 6254 = *IFayum* II 109 (102 BCE); *IFayum* II 134 (79 BCE); *GRA* III 221 = *SEG* 41:1638; *GRA* III 229 = *IFayum* II 122.

hand, a place established for the weavers to meet in Abydos was apparently covered by one individual (*GRA* III 271 = *SB* IV 7290; 256 CE).

Here it is worth giving attention to a more detailed Egyptian inscription regarding procedures to purchase. This was a situation in which the potential seller actually donated the land to the group, however. A synod of farmers at Psenamosis in the Nile Delta passed honours for a benefactor and, in the process, refer to how they came to access their meeting place (*AGRW* 287 = *GRA* III 160 = *IDelta* I 446; 67 BCE). The inscription outlines the synod's earlier plan to seek out property in order to build a gymnasium and a building (*oikos*) where they could engage in sacrifices and other activities. However, when they had found an appropriate place, the seller of the land actually decided to become the group's donor: 'he did not insist on receiving payment, but donated it and registered it as a free gift to the synod'. The farmers responded by granting him a statue in each of their two buildings and prime seating at the group's feasts, among other things.

One might be tempted to think that this case of a potential seller becoming a donor was an extremely rare occurrence, if not for another example from an earlier era from Rhamnous in Attica. In the early third century BCE, adherents of Sarapis there wrote to the owner of a piece of land, a wealthy citizen of Athens named Apollodoros, 'wishing to buy it so that they could construct a temple to Sarapis and Isis'. Not only 'did he not wish to be paid for it, but he even gave it to them without any charge, demonstrating extreme piety towards the gods and good will and zeal with regard to his fellow citizens' (*GRA* I 27 = *IRhamnous* II 59; 216 BCE).[29]

For associations that did come to possess and keep properties, there were the costs of maintaining, improving, renovating or expanding structures. Sometimes these expenses could be covered by an individual benefactor. There is the case of a donor at Lindos on Rhodes stepping in to help the 'association of Euphanorian devotees of Dionysos, Athena, and Zeus Atabyrios who are with Athenaios the Knidian' (*IG* XII,1 937; first century CE). Although the honorary inscription is fragmentary, it is clear that this group that included immigrants was, in its own words, 'being arrogantly abused in connection with its meeting places (*topoi*) and was wasting away 550 drachmas on these matters'. This may be a reference to costs in connection with a lawsuit (compare the Sarapis worshippers on Delos) or it may relate to damages inflicted by certain people (on which, remember the Judeans at Alexandria). In this case, a person stepped up to pay the necessary costs, promising 505 drachmas for the restoration of the meeting place, another 100 drachmas for the rooms and a further 100 drachmas for the expense of decoration. In Boiotia, in central Greece, there is the case of Antagoros (*IG* VII 2850; after 168 BCE). He was the appointed treasurer (*tamias*) of the synod of hunters (*kynēgoi*) devoted to the goddess Artemis at Haliartos, a city under Athenian control at the time. The hunters praised him and crowned him with a gold crown not only for fulfilling his duties by keeping the accounts in a 'righteous manner', but also for restoring the building (*oikos*) in which they met.

---

[29] Cf. Arnaoutoglou (2007).

Communal efforts to cover such costs are also clearly evident. Those devoted to the hero Amphiaraos (*Amphieraistai*) at Rhamnous on the eastern coast of Attica were particularly concerned about the disrepair of their temple, for instance (*IG* II² 1322 = *SEG* 33:145; after 229 BCE). The document that preserves an account of their meeting clarifies that 'the building (*oikos*) has no doors, the tiling has been broken, part of the wall which is opposite the altar has fallen down, the table of the god has been broken, and the portico is in danger of falling down'. In response, there was a special effort to raise funds, the sort of communal collection that we explore at length in Chapters 6 and 7. The participants together resolved 'to contribute towards the restoration of the temple as much as each was able, and that the names of those who contributed were to be inscribed on a stone slab and set up alongside the statue of the god'. More than twenty-seven names are listed as contributors. They also resolved to honour two specific donors: one had joined them in paying for the restoration of the temple itself and the other had granted an endowment that generated interest to pay for a specific yearly sacrifice.

Immigrants that formed associations in their society of settlement likewise engaged in such expansions or renovations, sometimes with the help of benefactors. Syrian immigrants illustrate the point.[30] The form of these inscriptions also points to some ways in which such ethnic associations acculturated to local, Greek honorary customs as well. In the third century BCE, the Sidonians settled in the Piraeus erected an inscription in their native language (with a short Greek summary). Despite the Phoenician language, the inscription nonetheless shows that such immigrants adopted local honorary customs. They honour 'Shama-baal son of Magon, who was president of the association in charge of the temple and in charge of the construction of the court of the temple, because he has built the court of the temple and has carried out every public function entrusted to him'.[31] Numerous contemporary Greek inscriptions from the Piraeus show that other ethnic groups and other associations likewise honoured those who built or enhanced their meeting places.[32]

A similar picture of immigrants and architecture emerges on the island of Delos. In the first part of the second century BCE, a society (*thiasos*) of Syrians had joined with the priest and priestess of their god in contributing towards the renovation and expansion of a shrine for Atargatis (*AGRW* 229 = *RICIS* 202/0194).[33] A Roman banker there contributed funds to help finish the construction of a sanctuary for the Berytian merchants around 150 BCE (*AGRW* 224 = *IDelos* 1520). There are hints in the Berytians' inscription that the group had found it difficult to afford the expenses

---

[30] On Syrian associations, see also Harland (2009: 99–122).
[31] Teixidor (1980). Harland's translation is based on Teixidor's French translation of the Phoenician part of the inscription. Cf. *IG* II² 2946 = Ameling (1990).
[32] See, for instance: *GRA* I 13 = *IG* II² 1271 (299/298 BCE): portico and pediment for those devoted to Zeus Labraundos. *GRA* I 18 = *IG* II² 1273 (265/264 BCE): 'house' built for those devoted to the Mother of the gods. *IG* II² 1282 (262/261 BCE): addition to the temple of the Egyptian god Ammon. *GRA* I 32 = *IG* II² 1324 (*c*. 190 BCE): repairs to the temple of the sacrificing associates of Bendis. *GRA* I 33 = *IG* II² 1325 (185/184 BCE): construction and then beautification of the temple of the Dionysos-devotees.
[33] See also Siebert (1968).

associated with the plans they had made for the sanctuary. So the benefactor, Minatius, helped to ensure that 'the building may be completed according to what was previously decided'.

Like Syrians settled elsewhere, Judeans in Greek cities had their buildings enhanced or renovated.[34] At Nysa in Caria, a benefactor arranged to have a building extended for what seems to be a Judean association (based on the usage of 'people' here): 'Menandros son of Apollonides arranged to have the area from the inscription to the east built for the people (*laos*) and the synod which is gathered around Dositheos son of Theogenes.'[35] Around 100 CE, Judeans at Akmoneia in Phrygia (if this 'synagogue' is Judean) honoured two men with the title of 'head of the synagogue' and another 'leader' (*archōn*) who had 'decorated the walls and ceiling, made the windows secure, and took care of all the rest of the decoration' (*AGRW* 145 = *IJO* II 168). The inscription also refers to the fact that the building (*oikos*) itself had previously been built by Julia Severa in the mid-first century. This implies that this local notable with important connections to the imperial elites had donated the structure itself to the Judeans and those associated with her family – perhaps as freedpersons – later improved it.[36]

While on the topic of immigrants from the Levant, it is also worth mentioning a case involving renovations for a temple used by a corporate body (*politeuma*) of Idumean soldiers settled in Memphis, Egypt. In a gathering (*synagōgē*) in 112 BCE, the soldiers honoured Dorion, a priest and leader of the troop (*plēthos*) of sabre-bearers. They did so primarily because of his piety towards their patron deity in improving the temple of Apollo, perhaps identified with the Idumean god Qos: 'Being piously disposed towards the deity, he has with much, abundant expenditure completed the plastering and whitening of the temple seen here by everyone' (*OGIS* 737 = *SB* V 8929).[37] In return, the Idumeans provided honours that might readily be understood as typically Greek, including a public proclamation at their sacrifices and a special crown during banquets of the group. Yet they also planned 'to remember him in the hymns' produced and performed by the priests and the temple-singers (*hieropsaltai*). As Dorothy J. Thompson Crawford observes, the hymns may well reflect Idumean ancestral customs.[38]

Archeological evidence provides momentary glimpses into the relative size and, therefore, cost of such buildings. Meeting places that have been excavated in the eastern Mediterranean range from more affordable, smaller structures to somewhat expensive or elaborate multifunctional buildings, likely reflecting the economic circumstances of the groups themselves, at least in some cases.[39] Peter Oakes' insightful study of houses at Pompeii considers how building sizes and quality might be a partial indicator of the

---

[34] On 'leader of the synagogue' (*archisynagōgos*) as benefactor, see Rajak and Noy (1993).
[35] *IJO* II 26 (first century BCE, according to Ameling in *IJO*). See discussion in Robert (1960: 261).
[36] On Severa and her family, see Harland (2013: 121–3) = ibid. (2003: 140–7).
[37] Idumeans are also attested in a dedication at Memphis (*SB* I 681). On Qos at Memphis, see *BGU* 1216, line 10 (110 BCE) and Thompson (1984). Cf. *AGRW* 258 = *IG* XII,3 6 (Idumean on Syme island).
[38] Thompson Crawford (1984: 1071).
[39] See *AGRW* B1–B28 for descriptions and bibliography. Cf. Bollmann (1998) on Italy, Trümper (2006) on Delos. Nielsen (2014) on mysteries, Ascough (2007, 2016).

economic status of those who inhabited them.⁴⁰ While we do not have such detailed information about association meeting places at any one locale, the relative sizes of buildings may be taken as a partial indication of the relative expenses involved in upkeep and may also reflect the resources of those who participated in some cases. Furthermore, the size of the building would also have implications for the number of people who could meet within such a space and, therefore, the number of potential contributors to the material well-being of the group. Cases where a *single* association is known to have owned and used a building are more secure indications of the relative resources of a certain association than are buildings that were frequented or rented by many groups, of course.

Several sanctuaries frequented or possessed by one particular association (or its patron deity or hero) are known at Athens and the Piraeus. The irregularly shaped sanctuary of the sacrificing associates of Amynos and Asklepios near the Areopagos at Athens, which dates to the fourth century BCE, measured about 250 metres squared.⁴¹ The meeting place of those devoted to Dionysos (*Dionysiastai*) in the Piraeus during the second century BCE consisted of a rectangular building measuring about 900 metres squared beside a courtyard surrounded by a hall measuring about 315 metres squared, for a total space of about 1,215 metres squared.⁴² From the mid-second century of the imperial era, the sanctuary of Bacchos at Athens (*AGRW* B2) was about 198 metres squared (11 x 18 metres) and consisted of a central nave and two aisles divided by two rows of columns, with an apse at one end where the altar stood.⁴³ Despite the smaller size of its meeting place, this group could, at one point, boast of having as its priest the very wealthy Claudius Herodes Atticus (*GRA* I 51 = *IG* II² 1368).

Further building evidence is forthcoming from Aegean islands, particularly Delos. Several meeting places of associations were located on the so-called 'Terrace of the Foreign Gods' (see Figure 4.1). We have already encountered the story behind the building of Sarapis sanctuary A (see building 91 on the plan = *AGRW* B7), which in its final, modestly built form measured about 302 metres squared (about 19.5 x 15.5 metres), including a small shrine or temple (4.1 x 3.2 metres) and a dining room.⁴⁴ A second sanctuary of Sarapis at Delos (Sarapieion B) was about the same size, including a small shrine or temple (7 x 4.5 metres; building 96). It seems that numerous associations met in this building, though (see *IG* XI,4 1227, 1229, 1226; second century BCE). The third Sarapis sanctuary C (building 100) was, by far, the largest at about 6,000 metres squared (120 x 50 metres). This sanctuary came to have close ties with the civic community of Delos itself (and is often described by scholars as 'public'), and is therefore not an indication of any one association's economic circumstances.

A society of Syrians met in the sanctuary of Atargatis (building 98) in this same neighbourhood of Delos.⁴⁵ This building was expanded over the years, pointing to the relative success of the sanctuary. Initially the building consisted of a courtyard with porticos dedicated to Pure Aphrodite and Zeus Hadad. An inscription published by

⁴⁰ Oakes (2009b: 46–68), building on earlier observations regarding house sizes at Pompeii by Jongman (1988: 239–41, 247–64). Cf. Wallace-Hadrill (1994).
⁴¹ Körte (1896), Wycherley (1970: 283–95). On this association, see *IG* II² 1252 + 999, 1253, 1259.
⁴² Dörpfeld (1884), Rider (1916: 222–4).
⁴³ Cf. Dörpfeld (1894), Schräder (1896), Schäfer (2002).
⁴⁴ Cf. White (1997: 32–7).
⁴⁵ Excavation report and plans in Will and Schmid (1985).

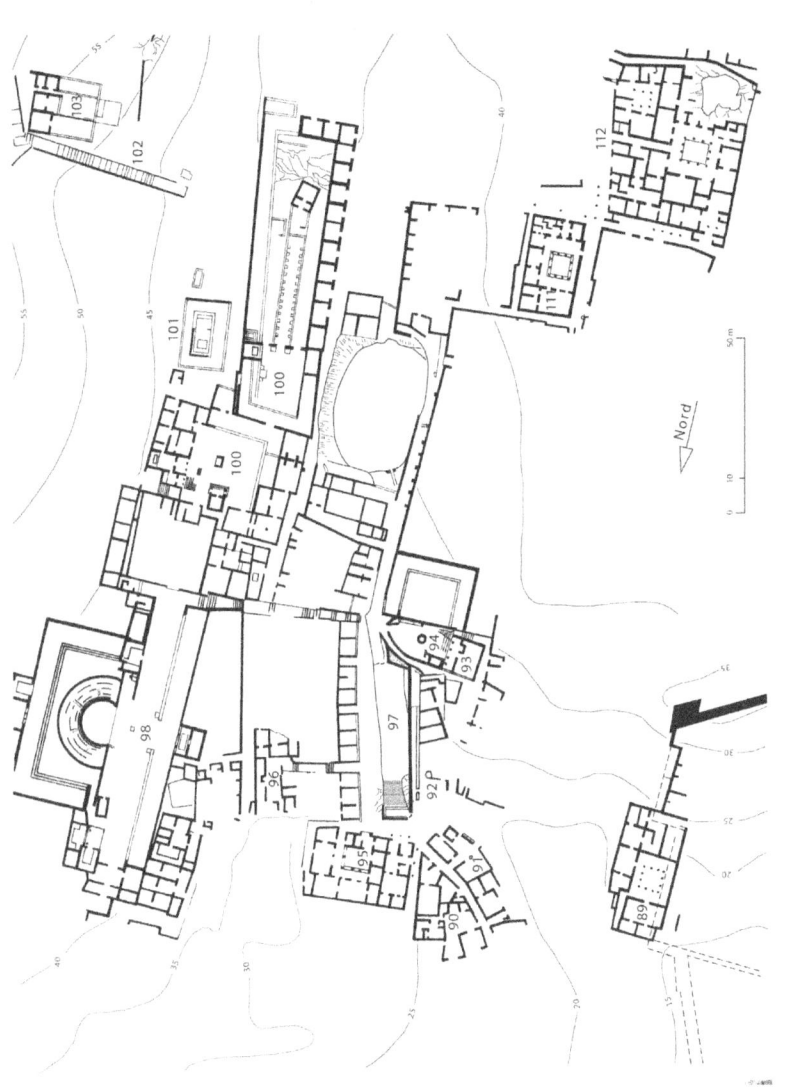

Figure 4.1 The so-called 'Terrace of the Foreign Gods' on Delos, showing various sanctuaries used by ethnic associations. Courtesy of l'École française d'Athènes / Brigitte Sagnier. Used with permission.

Gérard Siebert (*AGRW* 229 = *RICIS* 202/0194) comes from the first half of the second century BCE. It refers to the extension of a building (*oikos*) by the current priest and priestess and the society as far as the adjacent temple of Sarapis, what would expand to become Sarapieion C.[46] A further shrine within this sanctuary was dedicated to a god named Hadran in 92 BCE. In the following two years, the sanctuary was further expanded with another large portico, a theatre, and dining rooms fitted with benches at the north end. The building was likely destroyed by Mithridates in 88 BCE.

If inscriptions found on location in another structure on Delos are original to that structure, that building (GD 80) near the shore was used by adherents of the 'most high god' (*theos hypsistos*). This may involve either Israelites generally or Judeans specifically (although no inscriptions expressly mentioning either were found in the building). The rectangular building, which includes a large hall and courtyard, measures about 868 metres squared at most (28.3 x 30.7 m). It was likely used as a meeting place from the point of its construction in the second century BCE until the second century CE, according to Monika Trümper's recent detailed study.[47]

One of the largest meeting places used by a single association on the island of Delos, which suggests access to considerable resources at the time, is the building of the Berytian merchants (GD 57 = *AGRW* B8). This multi-functional structure located in a residential quarter measured about 1500 metres squared in total. It took the form of a peristyle house with two courtyards, three (then four) shrines devoted to the ancestral gods (and Roma), and a series of small- to medium-sized rooms.[48] It is likely that it served not only as a meeting place, but also for mercantile activities.

On the nearby island of Melos, there is the excavated building used by initiates (likely of Dionysos) in the first half of the third century CE.[49] This hall covered just over 191 metres squared (8.32 x 23 metres) and was surrounded by seven marble columns on each side. The eastern doorway led from the main hall into what was, in the view of the excavators, likely a shrine-like extension (*adyton*) opening into a place for rites and initiations.

Some of the few associative structures excavated in Asia Minor are adaptations of domestic quarters. The somewhat typical upper-class house at Priene, which was likely adapted for use by a group of Judeans (if the presence of a menorah points to such communal use) in the second century CE, measures about 510 metres squared (about 30 x 17 metres) in total.[50] But it seems that the open courtyard itself, measuring about 192 metres squared (14.8 x 13 metres), may have been the actual assembly hall. At Pergamon, a peristyle house built in the second century BCE came to be used and further adapted by the Dionysiac cowherds (*AGRW* B6). This measured 780 metres squared, including the banqueting room pictured in Figure 4.2, which was fitted with benches (hence the name 'Podium-hall') that measured 11 x 24 metres. The complex history of this building has now been documented in detail by Holger Schwarzer.[51]

---

[46] Siebert (1968).
[47] Trümper (2004). Binder (1999: 307–14) also argues (against White, 1997: 2.332–9) that it was not an adapted house. Trümper's reasons for excluding possible usage by a 'pagan' association seem less than convincing, however.
[48] Trümper (2002, 2006).
[49] Bosanquet (1898).
[50] See White (1997: 2.325–32).
[51] Schwarzer (2008). Cf. Radt (1988: 224–8), Schwarzer (2002), Nielsen (2014: 118–20).

Figure 4.2 Banqueting rooms of the cowherds at Pergamon. Photo by Harland.

So meeting places that seem to have been used by just one group ranged from about 191 to 1,500 metres squared in size, and can be ranked from largest to smallest to conclude this overview:

Berytian merchants on Delos:	1,500 metres squared
Devotees of Dionysos at the Piraeus:	1,215 metres squared
Devotees of the 'most high god' on Delos:	868 metres squared
Cowherds of Dionysos at Pergamon:	780 metres squared
Judeans at Priene:	510 metres squared
Sacrificing associates of Amynos and Asklepios at Athens:	250 metres squared
Sarapis sanctuary A on Delos:	302 metres squared
Devotees of Bacchos at Athens:	198 metres squared
Initiates of Dionysos on Melos:	191 metres squared

Writing and archiving

With the exception of excavated buildings and art, virtually all of the evidence for the activities of associations we have discussed so far consists in written materials, whether on papyrus, wood or stone. Thousands of extant sources produced by associations show that many could afford to write or hire others to write, or to hire an artist to prepare a statue or portrait. Regarding inscriptions in stone, the price of inscribing depended on the size and quality of the monument. The cost of purchasing a stone, having it inscribed and bringing it to its final destination seems to have amounted to approximately 10–20 silver drachmas in the early Hellenistic period.[52] To contextualize this figure, at this time 5–6 drachmas was the typical value of a dry measure (*medimno*) of wheat (measuring about 29.9 kg) and 3–5 drachmas was the value for the same amount of barley.[53]

Occasionally, inscriptions mention procedures or costs of having inscriptions prepared. In many cases, functionaries within the group were expected either to draw the money from a common fund or, less often, pay the cost of inscriptions from their own resources. With reference to honours voted for two 'monthly officers' (*epimēnioi*), Nikagoras and Lykaithos, an association devoted to Zeus on Kos ordered that 'the treasurers (*tamiai*) will have the decree inscribed on a monument of stone and set up alongside the altar of Zeus, and the cost that is incurred for the monument will be paid by the treasurers' (*IKosPH* 382 = *IG* XII,4.1 121; third century BCE).[54]

With hundreds of unofficial associations attested in the Egyptian papyri, it is remarkable that these documents, especially the financial accounts, rarely comment on scribal or inscriptional costs.[55] Nonetheless, in two day-to-day summary accounts of transactions from the Tebtynis record office (*grapheion*) dating to 45 or 46 CE, seventeen entries by the office mention payments of scribal and storage fees (*grammatikon*) by associations (*GRA* III 216 = *PMich* II 123–4).[56] Those who paid for storage of their regulations (*nomoi*) – rendering them binding – include a synod of an unnamed god for an unknown price, a synod gathered around an oil-manufacturer for the price of 4 liquid measures of oil (4 *kotylai* ≈ 1.08 litres); another synod gathered around Kronion for the price of 11 obols (6 obols = 1 drachma); the shepherds for 8 obols; and, the builders for 10 obols.[57] The varying scribal fees could reflect different lengths of documents being copied. A group of wool-workers paid 8 obols as a scribal fee when they stored a list of members, rather than a regulation.[58]

More expensive than regulations and lists were declarations (*cheirographiai*). An association of tenant-farmers on an imperial estate owned by Emperor Claudius paid 11 drachmas for such a document, while the guild of weavers paid 8 drachmas, as did the guild of wool-dealers.[59] When occupational associations registered bids for

---

[52] Nielsen et al. (1989: 411–20), Nolan (1981: 57–9), Lassère (2005: 1.4–10), Kloppenborg and Ascough (2011: 98–100).
[53] Reden (2010: 154).
[54] Similarly, the synod of Tyrian immigrants on Delos ordered their appointed leaders, the treasurers and secretary, to inscribe their decree, and specified that their treasurer and the head of the society should share the expense of the stone (*AGRW* 223, lines 51–4; 153/152 BCE).
[55] In *POslo* III 143 (1st century CE), a temple board of sacred object carriers (*pastophoroi*) at Oxyrhynchos documents 'writing expenses' at 4 drachmas, which amounts to one third the cost of their common meal (12 drachmas).
[56] Langellotti (2015: 125–6).
[57] *PMich* II 124 front [r.], II, lines 23–5; *PMich* II 123 front [r.], VI, line 18; X, line 6; XVI, line 12; XVII, line 38. On costs of storing regulations, see *PMich* II 123 front [r.], IX, line 45, and front XI, line 36.
[58] *PMich* II 123 front [r.], VI, line 19.
[59] *PMich* II 123 front [r.], III, lines 40 and 41, respectively.

obtaining concessions (*anagoria*), such as leasing public land or acquiring a fishing licence or selling salt, they registered them in the record office for a fee: 9 obols was charged to the dyers and 14 obols to the fullers, although it is not expressly stated that these workers formed guilds in these two cases.[60]

Outside Egypt, there are examples of associations storing copies of their documents in civic archives.[61] This probably means they paid a price charged by a copyist (*antigrapheus*), analogous to the scribal fee discussed above. Copyists are attested throughout coastal regions of Asia Minor, as are buildings where documents were copied and stored.[62] The dedication of the copy office in Ephesos includes mention of fees charged for copying documents (*IEph* 14, lines 17–18, 32).

Monumentalizing and honouring benefactors

As we discuss at length in Chapter 5, it seems that benefaction or patronage by local notables could be a source of income for certain groups, but there were also costs associated with maintaining such connections within local prevail would be to have the material and symbolic benefits of such connections well outweigh the costs, although rational decision-making would not necessarily prevail in many cases. Associations rewarded those who made such special material contributions with proclamations, crowns, monuments, statues, portraits or various other privileges, including exemptions, prime seating at meals and extra portions of food or wine. The cost of honouring a benefactor could be inconsequential if, for example, the reward granted was the best seat, but it could also amount to notable sums of money. The inscriptions often draw attention to the size, quality and duration of such honours. Each of these factors would have resource implications.

We begin by touching on documents that highlight where the money came from to fund the honorific activity of associations. It is sometimes difficult to determine whether an official within a certain group covered costs from a communal fund or from his or her own resources. This ambiguity is evident, for instance, when the sacrificing associates devoted to Dionysos at the Piraeus, 'resolved to inscribe this decree on a monument and to set it up beside the sanctuary of the god, and that the treasurer pay the costs of inscribing the monument and setting it up' (*GRA* I 33 = *IG* II² 1325; 185/4 BCE). Some documents do explicitly instruct that funds be taken from the common fund, however. An example of this from the same locale and era involves the decision of the sacrificing associates devoted to the Mother of the gods: 'Let the supervisors inscribe this decree on a stone monument and set it up in the sanctuary of the Mother. And the cost of both the plaque and the monument are to be paid from the treasury' (*GRA* I 35 = *IG* II²1327; 178/177 BCE).

---

[60] *PMich* II 123 front [r.], VI, line 16 and 17, respectively. See Langellotti (2016: 129–34) on associations and public concessions.

[61] See Harland (2009: 123–42) regarding Judean associations at Hierapolis.

[62] See Harland (2014: 176–7). For copyists in Asia Minor: *IEph* 1687 (31 BCE); *IErythrai* 122 (100 BCE), *IPriene* 111 (100 BCE); *SEG* 32:1149. For archives: *IKyme* 13.79 (130 BCE); *IPriene* 108.222 (129 BCE); *IEph* 14 + addenda, p. 1.

Specific individuals could take on responsibility for covering costs of monumentalizing in particular instances. Usually this was done on a voluntary basis, it seems. When initiates of Dionysos at Teos in Asia Minor honoured a Roman who served as Asiarch in the province, another person stepped up: 'Titus Aurelius Georgos Attalianos, who pursues honour in every way, has covered the cost for the statue and the altar from his own resources' (*IGLAM* 106; 117–38 CE). In such cases, the person who helped to pay for honouring someone else was himself or herself a benefactor to the group in covering costs. This illustrates the complexities involved in such social and economic exchanges.

The case of an Alexandrian immigrant on the island of Rhodes in the second century BCE is particularly instructive regarding the cost and nature of honours.[63] We know about Dionysodoros' connections with several associations (those devoted to Helios, to Pan and to Dionysos). This is because Dionysodoros of Alexandria collected together a dossier of his connections with these groups, having them reinscribed on one monument but not in chronological order. These three associations awarded Dionysodoros many crowns, which are variously described as gold, laurel and white poplar. There are further details regarding the longevity ('perpetual') and size ('largest possible gold crown') of these crownings.

The details of one particular crowning are illuminating. In the case of the association devoted to the god Helios, Dionysodoros had been a member for at least thirty-five years, and he was also the leader of the contributors (*archeranistēs*) for at least twenty-three of those years. This group resolved 'to praise and to crown perpetually with the largest possible gold crown – in accordance with our rule regarding the size of crowns – Dionysodoros the Alexandrian'. The membership had previously instituted a regulation limiting the size and expense of honorary crowns. The association resolved that 'three obols [= 1/2 drachma] be set aside (*exairein*) to pay for the crown at each meeting' (lines 22–3).

Even assuming a significant membership, half a drachma per meeting is not enough for a gold crown. A gold crown could cost anywhere from 200 to 1,000 drachmas (at least in fourth-century BCE Athens).[64] For instance, around 300 BCE, the sacrificing associates of Amynos, Asklepios and Dexion crowned two men each with a gold crown worth 500 drachmas (*GRA* I 6 = *IG* II² 1252 + 999; *c*. 300 BCE), and, in 332, BCE the Athenian merchants and shippers collaborated with the People to provide a gold crown worth 1,000 drachmas to a Sidonian named Apollonides for his goodwill towards the city (*IG* II² 343). As both Paul Foucart and Vincent Gabrielsen note, it seems likely that this association on Rhodes required that *each* contributing member set aside three obols *at each meeting*. This is the sort of regular collection practice that we explore more fully in Chapters 6 and 7, where we also deal with similar collection procedures in Pauline assemblies.[65] The crown for Dionysodoros was a perpetual one, which means that the honours were, theoretically, to be re-announced or re-enacted at meetings

---

[63] *AGRW* 255 = *IG* XII,1 155. Cf. *AGRW* 256 = *IRhodM* 46 (Dionysodoros' grave itself).
[64] See Gabrielsen (1994: 146 n. 19).
[65] Foucart (1873: 43), Gabrielsen (1994: 145). On the association's meetings, see *AGRW* 255 = *IG* XII,1 155, lines 23, 27–8, 57–8, 60–1.

forever. And so, at each gathering after the ratification of the proposed honours, the overseer and the sacred herald made a proclamation (lines 32-8) that mentioned the perpetual crown, but likely without presenting the actual crown.

Then, after Dionysodoros' death, the association's officers likely purchased the gold crown with the money having been set aside during the honouree's lifetime. These officials then made their proclamation at the special multi-day gathering 'on the second day after the sacred rites'. This proclamation was also to continue after Dionysodoros' death. In the month following this presentation of the crown, the association sold the gold crown, the overseer deposited the money from the sale into the common fund in the special assembly (*syllogos*), and this was all recorded: 'let the secretary write into the accounts (*apologoi*) the following: "Pertaining to Dionysodoros, the benefactor who was crowned with a perpetual gold crown: from the sale of the crown"' (lines 63-6). Following this procedure, the group also purchased a cheaper crown using funds collected from members in the month of Hyakinthios. This cheaper crown was placed on Dionysodoros' tomb each year in that same month (lines 66-9, 72, 85-9).

This intriguing glimpse into honorary procedures and expenses demonstrates the association's efforts to perform acts of reciprocity while carefully managing the costs and spreading those costs out among members and over time. The gradual collections for the perpetual crown and the sale of the crown after its presentation bring us into some of the behind-the-scenes strategizing and adapting about which most honorific inscriptions merely hint.

Burying or commemorating members

The Helios worshippers' posthumous honours for Dionysodoros bring us to another area of expenditure: funerary and commemorative expenses. As we noted in Chapter 1, it is now generally recognized that associations devoted solely to funerary purposes (*collegia funeraticia*) did not exist in the early imperial era.[66] Nevertheless, it was quite common for associations in various parts of the Mediterranean to take an active role in financially providing for the burial of an individual member or for a memorial monument or for a memorial gathering.

Modest monuments from Asia Minor illustrate the practice of setting up a memorial monument for a deceased member. In one from Prusa, 'sack weavers set this up for Ariston, their fellow society member, for the sake of remembrance' (*AGRW* 101 = *IPrusaOlymp* 1036; second century CE). And in another, 'fellow initiates (*synmystai*) set this up for Rufus son of Gaius for the sake of remembrance' (*AGRW* 102 = *IPrusaOlymp* 159; second or third century CE). Dozens of commemorative monuments from the village of Saittai in Lydia in the second and third centuries CE likewise have occupational or other associations setting up a monument to remember a deceased member: 'the synod of musicians (*mousikoi*) honoured Alypianos son of Epithymetes, who lived 11 years' (*ILydiaM* 145 = *SEG* 49:1683; 170 CE), or 'the guild (*synergasia*) of felt-makers (*pilopoioi*) honoured their friend Attallianos, who lived 27 years' (*SEG* 29:1195; 194

[66] See Kloppenborg (1996: 20-3), Perry (2006: 23-60), Bendlin (2011: 223-37).

CE). Similar customs existed as far away as Beroia and Thessalonica in Macedonia in the Roman imperial era, where there are several examples of an association remembering an associate with a monument.[67] Likewise, cases of a society or synod setting up a memorial for an individual deceased member constitute the bulk of our information for associations in the Bosporan kingdom, what is now southern Russia (e.g. *IBosp* 78–108, from Pantikapaion; *IBosp* 1259–86, from Tanais).

As we have already seen in the case of societies in Egypt and the Lanuvium group in Italy (Chapters 1 and 2), sometimes there would be regular contributions collected that would later be used to cover the costs of a member's burial or the costs of other funerary or memorial activities. Among devotees of the crocodile god in Tebtynis, for instance, participants in the association were to mourn for a deceased member and escort him together to the burial ground, covering the costs using members' funerary dues (*AGRW* 299 = *GRA* II 191 = *PCairDem* 30606; 158/157 BCE). Fines were outlined for not engaging in the communal mourning. Furthermore, members were expected to comfort members whose relatives had died: 'If one of our members has a son who dies at a tender age, we will drink beer with him and comfort his heart.' About three hundred years later in Athens, the expectation among adherents of Bacchos was that, when a member died and was presumably buried by family, the group would still cover the cost of a memorial wreath (worth 5 denarii) and a jar of wine for those who attended the funeral (*AGRW* 7 = *IG* II² 1368).

Although burial in a common tomb is not widely attested in Asia Minor, there are some instances. Collective burial places were used by a guild of flax-workers in Smyrna, a guild of bed-builders at Ephesos, a Judean group at Tlos in Lycia and several groups near Lamos in Cilicia.[68] The inscription on the common tomb at Smyrna specifies that: 'if anyone has been approved for membership, he will be placed in this vault by the guild (*synergasia*)' (*AGRW* 201 = *ISmyrna* 218). Communal burial by association was somewhat standard on some Aegean islands such as Kos and Rhodes. Earlier in this chapter, we have already mentioned the group of contributors on Rhodes who had each given towards the collection of about 1,000 drachmas to purchase land for a common cemetery.[69] In many other places, individual or familial burial was more common than collective tombs, but there, too, associations could engage in memorial activities.

Honouring deities and feasting with friends

A significant portion of our evidence for associations points to two interrelated purposes that were at the centre of meetings for many types of groups, whether familial, occupational, ethnic or otherwise: honouring gods and feasting with friends.[70]

---

[67] E.g. Beroia: *AGRW* 37 = *GRA* I 64 = *IBeroia* 372 (donkey-drivers, 2nd CE); *IBeroia* 371 (associates, 2nd–3rd CE). Thessalonica: *IG* X,2.1 288–9 (associates, 154–155 CE); *AGRW* 54 = *SEG* 60:665 (associates, 159 CE); *AGRW* 55 = *IG* X,2.1 291 (purple-dyers, late-2nd CE); *AGRW* 56 (mule-drivers, 150–200 CE).

[68] *AGRW* 201 = *ISmyrna* 218; *IEph* 2213; *IJO* II 223; *AGRW* 214–15 = *IKilikiaBM* II 190–202; cf. *IKos* 155–9.

[69] *ISelge* T48 = Kontorini (1989: 73–85, no. 10). See Gabrielsen (2001: 229–230).

[70] See Harland (2013: 45–70) = Harland (2003: 55–88).

Innumerable monuments entail honours for – or dedications to – deities, and we will detail many collective projects aimed at raising funds for gods and goddesses in Chapter 6. These honours and offerings were, in part, a response to favours received or expected, so the expense would, in the view of participants, be offset by other potential benefits. Of course, the cost of honouring deities could range from an offering of cake or animal for sacrifice, to a basic plaque or relief or altar, to the cost of a statue or an entire sanctuary.

To counter any notion that it was merely supposed 'religious' associations that were engaged in such honours for deities, dedications by occupational groups from various regions will illustrate these monumental honours that would entail expenditure. Among the many dedications by merchants from Berytos settled on Delos is a very substantial statue group that depicts Aphrodite, Eros and Pan, which was commissioned by an individual member (*AGRW* 225 = *IDelos* 1783; 153–88 BCE). Romans engaged in business on Cyprus dedicated a statue of Aphrodite of Paphos in her temple (*IGR* III 965; *c.* 100 BCE). And a group of men engaged in fisheries at Kyzikos dedicated a monument 'to Poseidon and Aphrodite of the Sea as a thanksgiving', depicting deities in relief (*IMT* 1539 = *RIG* 1225; first century BCE).[71] Cutlery manufacturers at Sidon in Phoenicia dedicated a monument to the 'Holy God' (Theos Hagios) in the late Hellenistic era, and clothing-dealers on the Aegean island of Kos set up a statue of Emperor Augustus depicted as Hermes (*IKosM* 466; 27 BCE–14 CE). In Greek settlements near the Black Sea, a benefactor set up an altar for the synagogue of small-wares dealers (or, possibly, oar-dealers) at Perinthos (*IPerinthos* 59; first–second centuries CE), a benefactor dedicated an altar to Herakles for the Nikomedian sculptors at Nikopolis (*IGBulg* 674), a grain-measurer consecrated a table 'to Herakles and the most sacred guild' at Philippolis (*IGBulg* 1401[2]) and a benefactor of the 'house' of shippers at Tomis commissioned a statue for Hestia (*ITomis* 132; second century CE). So individual members or benefactors could sometimes cover the cost of dedications, but at other times collective agency was involved.

Sacrifices, offerings and festivals for the gods, as well as meals that accompanied them, were a central expenditure for many types of associations. For the Hellenistic era, the honorary monument of the Berytian immigrant association on Delos is quite instructive regarding expenditures for ancestral customs and meals (*IDelos* 1520 = *AGRW* 224; 153/152 BCE). The inscription refers to Marcus Minatius' contribution of funds in order to invite 'all of us to the sacrifice, which he prepared for the gods to be accomplished for the synod, and he invited us to the banquet'. The association's honours, in return, include prime seating at a festival in honour of Poseidon and special celebrations in Minatius' honour in connection with a festival for Apollo. Among the expenses is a procession in which a specially chosen bull would be sacrificed on Minatius' behalf. The inscription goes into some detail regarding the role of the group's treasurers (*argyrotamiai*), who were to pay the herdsmen 150 drachmas for the processional bull and another 150 drachmas for a special reception for Minatius the day after the festival for Apollo. The

---

[71] Mordtmann (1885). An artistic error occurred in that the deities in the relief seem to be Apollo and Cybele.

treasurers were also to 'provide a written account of what funds they managed in the first meeting after the reception'. Any herdsman that did not follow the stipulations of the purchase would be liable to pay 1,000 drachmas. For the Roman era, see also our discussion of the gatherings of the hymn-singers at Pergamon and of the Herakles worshippers in Attica when we turn to income from participants' dues in Chapter 5.

When it came to meals, there was potential for some attendees to be concerned about the fare, which would help to explain why some communal regulations specify the amounts of food or drink that were to be supplied. So, for instance, the association founded by Epikteta at Thera specifies that those who officiate should 'provide enough imported wine for three cups per person' (*AGRW* 243 = *IG* XII,3 330; 210–195 BCE). Some centuries later, the salt merchants at Tebtynis in Egypt detail just how much beer each participant would receive (*AGRW* 302 = *PMich* V 245; 47 CE). And the regulation of the association of Diana and Antinous at Lanuvium ensures that each participant would receive a serving of four sardines and one loaf of bread at some banquets, as well as a substantial serving of wine (2 litres per person) at six of their yearly banquets (*AGRW* 310 = *CIL* XIV 2112; 136 CE).[72]

The records of associations detail a variety of sacrificial and commensal items that would need to be purchased.[73] There were different types of offerings for deities including libations, cakes and animals, such as sheep, pigs and bulls.[74] In many cases, sacrifice was accompanied by a communal meal. Food for the meals could include meat, seafood, beans, bread, eggs, nuts, fried figs, chick peas, laurel cakes, vegetables and fruits.[75] Excavators of the banqueting room of the Dionysiac dancing cowherds at Pergamon found bone remnants of beef, swine and poultry ground into the floor.[76]

Drinks would be an important component of gatherings, as some Egyptian documents show.[77] In fact, groups might allocate their funds towards wine and other drinks even if it meant a lack of food. We have already seen that one economically modest association at Tebtynis ensured sufficient wine at each of its gatherings but occasionally did without bread when funds were tight (*PTebt* I 118). Likewise, another association at Philadelphia refers to wine five times but never records food expenses (*SB* III 7182). A first-century papyrus of unknown provenance lists contributions for wine by members of the synod of donkey-drivers, ranging from 2 drachmas to 20 drachmas per person (*GRA* III 290 = *PAthen* 41). Beer was a viable alternative to wine, at least in Egypt. The president and secretary of a weavers' synod filed a contractual agreement (in the records office) to provide 92 drachmas to the association for the purchase of beer in a particular month.[78] And it seems that each member of the salt

---

[72] On food and wine here, see Bendlin (2011).
[73] For a recent discussion of association meals, see Öhler (2014).
[74] Libations: *AGRW* 295 = *PLond* VII 2193 (Philadelphia, Egypt; 69–58 BCE); cakes: *AGRW* 117 = *GRA* II 111 = *IPergamon* 374; sheep: *SEG* 33:147, line 18 (Thorikos; 4th century BCE); pigs: *GRA* I 14 = *Agora* 16:161 (Athens; *c*. 300 BCE); bulls: *AGRW* 317 = *IG* XIV 830 (Puteoli, Italy; 174 CE).
[75] E.g. *PPetr*. III 136, column III, lines 19–24 (Arsinoites; 231 BCE); *CIL* VI 33885; *GRA* III 194 = *PTebt* III 894.
[76] See Radt (1988), Schwarzer (2006, 2008).
[77] On wine, see most recently Öhler (2014: 489–92).
[78] *PMich* II 121 front [r.], IV abstract 6 = *GRA* III 210 and *AGRW* 302 = *PMich* V 245. Cf. *GRA* II 214 = *PTebt* II 401; *GRA* III 220 = *PMich* V 322b, from Tebtynis (beer merchant accounts mentioning associations).

merchants at Tebtynis were entitled to about six real pints (about 3.25 litres) of beer at each monthly gathering.[79]

Meals and sacrificial banquets could function not only to nourish members but also to broadcast social hierarchies within the group.[80] Such hierarchies were displayed and affirmed at association meals by provision of extra portions of food or drink to current officers or supporters, stationing them in the most honourable couches, toasting and wreathing them, and permitting them to invite guests of their choice.

There were various other expenses for gatherings, including entertainment, music and dancing, which could themselves be closely associated with honouring deities.[81] During meals, participants could listen to singers (e.g. *ICariaR* 162) and musical accompaniment (e.g. *SB* III 6319 back [v.], I, line 54; *SEG* 31:983) and observe dance performances (*ISmyrna* 654). The monument from Triglia in Figure 1.1 (see Chapter 1) pictures the activities of an association, with deities overseeing sacrifice led by the priestess Stratonike, along with the banqueting members and musicians. Dancing and musical accompaniment were particularly important in connection with mysteries and among groups devoted to Dionysos in particular, as the 'dancing' cowherds' self-designation illustrates.[82]

Conclusion

The varied aims of associations led to numerous expenditures, only some of which we have outlined here. We have not tried to be comprehensive in counting the costs, but this sketch does provide some context as we now turn to the ways in which such groups acquired resources to cover these and other expenses. Moreover, we will find that sources of income were both external and internal. Still, internal communal fundraising itself played a central role for many groups, including, but not limited to, those devoted to the Israelite god.

This survey of costs also points to the mundane daily decisions that would need to be made and to the various options that were available to associations and their members. There were options on where to meet, on what to eat, on how to honour external supporters and divine patrons and on how to honour members who passed away. All of these decisions could have material implications.

---

[79] *AGRW* 302 = *PMich* V 245. By 'real pints', we mean British imperial ones, not measly American ones.
[80] See Kloppenborg (2016: 174–7).
[81] On entertainment expenses in Egyptian villages, see Westermann (1932).
[82] Schwarzer (2006, 2008: 92–102 on collecting the inscriptions). Cf. *AGRW* L16 = Lucian, *The Dance* 15 and 79; *TAM* V 91 (Saittai); *SEG* 34:1266 (Nikomedia).

5

Acquiring Resources

The synod ... not only decrees appropriate honours for benefactors but eagerly promotes them, which is the most important thing.

IDelos 1520

Be it resolved also to inscribe the names of the fellow society-members who join, once they have contributed the share of the money that is their due in the fund, in accordance with the regulation.

IG II² 1298, from Athens

Introduction

The immigrants from Berytos (Beirut) who, in their honours for a local Italian notable, had the first statement inscribed seem very aware of how important it was to honour outsiders who financially supported the group's goals. And the other resolution by members of a society devoted to Artemis at Athens points to ongoing resources supplied by participants within the group. In this chapter, we begin to explore these and other external and internal sources of income that help us to understand the sustainability of unofficial groups in the eastern Mediterranean. Subsequent chapters delve deeper into the central importance of collective agency in the material well-being of many associations.

As with other issues, our ancient evidence seems like a snapshot rather than a moving picture. Furthermore, we are regularly presented with groups and individuals who were doing at least relatively well more so than those with very little means or those who were struggling, such as those groups facing precarious situations that we managed to find in Chapter 2.

Acknowledging variety in material circumstances, this chapter looks at three commonly encountered sources of income that helped to ensure the sustainability of many associations' activities. First, contributions by benefactors or donors – whether inside or outside the group – were a significant factor for many groups. There was a cultural system of benefaction which entailed both competition and cooperation among groups, families and the elites, with some groups being more successful than others in the competition. The preponderance of honorary monuments in our surviving evidence may give the false impression that individual external supporters were the essence of group life, however. This has sometimes led to the neglect of internal sources and collective agency in past studies. Second, internally managed funds, loans, properties and other assets could be an important source of income through rents or interest. Alongside such sources, there was a third, internal source of revenue: many groups drew resources from their own members through regular (usually monthly) contributions, fines, and other contributions or special communal collections. The following two chapters explore the importance of internal, communal fund-raising in some detail. Income from such external or internal sources could be collected within a common fund or treasury, being managed in a way that accomplished pivotal aims of honouring deities, feasting with friends, supporting members and recognizing benefactors.

Benefaction from external or internal supporters

Those who participated within certain associations could be very much aware of the importance of contributions from external benefactors for the well-being of the group. When Alkibiades made contributions to an association's temple at Athens, for instance, members interpreted this generosity to mean that 'the current circumstances of those devoted to Asklepios may continue without stopping for all time and may increase more' (*IG* II² 1293 + *SEG* 18:33; *c.* 250 BCE). So income generated from contributions by external supporters, benefactors or patrons (*euergetai* in Greek; *patroni*, m. *patrona*, f. in Latin) could be significant, particularly at critical moments in a group's history.[1] Although there was overlap in sociocultural systems of exchange from east to west, patronage was more characteristic of Italy and Latin-speaking areas and benefaction of Greek-speaking areas, with the latter being our principle focus here. Benefaction, which involved the exchange of benefits or resources in return for extremely valuable— although sometimes intangible—'honours' (*timai*), was at the cultural heart of cities in the eastern Mediterranean during the late-Hellenistic and Roman eras. This system of exchange – sometimes labelled 'euergetism' by scholars from the Greek word for 'doing good works' – helps us to understand not only a source of income for many associations but also the endurance of all kinds of groups, communities and institutions, including civic communities themselves.[2]

This system of reciprocity is perhaps best understood in terms of networks or webs of connections involving exchanges among individuals, families and groups at local, provincial and imperial levels of society. The substance of the favours or benefits offered by a benefactor could vary according to that person's status and the particular situation, as could the honours that were granted in return. In some cases, the benefits offered were primarily material. A donor could supply funds for a banquet or for purchasing oil in connection with gymnasial activities. She or he could supply a building, as was the case with women benefactors of Judean associations at both

---

[1] Cf. van Nijf (1997: 73–128 on Greek East), Liu (2008 on Latin West).
[2] On benefaction and honour generally, see especially: Veyne (1990), Lendon (1997), Zuiderhoek (2009).

Akmoneia and Kyme, for instance.³ More fortunate groups in the competition might also have buildings donated to them beyond what they needed for their own activities. Properties could then be rented out and become a further source of revenue, as was the case with the worldwide performers devoted to Dionysos, for instance (*AGRW* 184 = *IEph* 22; c. 142 CE). In that case, Aelius Alkibiades of Nysa had 'granted magnificent gifts of properties, including stabling facilities [at Rome], from which we reap the continuous, everlasting rent, distributing the rents among ourselves annually on the birthday of god Hadrian' (lines 19–20). An honorary decree by Nysa itself preserved on the other side of the same stone happens to refer to the same man's generosity in 'organizing (*systēsamenos*) a so-called "*collegium*" (*kollēgion*) consisting of his fellow citizens in the royal city of the Romans and dedicating communal properties' (*SEG* 4:418).⁴

Yet some benefactions did not directly entail what a modern person might consider material benefits. Often benefactors were praised for offering *services* to a group, including those focused on honouring deities (although even this, too, might entail the outlay of cash). In the Piraeus, for instance, devotees of the goddess Aphrodite initially commended their supervisor (*epimelētēs*), Stephanos, for administering the association with care and for conducting a procession in honour of Adonis, and there is no reference to financial donations (*AGRW* 14 = *GRA* I 9 = *IG* II² 1261, side A; 302/301 BCE). Similarly, five third-century decrees found on the adjacent island of Salamis have a society devoted to the goddess Bendis honouring internal treasurers or supervisors who had performed various services for the group in the previous year with no explicit reference to monetary contributions.⁵ The sacrificing associates of the Mother of the gods there similarly honoured their priestess for carrying out her *responsibilities* in an 'ambitious' and 'pious' manner (*GRA* I 28 = *IG* II² 1314; 213/212 BCE).

Centuries later at Prusias in Bithynia, members of a society (*thiasos*) honoured Anubion in connection with his services in honour of Isis, thanking him with eight paintings, a stone monument and ongoing announcements of his pious contributions (*AGRW* 97 = *IKios* 22 = *RICIS* 308/0301; first century BCE or CE).⁶ At Pergamon, a group of 'cowherds' set up a monument in honour of a man 'because of his pious and worthy leadership over the divine mysteries of Dionysos the Leader' (*AGRW* 115 = *IPergamon* 485; first century CE). A synod of initiates at Smyrna joined with the civic institutions in honouring two women 'for everything which they zealously offered with respect to piety toward the goddess and the festival of the initiates'. These women had served as 'theologians' (*theologoi*), expounders of the goddess's stories (*AGRW* 188 = *ISmyrna* 653; first–second centuries CE).

While it is true that those from wealthier segments of society often played the role of benefactors, in theory any person or group (including associations as a group and

---

[3] *AGRW* 145 = *IJO* II 168; late first century CE; *AGRW* 105 = *IJO* II 36; third century CE.
[4] Clerc (1885).
[5] Osborne (2004) = *IG* II² 1317 (Osborne no. 1), *SEG* 59:152 (no. 2), *IG* II² 1317b + addenda, p. 673 (no. 3), *SEG* 44:60 (no. 4), and *GRA* I 21 (no. 5). Cf. Osborne (2004) for similar examples on Salamis island.
[6] Cf. *AGRW* 98 = *IPrusaOlymp* 1028.

the members of associations as individuals) could offer benefits that were deserving of honours in return. In this way, associations were both recipients and suppliers of such benefits. So it is important to recognize that benefaction could be either a 'revenue' or an 'expense' for groups. One of the honorary lists of donors to the civic temple of Athena and Zeus on Rhodes, for instance, includes numerous collectives (all of which are associated with a man named Timopolis) that had gathered funds to donate to this civic sanctuary (*AGRW* 250 = *ILindos* 252, lines 222–7, 250–9; *c.* 115 BCE). An association devoted to Sarapis was among the donors to a project at Kamiros, also on Rhodes (*RICIS* 204/0216, column 3, lines 8–13 only; 200–150 BCE). The fishermen and fish-dealers who made contributions towards the building of the fishery toll-office at Ephesos in the mid-first century were, in part, taking on the role of a benefactor to the city and its patron deity (Artemis), as were the silversmiths and goldsmiths who restored a statue of Athena at Smyrna in the time of Tiberius (*AGRW* 160 = *IEph* 20; *AGRW* 186 = *ISmyrna* 721). Similarly, a group of those 'formerly from Judea' (likely Judean immigrants) made a substantial donation of 10,000 denarii to a civic project at either Smyrna or Erythrai (*AGRW* 194 = *GRA* II 139 = *ISmyrna* 697; *c.* 124 CE).[7] A society of shipowners and merchants at Athens could refer to its ongoing financial support of a shrine for Zeus, the Friend of Strangers (*AGRW* 5 = *IG* II^2 1012; 112/111 BCE). So, alongside income from benefaction, involvements in such exchanges could be an expense for associations.

A group's profile could rise to the attention of civic or imperial authorities and sometimes groups might solicit benefits from civic authorities or institutions. Such authorities could then function in the role of benefactors to such a group. So concepts of 'diplomacy' and benefaction overlap considerably, but the benefits received by an association were not always material. Recognition by civic or imperial authorities itself was a source of pride, as when adherents of Demeter at Ephesos proudly refer to previous interactions with authorities (*IEph* 213). Immigrant associations were also participants in this competitive arena. The Judean historian Josephus collects together many documents that illustrate Judean associations petitioning imperial or civic authorities and receiving certain benefits or favours in return, primarily a recognition of their continued performance of ancestral customs (see Chapter 7). And we have already discussed (in Chapter 4) those Thracian, Egyptian and Kitian immigrant groups who sought and received permission to own land from the civic authorities of Athens.

Diplomacy might, on occasion, result in some contributions from institutions to the sacrifices of particular local cults or associations.[8] The degree to which such partial financial contributions to an association's sacrifices or activities made such groups official organizations or civic boards themselves is debatable, however. Granted, it was possible that some groups that began in an informal manner gradually rose to take on a more official role in certain civic- or provincial-sponsored events or festivals, as seems to be the case with some groups of hymn-singers who on occasion sang in

---

[7] On this inscription, see the extensive commentary by Harland in *GRA* II 139.
[8] See Harland (2014: 264–6), Petzl (2009).

provincial celebrations (*AGRW* 160 = *IEph* 3801). Certainly there were cases when civic institutions fully or almost fully supported particular mysteries in a monetary way, and, in these cases, we can somewhat accurately speak of official or civic mysteries, as with the mysteries of the 'Maiden Saviour' at Kyzikos.[9] Yet we cannot assume such an official role for many other groups that labelled themselves 'initiates' (*mystai*), in our view.[10]

In studying economics in terms of the allocation of scarce resources, it is important to highlight the degree to which competition for resources from benefactors, whether institutions or individuals, was inherent in this system. Associations were participants in the competition.[11] The donations of the elites and ongoing links to specific influential people or collectives were, in a sense, limited resources sought by different groups.

The competitive dimension of this system of exchange can be illustrated using contemporaneous inscriptions from Delos (from 153 or 152 BCE) that happen to involve associations whose membership was based on both common ethnicity and shared occupation.[12] A group of merchants from Tyre honoured a member and leader who had, among other things, successfully acted as ambassador to Athens in securing the group a place to build a temple. Their resolution to honour him reflects motivations as it was done 'in order that he may provide in the future without being asked and the synod (*synodos*) may display its consideration for people who show goodwill toward it by returning appropriate favours to benefactors'. And the hope was 'that still other people may become zealous admirers of the synod because of the thanks shown toward that person and in order that those who show love of honour may compete for the favour of the synod' (*AGRW* 223 = *IDelos* 1519).

A second monument from Delos that illustrates the competitive dimension of this cultural system was set up by the synod of immigrants from Berytos that honoured Marcus Minatius. These Berytians state that they set up the inscription 'in order that the honours being given by the synod to Marcus may remain for all time, as is just, and that there are many who eagerly strive to display love of glory toward the synod, knowing that the synod is useful and that it not only decrees appropriate honours for benefactors but eagerly promotes them, which is the most important thing' (*AGRW* 224 = *IDelos* 1520). Members of such groups clearly understood that communal longevity depended, in part, on such external supporters.

So these two associations, alongside others, were quite self-consciously competing with one another. They honoured external financial supporters in a way that showed their awareness that benefactors, too, were competing with one another for beneficiaries, including but not limited to associations. Benefactors gained the symbolic capital associated with an increase in honour in competition with others.[13] Honorary monuments were, in part, one means by which groups advertised their valuable

---

[9] See Harland (2014: 103).
[10] Harland is grateful to Benedikt Eckhardt for discussions on this topic, although disagreements remain. Now see his current views in Eckhardt and Lepke (2018).
[11] Harland (2009: 145–60) = Harland (2005a).
[12] On instigating 'rivalry' among members as donors, see also *SEG* 56:203, from Athens (3rd century BCE), and *GRA* I 25 = *IG* II² 1301, from the Piraeus (219/218 BCE).
[13] Cf. van Nijf (1997: 116–20).

connections, seeking to present themselves to the wider community as special or important or worthy of further material support in competition with other groups and institutions.

Although local associations competed for supporters, this should not give the impression that winning the competition led to substantial material support such that members would be relieved from their own ordinary financial commitments. As we discussed with Epikteta and Symmasis in Chapter 3 and will soon see with funerary endowments below, benefactors were often specific about how their contributions should be used, limiting the association's freedom to cover other costs using the funds.

Rents, endowments and interest from loans

It is important to clarify how properties, buildings or other assets held by an association might be a source of income for certain groups, at least the more successful ones. Our knowledge of procedures around how associations rented or leased properties or buildings to others is somewhat limited for most times and places, so in this case we need to return to Attica in the Hellenistic era again in order to better understand rent income from leases. It is difficult to know the degree to which the situation in Athens and Attica is representative of procedures elsewhere, however. Nonetheless, this at least raises possibilities.

There are three known leasing agreements from the final decades of the fourth century BCE in which an association of sacrificing associates (*orgeōnes*) leased its own sanctuary or portions of property in order to ensure consistent income to engage in its sacrifices and other activities.[14] The best preserved inscription details how the sacrificing associates devoted to the hero Egretes leased out their sanctuary to a man named Diognetos. This lease was for a period of ten years at the substantial rate of 200 drachmas each year. In return, Diognetos gained the right to use both the sanctuary and the buildings on it. The person who leased the sanctuary was responsible for whitewashing the walls of the buildings but he was also permitted to add further structures, structures that were to be removed at the end of the lease. Diognetos was also responsible for taking care of the trees within the sanctuary, and replacing any that died during the span of the lease. The sacrificing associates were sure to specify that they were still permitted to use the sanctuary for a particular yearly festival with sacrifices and banqueting.

The sacrificing associates of the hero Hypodektes leased their sanctuary for ten years at a rate of 50 drachmas per year, ensuring that they would still be able to use the sanctuary for a specific yearly festival. And the sacrificing associates of the hero Iatros leased a garden for thirty years, specifying that the person who leased would need to ensure that the area was kept pure. The timing of payments in the Egretes and

---

[14] *GRA* I 7 = *IG* II² 2499 (306/305 BCE); *IG* II² 2501 = Ferguson (1944: 81–2) (no. 3) (*c.* 300 BCE); *SEG* 24:203 (333/332 BCE). See, especially, the summary discussion by Papazarkadas (2011: 191–211). On our limited knowledge of leasing procedures here and elsewhere, see Osborne (1988).

Hypodektes cases suggests that the funds were used to support the most important yearly festivals of these associations.[15]

Travelling outside of Attica, a first-century Egyptian document on papyrus shows that occupational guilds might also have income from leases (*GRA* III 208 = *PMich* V 313; 37 CE). In it, a group of public farmers – namely, those who, in part, leased crown land – led by elders (*presbyteroi*) and a secretary (*grammateus*) leased or subleased out a portion of land in the area of Tebtynis for two years to a man named Herakleides. The leasee then had the right to any produce on that land for that period, including reeds, arum, lotus root and 'so-called cannabis', and there is mention of some of this produce being useful as fodder for pigs. In return, the farmers gained income of 60 silver drachmas. The farmers retained use of the other half of the same plot of land (called 'the marsh of the god'), which would, of course, be another source of income for the farmers from the produce. Although we cannot generalize this situation of a guild leasing out farmable land (beyond farmers), the point here is that groups of various kinds that possessed land or buildings could engage in leasing as a form of income.

An act of benefaction could sometimes include granting use (*chrēsis*) or ownership (*ktēsis*) of properties, from which income could be generated.[16] An immigrant from Kyzikos (perhaps Nikasion) who had the right of residency on Rhodes either donated vineyards to Asklepios worshippers or allowed the group to benefit from income from the produce on those vineyards (early second century BCE).[17] Considering the importance of Rhodes in the wine trade, these vineyards may have been a significant source of income.

Similar donations of vineyards to associations are attested at Thessalonica in Macedonia in the Roman imperial era, but in both of these cases the vineyards were a bequest.[18] The earlier, first-century example demonstrates how properties and related assets might be considered to be owned by the god and used by an association (*AGRW* 50 = *IG* X,2.1 259). In this case, Gaius Julius dedicates one-third of five plethra of vineyards (one-third of about 4.4 square kilometres) to the god Zeus Dionysos Gongylos for the benefit of both current and future initiates (*mystai*) for 'as long as they are banded together'. He also specifies that the property must remain 'unsold'; this likely means that the property could not be mortgaged or offered as security in order to attain a loan (see Chapter 8).[19] However, he designates the initiates as recipients of income from the produce only on condition that they swear to hold three feasts each year, presumably in Julius' memory. Two of the three dates correspond to the Roman Parentalia and Rosalia festivals.

The second inscription from Thessalonica dates to the third century CE and contains contingency plans if the designated association does not fulfill the stipulations (*AGRW* 58 = *IG* X,2.1 260).[20] Euphrosyne, the priestess of Dionysos, leaves behind two plethra

---

[15] See also *AGRW* 11 = *GRA* I 4 = *IG* II² 1361 (330–320 BCE).
[16] On foundations generally, see Laum (1964 [1914]), Sosin (2000, 2001).
[17] Hiller von Gaertringen and Saridakis (1900: 109, no. 108); *IG* XII,1 127; *IRhodPC* 5. See Gabrielsen (2001: 231–3).
[18] See also the vineyard arrangement for initiates of the Zeus tribe at Amorion in Phrygia in connection with a festival of Mithras: Ramsay (1889: 17–23, no. 1).
[19] See Ascough in *GRA* I 76 and 81; Daux (1972), Kubińska (2001).
[20] See Edson (1948: 165–81).

(about 1.76 square km) of vineyards with irrigation ditches 'in order that sacrifices worth not less than 5 denarii may be burned for me from the income'. She designates this role to the initiates (*mystai*) who, like herself, belonged to the society of the holm-oak-bearers (*prinophoroi*). This is done on condition that they wear a crown of roses (purchased using income from the vineyards) in her memory during the Roman festival of roses. However, she also arranges contingency plans in the event that this society does not fulfil their responsibilities, designating secondly the society of oak-branch-bearers (*dryophoroi*) and thirdly the city of Thessalonica itself. Euphrosyne is among those women who played an important role in the material well-being of associations to which they themselves belonged (see Chapter 1).

Benefactions could also be monetary, as we began to see with foundations for familial associations in Chapter 3. In order to ensure longevity for an endowment fund, often associations would use only the interest or revenue, not the principal. So endowments are closely related to loaning practices, practices that we explore in terms of mutual aid among members in Chapter 8. Here we are primarily concerned with loans as a source of income, and later we will see how loans were one way participants in associations supported one another in difficult times.

The use of communal funds to gain revenue from interest-bearing loans is clear in several inscriptions particularly beginning in the fourth century BCE and continuing on in Attica, on Aegean islands, in Asia Minor and in the Black Sea region, at least.[21] These were loans that would be available to both outsiders and participants. Among the earliest clear indications from Attica are records of officials in charge of selling confiscated property (*pōlētai*) at Athens in the year 367/366 BCE.[22] This pertains to a loan of 24 drachmas made by a group of sacrificing associates – under the leadership of Aischines – to Theophilos, the father of Theosebes. The father had offered his house as security for the loan ('sold on condition of release') but had since deceased. The son, Theosebes, had been in possession of this house when he was charged with violation of the sacred (*hierosylia*) and had fled. The house was therefore seized as property of the Athenian People and was being auctioned by the selling authorities. The sacrificing associates brought forward a claim on the property in connection with Theophilos' unpaid loan, and the authorities granted their request. A similar claim regarding a loan to this now deceased man by the brotherhood (*phrateres*) of the Medontidians – a subgroup of an official civic tribe – occurs on the same inscribed record (lines 17–25). However, Crosby's speculation that the sacrificing associates were part of this official, descent-based brotherhood (phratry) is unfounded, as William Scott Ferguson also points out.[23] Theophilos, who received the loans, may well have been a member both of this brotherhood and of the sacrificing associates, although this is not expressly stated. If he was, then this may be a case of the sort of loans we detail in connection with mutual assistance among members of associations.

---

[21] For early hints, see the fragmentary *IG* I³ 369, lines 60–100, from 426/425 BCE.
[22] *SEG* 12:100 = Crosby and Young (1941: 14–27) (no. 1), lines 30–5. See also Fine (1951: 150–5). Cf. *Agora* 16, no. 161.
[23] See Ferguson (1944: 83), on Crosby and Young (1941: 22).

Other stones used as a record of mortgaging property in this early period clearly point to ongoing associations (rather than just temporary formations) offering loans. One marker from Athens which entails a society has been dated to the period 400–350 BCE by Stephen Lambert.[24] It illustrates well the basic form of these inscriptions: 'Marker (*horos*) of a property sold on condition of release to the society-members (*thiasōtai*) of Demotes for a loan of 100 drachmas.'[25] While it is possible that this was a subgroup of a more official descent-based body, Lambert clarifies that 'we lack grounds for supposing that every such thiasos was a phratry subgroup'.[26] Similarly, an undated stone refers to three loans where properties are offered as security: 'Marker of a property and house sold on condition of release to Hieromnemon from Halai subdivision for a loan of 500 drachmas – according to the agreement deposited with Lysistratos – and to the tenth-day celebrators (*dekadistai*) for a loan of 130 drachmas, and real security (*apotimēma*) to the contributors (*eranistai*) who are with Theopeithes from Ikarion subdivision.'[27] We will have much more to say about groups that designated themselves 'contributors' later.

There are clear indications of some level of continuity over hundreds of years in this practice of associations producing income through offering loans from communal funds. Around 200 CE, the regulations of those devoted to Herakles at Liopesi (also in Attica) include a stipulation that no one was to 'touch the endowment (*enthēkēs*) that has been deposited by the leader of the contributors (*archeranistou*) and whatever other endowment has been collected, beyond the interest (*tokou*) that accrues. The treasurer shall not expend more than 300 drachmas from the interest' (*AGRW* 9 = *NGSL* 5, lines 9–13).

Materials from Aegean islands and Asia Minor are suggestive of similar sources of communal income from interest on loans in other regions. Two relatively early inscriptions (with three loans) from Hephaistia on the island of Lemnos date to 314/313 BCE. These refer to associations offering loans from communal funds, although not necessarily in connection with an endowment. An association of sacrificing associates (*orgeōnes*) dedicated to the god Herakles offered two loans, with the borrower putting up property as security ('sold on condition of release') to ensure repayment:

> When Nikodoros was civic leader (*archōn*), marker (*horos*) of a property and house sold on condition of release for 1,000 drachmas to the sacrificing associates (*orgeōnes*) of Herakles who is at Kome according to the registry of the sacrificing associates.

> When Archios was civic leader, marker of a property and house sold on condition of release for 400 (?) drachmas to the sacrificing associates of Herakles who is at Kome according to the registry of the sacrificing associates.[28]

---

[24] See Lambert (1996: 77), who offers this date based on careful re-examination of the orthography.
[25] *IG* II² 2720 = Finley (1951: 132) (no. 43).
[26] Lambert (1996: 79).
[27] *IG* II² 2701 = Finley (1951: 129) (no. 32). See the detailed discussion in Biscardi (1983: 50–2).
[28] *IG* XII,8 19 = Finley (1951: 148–9), nos 107–8.

A second inscription from Hephaistia documents real security on a loan of 400 drachmas by another group of sacrificing associates in the same year (*IG* XII,8 21 = Finley, 1951: 149 [no. 109]). A case from Thera island clearly does involve use of an endowment for loans, in this case one provided by a local woman. Around 200 BCE, the overseers (*episkopoi*) in this association were responsible for lending 500 drachmas 'at interest with sufficient security' and they were to 'gather a gathering' (*synagesthai tan [synagōga]n*; *IG* XII,3 329 + *IG* XII,3 Suppl. 1295 on p. 284).

Turning to Asia Minor, the foundation established by Symmasis and his wife for the guild of coppersmiths outlines procedures for loans and the management of interest, as we briefly mentioned in Chapter 3 (*GRA* II 149 = *SEG* 58:1640): 'The managers of the funds which Symmasis has given will lend the funds out at interest very securely, writing down in the contracts that these funds come from the legacy of Symmasis.'[29] Less revealing than this Lycian material, although notable, is an imperial-era inscription from the area around Magnesia on the Maiander river which trails off with reference to 'whatever is lent out at interest (*ekdaneizetai*) by the ... initiates (?) ...' (*AGRW* 203 = *IMagnMai* 117; *c*. 100 CE). Unfortunately, no further details remain regarding financial procedures for managing loans in this group.

There is a very interesting case from the Black Sea region at the Greek colony of Kallatis (*IKallatis* 36 = *SEG* 45:902). This is an honorary inscription from around 200 BCE, in which members of a society (*thiasos*) honour a person named Bikon son of Dioskouridas. Bikon had been in charge of the communal fund and lending, but had also saved the group at a critical moment. The honorary inscription actually spells out much of the situation and reveals potential dangers in lending out communal funds: 'having been entrusted with the common resources and lending at interest in an advantageous manner, [Bikon] returned the money, along with the accruing interest. He did so despite the fact that, because of the circumstances, the societal money was lost and, according to the regulation, he was free from responsibility for the debt.' So lending out, even at interest, was not without risks and sometimes a potential source of income could threaten the financial stability of a group. Here, a member, as an internal benefactor, stepped in to save the day by offering mutual assistance to his associates.

Due to the predominance of funerary monuments in our surviving evidence, the purpose of most known endowments to associations – both in the western and eastern parts of the Mediterranean – was to have a group care for a family's grave or engage in specific memorial activities on a regular basis, usually yearly or biyearly. Numerous examples present themselves from Aegean islands and from the mainland of Asia Minor. We have already discussed the somewhat exceptional testament of Epikteta. Inscriptions from the subregions of Ionia and Phrygia illustrate the importance of funerary endowments there, although the precise customs could vary from one site to another. At Ephesos, for instance, a physician left behind 4,600 denarii so that the assembly (*synedrion*) of physicians from the sanctuary of the Muses could 'take care of' (*kēdontai*) the grave (*AGRW* 175 = *IEph* 2304). Another case from Ephesos involves a chief physician who chose the Judeans to take care of the grave (*AGRW* 174 = *IJO* II

---

[29] Side A, lines 35–40. Cf. A, lines 2–4; B, lines 9–21.

32; 150–250 CE). A silversmith and his wife left behind 500 denarii so that the assembly (*synedrion*) of silversmiths would take care of the gravesite from the proceeds (*AGRW* 161 = *IEph* 2212; 41–54 CE).

Funerary foundations took a more specific form at Hierapolis in Phrygia, where there is repeated reference to 'grave-crowning funds' (*stephanōtikon*) in the second and third centuries. This ceremony of crowning or garlanding the grave may have also included a meal. The somewhat extensive excavations of burial grounds that have been completed at Hierapolis provide an unusual opportunity to compare the amount of funds allotted for communal rites at the grave. The grave of Aurelius Zotikos Epikratos at Hierapolis, which spells out contingency plans, illustrates how such endowments would be dependent upon the association's fulfilment of its obligations: 'I leave behind 150 denarii to the guild (*syntechnia*) of nail workers for the yearly grave-crowning ceremony. But if they fail to provide the service, then the guild of coppersmiths will do so. But if they fail to provide the service, the funds are to be given to the purple-dyers for supervision of the grave.'[30] Publius Aelius Glykon's grant of 200 denarii to the presidency of the purple-dyers and 150 denarii to the assembly (*synedrion*) of carpet-weavers specifies that each of these groups was to participate in a grave-crowning ceremony during Judean festivals and a Roman festival using only the interest from the principal (*AGRW* 152 = *IJO* II 196; *c.* 150–250 CE; cf. *AGRW* 155 = *IHierapJ* 227).[31] Publius Aelius Hermogenes donated 1,000 denarii to the guild of dyers (*AGRW* 154 = *IHierapJ* 195). And Tiberius Claudius Kleon donated the largest attested amount for a grave-crowning ceremony at Hierapolis, granting 2,500 denarii to the civic elders' organization, rather than an unofficial association (*IHierapJ* 234). Although not always stated, it seems standard that only interest from the fund would be used to ensure continuation of memorial activities.

Moving beyond our geographical focus, Liu's detailed study of eighty-four endowments to associations (*collegia*) in the western part of the empire explores procedures in managing income from loans.[32] The majority of these foundations fell between 1,000 and 8,000 sesterces (= 250–1,000 denarii ≈ 250–1,000 silver drachmas), which is a range similar to that found at Hierapolis. When interest rates are mentioned, Liu points out, they usually fall between 5 and 12 per cent (rather than the 24 per cent interest that was common in Egypt, as we will see in Chapter 8).

Regular membership contributions and fines

Beyond donations and endowments, another source of income were recurring regular membership contributions, on the one hand, and fines paid by individual participants, on the other.[33] Before surveying evidence for this, it is important to acknowledge that, here, too, there could occasionally be potential struggles for individual members faced

---

[30] *AGRW* 158 = *IHierapJ* 133 (post-212 CE). Cf. *AGRW* 58 = *IG* X,2.1 260, from Thessalonica.
[31] On this case, see Harland (2009: 123–42) = ibid. (2006).
[32] Liu (2008).
[33] Cf. Poland (1909: 492–8).

with financial limitations and, if members failed to pay, difficulties for the group as a whole. In Chapter 1, we discussed the group at Tebtynis that was barely functioning above members' means, with the result that there were occasions when individual contributions may not have been enough to cover costs for food at banquets. There are also momentary glimpses of individuals concerned about how much was needed to participate in such gatherings. Once again, it is 'on paper' (papyrus) and not on stone that we witness such occasional personal hesitancies or difficulties.

Two letters on Egyptian papyri and a document that records unpaid contributions will suffice to illustrate potential problems. First, there is the case of Ptolemaios, living somewhere in the Memphites district (*GRA* III 240 = *PMich* VIII 511; 200–250 CE). In his letter to his father, Ptolemaios gives considerable space to the matter of how he can afford to participate in an upcoming banquet for Sarapis without spending too much.[34] Ptolemaios explains that the 'secretive' initiation payment for the feast (*siōpētikou tēs kleinēs*) was 24 drachmas and the cost of a seat was 22 drachmas (46 drachmas total). However, he noticed that those who took on the role of financial manager (*agoranomos*) were exempt from both costs while also receiving double portions at the meal. To take on the role, they were required to supply all the firewood that was necessary for the banquet, namely five loads of wood by donkey.[35] It is difficult to know what the cost of each load would be here. Using figures from up to a century later (edict of Diocletian in 301 CE) would provide a calculation of about 150 denarii ($\approx$ 150 drachmas) for five mule loads. This amount would be more than the costs Ptolemaios was attempting to avoid. But considerable inflation occurred in reaction to the reforms of both Aurelian in 274 CE and Diocletian in 294–296 CE, so the rates in the edict of Diocletian may be too high.[36] This inflation would have needed to be more than threefold for Ptolemaios to get a better deal than the regular cost for participation. It is also possible that Ptolemaios had ready access to wood at wholesale prices, so to speak. Costs would be reduced by his access to a donkey (from his father) instead of having to hire donkey-drivers to transport the wood (e.g. *AGRW* 37 = *IBeroia* 372). Either rightly or wrongly, Ptolemaios had thought that, for him, paying in kind by supplying the wood would be a less expensive avenue for participating in the gathering.

---

[34] A number of invitations to such banquets (especially *klinai*) have been found: Youtie (1948), Gilliam (1976); *NewDocs* I 1; *POxy* I 110, III 523, XII 1484, XIV 1755, XXXI 2592, LII 3693, LXII 4339; *PKöln* 57. Cf. Aelius Aristides, *Orations* 45.27–8 = *AGRW* L13.

[35] At Ioulis on Keos island, the worshippers of Sarapis honoured a man for supplying the money ('interest-free', which implies a loan) to pay for wood for the society (*IG* XII,5 606 = *RICIS* 202/0801; 3rd or 2nd century BCE). At Liopesi, the treasurer of the Herakles worshippers was responsible for arranging for firewood (*AGRW* 9 = *GRA* I 50).

[36] On the inflation, see Rathbone, Bowman and Wilson (2009: 319), Jones (1953). In the edict of 301 CE, a wagon-load of 1,200 Roman pounds (*librae*) of firewood was set at 150 denarii (i.e. 8 denarii per 100 pounds), a camel-load of 400 pounds was set at 50 denarii (i.e. the same rate), a mule load of 300 pounds was set at 330 denarii (i.e. the slightly higher 10 denarii per 100 pounds), and the donkey-load of 200 pounds was set on a missing figure, likely close to that of the mule (see Allen, 2009: 336; Mietz, 2016: 46–53). If we were to assume that the load amounts in our papyrus were the same, which is far from certain and may be doubtful, five loads of wood would be about 1,500 pounds and would cost 150 denarii, considerably more than the 46 drachmas ($\approx$ 46 denarii) in payment that Ptolemais was trying to avoid. However, the inflations after 274 CE may account for this discrepancy. On costs of wood, see also Blyth (1999).

And so he wrote to his father, who had a donkey, to see if his father could bring some of the necessary loads of wood. For, as Ptolemaios puts it, 'a man cannot refuse our lord Sarapis'.

A second case of individual difficulties is witnessed in the letter of Epiodoros to the supervisor and members of a synod, a letter on papyrus pictured in Figure 5.1 (*AGRW* 289 = *GRA* III 238 = *PMich* IX 575; 184 CE). The substance of the communication is quite blunt and can be quoted in full: 'To Thrax, the supervisor (*epimelētēs*), and to the members of the synod, from Epiodoros. Since I am in poor condition (*asthenōs*) and unable to make contributions to the common fund, I ask that you accept my resignation. Farewell.' It is possible that Epiodoros was a leader or benefactor who had promised funds but was unable to deliver; yet, as Liu clarifies, it seems more likely that he was a participant who here gives up his membership, ostensibly due to poor health and, therefore, poor financial conditions.[37]

Third, a document from the first decades of the third century produced by a synod in Talmis (Upper Egypt) draws attention to unpaid contributions by participants (*GRA* III 269 = *SB* I 4549; 226 CE). Several members, whose names are not preserved, had

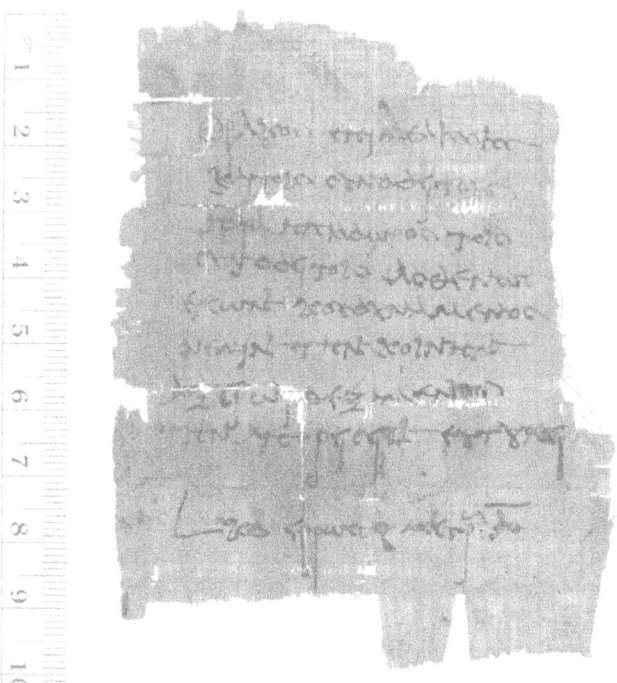

Figure 5.1 Epiodoros' letter (*PMich* IX 575, front [r.]). Courtesy of the University of Michigan Papyrology Collection, used under a Creative Commons licence.

---

[37] Liu (2016: 210 n. 41).

failed to supply their required contribution of wine and roosters for the meal, likely pointing to a lack of personal resources. The ruling of the group was that these people would need to pay double what they had originally owed if they wanted to remain members of the synod. So a steady stream of regular income would not always be coming from all participants in every association. But internal sources were still essential to sustainability.

The primary sources can be quite limited in what they reveal to us about regular (usually monthly) contributions from members and about fines for violation of communal rules. This is partly because graves, honorary monuments and dedications, which make up the bulk of our evidence outside of Egypt, are an unlikely place to find detailed explanations of membership costs. On the other hand, regulations are indeed a likely place to find reference to both regular contributions and fines. Yet the number of these legal documents that have survived in Greek pertaining to associations specifically is somewhat limited, and many were never inscribed in stone but rather written on perishable materials, especially papyri but perhaps also wooden tablets (since we know that membership lists were sometimes put on wooden tablets, too).[38] Income from recurring member payments and fines for violation of rules may have played a more important role in some groups than in others.

Starting with Asia Minor, one of the most substantial association regulations that has survived on stone pertains to a group based within a household at Philadelphia in the region of Lydia (*GRA* II 117 = *AGRW* 121 = *TAM* V 1539; first century BCE). However, this regulation, which takes the form of divine instructions received from Zeus in a dream, says nothing whatsoever about regular payments, fines or any other financial matter. Perhaps this is because the founder and the head of the household, Dionysios, was the supplier of the group's financial needs, as with other groups that began as an extension of the family (see Chapter 3).

Still, we do find brief mention of membership costs or fines elsewhere in Asia Minor. The regulation of those devoted to the god Sabbatistes near Elaioussa-Sebaste in Cilicia specifies fines for violating the stipulations (*AGRW* 213 = *GRA* II 152; time of Augustus). There is reference to members' contributions to the god (not necessarily the Israelite god), which may well be financial but voluntary. Moving beyond regulations themselves, a dedication from Smyrna makes direct reference to five members in a group of initiates devoted to Dionysos Breseus 'having paid the entrance costs' (*hoi peplērōkotes ta isēlysia*), but without mentioning amounts (*AGRW* 190 = *ISmyrna* 731; 83 CE; cf. *ISmyrna* 706). The Greek term used for entrance costs here (*eisēlysia*) was also employed by devotees of Bacchos at Athens and by the hymn-singers at Pergamon.

The altar found at Pergamon dedicated to Hadrian by the hymn-singers (*hymnōdoi*) of god Augustus and goddess Roma is by far the most detailed evidence for regular contributions we have from Asia Minor (*GRA* II 111 = *AGRW* 117 = *IPergamon* 374; 129–138 CE). This monument begins with a partially preserved list of participants, with twenty-seven of the thirty-four possessing the three names indicative of Roman

---

[38] On wooden tablets, see Meyer (2004, and on association lists, see p. 26 n. 27). On Greek regulations pertaining to sacred activities generally: Sokolowski (1955, 1969), Lupu (2005).

citizenship, but the others do not possess such citizenship and one is identified as an athlete. In conjunction with the costs of participating, this may suggest that a number of the participants were of higher socioeconomic status within Pergamon, particularly members of the Castricius family that participated and paid for the monument.

The outline of festivals that follows these names is important not only for regular membership payments, but also for contributions expected from persons who took on specific roles within the group. The inscription outlines five main festivals per year, along with monthly celebrations of Augustus' birthday and other meetings (e.g. birthdays of other emperors). The calendar specifies contributions of cash, food, wine and other necessary materials which each functionary was to provide, whether the 'keeper of order', the priest, the secretary, the 'appointed hymn-singer' or other members. So, for instance, the keeper of order (*eukosmos*), which seems to be the highest position, was to provide 1 mina (= 100 drachmas) for the Asian new year celebration on Augustus' birthday (23 September); 1 mina and one loaf (?) of bread for the first kalends of January (the Roman new year festival); 1 mina and one loaf of bread for the festival of roses in May; wine, 1 mina and one loaf of bread for the celebration of the mysteries; and, 1 mina and one loaf of bread for a gathering in honour of Augustus' wife, Livia. In addition, this functionary was to provide wreaths for the meeting place and wreaths for both members and their sons during the monthly celebrations in honour of Augustus, as well as cakes, incense and lamps. These are substantial contributions from the highest official in the group. The contributions of lesser officials were less substantial, although still significant. The priest (*hiereus*) and the secretary (*grammateus*) of the hymn-singers were not responsible for contributions for the new year celebration in September, but each was responsible for providing funds, wine, bread and table settings for other festivals. For sons of current members, entrance costs were 15 denarii to the gods and 7 denarii to each of the other members, as well as wine and a table setting. Other newly appointed hymn-singers were to contribute 50 denarii towards the images of the Augusti, which were presumably to be used in the mysteries of the group. This, then, is among the most extensive examples from Asia Minor of how an association's leaders and members helped to finance the activities of the group through specified material requirements.

A few surviving Greek regulations on papyri from Egypt provide further details regarding regular payments by members and fines for violation of rules.[39] There are three substantial regulations that have survived from Tebtynis in the Arsinoites district, all of them from the first decades of the first century and all of them from the same village records office (*grapheion*) that has supplied a significant portion of all discovered Egyptian papyri.[40] The regulation of one unknown association, which seems to consist of sheep- or cattle-raisers, outlines monthly membership dues of 12 silver drachmas for the monthly feast (*AGRW* 300 = *GRA* III 206 = *PMich* V 243; 14–37 CE). The regulation also specifies that the 'president (*prostatēs*) is permitted to exact a pledge from anyone who fails to pay his dues in these or any other matters'. In addition, special membership contributions were expected in the case of a marriage (2 drachmas), birth

---

[39] On norms and laws, see also Harland (2012).
[40] Cf. Boak (1937), Venticinque (2010: 285–8).

of a boy (2 drachmas), birth of a girl (1 drachma), purchase of land (4 drachmas), purchase of a flock of sheep (4 drachmas) and purchase of cattle (1 drachma). On the death of a member, each participant was to contribute 1 drachma and two loaves of bread for the funerary meal. In this same group, there are fines designated for: bad behaviour due to drunkenness (fine to be determined by membership); failure to attend meetings (1 drachma for meetings in the village or 4 drachmas for meetings in the city); failure to assist a member who is in trouble (8 drachmas); shoving or taking the seat of another member (3 obols, i.e. half of a drachma); taking legal action against a member (8 drachmas); engaging in intrigue against a member's household (60 drachmas); and, failure to attend the funeral of a member (4 drachmas). Comparison of this case with two other contemporary regulations from the same Tebtynis archive suggests that the range of payments and fines is quite typical for groups in this region, although the other regulations are less detailed on these matters (see *AGRW* 301–302 = *PMich* V 244–245). We will return to notions of mutual assistance reflected in these same regulations in Chapter 8.

Regulations that have survived from southern Greece suggest that the situation in the village of Tebtynis is not all that different from other regions, including Attica. From the Roman era in Attica, the regulation of Herakles worshippers at Liopesi – like the calendar of the hymn-singers – shows special concern for proper banqueting and sacrificial provisions (*AGRW* 9 = *NGSL* 5; *c.* 90–110 CE).[41] New members, whether adult or child, were to contribute in the form of pork for the meal (lines 38–40). The treasurer of the group was responsible for supplying the sacrificial victim (a boar) for the god once a year (line 37). If participants contracted to purchase the supply of pork or wine failed to furnish these supplies, they would have to pay back twice the amount, and those responsible for these duties were to provide sureties (lines 20–2). There is reference to four members who were to be chosen by lot for every feast day, two in charge of meat and two in charge of pastries (lines 31–3). Any improper handling of these arrangements by these designated members would result in a fine of 20 drachmas. Here, too, there were fines for engaging in fights: 10 drachmas for the instigator and 5 drachmas for anyone who joined in.

In the case of Bacchic adherents (Iobacchoi) at Athens, this well-known association had an entrance cost (*isēlysion*) of 50 denarii and a libation, with a 50 per cent reduced rate for sons of current members (*AGRW* 7 = *IG* II² 1368; *c.* 164/165 CE). There were fines for failing to pay the entrance cost, for fighting, for sitting in someone else's seat, for insulting another member and for speaking out of turn. Such fines were to be deposited in the group's common fund. The fact that the collection of such fines could be taken quite seriously is suggested by the procedure in another association. In that group of sacrificing associates in the Piraeus, supervising functionaries were to inscribe the names of those who owed money to the goddess to be displayed for all participants to see, and this would have obvious implications of dishonour for offenders.[42]

---

[41] See also Raubitschek (1981). Cf. *IG* II² 1339, Heroists at Athens, *c.* 55 BCE.
[42] *AGRW* 11 = *GRA* I 4 = *IG* II² 1361, lines 14–15 (330–323 BCE). Cf. *ISamos* 10, although not entailing an association.

At Laureion in Attica, a sanctuary was established around 200 CE by an enslaved Lycian for the Anatolian god Men (*AGRW* 22 = *GRA* I 53 = *IG* II² 1366). The regulations required participants to provide 'what is appropriate for the god' in connection with offerings and the meal: 'a right leg, a hide, a liquid measure (*kotylē*) of oil, a liquid measure (*chous*) of wine (i.e. about 3.25 litres), a dry measure (*choinix*) serving of cake, three sacred cakes, two servings (*choinikes*) of small cakes, and fruit'.

One of the few regulations that has survived from further north, in central Greece, pertains to a mixed society of male and female enthusiasts for Dionysos (*AGRW* 30 = *GRA* I 61 = *IG* IX,1² 670; *c*. 150 CE). Although the final part of the document from Physkeis is missing, we do see reference to the amount of 14 obols (i.e. 2 drachmas and 2 obols, as the obol was 1/6th of a drachma) that each participant paid, yet without specification of whether this was a monthly cost. This group also specifies a fine of 4 drachmas for any participant (male cowherd or female maenad) that attacked or abused another participant, and the same fine for anyone who failed to attend a meeting while in town. This inscription is one of the few that refers to the custom of gathering on the mountain to worship Dionysos (cf. *AGRW* 176 = *SEG* 17:503), and the fine for failing to attend was slightly more: 5 drachmas.

Avner Ecker and Benedikt Eckhardt's recent study of fines attested on fragments of pottery (ostraca) also surveys such fines in the Hellenistic era in both southern Greece and Egypt. They publish pieces of pottery from Maresha in Idumea that were reused as a sort of 'ticket', outlining particular members' fines within a Hellenistic association there.[43] One of these tickets on pottery is pictured in Figure 5.2 and reads: 'The association of Kosadar fines Rhodon 40 silver drachmas.'

Figure 5.2 Pottery fragment from Maresha reused as a 'ticket' stating a member's fine amount. Courtesy of Ian Stern, Director of the Maresha Excavation Project.

---

[43] Ecker and Eckhardt (2018: especially 200–3).

Beyond membership costs and other contributions, fines for violation of the grave were, in theory, a potential source of income for the common fund of an association. There were several methods by which families and other collectives sought to ensure the security of graves in the ancient Mediterranean. One was to include imprecations or curses against any potential violators of the grave, threatening that any vandals or anyone who attempted to add another body to the tomb would suffer dire consequences.[44] Another method was related to the role of associations as caretakers of a grave: unofficial associations or official institutions could be named as recipients of any fines for violation of a grave, suggesting a role in protecting the grave or a role in assisting the prosecution in cases of infringement.[45] So, for instance, families could threaten that potential law-breakers would have to pay fines to the people (*laos*) of the Judeans at Hierapolis (*AGRW* 151 = *IJO* II 206), or to the sacred assembly of sack-bearers at Kyzikos (*AGRW* 111 = *IMT* 1937), or to the guild of clothing-cleaners at Kyzikos (*AGRW* 112 = *IMT* 1801).

However, the degree to which fines for grave violation can be characterized as a significant source of income is questionable. The aim of any method to protect the grave was to ensure that there were no violations, and violations resulting in payment of fines would likely be rare. So the value of potential fines to a guild or association was more symbolic – publicizing connections with families in the local community – than actual.

With respect to regular contributions by participants in assemblies devoted to Jesus, scholars have a propensity to assume that these assemblies benefited from extraordinarily generous individual benefactors who covered literally every communal expense, and even did so perpetually.[46] Such a problematic scenario may be closely related to the broader scholarly tendency to assume individual rather than collective agency in historical explanation, as explained in Chapter 3 above. In this view, membership in an assembly would be free for all other participants, and survival would not be an issue to confront at all. Christian origins scholars who argue along these lines tend to contrast this situation with the 'fees' (a value-loaded term in such usage, it seems) charged by other associations. Furthermore, there are hints of such membership contributions in the Pauline material. For instance, it seems that some members from Paul's assembly at Thessalonica may have been concerned with unpaid recurring contributions, where certain members were attempting to negotiate (*periergazesthai*) extensions (2 Thess 3:6–12). Such extensions, which could, of course, result in outright non-payment, were apparently a common practice in some associations, as we saw with the Tebtynis group in Chapter 1. A synod devoted to Herakles in Attica similarly required members to pay twice their regular rate if a payment came in late, and there was recognition that sometimes members would not pay at all (*GRA* I 50 = *SEG* 31:122, lines 43–5). The punishment of expulsion could then follow.[47] Evidence in Paul's correspondence

---

[44] Cf. *AGRW* 175 = *IEph* 2304; *AGRW* 144 = *TAM* V 1148; *MAMA* I 437.
[45] See Harland (2009: 134–6).
[46] Last (2016a: 114–23), dealing with views of Theissen (1982 [1974]: 148–54), followed by Schmeller (1995: 66–73), Downs (2008: 101), Longenecker (2010: 271), Wanamaker (1990: 163), Malherbe (2012).
[47] On expulsions, see Kloppenborg (2011).

suggests that Paul may have advised a shaming mechanism, namely publicizing the names of debtors, as a strategy to ensure payment of regular contributions.[48] We return to techniques involving the posting of names to either shame non-payers or encourage those who contributed to communal collections in Chapters 6 and 7. When associations or institutions at other levels of society turned to shaming mechanisms for collecting overdue payments in the manner that the Thessalonians may have, it generally signalled the financially precarious condition of the organization itself (as opposed to obsessiveness in keeping members to their committed pay schedules).[49] Paul's letters to the Corinthians further indicate that regular membership payments may have been common in other assemblies devoted to Jesus as well.[50]

The common fund

Before turning to collections by participants within an association, it is important to say a few words about the concept of a common fund or treasury, the place where most income would be stored (with common Greek terms for this being *koinon, tamieion, thēsauros* and *eranos*).[51] We will further discuss storage containers for money soon, when we turn to collection receptacles (*thēsauroi*) in Chapter 6. It seems that many associations maintained a treasury or common fund and that regular contributions, fines and other sources of income were often deposited into it for safe-keeping. The existence of a common fund (or at least a specific collection) is implied in many inscriptions from Asia Minor simply in connection with members collectively paying for something, such as a monument, 'from their own resources' (*ek tōn idiōn*). So, for instance, those engaged in business in the slave-market at Sardis set up an honorary monument for T. Julius Lepidus 'from their own resources' (*AGRW* 124 = *SEG* 46:1524; late first or early second centuries CE).[52]

In other cases from the eastern Mediterranean, there is direct reference to the treasury or common fund itself.[53] In this respect, associations may have been replicating the structures of the city-state (*polis*), where the treasury and its treasurer (*tamias*) were quite important. Furthermore, this same Greek term for a treasurer is commonly attested within associations in Attica, in Asia Minor and on Aegean islands.[54]

The common fund seems to have held a similar importance in Italy and western provinces, where a treasury (*arca*) is mentioned in inscriptions and is assumed as standard by juristic compilers dealing with associations (*collegia, societates* or *corpora*),

---

[48] Last (2016c).
[49] Ibid. (2016a: 114–48), Lambert (2017, on the Thoudippos decree of 425/4 BCE).
[50] Last (2016c).
[51] See also Harrill (1998).
[52] Cf. *AGRW* 118 (Pergamon), 129, 133, 138 (Thyatira), 162 (Ephesos).
[53] *AGRW* 7 (Athens), 14, 20, 21 (Piraeus), 117 (Pergamon), 145 (Akmoneia), 215 (Lamos, Cilicia), 217 (Pessinous, Galatia), 224 (Berytians on Delos), 287 (Nile Delta, Egypt) 289 (Karanis, Egypt), 301 (Tebtynis, Egypt).
[54] E.g. *AGRW* 191 (Smyrna), 223, 224 (Delos); *AGRW* 2, 5, 6, 7 (Athens), 8 (Liopesi), 16, 17, 20, 21 (Piraeus), 40 (Kalambaki, Macedonia).

including the passage we cited in the last chapter (*AGRW* L43 = *Digest* 3.4.1).[55] Later on, the Roman jurist Aelius Marcianus (writing *c.* 222–235 CE) makes reference to imperial rulings concerning associations (*collegia*) formed by the non-elites (*tenuiorum*), likely soldiers here. These associations were likewise assumed to have such a common fund (*AGRW* L53 = *Digest* 47.22.1).

Conclusion

This preliminary survey of income points to the importance of resources coming from both external supporters and, perhaps more reliably, active participants. Yet there is much more to explore concerning collective agency by members in fulfilling group goals. The following two chapters therefore examine the importance of communal fund-raising within associations generally and within groups devoted to the Israelite god specifically.

---

[55] Cf. *AGRW* 310 (Lanuvium, Italy), 322 (Rome); Tertullian, *Apology* 39; Liu 2008.

6

Communal Collections

Part 1: Fund-Raising and Group Values

Do not be surprised when you see me looking fierce, oh stranger! For, patrolling day and night, I guard this divine offering receptacle without sleeping.

IG XI,4 1247

Introduction

The fierce bronze creature that speaks to you here was fashioned by an artist for devotees of Sarapis in order to protect their communal collection. The remains of the offering receptacle this creature protected are pictured in Figure 6.1. This association was not alone in relying on the contributions of participants towards particular goals or special projects. We have stressed the role of collective action over individual agency in our examination of group survival so far, but it is here and in the next chapter that we turn directly to communal fund-raising. These collections – designed for funding building repairs, purchasing wine for feasts and more – represent very important sources of income for many associations.

Yet collective efforts also deserve special attention here because their significance goes well beyond the material. Indeed, since these collections were in some sense volitional, they can provide a window into group values and into what individual members took to be important. In addition, the act of putting money into a special collection affirmed one's loyalty to the association and one's status within the group, and occasionally even helped to enhance the profile of an association within the wider community. For those participants who were able to contribute, collections would not necessarily be a financial burden, but rather an opportunity to perform membership and express one's sense of belonging in the group.[1] Since two factors in communal survival and longevity were the ability to generate sufficient income and to provide social benefits that would satisfy members and attract others, collections could enhance the viability of an association significantly. These are some of the reasons why collections can be taken as an important sign of group cohesion and stability.

---

[1] This is highlighted in Kloppenborg (2017: 323); cf. Ellis-Evans (2012).

Figure 6.1 Collection receptacle from Sarapis sanctuary A (*IG* XI,4 1247 = *RICIS* 202/0124). Courtesy of Laurent Bricault, Université Toulouse II.

Such collective endeavours by associations have implications for understanding gatherings of those devoted to the Israelite god, including adherents of Jesus. This is something we explore at length in the next chapter. For now it is important to state that there are clear indications that at least some groups devoted to the Israelite god also engaged in monetary collections for specific purposes, as when Judeans made collections to be sent to the temple in Jerusalem (before its destruction in 70 CE) and when members of Paul's groups raised funds to send to Judean followers of Jesus at Jerusalem. But these communal fund-raising practices seem to be only the tip of the iceberg, and it is important to place these practices within the framework of purposeful fund-raising among contemporary groups, which is the aim of this chapter.

We begin with a case study of Delos island, with special attention to the terminology associations used in reference to such fund-raising. This sets the stage for an investigation of procedures used elsewhere, again demonstrating both an important source of income and a sign of group values and group cohesion, often centred around honouring the gods. While in many cases deities were central to group values, the case of a collection by fishermen at Ephesos also shows how communal action by occupational associations, specifically, could in some ways simultaneously serve economic interests alongside other factors.

Collections on Delos and nearby islands in the Hellenistic era

The epigraphy of Delos is among the richest sources of archaeological information for associations at any one locale, and there are clear signs that communal collections were important to associations here in the Hellenistic era. This is particularly the case with respect to immigrant associations and cults for foreign deities. Numerous monuments from the final decades of the second century BCE attest to a cult of Syrian deities centred around the worship of the goddess 'Atargatis', also called 'Pure goddess' or 'Pure Aphrodite' (cf. *IDelos* 2220-304).[2] Several of these monuments indicate there was a group of 'servants' (*therapeutai*) of the goddess connected with this cult,[3] and that the cult was led by a priest and priestess. Most importantly here, one of the inscriptions refers to another 'society' (*thiasos*) in connection with both benefaction and a collection (166-88 BCE).[4] The inscription reveals that a priestly couple had arranged to cover most of the costs to reconstruct a sacred building for Atargatis adjacent to a temple of Sarapis.

Most notably for present purposes, members of this society of Syrians devoted to the same goddess had 'thrown together' or 'collected' (*symbeblēntai*) 50 drachmas to further support renovation of the building. It is notable that the inscription omits the names of individual contributors and the amounts each donor offered, unlike some other inscriptions. The implications of this anonymity are not entirely clear, but this could suggest an equalizing effect that solidified group cohesion as opposed to social hierarchy generated on the basis of competition among members. Since the priest and priestess are the only named donors, their role in funding the renovation is certainly elevated. Those involved in this ethnic association evidently continued to emphasize honouring the goddess from their Syrian homeland while also contributing to a local

---

[2] Will and Schmid (1985).
[3] *IDelos* 2224 (*c.* 105 BCE), 2229 (112 BCE), 2240 (95 BCE).
[4] *AGRW* 229 = Siebert (1968: 359–74); cf. *IDelos* 2225.

sanctuary that came to be frequented not only by Syrians but also by Greeks and resident Romans.[5]

Similar language of 'collecting' or literally 'throwing together' (*synballō*) is found among Sarapis worshippers on Delos (both Sarapieion A and B). An inscription from Sarapis sanctuary A that mentions Apollonios (hence *c.* 200 BCE) refers to those who threw together funds within a group of 'servants' of Sarapis (*hoi symbalomenoi tōn therapeutōn*) in order to dedicate a structure to the goddess Nike.[6] Furthermore, the 'association of servants who throw together' (*tōn therapeutōn symbalomenōn*) resources is mentioned in an inventory of treasures (*IDelos* 1417; 156 BCE). This same inventory also refers to an offertory or collection box (*thēsauros*) in the Sarapis sanctuary with a guard or decorative protector lying on it.[7] The earliest Sarapis sanctuary – Sarapieion A – on Delos happens to be the find-spot of just such a receptacle with an opening for the collection of coins, as we saw at the beginning of this chapter.

Such receptacles or treasuries (*thēsauroi*) came in block, cylindrical and pillar form, with an opening for inserting coins, and they were sometimes decorated with a protector, such as a serpent or other animal. An example of such a receptacle is pictured in Figure 6.1. These collection and storage containers would be heavy enough to prevent someone running away with the treasury, and often a small door for emptying the contents could be bolted and locked. Recent studies by Gabriele Kaminski (in German) and by Milena Melfi (in Italian) explore the evidence for such receptacles in various settings.[8]

The evidence from Delos alone suggests usage of such receptacles within various cults, including associations specifically.[9] The first of four offering receptacles used by associations on Delos (and mentioned in our introduction) was found in Sarapis sanctuary A. This was the sanctuary that was established while Apollonios II was priest and was used by 'servants' of the god (*hoi therapeuontes / therapeutai*).[10] This cylindrical offering receptacle itself was dedicated around the time of the founding of the sanctuary and was inscribed with the following (*IG* XI,4 1247 = *RICIS* 202/0124; *c.* 200 BCE):

> This is dedicated to Sarapis, Isis, and Anubis. Ktesias son of Apollodoros of Tenos island set up the offering receptacle and the base according to the command of the god. 'Do not be surprised when you see me looking fierce, oh stranger! For,

---

[5] Syrian expatriates were from Antioch (*IDelos* 2224, 2263, 2285), Hierapolis (nos 2226, 2261), and Laodikeia (nos 2259, 2262, 2264, 2270). Among other dedicants are an Alexandrian (no. 2225), an Athenian (nos 2251–2), a man from Marathon (no. 2245), and several Romans (nos 2255, 2266, 2269), on which see also Will and Schmid (1985: 140–2).
[6] *IG* XI,4 1290 = *RICIS* 202/0121. Cf. *IG* XI,4 1225.
[7] Side A, column 2, lines 131, 142, 154: *phylaka ep' e[m]phalou, ton epikeimenon epi tou thēsaurou en tōi Sarapieiōi*.
[8] Kaminski (1991: 63–181), Melfi (1998). See also Couch (1929), Martin (1940), Bruneau (1970: 365–7), *SEG* 41:182; *SEG* 49:222; *SEG* 55:2071; *SEG* 57:198 (receptacle for Aphrodite Ourania at Athens, *c.* 400 BCE); *SEG* 41:683 (Asklepios sanctuary on Kos); *SEG* 52:872.
[9] Bruneau (1970: 365–70). For other collection receptacles on Delos, see *IG* XI,4 1224; *IDelos* 372A = *RICIS* 202/0103, line 28; *IDelos* 442A = *RICIS* 202/0106, lines 156–7; *IDelos* 460t = *RICIS* 202/0109, line t 43.
[10] See *IG* XI,4 1299 = *RICIS* 202/0101; *IG* XI,4 1217 = *RICIS* 202/0115; *IG* XI,4 1290 = *RICIS* 202/0121.

patrolling day and night, I guard this divine offering receptacle without sleeping.'
'Yet you please me when you throw whatever your heart desires into my spacious body through my mouth.'

A bronze ornament of an animal, now lost, was positioned on the front as guard over the treasure within (cf. *IDelos* 1417, side A, column 2, line 142). The inscription playfully shifts to the perspective of the fierce creature that protects the offerings and then to the receptacle itself rejoicing whenever someone throws something into its mouth.

It is important to note that the verb used for contributing coins on this earliest receptacle, 'to throw in' (*emballesthai*), is widely attested and related to the verb 'to throw together' (*symballein*) that we encountered with the Syrian immigrant association which collected money for an expansion of Atargatis' sanctuary. The same 'throwing in' terminology is used regularly in reference to contributions to offering receptacles or treasuries for sacrifices and other ritual purposes in many other settings beyond the associations.[11]

A second receptacle for coin offerings found at Delos was set up by a priest of the Great Gods and of the Kabeiroi in the Samothracian sanctuary in 159/158 BCE (*IDelos* 1898). Although no evidence survives concerning associations that may have frequented this particular sanctuary, it would not be far-fetched to imagine participation by associations of merchants or devotees of Samothracian deities, like those attested in other locales.[12]

A third coin-collecting receptacle from Delos was dedicated in the second century BCE in the marketplace of the Competaliasts – namely, those dedicated to deities of the crossroads – by Gaius Varius son of Gaius, a freedman (*IDelos* 2575). Its find-spot in front of the Ionic temple of the Italians devoted to Hermes suggests the Competaliasts' connection to that building specifically, as Jean Hatzfeld also notes.[13] Those devoted to Hermes had built the temple around 140 BCE (*IDelos* 1731).

The commonality of associations beyond Delos using such coin collection methods is confirmed by other evidence. On the island of Thera, a man named Diokles and an association of 'royalists' devoted to Ptolemaic rulers as gods dedicated such a treasury to the Egyptian deities Sarapis, Isis and Anubis.[14] Another one of the fourty-four surviving examples of such offering receptacles (documented by Kaminski) was found within the meeting place of Mithras adherents at what is now Heddernheim, Germany.[15] These receptacles suggest anonymous contributions from a range of individuals who were connected – some more than others – to the association or sanctuary that managed the collection.

---

[11] *IPergamon* 255.13–16 (after 133 BCE); *IPergamon* 161a.8 (*c.* 150 CE); *LSAM* 73.30–3 (Halikarnassos, III BCE); *IKosS* ED 89.17–23 (first century BCE); *LSCG* 155 (Kos, 300–250 BCE); *IG* VII 235, lines 23 and 40 (Oropos in Boiotia, 387–377 BCE).
[12] Cf. *IEph* 20.67–71; *IG* XII,2 506, 506[1], 507; *IG* XII,1 43, from Rhodes; *IRhodPer* 115, 556; *ILindos* 285; *CIG* 3540, from Pergamon; *IRhodPer* 87, 471; Cole (1984: 83–6).
[13] Hatzfeld (1912: 202), Kaminski (1991: 162–3, no. II, 5).
[14] *IG* XII,3 443 (300–250 BCE). Cf. *IPriene* 195.37 (*c.* 200 BCE); *IG* IX,2 590 = *RICIS* 112/0502, from Larisa in Thessaly.
[15] See Kaminski (1991: 113).

Alongside the use of 'throwing in' language to speak of contributions to a treasury, Kaminski's study also observes the use of 'offering' language – particularly Greek terms such as *aparchesthai* – to speak of such contributions.[16] So the evidence for associations contributing to collections – with or without an actual offering receptacle – may provide a context for understanding two inscriptions from Delos that mention northern Israelites (or 'Samaritans'). Both inscriptions attesting to this association of immigrants from Israel use a similar self-designation, a designation that underlines the group's concern to collect contributions for a sacred site in their original homeland.

The earlier of the two inscriptions, which was very likely inscribed when a temple on mount Gerizim was still in use, reads as follows (*IJO* I Ach 66 = *AGRW* 222a; *c.* 250–175 BCE):

> The Israelites on Delos who contribute (*hoi aparchomenoi*) towards holy, sacred Gerizim honoured Menippos son of Artemidoros from Herakleia, himself and his descendants, who furnished and dedicated from his own resources on account of a prayer of god ... (*about two lines missing*) and they crowned him with a gold crown and ...

The second inscription, which may date to a later period (*c.* 150–50 BCE), confirms that this group somewhat consistently referred to itself as 'the Israelites on Delos who contribute to sacred Gerizim' (*AGRW* 22b = *IJO* I Ach 67). So the title of this immigrant association clearly indicates the centrality of the group's financial offerings to support rites for the Israelite god in the homeland, so much so that the act of collecting funds came to be integrated into the self-designation of the group.[17] This is yet another example of collections solidifying cohesion among members. It would be hard to imagine a closer relationship between financial collections and communal identification than this. Philippe Bruneau also provides a local context for the terminology employed by these Israelites. He points to the local use of similar terminology (*aparchai / aparchesthai*) in reference to 'offerings' sent to Delos in honour of Apollo, including those arranged by the civic institutions of Athens (*Hymn to Delos* 278, 299; *IG* II² 2336.34; 102–94 BCE).

Before moving on from collection receptacles and the semantic field of contributing to them, it is important to note other less common but related Greek terms for voluntary collections for a particular purpose, especially the Greek terms *logeia* and *logeuein* which can be rendered 'collection' and 'to collect'.[18] These concepts also have relevance for understanding collections within certain groups of Jesus adherents, especially with reference to 1 Corinthians 16:1–3, as we will see in Chapter 7.

Although these Greek terms could be used in reference to a collection of taxes, sometimes a 'collection' (*logeia*) of this sort was made for a particular purpose related to the gods. A third- or second-century BCE inscription from the island of Paros

---

[16] Cf. *IOlbiaD* 88 = *SEG* 3:587; *c.* 230 BCE. Kaminski (1991).
[17] Cf. Bruneau (1982: 480).
[18] Cf. Deissmann (1922 [1909]: 104–7), Downs (2008: 129–31).

(located about 35 kilometres south of Delos) is a noteworthy example (*IG* XII,5 186 + addenda, p. 310). This is a list of contributions by a group of at least sixty-five women, perhaps members of an association, although not likely an association of prostitutes devoted to Aphrodite as the original editor, Ernst Maass, imagined.[19] The relationship to a temple is clearly indicated by the opening of the inscription, which is dated not only by the civic magistrate (archon) but also by the temple warden and the priest of the sanctuary. The text then states that 'it (the association [?]) made a collection (*elogeuse[n]*) for the restoration of the fountain, the altar, and the shrine (*thalamos*) ...' Then follows the list of female contributors, with amounts ranging from 1 obol (1/6th of a drachma) to 31 drachmas per donor.[20] The use of this noun for a 'collection' (*logeia*) is found in several other cultic contexts, including a cult of Helios Apollo at Smyrna (first century CE), a cult at Physkos on the Carian coast (*c.* 100 BCE) and a cult of Isis at Thebes in Egypt.[21] So this terminological usage was not uncommon.

Organizing collections

Beyond the existence and use of receptacles for gathering funds together, the inscriptions we have considered so far indicate little regarding actual procedures used in gathering funds for a particular purpose. Several other inscriptions do provide more details regarding fund-raising for various purposes, including gaining supplies for meals, purchasing land for burial or other purposes, and constructing a meeting place or acquiring a sanctuary. These may reflect the sort of procedures that took place within other associations about which we know less. In many cases, honouring deities stands out as a principal motivating factor in the evidence for collections, but not the only factor.

Often, the cost of a group's meals could be covered by regular dues paid by members or by occasional donations by benefactors. But there is some evidence that, on occasion, special collections could be done to cover the cost of certain supplies for banquets. More or less voluntary communal collections were sometimes done in addition to and apart from regular membership payments.[22] In particular, there are papyri that record members' donations to a collection for the cost of wine at meals.[23] One papyrus identifies itself as a 'list of wine-payments of a synod of donkey-drivers' (*PAthen* 41; first century CE). There were nineteen members whose contributions are listed with amounts ranging from 1 drachma (and 1 obol) to 20 drachmas. In these record-keeping lists, contributors and their donations were organized chronologically rather than based on the amount given. We generally lack this sort of evidence for other regions such as Greece, Asia Minor and Aegean islands, in part, because such special collections for wine or other supplies were not likely to be inscribed in stone.

---

[19] See Maass (1893: 21–6), corrected by Wilhelm (1898: 409–40). Cf. Rudolf (1899).
[20] Cf. Taylor (2011: 709–10), Berranger (2000: 177–9), Stavrianopoulou (2006: 242–3).
[21] *ISmyrna* 753, lines 24–6; *LSCG* 143 = *IRhodPer* 501, line 6; Deissmann (1922 [1909]: 104–7).
[22] Last (2013: 93–5).
[23] E.g. *PTebt* III 894, frag. 3 back [v.], I, lines 1–19 (see Chapter 2).

Communal collections were sometimes aimed at larger projects, including acquiring property for buildings. Funerary functions were of course an important dimension of group life as well. On the island of Rhodes, references to the purchase of a 'place' (*topos* in Greek) sometimes pertains to the acquisition of a communal burial 'plot'. Communal burial was not widespread across much of the ancient Mediterranean, where individual or family graves were the norm. But on the island of Rhodes and some other Aegean islands such as Kos, collective burial by association was common in the Hellenistic and Roman eras, alongside familial burial.[24]

An example of collective action is provided by an association consisting of a mixture of at least twenty-nine immigrants and seven Rhodian sculptors.[25] These members were headed by a priest and they worshipped the Samothracian gods and Hermes, among others. Together, the 'contributors' (*eranistai*) raised a fund (*eranos*) in order to purchase a 'place' which, in light of its location in a necropolis near Ialysos on Rhodes, was to be used for a communal burial plot. We will return to the importance of Greek concepts related to contributors (including the Greek term *eranos*) in Chapter 8, but for now we should note that the total amount of the purchase (excluding the few missing names or amounts) was 930 drachmas. The inscription clarifies that each member first voluntarily promised (*epaggellesthai*) to contribute a certain amount, ranging from the very few who donated as much as 280 drachmas to the many (eighteen) who donated 5 drachmas. Apparently, everyone had fulfilled their promise. The benefactor of the group, Ktesiphon from Chersonessos on the mainland of Asia Minor, was also a member who donated 250 drachmas, and he dedicated the monument itself.

For Greek-speaking sites beyond Aegean islands, there is notable epigraphic evidence for communal fund-raising for the purpose of constructing, purchasing or renovating a meeting place or sanctuary. Among the earlier ones is an inscription from Kallatis, a longstanding Greek colony on the western coast of the Black Sea (*AGRW* 73 = *IKallatis* 35). Ancient Kallatis was located near what is now the city of Mangalia in Romania. This Greek inscription, dating around 200 BCE, provides the names and amounts of donations, unlike the case of the Atargatis devotees on Delos. In this case, the male members of a society (*thiasitai*) resolved to build a temple (*naos*) for their patron deity, likely Dionysos in light of reference to a 'triennial festival'. The decree of members goes into some detail regarding how the funding was to be raised. Contributors from the society were 'to promise' (again, *epaggellesthai*) a certain donation towards the costs. There would also be a reward system in place to encourage giving. Those who contributed larger amounts were to be granted special honours. In this case, those who donated a gold coin were to be granted a 'crown of honour (*philotimias*) *for life* and their name inscribed on the monument'. Those who promised less than a gold coin but

---

[24] Fraser (1977: 58–70).
[25] *SEG* 39: 737 (185 BCE; cf. *SEG* 53:822 from Rhodos) = Kontorini (1989: 73–85, no. 10). The immigrants are from Athens, Rhodian coastal territory (Chersonesos), Aegean islands (Chios [2], Samos, Thera), Asia Minor (Halikarnassos, Ephesos [2], Miletos [2], Kyzikos, Laodikeia [if not in Syria], Herakleia [3] [if not the town in Thrace], Etenna in Pisidia, Selge in Pisidia, 'Pisidian', Phaselis in Lycia, 'Cilician', Amisos in Pontus), Armenia ('Armenian'), and Egypt (Alexandria). On 'Rhodians' as sculptors, see Gabrielsen (1993).

more than 30 silver drachmas were to be similarly granted a crown, but a lesser 'crown of approval' (*apo*[*doxa*]*s*) during the triennial festival every other year – but, again, for life. Finally, those who contributed less still were to have only their names inscribed on the monument, but this nonetheless gave these lesser donors publicity for giving. So here the public presentation of the donors' names was taken to be a motivating factor. Added to this was an incentive to contribute as much as possible in order to receive one of the two levels of prestigious crowns presented in the ongoing meetings of the society (on which, see the earlier discussion of the crown for Dionysodoros).

The level of organization in fund-raising went even further within this group. As with some other cases discussed below, members of the society also arranged to have a special team chosen to collect the promised funds. In this case, three men were to be 'appointed (*kataskeuasthē*) from among all the society members to ensure that the temple (*naos*) is constructed magnificently and quickly'. These appointed collectors would receive the promised funds and 'administer the expenses', keeping a written account of the funds that were managed. These functionaries, too, were given an incentive for overseeing the collection and construction. They would be granted crowns during the triennial festival of the association. We know from many other inscriptions that those who took on responsibility for managing finances could expect to receive special honours for their appropriate care of communal funds.[26]

The decree from Kallatis then lists thirty names of members who had contributed towards the building of the temple. The incentives seem to have worked, as at least twelve of the thirty legible participants clearly contributed 1 gold coin each, at least six contributed 30 silver drachmas and many members contributed in other ways. In particular, some donors contributed significant materials. Damosthenes paid for the construction of a vaulted structure, leading to the main doorway. Several others offered a labour force for the construction itself, with members supplying ten, fifteen or even thirty labourers (either hired workers or enslaved persons), and one supplying a horse as well.

A similar level of communal effort is reflected in a first-century inscription from Kyme on the western coast of Asia Minor. The monument contains a record of purchase for buildings that were to be used as a sanctuary by a group of initiates in mysteries for a deity whose identification remains uncertain due to damage to the stone (*GRA* II 105 = *IKyme* 37). Thankfully for our purposes, this record also refers to the earlier process of raising funds for the purchase. Considerable attention was given to organizing the collection of funds, as a team of ten 'appointed collectors' (*praktores*) had been established by the initiates.

This term for functionaries with some financial role within an association is attested elsewhere, although the responsibilities are not spelled out as clearly as at Kyme. The synod devoted to Herakles at Liopesi likewise had ten 'collectors'. At Liopesi these were responsible for the group's finances in some way, presumably under the direction of the 'treasurer' (*tamias*) and under the watch of the 'auditors' in that case (*eglogistai*; *SEG* 31:122 = *GRA* I 50, lines 27–9; *c.* 100 CE):

---

[26] E.g. *IG* II² 1271 = *GRA* I 13 (299/8 BCE) and *IG* II² 1329 = *GRA* I 37 (175/4 BCE), both from the Piraeus.

It is necessary to appoint from the synod ten collectors. If they do not wish to be collectors, let ten be chosen by lot from the general membership (*tou plēthous*). Likewise, when the treasurer provides an accounting, after a meeting has been called, they shall appoint three auditors and the auditors shall swear by Herakles, Demeter, and Kore.

Although not clearly stated, it may be that the collectors at Kyme were also members of the association, as had been the case at Kallatis as well.

An opponent of the movement known as the 'new prophecy' (or, Montanism) in Phrygia critiques these other Jesus adherents for the way in which they received or managed funds, mentioning that one of the leaders, Montanos, appointed 'collectors of funds' (*praktēras chrēmatōn*, as cited in Eusebius, *Church History* 5.18.2). While this opponent's (Apollonios') sustained accusation of greed and banditry (throughout 5.18.2–11) is not to be taken at face value, this may well make reference to actual procedures for collections to support communal activities or leaders within that setting as well.[27]

As head of the team of collectors back at Kyme, Herakleides Olympikos led them in gathering funds from 'those participating in the sacred rites' (*tōn metochontō[n] tōn hi[erō]n*, in lines 13–14), who had each promised a standard amount of 103 denarii. When the collectors brought the funds, Herakleides then made the purchase of the temple on behalf of those participating in the sacred rites, but the title of the property seems to have remained in Herakleides' name. Herakleides was also to manage and spend the funds at the appropriate times. After purchasing the temple, Herakleides dedicated the rooms and surrounding areas as sacred to the deity. There are also indications that this team was to continue to have responsibilities in the sanctuary as they were to 'consider and care for the sacred things and the buildings'.

The document underlines just how important the mysteries were to those who contributed funds to have this sanctuary purchased and dedicated: 'May those who take part in the mysteries, accomplishing and protecting them perpetually, acquire accessible and fruitful land, the birth of legitimate children, and a share in all good things. But for the one who does not consider these things, the opposite will happen.' Implied is that those who supported the construction would receive such benefits in return from the deity or deities in question. The inscription concludes with a list of at least thirty-nine people (beyond the collectors) who had contributed money to the collection, most likely initiates themselves in light of the preceding blessing and curse. At least twenty-seven contributors were women, pointing to the prevalence of women in this particular group of initiates.

Fishermen at Ephesos and communal economic interests

Although far less detailed regarding procedures for gathering funds, there were other clear cases of members in an association collecting together materials or funds

---

[27] See Trevett (1996: 48–9), who seems to believe the accusation that the leaders were benefiting financially.

specifically for the construction, purchase or renovation of a sanctuary, meeting place or other building. Aims beyond honouring the gods could play a role, pointing to other values held in common by members of such groups. In the mid-first century CE, the fishermen and fish-dealers at Ephesos dedicated the fishery toll-office to imperial figures and, likely, to Artemis of Ephesos as well (*AGRW* 162 = *GRA* II 127 = *IEph* 20; 54–9 CE).[28] The monument is pictured in Figure 6.2. The opening of the inscription on the monument reads as follows:

> This was dedicated to Artemis Ephesia (?) (as in Lytle's reconstruction) ... to the emperor Nero Claudius Caesar Augustus Germanicus; ... to Julia (?) ... Agrippina Augusta, his mother; to Octavia, the emperor's wife; to the People of the Romans; and, to the People of the Ephesians. The fishermen and fish-dealers set this up from their own resources (*ek tōn idiōn*), having received the place by decree from the city and having built the fishery toll-office.

The dedicatory monument then lists those who had contributed the necessary materials and funds for building the structure, along with amounts from largest to smallest. Regarding the status of membership in this group, studies by G. H. R. Horsley and Steven Michael Baugh show that, if these donors are in fact members (see below), there is a fair cross section of socioeconomic levels within this group's membership.[29] There are Roman citizens of freed and free status (43–4 members, approximately 50 per cent of the legible names), persons of non-servile status (36–41 members, about 45 per cent) and several enslaved persons (2–10 members, 3 per cent or more). It may be that some other guilds, for which we lack such a detailed list, included such a mixture of people of free, freed and servile status with differing levels of resources.

Ephraim Lytle claims that the names listed were not, in fact, members of the association of fishermen and fish-dealers, but rather *additional* contributors from outside of the group.[30] Lytle notes that, although the Greek verb used before the list of contributors (*proskatapherō*) is not otherwise known, the combination of the two prepositions (*pros* combined with *kata*) in line 11 'almost always conveys the sense of "in addition to" or "besides": individuals listed provided funds *in addition to* the contributions of the association of fishermen and fishmongers'.[31] Yet this remains uncertain. If taken literally, lines 9–10 would argue against Lytle's interpretation: there the fishermen and fish-dealers do expressly claim to be setting up this building 'from their own resources'. This could be interpreted to mean exclusively so. Others such as Horsley (*NewDocs* V 5) take these donors to be *members* of the fishermen and fish-dealers, as we do here. If this is so, then it seems that the composition of membership in this association reflected a range of socioeconomic levels (see commentary on *GRA* II 127). Many of the larger contributions are in kind, with donors and their families offering building materials, including columns, paving stones and tiles. The monetary

---

[28] Cf. Keil (1930, initial publication).
[29] Horsley in *NewDocs* V 5; Baugh (1990).
[30] Lytle (2012a: 213–24).
[31] Ibid., 220.

Figure 6.2 Fishermen and fish-dealers' monument, now in the Selcuk Archaeological Museum. Photo by Harland.

donations then range from the five donors who offered 50 denarii to the approximately thirty donors who offered just 5 denarii, with those who gave 25, 20 or 15 denarii in between. Three men who provided 2,000 or 1,000 bricks are placed in the list after those who gave 25 denarii, which may be an indication that this number of bricks would cost around or less than 25 denarii.

So far, most of the cases we have considered had members of an association joining together to financially support honouring deities, and this points towards the importance of such deities in communal self-understanding and cohesion. The fishery toll-office as a whole was not mainly designed as a sanctuary. Yet the building may have been dedicated to Artemis (depending on the restoration of the opening lines), and it is important to note that there are indications that certain parts of the building were indeed designed for honouring deities. The final lines on side A (lines 67–71) of the monument clarify that, 'along with his wife, L. Fabricius Vitalis – who superintended the works and procured the construction of the work – also dedicated at his own expense two columns together with the adjacent altars beside the Samothracian shrine'. So there was a sacred area dedicated within the building. It is not surprising to find fishermen honouring these deities who were especially known for protecting those who travelled by sea or whose livelihood was linked to maritime trade.[32] From a later inscription, we know that the goddess Isis – also a favourite of those who navigated by sea – was honoured in the building by workers in the toll office as well (*IEph* 1503).

Particularly noteworthy, however, are the potential *economic* purposes of the construction, which suggest that members of the group expected some financial or professional advantage by erecting the building. Horsley raises the question of why the fishermen and fish-dealers at Ephesos would want to support the foundation of this building, a building presumably devoted to collecting dues, tolls or taxes on the fish that this very group caught and sold. In Horsley's view, the association may have been here investing in what might be labelled a 'cartel' of sorts. The group was, in this view, attempting 'to ensure that those who were not members of the group at Ephesos were barred from bringing their catch ashore there and marketing it in the city' (*NewDocs* V 5, p. 103). As to what type of fisheries were involved, Horsley refers to a passage in Strabo about a dispute over the collection of taxes at Ephesos specifically (Strabo, *Geography* 14.1.26). According to this passage, those assigned to collect taxes for the Roman imperial regime (the *publicani*) had attempted to control revenues from fishing in lakes owned by the goddess Artemis, and an Ephesian embassy to Rome had successfully regained these revenues for the goddess. Horsley proposes that the tolls collected in this new structure built by the fishermen would be those for the goddess and would pertain primarily to *freshwater* fish caught in her sacred lakes, not sea fisheries. On a separate matter that relates to economic advantages for the guild, Horsley also points out that some of the architectural features mentioned in the donations, especially the porticoes, are in keeping with the simultaneous use of the building for the sale of fish, either wholesale or retail. This would also financially benefit the members of the group.[33]

Lytle likewise emphasizes the importance of these shops as one of the reasons why the fishermen were involved in building the structures.[34] Lytle differs from Horsley in convincingly arguing that the location of the toll building on the waterfront would suggest, instead, sea-fishing: 'the very existence of such a building project best agrees

---

[32] See Cole (1984).
[33] Horsley, *NewDocs* V 5, p. 104.
[34] Lytle (2012a: 218–19).

with a scenario whereby fishermen wishing to have access to the city's markets had to deliver their fish at the docks in the harbor and pay in the process a duty on the value of the catch'.[35] In particular, Lytle argues that, although fish caught *at sea* were considered free of taxation, cities could still impose duties on any fish brought into the *local* market.[36] So the tolls collected in this building at Ephesos likely went not to the Romans and not to Artemis of Ephesos specifically, but to the civic institutions. It was a 'simple duty assessed on fresh seafood entering the local market'.[37] Challenging Horsley's notion of a fishing cartel, Lytle suggests that economic advantage still does explain, in part, the fishermen and fish-dealers' contributions to this building: the move to the harbour would allow the group its own space to coordinate unloading fish, paying dues to the city and selling wholesale, all in one location. 'The benefits of such specialization, especially tangible when dealing with a non-durable good like fresh seafood, would have soon exceeded the costs of construction,' as Lytle puts it.[38]

Whether one accepts Horsley's or Lytle's interpretation, the point remains that we have here fund-raising aimed at furthering the corporate financial well-being of persons of a common trade, although not without a place for the gods as well. This suggests that the members of this guild placed some degree of importance on protecting their economic interests and that such interests also played a role in group cohesion.

The notion that the fishermen at Ephesos engaged in collective action to, among other things, protect their material interests brings us to another potential economic dimension to associative life that deserves mention here. Early scholarship that considers the issue tends to heavily downplay economic goals of ancient guilds, often thinking of medieval guilds or modern labour unions as a sharp contrast, and much subsequent research tends to do the same. Jean-Pierre Waltzing's hesitancy about guilds serving either 'an economic goal or protection of the profession' echoes quite clearly in Moses Finley's assertion that 'not only were there no guildhalls in antiquity, there were no guilds, no matter how often the Roman *collegia* and their differently named Greek and Hellenistic counterparts are thus mistranslated'.[39] By this, Finley seems to mean that ancient guilds, unlike medieval ones, did not function to protect the economic interests of members. Similar views are expressed by Ramsay MacMullen, who stresses social in opposition to economic purposes.[40] Van Nijf and Liu rightly point out that medieval guilds themselves were not nearly as focused on protecting their members' economic interests as such ancient historians imagine, but rather served a variety of social and other purposes as well.[41]

Building on H. W. Pleket's critique of Finley's primitivist economic model, recent scholarship since van Nijf tends to carefully critique this exclusion of collective

---

[35] Ibid., 220. Cf. Pleket in *SEG* 39:1211.
[36] Cf. Lytle (2012b).
[37] Ibid. (2012a: 218).
[38] Ibid., 220.
[39] Waltzing: 'On ne parle pas d'un but économique, ni de la protection du métier, ni de la conservation des procédés, ni de l'exercice d'une industrie en commun' (1891: 173). Finley (1973: 138). Cf. Waltzing (1895: 345–9).
[40] Finley (1973: 81), MacMullen (1974: 19), Ausbüttel (1982: 99).
[41] van Nijf (1997: 12–18), ibid. (2002), Liu (2008: 16).

economic or professional interests in a number of ways.⁴² Matthew Gibbs, Koenraad Verboven and others build on van Nijf's observations and argue that guilds did, at least on occasion: engage in collective bargaining, attempt to monopolize local trade, fix prices, control membership by means of licensing and seek to introduce regulatory practices.⁴³ And so van Nijf points to a decree from Smyrna, in which civic institutions take action against ferrymen who had been price-fixing and preventing 'many from taking part in the ferry business' (*ISmyrna* 712; 1–2 CE). At Pergamon, imperial authorities in the second century responded to complaints regarding unfair surcharges added by money-changers, particularly in connection with fish-dealers (*IGR* IV 352). Whether or not we can call the action by bakers at Ephesos a 'strike', the proconsul's edict nonetheless reveals concerted action by those of a common trade (*IEph* 215; cf. *PSI* VII 822). The author of Acts imagines as realistic a work stoppage and riot by silversmiths in reaction to a threat to sales, namely Paul's teaching that gods made with hands – statues of Artemis included – are not gods (Acts 19).

Gibbs also discusses several cases of such economic interests from Egypt, including the famous regulations of the salt merchants at Tebtynis, who attempted to license those of a trade, fix prices and establish exclusively assigned trade boundaries (*AGRW* 302 = *PMich* V 245; 47 CE). Gibbs and Verboven also highlight the role of licensing or concessions in the form of local and periodic control over the supply of a product or service, approaching the idea of local 'monopolies'.⁴⁴ As Verboven shows, Egyptian papyri indicate licences for fixed periods in connection with hunting, fishing, fish-breeding, salt-trading and even weaving, and he suggests that similar situations may have existed in other provinces.⁴⁵

None of the above discussion of guilds serving the purpose of economic protection is to suggest that these were necessarily typical situations. Yet these instances do point to problems with scholars excluding collective economic action from consideration. Clearly, this material also provides further evidence regarding the importance of collective agency for associations overall.

Conclusion

It is worth noting that our observations above regarding communal collections as an expression of group values and cohesion relate to some recent findings related to donation lists or subscriptions in other contexts.⁴⁶ John S. Kloppenborg notes the importance of distinguishing between association collections that were exclusive to members and those that were open to external supporters in the local community. While the former, internal, ones helped to define group boundaries and cohesion, the

---

⁴² Van Nijf (1997: 12–18, 87–107). Cf. van Minnen (1987), Patterson (2006: 252–4), Gibbs (2011).
⁴³ Van Nijf (1997: 12–18, 87–107), Gibbs (2011: 297–9), Verboven (2011a), Tran (2011), Broekaert (2011), Verboven (2012, 2016). Cf. Adams (2007: 100).
⁴⁴ Gibbs (2011: 298–300), Verboven (2016: 183).
⁴⁵ Verboven (2016: 183–4).
⁴⁶ Ellis-Evans (2012), Kloppenborg (2017).

latter served to assert the association's sense of belonging in the wider community.[47] Kloppenborg also distinguishes between cases when names and amounts are mentioned, which might serve to promote competition in giving to the communal effort, and cases when there is less concern with singling out individuals and more on the group as a whole.[48] In addition, Aneurin Ellis-Evans' study of subscriptions (*epidoseis*) in the civic context generally shows how such lists of contributors served to portray certain demographic cohorts in particular ways and 'to encourage members of the *polis* community to reproduce civic values by publicly acting them out'.[49] This performative dimension to the display of contributors would also play a role for associations and their members.

Many collections discussed in this chapter pertain to raising funds for sacred purposes specifically, including sacrifices, temple renovations, and other dedications to gods and goddesses. This evidence clarifies the highly important place of deities within the lives of many associations and their members. Participants within these associations placed considerable value, sometimes expressed in material terms, on both honouring and being seen honouring gods and goddesses. Collecting funds to honour these deities was one way in which such groups could publicize who they thought they were within a broader civic context, demonstrating the role of the group in maintaining positive relations with divine powers who helped to protect the broader community.

In some cases, ethnic identifications came to the fore in the financial choices that were made by members of an association in, for instance, renovating or establishing a sanctuary or erecting a monument for a deity that was the patron deity of their original place of origin. For immigrant associations in the diaspora, collections could be used both to express belonging within the local community and to reassert the members' ties with their homeland and its ancestral customs, as we have begun to see with those devoted to the foreign, Israelite deity on Delos. Taking a look at further groups devoted to this foreign god in the diaspora will enrich our picture of collective action, group cohesion and honours for deities.

---

[47] Kloppenborg (2017: 323–5).
[48] Cf. ibid., 321–2.
[49] Ellis-Evans (2012: 112).

7

Communal Collections

Part 2: Associations Devoted to the Israelite God

Let each one of you individually make a deposit, storing whatever amount if a person makes a profit, so that collections do not need to be made when I come.
1 Cor 16:1–3

Introduction

In addressing those who participated in an assembly at Corinth in southern Greece, Paul takes for granted the communal custom of gathering collections but specifies how he would like such practices to be implemented for a particular project. Our discussion of collections by associations in the previous chapter provides a framework for comparing practices within groups devoted to the Israelite god, such as the collections facilitated by Paul, who himself identifies as Israelite or Judean. Conversely, the customs of these groups devoted to a foreign deity may shed further light on other immigrant gatherings and cultural minority groups and on associations generally.

Yet there are some obstacles facing the social historian who wishes to assess financial collections among those devoted to the Israelite god in relation to other associations. First of all, the majority of our evidence for collections by Judeans and by groups of mixed ethnicity that adopted the Israelite deity is literary, while almost everything we know about other associations comes from inscriptions or papyri. The difficulty here is that, as social historians, we should not expect these two quite different types of sources to supply us with the same sorts of socioeconomic information. On the other hand, while there are many inscriptions that have survived concerning Judean gatherings in the diaspora, only a handful happen to provide insights into communal fund-raising or the procedures involved. Similarly, the earliest monuments set up by followers of Jesus (which only begin to be noticeable following 190 CE) generally do not happen to mention communal financial customs. If we were to rely solely on epigraphic evidence for Judeans and adherents of Jesus, then, we would have to admit that we generally lacked evidence that these groups engaged in collections much at all, in contrast to the noticeable epigraphic evidence for these financial practices in other associations. Still, we do indeed have literary sources that refer to such practices among groups devoted to the Israelite god.

The other side of the coin here is that these apparent obstacles can actually be seen as an advantage from another angle. In terms of quantity, the literary and epigraphic evidence for groups of people in the diaspora identified as 'Judeans' (*Ioudaioi*, traditionally rendered in English as 'Jews') exceeds that for virtually any other set of immigrant associations engaged in ancestral customs of a particular homeland (e.g. Syrians, Italians, Phrygians, Egyptians). We have further literary evidence pertaining to those of other ethnic backgrounds who joined cultural minority groups devoted to the Israelite god, along with an additional focus on Jesus as that god's emissary or anointed one. So these associations provide another angle on our questions, providing an important piece in the puzzle of how unofficial collectivities of various kinds could manage their material situations and survive.

So, for these groups devoted to the Israelite god, we often need to rely (carefully) on the educated literary types who happen to incidentally refer to such financial practices in limited ways and with specific purposes in mind. Because it aligned with Josephus' agenda of defending Judean cultural practices, Josephus happens to make multiple references to diaspora Judeans' collections used to support ancestral customs. In particular, there is significant evidence regarding diaspora Judeans' material support for sacrifices and activities at the second temple in Jerusalem, before its destruction by the Romans in 70 CE.[1] Beyond yearly temple-contributions, which are also mentioned in other contemporary Judean and Roman sources which we will discuss, references to communal fund-raising are not very common in Judean literature, but we will find some other hints.

While Josephus was engaged in a form of apologetic historiography, the Judean Paul wrote letters to specific groups consisting of Greeks and others devoted to the Israelite god. It is only because one specific type of collection was key to Paul's central aim of including Greeks and other non-Judeans in a movement devoted to the Israelite god that we know much at all about fund-raising among groups in Macedonia, Achaia and, less so, Galatia. While there are other passages in literature of the second and third centuries that will occupy us in the next chapter on mutual aid, it is Paul's letters that occupy us here on the issue of communal collections among groups of Jesus adherents in the mid-first century.

Judean collections to support ancestral customs

The most substantial evidence for associations of Judean immigrants collecting together money pertains to periodic contributions for ancestral customs, particularly relating to the Jerusalem temple. So it is important to provide some background on this practice. As a Jerusalemite of a priestly family, Josephus could speak proudly of the wealth of the temple in Jerusalem, and he pinpoints contributions by Judeans 'throughout the world' as part of the reason for this. Judeans 'from Asia and Europe had

---

[1] See Mandell (1984), Horbury (1984), Trebilco (1991: 13–16), Barclay (1996: 238, 265–7, 417–24), ibid. (2006), Richardson (2004: 244–7).

Figure 7.1 Tyrian shekel dated 31/30 BCE, with bust of the god Melqart and eagle. Courtesy of the Art Institute of Chicago, used under a Creative Commons Zero licence.

been contributing (*sympherontōn*) to the temple for a very long time', he states (*Ant.* 14. 110–11). The yearly temple contribution or first-fruits offering, which was based on a passage in Exodus (20:11–16), was a half-shekel (≈ 2 drachmas or 2 denarii in the first century) that was, in theory, paid by male Israelites who were more than 20 years old (cf. Matt 17:27). The Tyrian shekel – often used by those who actually made the trip to Jerusalem in order to pay the temple contribution (e.g. *T. Ketub.* 12) – is pictured in Figure 7.1. Such contributions in the form of other coins or precious metals from the diaspora were sent to Jerusalem to support the sacrificial system of the temple in honour of the Israelite god, even if a person did not make the journey. The beginning point of such yearly monetary contributions is not known, but the custom likely dates after the construction of the second temple (after 500 BCE) and may be as late as the Hasmonean period (post-160s BCE), as William Horbury argues.[2]

Philo of Alexandria in Egypt claims that these contributions (*aparchai*) were 'given with utmost zeal' and that the donors brought them voluntarily, believing that the donor would receive special protection or benefits from the god in return (Philo, *Special Laws* 1.76–8). Similarly, Sara Mandell points out that there is no evidence to suggest that this payment was considered mandatory for all Judeans.[3] A corollary is that the scholarly terminology of 'temple tax' may mislead, we suggest. This changed when the Romans transformed this payment with the institution of their version of a 'Judean tax' (*fiscus iudaicus*) after the second temple was destroyed in 70 CE. Members of Judean gatherings in the diaspora identified with the homeland and with fellow Judeans at the local level, in part, by raising funds to maintain ancestral customs for their ancestral deity, as was also the case with the Italians, Syrians, Tyrians, Berytians, Idumeans and Israelites discussed in previous chapters.

---

[2] See Horbury (1984: 277–82).
[3] Mandell (1984).

Evidence for the collection of the yearly temple contribution is primarily limited to literary sources, and in most cases apologetic ones. These same sources also point to collections for other local purposes as well. Although the materials presented by Josephus are error-prone on the names and titles of officials, for instance, it seems that Josephus is reliable with regard to the overall practice among Judean associations, as sometimes confirmed by both Cicero and Philo.[4] The literary materials are also rather limited in terms of geography: one passage in Josephus' writings deals with Cyrenaica and virtually all the others pertain to the province of Asia (western Asia Minor) or nearby Aegean islands. Furthermore, most of what has been documented in literary sources pertains to the anomalous problems particular to the politically and financially turbulent first century BCE, when instability among the Roman elites (civil war) sometimes led to instability in provinces such as Asia, as John M. G. Barclay clarifies.[5] Still, we can discern several important things about procedures from these relatively limited materials.

The earliest incident pertaining to monetary collections by Judean gatherings relates to Mithridates VI Eupator and the island of Kos (c. 88 BCE). Josephus cites a source by Strabo to the effect that, when Mithridates captured Kos, he seized money. Josephus claims that 800 talents of this stolen money had belonged to Judeans (*Ant.* 14.111–12). With 1 talent equalling 6,000 drachmas, this would amount to 4.8 million drachmas, a massive and somewhat unbelievable sum. So one may doubt Josephus' numbers and this may have included collected money beyond funds for the temple. Anyhow, Josephus claims that this was earmarked for the god, likely for the temple in Jerusalem. Josephus goes on to argue that this money was transferred from the Judeans in the cities of Asia to Kos for safekeeping.

Chronologically, our next glimpse into collections by Judeans in Asia once again entails difficulties in achieving aims of supporting ancestral sacrifices in the homeland. As proconsul of Asia in a financially problematic time, L. Valerius Flaccus had decided to enforce a previous decision that gold should not be exported from the province. In the process, he seized over 100 pounds of gold headed for Jerusalem that belonged to Judeans from Apameia and Laodikeia in Phrygia and from Adramytteion and Pergamon in Mysia, according to the defence lawyer, Marcus Tullius Cicero (*For Flaccus* 28.68). As Barclay notes, 100 pounds of gold would amount to over 100,000 drachmas, a considerable sum that would likely be the result of several years' worth of temple funds from numerous Judean groups, if this number is accurate.[6]

The fact that the four cities that are named in the legal case were on the proconsul's assize circuit – namely, his pattern of holding legal hearings – may suggest a rather developed system of collection by Judean groups in Asia modelled on provincial networks. Smaller communal collections may have been sent by a team of local Judeans to significant centres before the transportation of larger sums to Jerusalem, again by a team of Judeans.[7] So there are hints of collection procedures in the evidence and signs of some organization.

[4] See the excellent discussion of the Josephus material by Barclay (1996: 262–81).
[5] See Barclay (1996: 259–319).
[6] Ibid., 266.
[7] Cf. Trebilco (1991: 14).

In light of the Israelite immigrants on Delos who made contributions for rites at mount Gerizim in Samaria (see Chapter 6), it is noteworthy that Judeans on the island of Delos seem to have likewise made collections. In a letter attributed to Julius Caesar (*c.* 46 BCE), Josephus reports that Judeans on Delos had appealed to Roman authorities because local civic leaders had changed policy for some reason. According to the complainants, these authorities were no longer allowing Judeans 'to live in accordance with their customs and to contribute money to common meals and sacred rites' (*Ant.* 14.213–16). Overall, the concern of the letter, as with most of these documents relating to diplomacy with the Romans, was to permit the observation of 'ancestral customs and sacred rites (*tois patriois ethesi kai hierois*)'. In the case of the Delian Judeans, there is no reference to the temple contribution in particular. So these financial contributions may have been put to purposes beyond support of the temple, both commensal and ritual. Another roughly contemporary document (attributed to Dolabella) likewise emphasizes Judeans' rights to follow ancestral customs, including the right to gather funds 'set aside (*aphairēmatōn*) for sacrifices', likely a reference to funds for sacrifices in the Jerusalem temple, not local ones (*Ant.* 14.223–7).

The Roman authorities' recognition of a group's right to maintain ancestral customs was by no means limited to the Judeans, so we should not imagine this allowance to be special treatment for Judeans in particular compared to others who sought acknowledgement or specific favours (see also the discussion of 'diplomacy' as benefaction in Chapter 5).[8] Tessa Rajak quite some time ago thoroughly demonstrated major problems with imagining the Romans granting to Judeans special treatment in the form of a legal charter of protections or 'Magna Carta' of sorts.[9] There are many other clear examples from Asia of local associations or cults engaging in diplomatic relations by appealing to proconsuls or other Roman leaders in order to maintain traditional rites.[10] In some cases, this diplomacy with Roman authorities was done in the face of opposition from the current civic leadership who had made some change that hindered a group's ability to engage in such traditional customs. So the Judean case is not unique in that respect (see *GRA* II 128, with commentary). What is most notable here is that Roman authorities typically gave positive responses to any request to continue already established rites and practices, often described as 'ancestral customs' by those making the request. It did not matter much what the content of those ancestral customs was. Judeans were peculiar in that their ancestral customs focused attention on their own patron deity usually to the exclusion of other gods.

Josephus presents further instances of Judeans engaging in collections as reflected in several other Roman imperial letters or pronouncements from the time of the first emperor, Augustus (27 BCE–14 CE). These documents pertaining to Ephesos, Sardis and, more generally, the province of Asia once again underline the ongoing significance of communal fund-raising among Judean associations into the imperial era. These documents also provide some further details regarding procedures. Several of these diplomatic sources are concerned specifically with affirming the Judean freedom to

---

[8] Cf. Harland (2013: 192–6) = ibid. (2003: 220–4).
[9] Rajak (1984).
[10] See commentary on *GRA* II 128. Cf. *IMilet* 360 (80–82 CE).

collect and transport sacred funds to the temple in Jerusalem 'in accordance with their ancestral customs' (*kata ta patria*) and with forbidding the theft of 'sacred monies' (*hiera chrēmata*), as in Agrippa's correspondence with Ephesos.[11] A decree of Augustus himself, which was apparently to be set up in the temple of the provincial League of Asia, further adds that sacred monies taken up to Jerusalem should be considered 'inviolable' (*asylia*).[12] Any attempt to steal such funds would therefore be subject to the usual laws for temple robbery (*hierosylos*).

Augustus' decree refers to local structures (*sabbateion, aarōn*, or *andrōn*), where the money and sacred books were stored for relative safety. The use of some sort of treasury or secured receptacle comparable to those discussed in the previous chapter is implied by Philo's statement that: 'practically in every city there are treasuries for the sacred money' (*tamaiea tōn hierōn chrēmatōn*; Philo, *Special Laws* 1.77–8).

Another document concerning Ephesos that is presented by Josephus further clarifies certain procedures in managing the funds. The proconsul Julius Antonius gives permission to Judeans 'to follow their own laws and customs, and to bring the offerings (*aparchas*), which each of them makes voluntarily out of piety towards the god'.[13] But he also speaks of them 'travelling together under escort without being hindered in any way' (*Ant.* 16.172–3; 9–2 BCE). It is noteworthy that the root for 'offerings' here is that found in the inscriptions of the Israelites on Delos discussed earlier and in other Delian inscriptions pertaining to offerings for Apollo, so a variety of communities shared a common semantic field for contributions to a deity.[14]

Other Judean collections

So there are clear signs that at least some Judean gatherings made collections for the purpose of sending funds to the Jerusalem temple before its destruction in 70 CE. We have also seen hints of other similarly organized collections for the local performance of ancestral customs. Yet collections by Judean groups for other purposes are not widely attested. However, a case from Berenike in Cyrenaica in the mid-first century is suggestive of the possibilities among these immigrants settled throughout the Mediterranean. Like other immigrants, Judeans at Berenike had formed themselves into an association, and we know about the group from inscriptions on three monuments (*CJZC* 70–2).[15] The group apparently used two different self-designations for an association: 'corporate body' (*politeuma*) and 'gathering' (*synagōgē*). The inscription that most interests us here was set up to document renovations to a building, and the building itself seems to be designated a 'synagogue'. This is among the

---

[11] Josephus, *Ant.* 16.167–8; cf. *Ant.* 16.171, on Sardis (18–12 BCE); *Ant.* 16.166 (18–16 BCE); *Ant.* 16.169–70, on Judeans at Cyrene.
[12] *Ant.* 16.162–5, 12 BCE. Cf. Philo, *Embassy to Gaius* 311–15.
[13] Cf. Philo, *Special Laws* 1.7, regarding *aparchai*.
[14] For a relatively early use of *aparchai* for offerings, see Athenian decree on supervision of wheat and barley *aparchai* dedicated to Demeter and Persephone at Eleusis (*IEleus* 28A = *SEG* 42:17; Athens, c. 435 BCE).
[15] Reynolds (1977: 242–7, nos 16–18).

earlier uses of a common self-designation for a 'gathering' (*synagōgē*) to refer to a *building* in which the gathering took place, but the earliest usage in this way may be the 'synagogue of Zeus' near Apameia in Bithynia (if that is a reference to a building and not only to a gathering).[16]

The Judean inscription from Berenike begins by stating that it 'seemed good to the synagogue of the Judeans in Berenike that they should inscribe on a monument of Parian stone the names of those who contributed towards the restoration (*eis episkeuēn*) of the synagogue'. The names of at least eighteen contributors to the project then follow. Ten of the legible names are identified as leaders (archons) and one as a priest, and there are at least two women contributors. In this case, the donation values are not presented in descending order. One person contributed 28 drachmas, two others gave 25 drachmas, ten gave 10 drachmas and four others, including the two women, gave 5 drachmas. Much like adherents of the goddess Atargatis on Delos and many other associations dealt with in the previous chapter, these Judeans made a collective effort to raise funds in connection with their meeting place. There is very little to distinguish the procedures and monumentalizing customs of these Judeans from the standard associative approach. These may also be the sort of communal collections that also preceded the construction and corporate dedication of Judean prayer-houses in Egypt, which we discussed in an earlier chapter.

The methods used to collect yearly temple payments or to renovate or construct buildings like the ones at Berenike or in Egypt could presumably be adapted for other communal projects, even though we rarely have evidence of these. There are hints of this in Rabbinic sources, though. If Tannaitic prescriptions reflect some reality, Gregg Elliot Gardner's recent work on what he casts as 'organized charity for the poor' in Rabbinic literature may provide other instances of collections.[17] There is a sense in which we could reserve discussion of these materials to the next chapter on mutual assistance, so this Judean case should be remembered there. But here we are more concerned with procedures surrounding communal collections for various purposes.

There are two main concepts in Rabbinic materials that may be interpreted in terms of the development of procedures (Gardner ambitiously calls them 'institutions') aimed at helping attendees with lesser means within some Rabbinic Judean settings from the early third century CE, perhaps including synagogue settings. The Rabbinic writings known as the *Tosefta* provide the clearest references to the 'basket' (*quppa*) and the 'dish' (*tamhui*) in the sense of a communal 'fund' and a 'soup kitchen' for the poor respectively, as Gardner interprets these concepts. The latter term apparently reflects the practice of redistributing food to the poor as prescribed by certain rabbis. *Tosefta Peah* (4:9) suggests that such redistributions of food could take place on any day of the week. This may then reflect an instance of mutual aid among Judeans. Yet the passage in *Tosefta* does not make it clear where these redistributions took place, whether among members of a specific diaspora gathering or among people in a Palestinian village or town setting, so an association context is not guaranteed.

---

[16] *IApamBith* 35 = *GRA* II 99 (119 or 104 BCE).
[17] Gardner (2009), a dissertation revised and published as Gardner (2015).

The former term, 'basket' (*quppa*), does seem to suggest a communal collection of money that could be drawn from on Sabbath evenings specifically (*Tosefta Peah* 4:9). A corresponding Mishnah passage advises that this was to be collected by at least two people and managed or distributed by at least three (*Mishnah Peah* 8:7). Furthermore, as Gardner argues, the social settings in which needy members were to draw on such a communal fund do seem to include 'the sabbath in the synagogue', at least for those in line with the opinion attributed to the House of Hillel (and not the House of Shammai, according to *Tosefta Shabbat* 16:22a–g). Unfortunately, as far as we can find, none of the inscriptions pertaining to Judean gatherings happen to confirm that such prescriptions in Rabbinic writings were actually implemented at any particular diaspora locale in the first three centuries, including Aphrodisias. There is a possibility of a 'soup kitchen for the poor' (if that is what the Greek *patella*, literally 'dish', means) in an inscription from Aphrodisias (*IAph* 11.55).[18] However, the inscription is now usually dated to the fourth or fifth centuries rather than the late second, and the soup-kitchen interpretation is questionable.[19]

Jesus adherents and collections

The discussion of associations and Judean gatherings so far provides a framework for understanding financial collections in groups focused on Jesus, including Paul's collection for Jerusalem. Details of procedure in Paul's letters may also shed light on associations generally. Last's earlier book on the financial workings of the Corinthian assemblies in comparison with associations generally shows just how problematic it is to imagine these assemblies with 'no organized system of finance' or no economic structures.[20] Some degree of economic organization was 'a necessity rather than a luxury', as we have shown in the previous chapters, and so there is value in considering material conditions in these assemblies alongside other associations.[21]

The earliest references to such collections are, of course, found in Paul's letters. Paul refers to an agreement that was made early on (perhaps around 50 CE) with the 'so-called' pillars at Jerusalem that he would 'remember the poor (*ptōchoi*)' (Galatians 2:10).[22] This is not the place to engage fully the extensive scholarship on this topic, except to say that this financial collection for 'the poor' or 'the holy ones' in Jerusalem was not a side issue for Paul.[23] And the reasons for the collection's importance went well beyond mere material relief or 'charity', if we can even appropriately use such a term. Rather, this was central to the whole legitimacy of Paul's aim to include Greeks

---

[18] On which, see Reynolds and Tannenbaum (1987: 26–8).
[19] See Chaniotis (2002). Cf. Williams (1992).
[20] Conzelmann as cited by Last (2013: 80) = ibid. (2016a: 115).
[21] See, especially, Last (2013: 29–37, 79–80). Cf. ibid. (2016a: 114–15).
[22] Unlike Downs (2008: 35) and Bruce Longenecker (2010: 157–82), we see this reference to assisting 'the poor' in Jerusalem (Gal 2:10; Rom 15:26) as directly connected to other passages regarding collections in these assemblies, rather than as Paul's general principle regarding material aid for those who were poor in other contexts (beyond Jerusalem).
[23] For discussion, see Georgi (1992 [1965]), Hurtado (1979), Joubert (2000), Wedderburn (2002), Downs (2006, 2008), Friesen (2010), Ogereau (2012).

(and other non-Judeans) in a movement devoted to a foreign god, the Israelite god. For this reason, the collection was pivotal to the self-understanding of these groups as Paul conceived that.[24]

The link between Paul's primarily Greek-speaking groups devoted to the Israelite deity and the Judean homeland was important. Having these uncircumcized adherents of Jesus collect money for Judeans at Jerusalem was one way that Paul sought to lessen tensions and bridge a connection between Judeans and Greeks. This may have had something to do with Paul's Judean apocalyptic notions: the end was near and 'gentiles' or 'peoples' (*ethnē*, namely all non-Judean peoples) would play some role – an important one in Paul's particular view – in the unfolding of the Israelite god's final plan.[25] The legitimacy of Paul's efforts was at stake in the relationship with Jerusalem leaders. These leaders included James, the brother of Jesus, and some of the disciples who had accompanied Jesus while he was alive – a close connection that Paul could not claim (see, especially, Gal 1–2).

This backdrop is one of the reasons why references to the collection of money recur with some urgency in Paul's letters. In writing to those in Galatia, Paul mentions his initial meeting with leaders ('so-called pillars', in his terms) of the movement at Jerusalem, where the plan for raising funds to send to 'the poor' (*ptōchoi*) in Jerusalem was established (Gal 2:10; cf. Rom 15:26). It is not clear whether 'the poor' here is meant as a reference to those who were literally destitute or rather to those who designated themselves 'the poor' in the sense of being 'the righteous' or 'the pious', since Israelite and Judean literature regularly uses the term with connotations beyond the material.[26] Whatever the case may be, the issue of such collections comes up again and again in Paul's correspondence, from the beginning to the end of his travels. For key passages beyond Galatians 2, see: 1 Corinthians 16:1–4; 2 Corinthians 8:1–9:15; Romans 15:14–32.

The success of Paul's collection remains unknown, but the last time he refers to it (probably in the early to mid-60s CE), he seems worried that this gift or offering or benefaction (depending on how one interprets the action and from whose perspective) may not be accepted by those in Jerusalem. This despite the fact that the Macedonians and the Achaians had been successful in gathering funds, although the Galatians are conspicuously absent in the key passage (Romans 15:25–32):

> At present . . . I am going to Jerusalem in order to be a service to the holy ones. For Macedonia and Achaia have been pleased to form a partnership (*koinōnian*)[27] for the poor among the holy ones at Jerusalem. They were pleased to do it. Indeed, they are in debt to them, for if the peoples have come to be a partner in their spiritual

---

[24] See now Kloppenborg (2017: 307–11) for an overview of five theories regarding the motivations for the collection.

[25] Munck (1959), Donaldson (2007) Fredrickson (2017).

[26] See, for instance, the custom among members of the Dead Sea sect: 1QH 5.1, 21; 18.14; 1QM 14.7; 1QpHab 12.3, 6, 10. Cf. *Psalms of Solomon* 5.2, 13. See also Skarsaune (2007: 424–7, on Ebionites, although he does not think this logic should be applied to the Jerusalem group in Paul's time). For the application to Galatians, see Richard N. Longenecker (1990: 104–5).

[27] On translating 'partnership' or 'participation' or 'sharing' (rather than 'contribution', as is common), see Ogereau (2012: 366–71). Ogereau's claim that Paul creates a 'new order of socioeconomic equality and solidarity' seems theologically motivated, however.

benefits, they should also be of service to them in material benefits ... I appeal to you, brothers, by our Lord Jesus Christ and by the love of the spirit, to strive together with me in your prayers to god on my behalf, that I may be rescued from the disobedient ones in Judea, and that my service for Jerusalem *may be acceptable* to the holy ones. This would have the result that, by god's will, I may come to you with joy and be comforted by you.

Paul is apparently asking the Romans to pray that the communal collections by assemblies associated with him not be rejected by the Jerusalem leadership due to the ongoing tensions surrounding Paul's inclusion of other peoples without requiring circumcision (see Galatians as a whole). That will need to suffice as an overview of the situation behind Paul's collection here. For what matters more to us are some of the actual procedures involved in making collections within associations established by Paul. These procedures may well have influenced subsequent fund-raising for other purposes in these same groups.

The most crucial passages for understanding the connection between the associative practices we have seen in the previous chapter and the practices within groups founded by Paul are encountered in his letters to those at Corinth. It is important to notice the use of similar terminology to what we have encountered in earlier chapters. Paul instructs those at Corinth regarding weekly collections for the 'holy ones' in Jerusalem in the following way (1 Cor 16:1–3):

> Now concerning the collection (*logeias*) for the holy ones: just as I directed the assemblies of Galatia, so you are likewise to do. On the day after the Sabbath, let each one of you individually make a deposit, storing (*thēsaurizōn*) whatever amount if a person makes a profit, so that collections (*logeiai*) do not need to be made when I come. Whenever I arrive, I will send those whom you approve (*dokimasēte*) by letter to carry your gift to Jerusalem. If it seems appropriate that I should go as well, they will come with me.

In this passage, Paul refers to his proposed procedure for fund-raising among members of the groups with whom he interacts. They were to gradually gather the funds, storing whatever amount they could each week. This was done to avoid the problem of raising funds for a project on the spur of the moment when Paul came to visit. Still, he speaks in a way that suggests that sometimes this more spontaneous approach was, in fact, the procedure in these same groups.

Paul also employs terms familiar to us from epigraphic evidence for fund-raising activities of associations and other contemporary cults. We have discussed the use of the Greek term he uses in this passage (*logeia*) for a 'collection' in several cases. For instance, we found a group of women on Paros island employing the corresponding verb to describe collecting money to restore their sanctuary. Furthermore, Paul's instruction to 'deposit' and 'store' weekly contributions uses a verb (*thēsaurizōn*) corresponding to the noun for an offering receptacle or treasury (*thēsauros*). We have seen just how common such collection and storage procedures were in a number of settings.

On a more specific detail which is significant, although not essential, to our argument here, there are two main ways in which the phrase which literally means 'by himself' or 'by itself' (*par' heautō*) – but has several extended meanings – has been interpreted recently. Paul recommends 'putting' (*tithetō*) 'aside' (*par' heautō*) the money, with the main concern being that the group store (*thēsaurizōn*) the money separately from other funds they collected for other purposes.[28] This concern over the placement of the funds may reflect a broader associative practice of keeping collections separate from regular membership contributions and other income in order to avoid misuse of the funds.[29] While several previous interpreters have also taken the prepositional phrase in this way, the Greek does not permit any conclusion to be made on where *precisely* these collections were to be stored, whether at home or paid to the group's treasurer, for instance. Paul does not seem to micromanage the collection to that degree. In this interpretation, the main practical consideration addressed in 1 Corinthians 16:1–2 seems to be the act of keeping the funds separate from other collections.[30] Paul's unstated assumption on this model, of course, is that members were bringing in regular contributions ('fees') and other income, as well.

On the other hand, if the phrase (*par' heautō*) is taken to be qualifying the preceding subject – 'each of you' (*hekastos hymōn*) – then this may merely be understood to reinforce the point that each member should 'by himself', that is, 'separately' or 'individually' (*par' heautō*), contribute some funds to the collection – a point that could be made by 'each of you' (*hekastos hymōn*) alone.[31] S. R. Llewelyn offers several literary instances of this usage.[32] David J. Downs offers epigraphic ones, including a stipulation in an inscription from Delos that 'each of the cities *individually* (*tas poleis hekastas par' heautais*) should engrave the decree and make dedications in their temples, which is their custom'.[33]

In either of the above interpretations of Paul's phrasing, the funds were supplied individually by each member. Both interpretations also allow for the contributions to have been provided *during the meeting*. If either of these interpretations is adopted, then, by the mid-first century, those at Corinth, at least, had a meeting or a communal meal on the day after Sabbath, on Sunday or the 'Lord's day'.[34]

If Paul's recommended procedure was to take place during a meeting rather than at home, then the evidence for associations using offering receptacles provides a very close analogy for what Paul was proposing. Each week, on a day when the group met (Sunday), members of the assemblies were, individually, to deposit a portion of their

---

[28] Last (2016a: 137–8). Cf. Fee (1987: 813), Young (2003). In this interpretation, the prepositional phrase (*par' heautō*) is the verb's locative indirect object ('to put aside'), as is common when it occurs elsewhere. See, for instance, Xenophon, *Cyropaedia* 1.2.8 and 6.1.49.
[29] Last (2016a: 141–6). On misappropriation, see Kloppenborg (2017: 312–18).
[30] Last (2016b: 141–6).
[31] Cf. Llewelyn (2001: 209).
[32] E.g. Aristotle, *On Sterility* 511b; Dio Cassius, *Roman History* 63.28.5.
[33] *IG* XI,4 1040, lines 21–3 (287 BCE). Cf. *SEG* 43:26, from Acharnai (315 BCE). Downs (2008: 128 n. 29).
[34] Cf. Acts 20:7; Rev 1:10; *Didache* 14.1; Ignatius, *Magnesians* 9.1–3 (*c.* 110 CE); *Gospel of Peter* 35, 50 (*c.* 150 CE). On the question of the meeting day, see most recently, Llewelyn (2001) vs Young (2003). Cf. Downs (2008: 127–9).

profits into a common treasury or offering receptacle for safe keeping for 'the poor' at Jerusalem. The terminology that Norman H. Young employs when he objects to the notion that Pauline groups would have a 'central ecclesiastical bank' betrays a lack of knowledge of the less institutional uses of secured, collection receptacles within associations as we outlined in the previous chapter.[35]

Although Downs gives some attention to associations, he also seems to miss the potential value of the associative materials here for interpreting Paul's use of depositing and storing terminology. This may be due, in part, to Downs' attempt to argue that Paul was advocating for an approach that would subvert normal expectations or values associated with benefaction or patronage.[36] The tendency to see Paul rising above or fighting against local cultural customs sometimes leads to the neglect of other more mundane explanations or analogies.

Furthermore, in this same passage in 1 Corinthians, Paul refers to the approval of a team to bring the funds to Jerusalem. This is what we should expect if a key issue in 1 Corinthians 16:1–2 is potential misappropriation of funds. It seems that those given this responsibility would be drawn from and 'approved' (with the use of *dokimazō* to indicate choosing after scrutiny) by members of an assembly at Corinth. Our earlier discussion of associations at Kallatis, Kyme and Liopesi shows that it was not unusual for members of an association to appoint collectors in conjunction with fund-raising for a particular purpose, or even as ongoing officers within the group. Such functionaries were responsible for collecting and managing funds, but also ensuring that such funds reached their proper destination and were disbursed in the ways that were arranged by the group or its leaders. Similarly, with ethnic associations of Judeans, there were signs that certain people would be appointed to ensure the proper delivery of contributions for the temple. And prescriptions regarding the 'basket' collection in later Rabbinic sources likewise envision a group of at least two collectors and three managers of the funds. So Paul's procedures here may be placed within this broader framework of careful management of communal funds.

Also important are the factors that served to encourage or motivate financial giving in groups such as those founded by Paul. The case of the procedures in an association at Kallatis, where the incentives for honorary crowns were set out clearly, were perhaps the most obvious on this point. Publicity and the honour or recognition it brought were among the benefits that might be expected by contributors. In some cases, the method to achieve this was to have a list of contributors inscribed and displayed, and a list of those who failed to pay might also be made. Correspondingly, the absence of one's name from a list of members who had offered funds might lead to dishonour, thereby affecting one's status within that social setting. So there would be social pressure to give in such circumstances.

Moreover, in parts of 2 Corinthians, Paul attempts to place some social pressure on participants within the assemblies in order to have them put even more effort into gathering funds. Paul does so by comparing Jesus adherents at Corinth to the

---

[35] Young (2003: 114).
[36] See also Friesen (2010: 49–52), who agrees with Downs.

materially less well-situated Macedonian adherents. Perhaps the manual labourers at Thessalonica rather than the Philippian adherents are in mind (see 1 Thess 2:9-12; 4:11). Paul says that, despite limited means, the Macedonians had given 'beyond their means, of their own free will (*authairetoi*), pleading with us for the favour of partnership (*koinōnian*) in this service to the holy ones' (2 Cor 8:3-5; cf. 2 Cor 9:13; Phil 1:4-6).

There are further hints of publicity and an honour-shame context for motivating giving. In what might be a separate letter to the Corinthians, Paul once again raises what the Macedonians might think about the Corinthians' collection. Here he mentions that he has been using the Achaian case to encourage the Macedonians in giving as well. So they had better live up to the expectations in case some Macedonians come along the next time Paul visits Corinth (2 Cor 9:3-5): 'I am sending the brothers so that our boasting about you [Corinthians] may not prove pointless in this case, so that you may be ready, as I said you would. I do this in the event that, if some Macedonians come with me and find that you are not ready, we be shamed (*kataischynthōmen*) – to say nothing of you – for being so confident.' The implications are quite clear here. Paul is providing the Corinthian addressees an opportunity to be publicly recognized for giving generously to the collection, thereby gaining a positive reputation among assemblies elsewhere. The idea seems to be that the Corinthians' relative success or failure in comparison with the Macedonians would result in honour or its opposite. So, although there may or may not have been a list of contributors with amounts inscribed in stone and set up for all to see at Corinth, there is the notion that contributions would be publicized and there are signs that the perception of others was a factor which motivated giving.

The competitive implications of this situation are not often recognized: Paul seems to be in some sense encouraging competition (for the benefit of the collection) among these assemblies. Paul does describe the collection not as an exaction (*pleonexia*) but as a voluntary gift (*eulogia*). Yet, as with collections in other associations, it seems that social or peer pressure accompanied the call for 'voluntary' contributions, and the pursuit of honour (*philotimia*) and the avoidance of shame (*aischynē*) would play some role – either with or without Paul's encouragement. So honour both here in these assemblies and in other associations was among the rewards for making material contributions.

There are other important observations to be made concerning the *meaning* of collections in Pauline settings and expressed *motivations* for giving. As with some cases of fund-raising in associations, there are signs that material contributions were part of a system of exchange that included the expectation of benefits of various kinds in return. Such benefits included but were not limited to individual member's honour and status in relation to the group. On the other hand, giving could also be expressed as a *response* to benefits already received, as when members of an association paid to have a monument set up in fulfilment of a vow to the gods, for instance (e.g. *TAM* V 536-7, from Maionia in Lydia). For Paul and for those in the assemblies that accepted his approach, the resources that were to be sent to the 'holy ones' in Jerusalem were, in part, an exchange of *material* benefits for *spiritual* benefits and, as such, can be understood in cultural terms of benefaction and the exchange of benefits.³⁷ As Paul puts it, the Macedonian and Achaian followers of Jesus 'owed' (*opheiletai*) the Judeans. For if the non-Judean peoples had a share in spiritual things as a result of this interaction, they were to contribute material things in return (Rom 15:27). Further benefits would continue in return, however, as those who gave 'bountifully' and not 'reluctantly' could expect an abundance of favours from the deity (2 Cor 9:6–12).

Earlier, we observed that, with many cases of fund-raising in associations, a principal aim was to honour – and *be seen* honouring – such deities. Material matters were closely linked with ritual matters of honour, to put it another way. Like an association that collected funds or materials to build an altar or to construct, purchase or renovate a sanctuary, the collection could also be considered an act of piety or honour for the patron deity that reinforced the importance of that deity for group cohesion. In Paul's case, the offering from non-Judeans would also potentially create greater cohesion with Judeans who were adherents of Jesus. The interpretation of material contributions as an act of honour in relation to a deity was also particularly evident in the case of the Israelites who made contributions for ancestral customs on mount Gerizim and the Judeans who gathered funds that supported sacrifices in Jerusalem. There are many similar situations to be found in dedications of sacred objects, monuments and buildings to gods and goddesses by other associations, of course.

There are clear signs that Paul himself and any of his addressees who adopted Paul's perspective could also interpret the financial service for Jerusalem as an act of piety and thanksgiving towards the Israelite god (see, especially, Rom 15:14–21; 2 Cor 9:11–14). Downs argues strongly that Paul's rhetoric surrounding the collection draws heavily on ritual imagery in a way that expresses the collection as an 'offering to god', an offering by 'the peoples' (non-Judeans) to the Israelite god.³⁸ And, in 2 Corinthians 9, Paul states clearly that the collection not only materially supports those at Jerusalem 'but also overflows in many thanksgivings to god' (v. 12). For Paul, his entire mission was to bring the message to non-Judeans in expectation of the Israelite god's final intervention. Furthermore, the collection was an important component in establishing both the legitimacy of this mission and the link between Judeans and non-Judeans. So the collection could be interpreted as part of the 'work for god' in Paul's 'priestly service of the message of god' (Rom 15:17).

Beyond the collection for Jerusalem, we do not have many details about other fund-raising projects within groups established by Paul. There are, of course, Paul's ongoing issues with materially supporting his own teaching activities. While he rejects benefactions or financial support from those at Corinth (1 Cor 9; 2 Cor 10–13) and engages in manual labour while at Thessalonica, at least, he accepts 'gifts' multiple times from those at Philippi in Macedonia (especially, Phil 4:14–20). Yet the Philippian letter itself gives no indication of how these 'gifts' were gathered together. The 'super-apostles'

---

[37] Downs (2008: 92), like Longenecker (see Chapter 2) unconvincingly claims that Paul (like Philo and Josephus) 'condemned' the ideology of 'pagan benefaction'. For a more balanced approach to Paul, patronage and benefaction, see, especially, Crook (2004). Cf. Joubert (2001), MacGillivray (2009).

[38] Downs (2008). Downs seems on most solid ground in explicating Rom 15:14–32. See also Ascough (1996) on Paul's use of *epiteleō* in 2 Cor 8:1–15.

at Corinth – in relation to whom Paul defends himself – likewise received financial support from a subgroup at that locale (2 Cor 10–13; cf. 1 Cor 9). It is quite possible that the Philippians and Corinthians engaged in concerted communal fund-raising efforts (similar to the procedures used to gather collections in other cases) in order to support the travels and teaching of Paul or other leaders, like the so-called 'super-apostles'. Still, in some cases, material support may also have been a benefaction from one or several wealthier members of the congregation (e.g. Phoebe), rather than a broader communal effort. What is clear is that Paul interprets the contributions by those at Philippi, like the collection for Jerusalem in some respects, as a 'fragrant offering, a sacrifice acceptable and pleasing to god' (Phil 4:18). In return, the givers could expect benefits from the Israelite deity. For Paul, both the collection for Jerusalem and the issue of materially supporting his own teaching activities were intimately connected with the success of his 'call' to the 'peoples', mostly Greeks (Gal 1:15–17).

Conclusion

Devotees of the Israelite god, like many other immigrant associations and other unofficial groups, expressed their sense of belonging together and their common group values by, in part, engaging in communal collections for purposes that were important to them and, in their view, to the god they honoured. There were considerable overlaps in the purposes and procedures adopted by different groups, even though each and every group – whether associated with the Israelite god or not – would have its own more specific techniques, concerns and ways of expressing or justifying what they were doing. Approaching groups devoted to the Israelite god from the social-historical perspective of down-to-earth material factors and socioeconomic procedures helped to highlight often missed aspects of communal life and to cut against the grain of ideologically or theologically motivated explanations of ancient participants and, sometimes, modern scholars. Our attention to social practices and behaviours, rather than on how those engaged in them framed them in ideological or moral terms, will be important as we now turn to the hotly debated issue of mutual aid in unofficial associations.

8

Mutual Assistance and Group Cohesion

We will stand by the man among us who is involved in an unjust legal dispute...[1]
PCairo II 30605

Introduction

Early on, Theodor Mommsen (1843) claimed that associations (*collegia*) served an important function in offering material aid to members, particularly, although not solely, by covering the expense of burial. 'The treasuries of the guilds,' Mommsen states, 'were designed to furnish help to the associates who had need of assistance; they were the ordinary refuges of the orphan and poor, and it was to these treasuries that one left charitable legacies.'[2] More influential than this somewhat Christianizing approach to associations (e.g. the reference to orphans), however, were scholars who strongly challenged the 'charitable' function of 'pagan' associations. Usually, modern moral or theological investments played a role in such challenges as well: 'Roman guilds had organized to secure to their members mutual assurance of a decent funeral, but they did not aid them in the needs or reverses of life.' Furthermore, '*they did not even practice purely human benevolence*'.[3] Writing in 1895, Jean-Pierre Waltzing draws a stark contrast between a superior form of 'charity', which he finds solely among early Christians, and the insignificant support provided to members of other groups: 'Christianity had not given the world a superior conception of charity, a charity which not only inspires in men pity for their unfortunate brothers, but obliges them to offer effective aid and to give, themselves, without reserve.'[4] In other words, participants in most associations did not 'stand by' their fellow members in times of trouble or need – to refer to a contrary statement in a regulation we quoted at the outset of this chapter. The spread of the Jesus movement through the lower classes, Waltzing suggests, promised the development of mutual aid societies informed by the 'Christian spirit'.[5]

---

[1] Translation adapted from Monson (2006: 236).
[2] Mommsen (1843: 91), as cited by Waltzing (1895: 348), an English translation of Waltzing (1895–1900: 1.300–21).
[3] Waltzing (1895: 362, emphasis added).
[4] Ibid., 348. Cf. Hatch (1881: 35–6): 'Other associations were charitable; but whereas in them charity was a accident, in the Christian associations it was of the essence.' On 'charity' and Waltzing's social and political context, see Perry (2006: 85–8).
[5] Waltzing (1895, overall). See Perry (2006: 87).

152   *Group Survival in the Ancient Mediterranean*

More than one hundred years later, Waltzing's sentiments (more so than Mommsen's) continue to echo within Classical Studies, Ancient History, Jewish Studies, and Christian Origins scholarship, where it is still not unusual to find an oversimplified contrast between 'pagan' associations and groups devoted to the Israelite god on the subject of mutual support or 'charity'. Justin Meggitt, Judith Lieu and Pieter van der Horst, for instance, sound a lot like Waltzing when they comment on 'pagan' groups and, instead of considering evidence, dismiss these other associations as irrelevant to the study of economic practices and reciprocal aid among Judeans or Jesus adherents.[6] For Meggitt, only groups devoted to Jesus, and not other associations, adopted 'mutualism as a survival strategy'. Meggitt includes the collection by assemblies associated with Paul as a prime example of such mutualism.[7] Despite the difficulties here, it is notable that Meggitt, unlike others such as Bruce Longenecker, gives particular attention to economic interchanges among the lower strata rather than heavily emphasizing wealthier benefactors within groups devoted to Jesus.[8] But the problematic contrast with other associations – without actually investigating the evidence – remains.

Closely related to these tendencies, it is quite common to encounter groups devoted to Jesus – but not other associations – portrayed as tightly knit, cohesive communities of 'brothers' and 'sisters' in a fictive family, whose extensive engagement in mutual aid was central and *unique*. A study of familial terminology within associations shows some of the fault lines in this scholarly trajectory, but so does attention to mutual aid.[9] Longenecker's recent study on treatment of 'the poor' is more nuanced than Waltzing and others in offering qualifications.[10] Yet Longenecker still employs Christian language of 'charity' (primarily in terms of wealthier members assisting those of lower economic status) and tends to posit a lack of 'charitable initiatives' in the 'pagan' world.

The other side of the coin is that some of the scholars who neglect evidence of associations tend to take certain moral exhortations or apologetic claims in literature produced by devotees of the Israelite god (including Jesus adherents) at face value.[11] Sometimes, scholars consider such rhetoric as representative of day-to-day social realities, rather than carefully considering rhetorical settings and functions.

While recent studies of attitudes towards wealth and poverty among Jesus adherents do briefly mention associations or at least do seek to place such attitudes within broader 'Greco-Roman' or Judean cultural contexts, no careful comparative study of mutual material assistance in unofficial group settings in the eastern Mediterranean has been done.[12] So any scholarly generalizations about what 'pagan' groups or associations

---

[6] Meggitt (1998: 91–2, 170–3), Lieu (2004: 164–9), van der Horst (2016: 119).
[7] Meggitt (1998: 157 and 157–61 generally).
[8] Now see Schellenberg (2018).
[9] On this problem, see Harland (2009: 61–96) = ibid. (2005b).
[10] Longenecker (2010: 68–70, 98–9).
[11] For instance, Lieu cites Aristides' *Apology* 15.7–9 (discussed towards the end of our chapter) as though Aristides offers a descriptive statement of social behaviours of mutual support among Jesus adherents rather than a defensive one. This seems contrary to Lieu's own warnings just a few pages later against taking such literary sources at their word. Lieu (2004: 165, 168).
[12] E.g. Holman (2008), Longenecker and Liebengood (2009), Longenecker (2010: 68–70, 98–9), Rhee (2012).

supposedly did would be premature, to say the least. Some works by ancient historians do begin to touch on such matters, including Marie-François Baslez's brief article about 'mutual aid' in associations of Attica and Andrew Monson's, Philip F. Venticinque's and Matthew Gibbs' insightful studies on what Egyptian associations offered their participants.[13]

More than a century after Waltzing, we are in a better position to reconsider mutual material support among members with careful reference to papyri and inscriptions from places like Egypt, Asia Minor and Greece. Few scholars of Christian origins, Jewish Studies or Ancient History today have made themselves familiar with this looming evidence. And so it is time to reassess the issue of mutual aid among participants in associations based on analysis of this evidence. Simultaneously, we need to carefully avoid modern theological or moral judgements that often stand behind discussions about concepts such as 'brotherly love', 'charity' and 'almsgiving', value-loaded Jewish or Christian insider terms. Such terms need to be set aside as unhelpful, at least as analytical or scholarly categories. Scholars' employment of such terms tends to load the deck in favour of the 'uniqueness' of Judeans or Jesus adherents from the outset, when the social historian is better off not loading the deck at all. Instead, here we employ the intentionally neutral terms 'mutual aid', 'mutual assistance' and 'socioeconomic assistance' as synonyms to refer to evidence of *actual practices* or *behaviours* that involve one participant in a group – or a group as a whole – helping another participant in some material way.

There are indications that mutual socioeconomic assistance in this sense was an important principle for at least a substantial portion of associations in the eastern Mediterranean beyond gatherings devoted to the Israelite god. While cultural precedents or ideological explanations (along with insider terminologies) for such behaviours could, of course, vary depending on a specific group's self-understanding or on local cultural norms, a similar range of evidence reflecting *actual practices* is found in a variety of groups. These practices both flow from, and help to explain, the significant ties that formed and held members together, contributing to group sustainability and longevity. We argue that, in this way, mutual aid is intimately related to group cohesion and survival.

Defining social capital

In considering the implications of social bonding for access to material or non-material resources, we are treading on theoretical ground covered by the sociological concept of 'social capital'. This is a scholarly (etic) concept that pertains to the trust or 'goodwill that is engendered by the fabric of social relations and that can be mobilized to facilitate action'.[14] It has to do with 'actual and potential resources embedded within, available

---

[13] Baslez (2006), Monson (2006), Venticinque (2010), Gibbs (2011). Garnsey and Saller (1987: 156), sound more like Mommsen than Waltzing: '*Collegia* ... were essentially mutual aid societies formed to meet basic needs of their members.' Anneliese Parkin helpfully surveys Greek and Roman *elite* perspectives on begging and on giving to the poor, but this provides little insight into the view from below (Parkin, 2006). Cf. Hands (1968) and Bolkestein (1939).

[14] Adler and Kwon (2002: 17).

through, and derived from the network of relationships possessed by an individual or social unit'.[15] Such resources are by no means limited to the material, however. Some studies of social capital focus attention on resources accessed by a group through external ties, also known as *bridging* forms of social capital. This is along the lines of what we have witnessed in interactions between an association and an external supporter. Other studies in this area emphasize internal, *bonding* forms of social capital.[16] With bonding forms, social capital primarily dwells within the close internal ties among members of a group, ties that hold members together as a cohesive whole and that foster the pursuit of collective goals.[17] It is primarily this latter, internal dimension of bonding that occupies us in this chapter and that dovetails well with our concern to understand and explain the survival of associations in the ancient Mediterranean.

Internal benefactions as mutual support

In discussing benefaction, we have already seen that donors could be people from outside of the group. In these circumstances involving bridging forms of social capital, participants reached out into external networks in a way that afforded access to resources, sometimes material. Yet there were also internal benefactors, as when members helped to finance a group's activities. These provide another example of mutual aid as one member engages in behaviour that supports other participants or the group as a whole.

Members of associations could be very much aware that they were competing not only for resources from external supporters but also for voluntary contributions and assistance from fellow associates, as illustrated here by two instances from the Piraeus, port city of Athens, and one instance from Teos in Asia Minor. First, an association devoted to the 'Good goddess' at Athens praised a woman who, in her supervisory role, had contributed twice as much from her own funds than what was drawn from the common fund. This was done for the purpose of covering the cost of sacrifices and other services for the goddess: 'in order that there may be a rivalry among those in the assembly who want to be honour-loving, knowing that whoever displays love of honour will receive appropriate favours ... it was resolved by the society-members to praise Bakchis' (*SEG* 56:203; third century BCE).[18]

Similarly, a man named Hermaios had served as treasurer (*tamias*) of a group of sacrificing associates of the Mother of the gods for several years leading up to 178 BCE (*GRA* I 35 = *IG* II² 1327). The membership, which included Athenian citizens, voted to honour him, enumerating his many contributions to the well-being of the group. According to the inscription, not only had Hermaios paid from his own

---

[15] Nahapiet and Ghoshal (1998: 243).
[16] On bonding and bridging forms, see Adler and Kwon (2002).
[17] Ibid., 21.
[18] See Tsirigoti-Drakotou (2006). Now also see Eckhardt (2017c). However, his suggestion that this 'private' group became integrated into a 'civic cult' is less than secure.

resources for the customary sacrifices on some occasions, but he had also paid for a tomb for deceased members at a critical point when the common fund (*koinon*) was empty, ostensibly saving the group from financial ruin. Furthermore, he covered expenses for repairs to the meeting place and also organized for a special collection of contributions (an *eranos*). Particularly important for our point regarding these actions as mutual support – not only for the group as a whole but also for specific individual members with some need – is the language attested here and in other such inscriptions: 'he has proved himself generous to the sacrificing associates *both collectively and individually* (*koinei ... kai idiai ekastōi euchrēston auton*), putting himself at the disposal of each' (lines 6–7).[19] A similar sentiment appears in honours for a priestess within an association at Koloe in Lydia, where Stratonike is commended for behaving 'in an honour-loving manner towards both the collective (*koineion*) and each member individually during the gathering of the association' (*ILydiaHM* 96).[20]

A third and final example of this type of mutual assistance comes from Teos in Ionia, on the western coast of Asia Minor. This is a decree that summarizes the lifelong contributions that a particular member, named Kraton son of Zotichos from Kalchedon, had given to his associates in a group devoted to Attalid royalty (the *Attalistai*). The amounts of Kraton's contributions are somewhat exceptional, but not his behaviours in supporting the association to which he belonged. Although numerous inscriptions mention Kraton, clarifying that he was a member of both the Ionian Dionysiac performers (as a flute-player) and the Attalists in the first half of the second century, it is the final decree of the Attalists after Kraton's death (probably between 146 and 133 BCE) that is most pertinent here.[21] In the decree, the Attalists acknowledge Kraton's service as priest and highlight his success in gaining the group favours and gifts from the Attalid king himself. The decree also refers to Kraton's final arrangements (a 'sacred regulation') before his death, which had been sent to the association by the king himself. The arrangements clearly indicate Kraton was a very wealthy man by the time of his death. These final gifts to his associates included the dedication of a sanctuary for Attalos – an Attaleion – near the theatre (in either Pergamon or Teos), as well as another building near a royal residence.[22] It also entailed a massive endowment worth 10,500 Alexandrian drachmas. This was to produce interest that would pay for sacrifices and meetings. Beyond the money, Kraton supplied enslaved persons and equipment to

---

[19] On this notion of both collective and individual assistance, see also *AGRW* 16 = *GRA* I 11 (internal secretary of a society at the Piraeus); *OGIS* 737 = *SB* V 8929 (internal priest of Idumean soldiers at Memphis); *AGRW* 287 = *GRA* III 160 = *IDelta* I 446 (external benefactor of farmers at Psenamosis); *AGRW* 298 = *OGIS* 51 (external benefactor of perfomers at Ptolemais Hermiou); *AGRW* 306 = *IBerenike* 17 (external benefactor of Judeans); *AGRW* 305 = *IBerenike* 18 (external benefactor of Judeans); *AGRW* 181 = *GRA* I 134 = *IMilet* 939 (athlete / external benefactor of linen-weavers).

[20] See also Jones (2008).

[21] *GRA* II 141 = *CIG* 3069 = *OGIS* 326 (final decree); *CIG* 3071 (reverse of same monument with list of items); Boulay (2012: 269, no. 12; mention of Attalists with Kraton; *c*. 150 BCE); *CIG* 3070 = *OGIS* 325 (fragment of Kraton's letter to performers; 153/152 BCE); *CIG* 3068 (Dionysiac performers' honours, before 158 BCE). See comments and bibliography in *GRA* II 141. Cf. Stang (2007: 268–71), Le Guen (2007), Michels (2011).

[22] See Schwarzer (1999: 271–2).

assist the group in its sacrificial and feasting activities.[23] The inscription begins to trail off as the Attalos devotees' honours for their exceptional member, Kraton, are mentioned, but it is clear that a day was established in this participant's honour. The scale of these contributions suggests that we are dealing with a rather wealthy group, with plenty of resources to spare after this donation, if not before. But this is still a further case of a member contributing to the well-being of other members in the group.

So these sorts of behaviours on the part of a participant within an association could well be considered under the rubric of mutual material assistance in many ways: Bakchis, Hermaios and Kraton were helping their associates, both as a group and sometimes individually. Rather than dwell on numerous such cases of members as benefactors of their own group in this sense, this chapter turns instead to other neglected signs that participants within associations could count on material assistance from other members or from the collective as a whole.[24] For reasons that will become clear and may be familiar to you already, our most substantial evidence for such activities happens to come from papyri found in Egypt, particularly at Tebtynis. Nonetheless, there is substantial corroborating evidence from elsewhere.

Egypt in the Hellenistic era

It is only in very dry climates that papyri survive, and it is on papyri – the impermanent paper-like material of the ancient world – that we are more likely to encounter regulations, loan contracts, letters and other daily transactions relating to economic exchanges. Like other parts of the Mediterranean, concrete *epigraphic* evidence for internal socioeconomic assistance – beyond burial – is scant in Egypt. In fact, such *monumental* evidence regarding mutual aid in associations may even be non-existent for Egypt, as far as we have been able to determine in surveying the inscriptions. This should caution scholars who tend to be over-confident that a lack of widespread evidence (epigraphic or otherwise) reflects a lack of social practice. Nevertheless, documents on Egyptian papyri do offer a fresh vantage point on certain social realities, including the significance of mutual aid for associations in places like the Fayum region, then called the lake district (nome) or district of Arsinoites.

It should be clarified that the majority of published Egyptian papyri (dating from the eighth century BCE to the eighth century CE) comes precisely from this Arsinoites district. This district supplies about 45 per cent of documents at our disposal: 17,519 out of 39,315 published papyri with an identifiable district as find-spot came from Arsinoites when Herbert Verreth produced his study (in August 2009).[25] Of locales in this district, the village of Tebtynis (2,407 papyri), in particular, comes second only to Philadelphia (2,575 papyri) in terms of the *quantity* of published evidence, with each

---

[23] Fragments on the reverse side list materials for banquets: carpets, linen elbow-cushions, tables, a jar, a jug, a cup, a tray for cups, a lamp, a stool of ebony, a shield and a spear (*CIG* 3071). See Rigsby (1996).
[24] For further examples, see *GRA* I 11, 13, 15, 24, 25, 32, 33, 35, 36, 39, 48, 73, 83.
[25] See Verreth (2009: 167–87). Cf. Kelly (2011: 20).

of these sites supplying about 6 per cent of all available Egyptian papyri. The Oxyrynchites district comes in a distant second, supplying us with 21 per cent of the total number of published papyri whose district of provenance is known. Next in line, the Hermopolites and Herakleopolites districts each have less than half of what the Oxyrynchites supplies. Not surprisingly, then, it is precisely from the two districts of Arsinoites and Oxyrhnchites that most evidence for mutual aid and loaning practices within associations derives. In light of these circumstances, the fact that this evidence for these practices comes from a limited number of sites should *not* be assumed to mean that such customs were rare or geographically limited. In fact, this more detailed papyrological evidence provides a new perspective on scattered, although significant, epigraphic material that is found elsewhere in the eastern Mediterranean, even though regional variations in cultural and associative practices would certainly exist.[26]

Traditions of mutual assistance in Egyptian associations can be traced as far back as the third century BCE, during the Ptolemaic era. Rather than isolated rules, however, the idea of coming to help associates in difficult circumstances was often a guiding principle that informed numerous regulations and customs within associations in the district of Arsinoites, with most evidence coming from the village of Tebtynis. In fact, Monson's study of Demotic regulations draws on Charles Tilly's model of the 'trust network' to argue that these documents were an institutionalization of typical norms of mutuality in such a way that the association served as a more trusted group for its members in comparison with other local social networks.[27]

There is a sense in which these regulations embody principles of social capital in that rules regarding assistance encapsulate in written form the mutual expectations that participants in this small, cohesive social unit held. These expectations included access to material and non-material resources at critical moments in an individual's life and at death. The fact that such regulations were most often passed by vote of all members further underlines how group cohesiveness could facilitate adherents' access to valuable resources, further reinforcing bonds within the group.

There are at least eight somewhat well-preserved association regulations from Tebtynis in Demotic, a late phase of ancient Egyptian.[28] A distinction should be made between official boards of priests and other associations that did not consist entirely of priests but could include priests as members, as Monson clarifies.[29] The latter, more unofficial groups, are pertinent here. Membership in these associations usually ranged from fifteen to thirty persons. Five of the regulations for these associations date between 178 and 145 BCE and pertain to one particular association devoted to the crocodile god, Sobek or Souchos, also regarded as 'lord of Tebtynis'.[30] Three other

[26] On local cultures and associations, see Harland (2014).
[27] Monson (2006).
[28] See Cenival (1972: 46–81, 83–102, 215–36), Monson (2007b), Monson and Arlt (2010), Monson (2013).
[29] See Monson (2007b) and ibid. (2007a), challenging a previous view espoused by Cenival (1972). Cf. Monson and Arlt (2010: 118–19).
[30] Five regulations pertaining to one association: *PMilanVoglDemotic* inv. 77–8 (178 BCE); *PCairo* II 30606 = *AGRW* 299 (157 BCE); *PHamburgDemotic* 1 (151 BCE); *PCairo* II 31179 (147 BCE); *PCairo* II 30605 (145 BCE). On these five, see Monson (2007a: 183–7). There are also fragmentary regulations, such as *PStanfordGreenDemotic* 21 = Monson and Arlt (2010).

documents dating to 137 BCE deal with two different groups which were also devoted to this same local deity.³¹ There is one quite fragmentary, earlier regulation dating around 250–210 BCE.³²

Regarding members' treatment of one another, these regulations include negative rules that help to ensure that participants avoid harming one another or harming the unity of the group as a whole. So, for instance, there are prohibitions against insulting others (e.g. *PCairo* II 30606), against fighting with one another or with leaders (e.g. *PPrague*), against stealing from the group,³³ and against going to outside authorities to settle a dispute with an insider (e.g. *PCairo* II 30606). Similar negatively stated rules about members' treatment of one another are found in regulations from later periods and from other parts of the Mediterranean, including the well-known second-century rules of the Bacchic group at Athens and the association at Lanuvium.³⁴

On the other hand, there are three types of positive stipulations in the Demotic regulations that confirm mutual aid as a fundamental group norm. These show us how goodwill or trust arising from close social ties could be translated into concrete forms of assistance. In these cases, access to such social capital was encapsulated in rules. These three types of assistance are also attested in roughly contemporary *Greek* papyri from Tebtynis and elsewhere in Egypt, as we will see.

First of all, there are rules on supporting an associate in financial need when one encountered that person in a variety of contexts. One such rule from Tebtynis (dating to 145 BCE) reads as follows: 'The man among us who finds a man among us at the landing place or a similar place saying "Give to me because of my misfortune," and he does not give to him, his fine is 25 deben unless he swears before Sobek saying, "I was unable to give to him"' (*PCairo* II 30605, lines 22–4).³⁵ The reference to a landing place implies that the fellow member was on the road, as in *PCairo* II 31179 (147 BCE), where the phrase is 'on a road, a landing place, or the like, a boat or a canal'; but this call to offer material support is generalized with reference to similar situations.³⁶ A deben in weight was the equivalent of 20 drachmas or 5 staters.³⁷ In bronze coinage, 25 deben would be the equivalent of 500 bronze drachmas, which would be worth about 2.08 silver drachmas in this era (240:1 ratio using Reden's figures for the period 164 BCE– 130 BCE). This amount is similar to, although less than, Roman-era fines within Tebtynis regulations such as the regulation of a guild of sheep- or cattle-raisers (?),

---

³¹ *PCairo* II 30618 and 30619 (same group in both of these documents); *PPrague* = Erichsen (1959).
³² *PTebtunisSuppl* 1578 = Monson (2013).
³³ E.g. Monson and Arlt (2010: 115).
³⁴ *IG* II² 1368.73–96, 136–46 (164 CE); *CIL* XIV 2112.25–8 (136 CE). Cf. *SEG* 31:122, lines 5–8; *PLond* VII 2193; *PMich* V 243; Harland (2012: 80–2).
³⁵ Translation based on Monson (2006: 236), with adaptations arising from comparison with the German translation of Spiegelberg (1908: 23), and the French translation of Cenival (1972: 73–8, 222–5, at 73).
³⁶ See Monson and Arlt (2010: 119), on *PStanfordGreenDemotic* 21 and *PCairo* II 31179 (147 BCE), where the fine amounts are 10 and 15 deben, respectively. Also see *PCairo* II 30619. Thanks to John S. Kloppenborg for his thoughts on interpreting this passage in light of other Greek papyrological references to disembarkation. For the equivalent Greek term for a landing place (*hē ekbatēria*), see *PTebt* I 33, line 8 (112 BCE) and *PPetrie* III 39, column 2, line 10 (3rd century BCE, also from the Arsinoites).
³⁷ Maresch (1996: 34).

Mutual Assistance and Group Cohesion 159

where the fine for failing to assist a member who was in trouble or for taking legal action against an associate was 8 silver drachmas (*AGRW* 300 = *GRA* III 206 = *PMich* V 243; see Chapter 5).

A second type of mutual aid is attested in numerous regulations that include a special rule for assisting someone who was in legal trouble, imprisoned or held captive. John Bauschatz's study of prisons in Ptolemaic Egypt argues that arrests were more common than previously believed and that imprisonment for debt (either debt to the government or to other individuals) remains most prevalent in the papyrological sources.[38] However, there were a number of other less noticed reasons for being in jail, including minor misdemeanors, theft, assault and disturbing the peace. A somewhat unusual case involves the carpet-weaver in Philadelphia, who somehow had his fellow worker imprisoned due to poor workmanship and less than honest means of weighing finished carpets (*PCairZen* III 59484; third century BCE). Such imprisonments tended to be short (usually days and rarely more than a month), and release would generally follow appearance before an official or payment of debts, if that was the issue. So the following instances where associations anticipate the possibility of imprisonment may well relate to debt, since there is a need for funds, but reasons for arrest are not specified in most cases.

A recurring phrase in regulations of associations was that, when a member was arrested, his fellows should 'stand by him'. For example: 'We will all stand by the man among us who is imprisoned unjustly, and will each give to him up to 50 deben with interest for his legal dispute until they ... acquit him (?).'[39] Bauschatz documents many claimed cases of arbitrary or 'unjust' imprisonment in the papyrological record. Some sources do reveal improper behaviour on the part of officials who falsely detained people, but it is difficult to know when claims of 'injustice' by an imprisoned person were in some sense accurate.[40] Anyhow, as with the person in financial need, a member was to use his own funds – rather than the common fund – to help a fellow member in this particular association. The amount of 50 deben in bronze coinage would be the equivalent of 4.16 silver drachmas (at 240:1, assuming the date of 130 BCE is secure).

Yet there are variations on this concept of assisting those in legal trouble. Sometimes there is reference to the use of communal money (rather than an individual associate's funds), presumably drawn from the group's treasury, as in the rule cited at the beginning of our chapter: 'We will stand by the man among us who is involved in an unjust legal dispute and will give him the funds that the members of the association have agreed on in order to acquit him.'[41] Another regulation provides further details on the aim of this assistance: 'We will assist the man among us who will be implicated in an unjust legal case and we will give him membership contributions, which those of the association have agreed to give, in order that he is acquitted and the representative of the association

---

[38] Bauschatz (2007). Cf. Bertrand-Dagenbach (1999). For prisons in the Roman era, see Krause (1996) and Rapske (1994).
[39] *PPrague*, lines 25–6 (137 BCE) = Erichsen (1959) (translated by Monson, 2006: 236). Cf. *PCairo* II 30605, line 18 (145 BCE); *PCairo* II 30619, line 7 (137 BCE); Monson Arlt and (2010) = *PStanfordGreenDem*. 21.
[40] Bauschatz (2007: 9–11, 23–4).
[41] *PCairo* II 30605 (translated by adapted from Monson, 2006: 236).

will assist him and we will raise for him ten rations.'[42] The implication here is that the group would financially assist the member until the case was cleared, a principle that is also stated in another regulation (*PCairo* II 30619, line 7, 137 BCE). The reference to providing rations means that participants would ensure that the imprisoned person received food while jailed. This idea of offering assistance to others and feeding those in prison could even extend to those who were imprisoned for a seemingly legitimate reason, in some cases (assuming that there is not a scribal error in the phrasing of another regulation): 'The representative of the association will stand by the man among us who is *justly* imprisoned ... we will provide for him (?) ... ten rations.'[43]

For point of comparison with the above principles of mutual aid, it is worth quoting part of another regulation, not from Tebtynis but from Pisais, also in the Arsinoites district. This pertains to an association devoted to the god Horos and dates to 223 BCE. In that regulation, there is considerable detail regarding the need for assistance in cases of legal trouble or imprisonment, comparable to the Tebtynis regulations we have just discussed:

> If one of us finds a member who is involved in a trial and evades his responsibilities to him and offers testimony against him, if the case is proved against him, his fine shall be 4 kite (= 8 drachmas). If one of us is unjustly arrested, without the appeal to the altar of ... we will ensure that the representative of the 'house' levies a ration for him of food that he will receive every day of his imprisonment until the god pardons him (?). We will offer testimony in the trial – all of us – and we will appeal for him, up to the ten days. If we are able to obtain his release, we will obtain his release. If anyone of us is ... ill (?) ... or in prison or has taken refuge in the temple of the god, or in a place of supplication, or has been arrested as the object of a pledge during the period mentioned above, we will ensure that the representative of the 'house' comes to his assistance; and whoever decided against him will have decided against us.
>
> GRA III 188 = *PLilleDemotic* 29, lines 14–17[44]

Overlapping with these first two types of socioeconomic support, five contemporary documents written in Greek confirm that members of guilds in the Ptolemaic period could access resources in the form of loans, whether interest-free or interest-bearing. One Greek papyrus from an unknown location preserves three receipts from individuals who had each received a monetary loan drawn 'from the common funds' (*apo tōn koinōn chrēmatōn*) of what was likely a guild or association to which they belonged.[45] These receipts, which date to either 182 or 158 BCE, say nothing about interest, which leaves open the possibility that these were, in fact, interest-free loans. In each case, the document is a statement by the debtor that he has received funds of a certain amount and that he agrees to repay within six months. A loan received by Menestheus is illustrative here:

---

[42] *PCairo* II 31179, lines 16–17 (147 BCE; translated by Monson and Arlt, 2010: 120, with adaptations).
[43] *PPrague* (137 BCE; translated by Monson, 2006: 236).
[44] Translated by Kloppenborg with adaptations, based on the French of Cenival (1972: 3–10).
[45] *GRA* III 286 = *PTexas* inv. 8 = Martinez and Williams (1997).

Menestheus son of Chares to Herakles, leader of the people (*dēmosiarchēs*, here an internal functionary), greetings. I agree that I have received from the common funds ... *x* talents and five thousand ... drachmas of copper, which I will repay you in the month Mesore of the twenty-third year and, if I do not repay, you may seize me without accountability in any way you see fit. Farewell. In the month of Phamenoth ...[46]

The amounts of the other two monetary loans were 3,093 bronze drachmas (or more) for Asklepiades and 859 bronze drachmas and 3 obols for Xenikos. The ratio of bronze to silver drachmas is thought to have shifted from 60:1 before 180 BCE to 120:1 after that date, so Xenikos' loan would roughly be the equivalent of either 14 or 7 silver drachmas.

A fourth Greek document is most likely from Philadelphia in the Arsinoites district. This is a ledger of debts that had been drawn from the 'common funds' (*[e]pikoina chrēmata*; *PRyl* IV 589, especially lines 84–91; 180 BCE). These funds seem to belong to an association whose members engaged in at least some activities within a gymnasium, as the original editors argue based on the references to oil.[47] Several of the loans are described in terms of the debtors being outsiders (*xenous*, in lines 62–72). But the more substantial ones were made to adherents of the group, who were charged the customary (in Egypt) 24 per cent interest (lines 84–91).

Similar loaning practices are attested on Greek papyri elsewhere, including some from Oxyrhynchos. The clearest case, dating to 99 BCE, is apparently an instruction for the person to repay the loan: 'Let Demetrios repay the 53 talents and ... *x* thousand drachmas of copper with interest to the lenders or to the ... treasurer (?) ... of the association (*tou koi[nou chrēmato]phylaki*)' (*AGRW* 304 = *GRA* III 248 = *PRyl* IV 586, lines 7–12; cf. line 24).[48] Here the interest rate on the loan is, once again, the Egyptian standard of 24 per cent per year. The fact that it is never specified which association was involved suggests that Demetrios was a member of the group; therefore, there was no need to name the corporate lender. Although interest is involved with some of these loans, the practice of lending communal funds at all can still be seen as a way of financially assisting those who belonged to the group. This gave participants in these internal social networks ready access to resources to which they might not otherwise have access and, potentially, in difficult circumstances.

Returning to regulations in Demotic, the third type of rule which embodies the principal of support here pertains to assistance by members at the death of a member: 'We will mourn for the man among us who dies during the period mentioned above, we will give 5 deben (= 100 drachmas) per person for his burial, we will raise ten rations of grief ... for his household (?) ..., and we will invite his son, father, or father-in-law to drink with us in order to sooth his heart.'[49] The expectation that participants

---

[46] Translation by Martinez and Williams (1997).
[47] Turner and Neugebauer (1949: 81–2). Cf. van Minnen (1987: 65–6).
[48] See also *PGrenf* I 31 from Pathyris (101–100 BCE). This is a loan contract, in which Herianoupis and the members of a society (*synthiasitai*) lend money to a man named Nechoutes, who may or may not be a member. In that case, the loan was to be paid in kind (produce, likely barley).
[49] *PPrague* (137 BCE; translated by Monson, 2006: 229, with adaptations). Cf. *PCairo* II 30605.

should assist another member or a member's family in times of mourning also extended to the death of family members.⁵⁰ The amount specified here as a contribution for a member's funeral (100 bronze drachmas = 0.416 silver drachmas) is significantly less than the amount that each participant in the same group was expected to bring forward to assist someone in legal troubles (1,000 bronze drachmas = 4.16 silver drachmas). But the latter amount was to be taken as a loan and would, in theory, be repaid. In Chapter 2, we have already encountered two petitions to Ptolemaic authorities (written in Greek) that confirm that associations of various types – in these cases, 'societies' (*thiasoi*) – played a role in helping to pay for the funeral of members in this same era, but that in some rare cases a group might fail to fulfil its obligations.

Egypt in the Roman era

For the Roman imperial period, two out of three association regulations that have been found at Tebtynis (*PMich* V 243–5) illustrate the continuation of mutual assistance as an underlying principle of group life.⁵¹ These documents show how membership in such groups provided access to resources, both material and non-material. One of the main reasons why the best preserved association contracts happen to come from this one particular village and not from various locales is that these and three other incomplete drafts of contracts by associates (*PMich* V 246–8) come from the official archive of the Tebtynis writing office (*grapheion*). And this Tebtynis archive is, at present, apparently the only substantially preserved village records office archive from all of Egypt, preserving a total of 192 documents from the period 20 BCE–56 CE.⁵² The fact that these archived regulations were in official storage means that there was a higher likelihood that they would be preserved together. So these documents are just the tip of the iceberg, it seems. We should not jump to the conclusion that these were anomalies or regionally peculiar in terms of the customs they reflect. Furthermore, even though they were stored in the records office, it is important to emphasize that these Tebtynis regulations were not imposed by some authority. Rather, they were the result of a vote of all members in the association, who would, therefore, be directly invested in maintaining prescriptions and proscriptions.

All three types of social assistance found in the Demotic regulations and in contemporary Greek documents of the Ptolemaic era continue to be attested within two of the three surviving Tebtynis regulations from the reign of Tiberius (14–37 CE; *PMich* V 243–5 = *AGRW* 300–3). Two of the contracts end with a series of statements regarding the third main type of mutual aid: the need for each member to participate in, or financially contribute towards, funerary rites when a member passed away. This is a form of mutual support that is very well attested across the ancient Mediterranean.

---

⁵⁰ E.g. *PCairo* 30606 = *AGRW* 299 = *GRA* II 191 (158 BCE).
⁵¹ On these associations at Tebtynis, see also Boak (1937: 217–18), Préaux (1948), Schnöckel (2006 [1956]), Venticinque (2010: 282–4), Alston (2002: 207–12).
⁵² We are grateful to Ben Kelly, York University, who clarified important information regarding patterns of survival with respect to the papyri (cf. Kelly, 2011: 43–4). On this archive, see Boak (1923), Husselman (1970), Beek (2013).

The first two types of financial assistance need more attention here. The most pertinent document belongs to a guild of fifteen members whose precise occupation has been lost, but these may be raisers of sheep or cattle based on references to livestock (*AGRW* 300 = *GRA* III 206 = *PMich* V 243; 14–37 CE).[53] The front of this document is pictured in Figure 8.1. This regulation suggests the importance of members having a positive disposition towards other members, providing help when needs arose and, corresponding to this, avoiding conflict.[54] For instance, 'if a member ignores someone who is in distress and does not assist in helping him out of his trouble, he shall pay 8 drachmas'. Furthermore, 'if a member prosecutes or calumniates another member, he shall be fined 8 drachmas'. Several Demotic regulations of the Ptolemaic era likewise clarify that disputes were to be settled internally and that adherents were not to bring complaints about other members before officials outside of the group.[55] There are cases from other regions in which an association similarly stipulates that participants were not to take disputes to external authorities or courts, as with Bacchic devotees at Athens and with any adherents in assemblies at Corinth who may have listened to Paul's advice.[56] These other situations may reflect a similar concern to foster positive relations among adherents and to protect the reputation of the association.

Furthermore, in the sheep-raisers' (?) guild at Tebtynis, 'If a member commits intrigue against, or corrupts the home of another member, he shall pay sixty drachmas.' Notice the inflation of the fine here (60 drachmas compared to 8 drachmas), which indicates a heightened importance for this violation. The reference to avoiding intrigue and corruption of other's homes at Tebtynis could be compared to the prohibition of stealing another man's woman in the regulation of an association of Zeus Hypsistos at Philadelphia (*PLond* VII 2193 = *AGRW* 295; 69–58 BCE). It also has some affinities with a regulation for a domestic association from another Philadelphia – the one in Lydia (*AGRW* 121 = *GRA* II 117 = *TAM* V 1539; *c*. 100 BCE). The Lydian regulation from Asia Minor outlines several other prohibitions that were aimed at people avoiding harm to other participants, and any who were aware of such plans to harm others were to expose the guilty parties. Although these stipulations in Lydia are in the negative, speaking against inappropriate treatment of other participants, the general framework in which they are presented – the need for participants to show 'goodwill towards this house' – points towards an underlying guiding principle of mutuality and cohesiveness.

In the sheep-raisers' (?) guild at Tebtynis, there were also provisions for paying bail if a member had been arrested.[57] The member was to reimburse the association within a month: 'If a member has been arrested for a private matter, they (i.e. associates) shall stand surety for him for up to 100 silver drachmas for thirty days, during which time he shall release the men from their pledge' (*PMich* V 243, line 9). The second document

---

[53] The identification as sheep- or cattle-raisers is based on reference to these animals in line 5. Such livestock raisers are attested at Tebtynis: see *PMich* II 123 front [r.] III, line 40 and VIII, line 26. Cf. *GRA* III 235 = *PHamb* I 34, from Euhemeria.
[54] Cf. *IG* II² 1275, from the Piraeus in Attica (*c*. 325–275 BCE); *PLond* VII 2193, from Philadelphia in the Arsinoites district (69–58 BCE).
[55] Monson (2013: 212).
[56] *AGRW* 7 = *IG* II² 1368, lines 90–5; 1 Corinthians 6:1–11.
[57] On bail, see Bauschatz (2007: 21–2).

Figure 8.1 Regulation of the sheep-raisers' (?) guild (*PMich* V 243, APIS inv. 720, front [r.]). Courtesy of the Papyrology Collection, Graduate Library, University of Michigan, used under a Creative Commons licence.

from Tebtynis – the regulation of the 24 tenant farmers (?) who claim some sort of exemption (*apolysimoi*) – similarly makes provisions for helping a member who was arrested. Yet, in this case, the period for repayment was doubled: 'If any of the undersigned men is arrested, the association will stand surety for him up to the amount of 100 silver drachmas for a period of sixty days' (*AGRW* 301 = *GRA* III 212 = *PMich*

V 244, lines 9–11; 43 CE). Once again, it should be remembered that imprisonment for debt is among the most attested reasons for arrest in other Egyptian sources, but these regulations are more wide-reaching in that they do not specify what legal offences would result in help.

The fact that procedures like those at Tebtynis were practised elsewhere in the district is confirmed by another papyrus from the time of the emperor Tiberius, this one from the village of Euhemeria, also located in the district of Arsinoites (*GRA* III 205 = *PRyl* II 94).[58] In this case, detainment was not necessarily the result of debts. The document is a letter from the leader (*hēgoumenos*) and the secretary (*grammateus*) of the weavers (*gerdoi*) to a village official (*exēgētēs*). The leaders of the guild put themselves forward as sureties, offering bail for the release of five imprisoned members of the guild. These five members were faced with (now) unknown charges brought forward by what was likely a wool-worker (*eriourgos*). In acting as sureties, the leaders of the guild would be responsible to guarantee the appearance of these weavers when the case was heard before village authorities. Since records of persons providing surety or bail would often be made on perishable materials (such as papyri), we rarely witness this outside of Egypt. Nonetheless, there are hints of this in Attica, as we shall see, and there is the senatorial decree dealing with Bacchic groups in Italy in the early second century BCE which seems to specifically forbid members of such groups from either giving or taking surety (*fidem inter se dare*; *ILLRP* 511, lines 10–14; 186 BCE).[59] Wim Broekaert discusses the likelihood that Roman merchants and shippers commonly looked to their fellow members in the association for surety, loans and other economic assistance.[60] Unfortunately, epigraphic evidence from Italy and the West (like the *epigraphic* evidence from Egypt itself) does not supply any further clear cases of such practices, as far as we have been able to determine at this point.[61]

Beyond the offer of surety, other papyri confirm the related practice of offering adherents loans in the Roman imperial period. This is a topic that we address at some length below in connection with so-called 'friendly loans' (*eranoi*) in Greece and on Aegean islands. An early first-century Egyptian instance involves an association in Alexandria financially assisting a member who faced economic difficulties.[62] The papyrus is a record of a decision by a synod devoted to god Augustus concerning a member and imperial enslaved person named Syntrophos (dating to 6 CE). Syntrophos owed 120 silver drachmas to another enslaved person of Caesar whose name is now missing. The common consent of the membership was that the synod's priest (Iucundus), who was evidently also the treasurer in charge of the group's communal fund, should provide Syntrophos with a loan of 120 drachmas, including interest in order to pay his debt. The member was then expected to repay the synod (lines 12–16). This is a clear use of the group's common funds to supply a loan to a member in need,

---

[58] Cf. Venticinque (2010: 283).
[59] See Rauh (1993: 251–87, especially 254).
[60] Broekaert (2011: 236–42).
[61] Jinyu Liu and Jonathan Scott Perry both helpfully responded to inquiries, indicating that they could not think of any further cases of an association or its members offering sureties or loans in Italy or in western parts of the Mediterranean generally.
[62] *AGRW* 281 = *GRA* III 168 = *BGU* IV 1137 = Brashear (1993).

although it seems that interest was involved (if *atokos* is to be interpreted as 'including interest' or 'interest built in' in Egyptian papyri, rather than 'interest-free').[63]

The eastern Mediterranean

A situation of mutual support among members of groups is not peculiar to Egypt, as we have already begun to see. Internal bonds among associates facilitated access to resources of different kinds, and the precise manifestations of support could vary from one region to another and from one group to the next. As with the Egyptian evidence, principles of reciprocal assistance begin with our earliest evidence for such groups in southern Greece (Attica) and on Aegean islands, and continue on into the Roman imperial era. The notable parallels in the types of assistance that members were expected to give to one another suggest that cultural traditions found in Egypt are not peculiar. Instead, there are considerable overlaps in communal principles that were at work within groups in various villages or Greek cities. Internal bonds provided individuals access to material or non-material resources they might not otherwise have accessed so readily.

As we will soon see, evidence for such socioeconomic customs in Greece and the Aegean, although more fragmentary, begins about a century or more *earlier* than in Egypt, beginning in the mid-fourth century. A partially preserved monumental record of members' obligations in a society (*thiasōtai*) at the Piraeus (*c.* 325–275 BCE), for instance, clarifies that members were expected to attend funerals of members' families. Furthermore, the practice of providing communal funds for the funeral of members is attested in a roughly contemporary document from Attica (*IG* II² 1278 = *GRA* I 17; 272 BCE).

There are indications that this was part of a general principle of mutual aid, comparable to the situation in Egypt. For the same Piraeus regulation subsequently stipulates that participants should help one another in cases of difficulties: 'if a member should be wronged, they (i.e. the society-members) and all the friends (i.e. perhaps another level of participants) shall come to his assistance, so that everyone might know that we show piety to the gods and to our friends. To those who do these things, may many blessings come upon them, their descendants, and their ancestors' (*IG* II² 1275 = *GRA* I 8 = *AGRW*, lines 7–12). We know from the Attic orators that small groups of friends or 'clubs' (*hetaireiai*) in the late-fifth and fourth centuries BCE could assist members in legal cases, sometimes by raising money or by testifying on behalf of a fellow member, as George Miller Calhoun discusses at some length.[64] So the association at the Piraeus may well have in mind assistance in legal or other troubles along these lines. It is noteworthy that mutual assistance in this association is also connected with *piety*, and deities are imagined to reward positive interrelations among members in the

---

[63] On this, see Pestman (1971), Modrzejewski (1997: 118), Reden (2007: 159–61).
[64] Calhoun (1913: 40–96). Note, however, that some of the legal examples that Calhoun assembles do not expressly involve *hetaireiai*. Cf. Jones (1999: 223–7).

group, which is a rarely attested concept in inscriptions.⁶⁵ Further on, the document clarifies that these rules were to be ratified and enforced by adherents themselves. Participants were to report any transgressions and to determine any penalty for violation (lines 12–17).

We have already witnessed associations providing loans when we dealt with income from endowments and communal funds (Chapter 5) and when we surveyed mutual aid in Egypt (in this chapter), and further valuable evidence is forthcoming from Attica and islands of the Aegean. The practice of associations offering loans sometimes has important implications for mutual aid, particularly in cases when it is a member or participant who would have access to such loans from the association to which he or she belonged. In this way, members could receive material assistance in difficult circumstances from those beyond their own family, and the expectation that one's association might offer such financial help would also reinforce bonds among participants.

These loaning practices need to be understood within the context of other cultural and socioeconomic practices of the Hellenistic era, particularly practices associated with the Greek term *eranos*, that is, the 'collection', 'contribution' or 'friendly loan'.⁶⁶ This Greek term, which also came to be used as a designation for an ongoing 'contribution-society' (*eranos*) to which one made contributions, was also used to refer to 'contributions' to a common meal and continued to be used in this way as well.⁶⁷

Beginning in the fourth century BCE in Attica, this Greek term (*eranos*) was commonly used in reference to a specific type of 'loan' (sometimes, although not necessarily, interest-free). This type of loan was either (1) solicited by a person in need from various connections, usually friends (*philoi*) and neighbours (*geitones*); or, (2) generated by a group (*koinon*) of 'lenders' or 'contributors' (as we translate the Greek term *eranistai* here).⁶⁸ Such loans were aimed at supporting a borrower's specific needs in emergency situations, situations such as difficulties in paying fines, taxes, dowries, expenses incurred through civic service roles and costs associated with manumission from slavery.⁶⁹ As Paul Millett clarifies, these loaning practices emerged, in part, out of the common belief that people should practice significant levels of reciprocity, assisting and being assisted by immediate neighbours (e.g. those on one's street, or members of one's deme or subdivision).⁷⁰ In this view, neighbours and friends held an intermediate position between the household and the civic community. We would suggest this is an intermediate social position similar to that held by more permanent unofficial associations in the Hellenistic and Roman eras, many of which were, in fact, formed from network ties in neighbourhoods.

---

[65] Cf. Kloppenborg in the comments to *GRA* I 8; Longenecker (2010: 98–9).
[66] On such loans and security-markers, see Fine (1951), Finley (1951: especially 100–6), Vondeling (1961), Maier (1969), Harris (1988), Millett (1991), Harris (1993), Rauh (1993: 251–87), Harrill (1998: 167–70), Arnaoutoglou (2003: 66, 69–87, 122–3), Faraguna (2012). On women and loaning practices, see Harris (1992) and Harris and Tuite (2000).
[67] Cf. Hesiod, *Works and Days* 722–3; Homer, *Odyssey* 1.226; 11.415; Plato, *Laws* 11.915E.
[68] See Millett (1991: 153–9). On the two types, see Thomsen (2015).
[69] See Rauh (1993: 263–9), Harrill (1998: 167–2), Faraguna (2012: 138).
[70] Millett (1991: 139–53).

Despite informal dimensions of these loans and signs of flexibility in paying back the loan, there could still be some pressure laid to bear in ensuring repayment, so the 'friendly' aspect needs some qualification.[71] Mechanisms to ensure repayment are evident in the fact that a formerly enslaved person who had been manumitted but failed to repay a friendly loan could potentially face re-enslavement, as indicated in some Delphic manumissions (c. 200 BCE–70 CE).[72] Furthermore, and more importantly here, a considerable source of information for such loans are boundary or mortgage stones (*horoi*) that were used as records of securities offered in return for such loans, mortgage stones which we have already encountered in the discussion of income (Chapter 5).[73] In Attica and on some Aegean islands, these mortgage stones date mainly from the mid-fourth BCE to the second century BCE, after which the means of documenting mortgages apparently shifted away from boundary stones.

This overall cultural and socioeconomic milieu means there were precedents in place for a group of friends collecting funds together for a friend or acquaintance, and so such notions of mutual assistance naturally came to play a role in a variety of social settings, including ongoing associations. In fact, building on the arguments of Johannes Vondeling, other scholars, including Ilias Arnaoutoglou, Michele Faraguna and, now, Christian Thomsen, put forward a new and convincing understanding of the situation. These scholars argue that many references to an 'association of contributors' (*koinon eranistōn*) on security stones and on entries on the so-called freedperson's bowls from Attica represent more *permanent* associations engaged in offering loans. Previously, such groups had been characterized as *temporary* affiliations in an influential study by Moses Finley that was followed by Millett and others.[74] Finley proposed this due to his belief that there was a century-long chronological gap between the earliest security stones referring to people offering a friendly loan (c. 350 BCE, in his view) and the emergence of permanent associations of 'contributors' (after c. 250 BCE, in his view).[75] Closely related to this notion of timing is the common but questionable assumption that unofficial associations only began to emerge as a direct consequence of the supposed decline of the Greek city-state (*polis*) and its social structures after the time of Alexander the Great (died 322 BCE).[76]

---

[71] On informality, see Plato, *Laws* 11.915E as discussed in *GRA* I 19 and by Arnaoutoglou (2003: 74–8).
[72] E.g. *SGDI* 1791, lines 11–12; *SGDI* 1804, lines 3–4; *SGDI* 1878, lines 12–13; *SGDI* 2317, lines 8–11. See Harrill (1998: 168–70), Kamen (2014: 293–5). Cf. *IG* II² 1553–78), *IG* VII 3376 (from Chaironeia in Boiotia).
[73] On the *horoi*, loans and security generally, see Fine (1951), Finley (1951), Biscardi (1983), Harris (1993).
[74] Vondeling (1961: 126–32), Arnaoutoglou (2003: 70–87), Faraguna (2012), Thomsen (2015). For the security stones, see Finley (1951: nos 8, 30, 31, 32, 40 , 42, 44, 70, 71, 110, 112, 113, 114, 31A, 114A; *SEG* 32:1982. For translations of the bowl inscriptions, see Meyer (2009), who proposes that these do not have to do with manumissions but rather with payments by metics. The usual formula on the bowls is: '*Person's-name*, living in *district*, having escaped *Person's-name*, a bowl weighing 100.'
[75] Finley (1951: 100–6, especially 101 with n. 60). Cf. Jones (1999: 307–8). On problems with theories of decline and associations, see Harland (2013: 71–94) = ibid. (2003: 89–114).
[76] Nicholas Jones' (1999: especially 123–50, 307–10) treatment of the relationship between official, descent-based civic structures or associations of the classical era and the emergence of unofficial (or 'voluntary') associations is far more sophisticated than those that precede it. But he still seems to give considerable credence to the notion that Alexander the Great set in motion an overall decline (rather than evolution) of the *polis*.

Now Thomsen's thorough study confirms how little time there is between our earliest evidence for friendly loans and our earliest evidence for permanent, non-descent-based associations. As Thomsen notes, the early existence of such ongoing (rather than temporary) associations of 'contributors' (*eranistai*) that also engaged in activities such as meals and honours for deities is, in fact, clearly indicated in an important passage in Aristotle's *Nicomachean Ethics* 1160a19–20, which likely dates between 334 and 322 BCE: 'Some associations (*koinōniōn*) seem to be formed on the basis of enjoyment (*hēdonē*), such as society-members (*thiasōtai*) and contributors (*eranistai*).'[77] Roughly contemporary with Aristotle are two Attic dedications to deities (one to Zeus Philios and the other to another deity) from the final decades of the fourth century by groups of 'contributors' (*eranistai*), which likewise seem to be ongoing groups rather than temporary formations (*IG* II² 2935 and 2940). Thomsen argues that virtually all groups (*koina*) of contributors (*eranistai*) on the Attic mortgage stones (22 cases) and on lists of bowls dedicated either by manumitted persons or by prosecutors in trials related to 'registered foreigners' or metics (17 cases from the 330s–320s BCE), were likely permanent associations engaged in offering loans to associates and others, alongside other ongoing commensal and ritual activities.

A boundary marker from Arkesine on Amorgos island dating around 300 BCE provides an early example of an organized group where the language of contributors and friendly loans is present. This case also offers more details regarding procedures and so is worth presenting in full here:

> Boundary marker (*horos*) of the properties which are in ... and of the houses and gardens of Xenokles situated in Phylincheia and of the registered securities. These were mortgaged with the consent of his wife Eratokrate and her guardian (*kyrios*), Broukion; to the contribution-society (*eranos*); to Aristagoras the leader of the contribution-society (*archeranos*); and, to his wife Echenike (?)..., as the surety for which he recorded Xenokles in the matter of the friendly loan (*eranos*), which Aristagoras had collected in accordance with the law of the contributors (*kata ton nomon tōn e[ranis]tōn*).
>
> *IG* XII,7 58[78]

As Thomsen points out, this inscription employs the Greek term *eranos* both in reference to the ongoing group itself – the 'contribution-society', as we translate the term – and in reference to the fund that was raised to offer as a 'friendly loan'.[79]

Returning to Athens itself, there is a decree from the early third century BCE by sacrificing associates who participated in two different associations, one devoted to the hero Echelos and the other to the heroines (*AGRW* 1 = *GRA* I 14 = *Agora* 16:161).[80] The resolution refers to moneys owed by members to the associations. While it may be

---

[77] Thomsen also points to two groups of contributors around 300 BCE: *SEG* 41:171 and *IG* II² 1265.
[78] Based on Thomsen's recent reading of the stone (2015: 169–70). Cf. *SEG* 29:36, c. 350 BCE; *IG* II² 2721.
[79] Thomsen (2015: 168–9).
[80] Cf. Ferguson (1944: 76–9).

that some of the funds owed were for regular participation payments, the reference to principal and interest suggests strongly that loans were regularly made to participants and there had been some shortcomings in repayment:

> In order that the partnership (*koinōnia*) in the sacrifices be maintained for all time for the association (*koinon*) that is near Kalliphanes' property and that of the hero Echelos, it was resolved to inscribe the names of those who owe anything to the partnership – both the principal and the interest, as much as each owes – on a monument and set it up by the altar in the temple, and to inscribe the ancient decrees on the monument.

So the practice of ongoing associations offering loans or so-called friendly loans is firmly established and began much earlier than Finley and others imagine. Fourteen of the associations of contributors on the mortgage stones designate themselves by the person they are with, using the prepositions 'with' (*meta*) or 'around' (*peri*): e.g. 'contributors who are with Aristophon of Eiresides district'. This is a further sign of an ongoing group as this phrasing is common among ongoing associations with some degree of permanency, as we discussed in Chapter 3.[81] A corollary of this overall situation is that other associations using the self-designation 'contributors' (*eranistai*) outside of Attica – as at Hyllarima, Kos, Rhodian Peraia and the island of Rhodes itself – may also have engaged in collections for the purpose of lending, even though we happen to lack specific instances in the surviving inscriptions.[82]

Some associations of contributors attested on the security stones in Attica refer to the collected fund itself (using the Greek term *eranos*). Around 250 BCE, an 'association of contributors' (*to koinon tōn eranistōn*, lines 15–16, 20) devoted to Zeus and Herakles mentions a 'fund' (*eranos*, line 7) which, distinguishable from another 'common fund' (*[to a]rgyrion t[o] koino[n]*, line 4), had been appropriately managed by the group's treasurer (*tamias*; *GRA* 19 = *IG* II² 1291; cf. *IG* II² 1298).

Arnaoutoglou argues that there may be a reference to a collection for a friendly loan by worshippers of the Thracian deity Sabazios in the Piraeus in 100 BCE (*GRA* I 43 = *IG* II² 1335).[83] In this inscription, the group is designated 'the Sabazios-devotees', and yet the resolution was to have the names of 'the contributors' (*eranistai*) inscribed on the monument. The implication is that 'the contributors' on this inscription was not a self-designation for the group but rather a term for those who contributed to a specific collection: 'The Sabazios-devotees resolved to inscribe the names of the contributors (*eranistai*) on a monument and to erect it in the temple' (lines 4–5). It is noteworthy that the fifty-one contributors (all men) who belonged to the association consisted of a mixture of citizens and immigrants with 'registered foreigner' (metic) status, including those from Antioch (two), Miletos (three), Laodikeia (one), Macedonia (two), Herakleia (one), Maroneia in Thrace (one), Aigina island (one) and Apameia (one). There was at

---

[81] Thomsen (2015: 166–7).
[82] E.g. *IHyllarimaMcCabe* 18; *IKosS* EV 278; *IG* XII.1 155, from the town of Rhodes; *IRhodB* 12 and 155, from the Rhodian Peraia in Caria. See Gabrielsen (2001).
[83] Arnaoutoglou (2003: 86). Cf. *GRA* I 47 = *SEG* 54:235, from Epano Liosia (mid-1st BCE).

least one enslaved person of the People and others without mention of place of origin or Athenian subdivision, which points to servile origins (enslaved persons or formerly enslaved persons).[84] In this case, it is possible to imagine these enslaved persons employing a friendly loan for manumission.

Advancing to the Roman imperial era, there is an important case of loans as a matter of course within an association that chose Herakles as patron at Liopesi in Attica (*GRA* I 50 = *SEG* 31:122; *c.* 100 CE).[85] The difficulty here is that it is not stated whether the loans were for insiders or for outsiders, but Antony E. Raubitschek and others argue that members were likely in mind.[86] There is no mention of interest here, so either these were interest-free friendly loans or typical interest charges were taken for granted. This group designated itself both a 'synod' and a 'contribution-society' (*eranos*). The leader of this group devoted to Herakles was called 'head of the contribution-society' (*archenanistēs*).

The evidence for loaning practices here is direct. In specifying procedures in the management of endowments, the regulation states: 'Let the head of the contribution-society choose three people – whomever he wants – from the synod to assist him in loaning out the endowment (*[[eis to syneg]]danisai tēn enthēkēn*).'[87] So a team of three members was formed to manage such loans. A second reference to the loans this group offered to its members or to others comes further on: 'The dues must be brought to the treasurer so that loans can be made (*is tas egdosis*). Whoever does not pay shall be fined a double amount. Whoever does not pay at all shall be expelled from the contribution-society (*exeranos*).'[88]

Moving to Greek cities in Asia Minor, another piece of evidence provides clarity regarding the commonality of associations in this region, too, functioning to financially assist members using corporate funds, potentially including loans. This despite the fact that we happen to lack references to *interest-free* loans in the inscriptions of Asia Minor, as far as we have been able to establish (for interest-bearing loans, see *IMagnMai* 117 and the discussion in Chapter 5). Among Pliny the Younger's dealings with associations during his time (*c.* 112 CE) as specially appointed legate in the province of Bithynia-Pontus is his response to a request from people at Amisos.[89] Pliny's letter to the emperor Trajan suggests that Roman authorities, like others, recognized the important role of associations in providing members with access to resources in times of need, even though these same authorities could also be suspicious of people gathering together. Pliny first writes to Trajan regarding a petition from inhabitants at Amisos regarding the formation of 'contribution-societies' (*eranous*), with Pliny employing the plural

---

[84] See the discussion by Kloppenborg in *GRA* I 43.
[85] See also Raubitschek (1981), Lupu (2005: 181–2).
[86] Raubitschek (1981: 96) takes it for granted that these loans were for members, even if there was interest.
[87] The root of the verb used here, *daneizō*, was regularly used in reference to lending out funds, as we have translated here (see LSJ).
[88] Taking *ekdosis* as a reference to lending here, as do Raubitschek and John S. Kloppenborg (notes to *GRA* I 50), seems to fit the overall context better than Lupu's (2005) suggestion that 'contracts' for supplies are in mind (still, Lupu does nonetheless agree that loans are involved in lines 34–5).
[89] On associations, see Pliny the Younger, *Letters* 10.33–4, 92–3, 96 = *AGRW* L40. Cf. Harland (2013: 153–5) = ibid. (2003: 169–73).

of the Greek term (even though writing in Latin) that is so familiar to us now (*Letters* 10.92).

Even more significant is Trajan's response, which clarifies that both he and Pliny took it for granted that one of the most notable aims of such groups was to support members in material ways: 'If the citizens of Amisos ... are allowed by their own laws ... to form a contribution-society (*eranum*), there is no reason why we should interfere, especially if the collections (*collatione*) are not used for riotous and unlawful assemblies, but to support the needs of people in the lower strata' (*sed ad sustinendam tenuiorum inopiam utuntur*; *Letters* 10.93). Financially assisting members by means of loans, meals or burials is likely in mind here with these contributions or collections. Yet, there is nothing in this correspondence that would suggest the support was limited to burial, as often assumed by scholars working with the problematic category of 'burial clubs' for the poor (see Chapter 1). Trajan then suggests that in other cities without these privileges such contribution-societies should not be formed due to the potential for disturbances.[90]

So, although evidence from cities in Greece and Asia Minor provides only momentary and suggestive glimpses (although more than *epigraphic* evidence from Egypt), there are clear signs that the principle of mutual aid was at work in groups here, as in parts of Egypt. Still, there are further noteworthy inscriptions to consider regarding the involvement of associations in the third main type of assistance for members: burial- or memorial-related support.

Despite a dearth of evidence for groups whose *principal* purpose was burial, it is still true that funerary functions played a more or less significant role within associations all over the Mediterranean, including Italy, Greece (both Attica and Boiotia), Asia Minor, the Bosporan region and, as we have already seen, Egypt.[91] A few more words are in order, then, concerning mutual aid in connection with burial, a topic we have encountered piecemeal in the discussion of papyri from Egypt, inscriptions from Attica and group expenditures in Chapter 4.

Early on, members of 'societies' (*thiasoi*) in Attica, for instance, were expected to attend the funeral of fellow members. By the third century BCE at least, some societies had their treasurers pay out a benefit (*taphikon*) to assist in the cost of funerary customs, something that we also witnessed in Ptolemaic Egypt.[92] There were also many instances in Greek or Hellenized cities of Boiotia, Asia Minor, the Bosporan region and Syria when associations of various kinds collected together funds to erect an *individual* memorial for a deceased member, including graves erected by guilds, fellow initiates in mysteries, societies and ethnic-based associations of soldiers.[93] So, for example, worshippers of Dionysos at Tanagra in Boiotia buried Galatas in the third century BCE, the archers devoted to two goddesses buried Euklides in the second, and the butchers

---

[90] Harland (2013: 141–56) = ibid. (2003: 161–76).
[91] Ibid. (2009: 134–6), ibid. (2014: 410–17), Bendlin (2011) on the West.
[92] E.g. *GRA* I 8 = *IG* II² 1275 (325–275 BCE); *IG* II² 1277 (in the comments to *GRA* I 15); *GRA* I 17 = *IG* II² 1278.2 (272 BCE); *GRA* I 30 = *IG* II² 1323.10–11 (194 BCE).
[93] See Harland (2014: 410–17) in connection with *GRA* II 150; Macridy (1904) = *AGRW* 271–4 (groups of soldiers at Sidon); *AGRW* 257 (a group of transporters at Askalon).

buried Hippomachos in the second or first.⁹⁴ At Pantikapaion in the Bosporan region there were numerous individual tombs set up by fellow members of the society. One of them happens to highlight the familial terminology that was commonly used within the association that set up the memorial: 'Those gathered around the priest, Valeris son of Neikostratos, and the father (*patēr*) of the synod, Kallistos the second, and the rest of the members of the synod honoured their own brother (*adelphos*), Symphoros son of Philippos' (*AGRW* 88 = *IBosp* 104; 200–250 CE).⁹⁵ So burial was part of a larger pattern of group cohesion.

What is less well attested, but still important to note in connection with mutual aid, is that certain associations in some regions might also purchase or receive their own *collective* tomb or communal burial plot reserved for members of the group.⁹⁶ It is difficult to generalize, but in some cases, this practice may reflect the lower socioeconomic status of members, suggesting those who may not have been as readily able to afford an individual family grave. This may have been the case with the bed-builders at Ephesos (*IEph* 2213) and the guild of flax workers at Smyrna (*ISmyrna* 218) who both had communal tombs. There also seem to be regional cultural traditions at work, as communal burial is very well attested in southern Asia Minor and on Aegean islands off the south-western coast of Asia Minor, particularly on Kos and Rhodes.⁹⁷ It is less well attested elsewhere.

Rhodian material is illustrative here, particularly as there are signs of corporate collections for burial purposes, combining our interests in mutual material assistance and funerary support. In Chapter 6, we already discussed the association of immigrants and Rhodians who, around 185 BCE, raised a fund (*eranos*) to purchase a place for a common grave (*SEG* 39:737).⁹⁸ Two other Rhodian documents from the second century BCE provide further insight into such communal burial. These show that an association devoted to Aphrodite and led by Zenon of Selge owned burial plots (*taphiai*; *IRhodPC* 18 = *SEG* 3:674).⁹⁹ Here there was concern to give all contributing members (*eranistai*) of the group equal access to burial on this land. Another inscription from Rhodes has such contributors promising funds to restore their communal memorials that had been damaged during an earthquake (*IG* XII,1 9). So communal burial is one further instance of mutual aid that is found in connection with at least some groups in certain regions. For many other groups, the association provided funerary support in less fundamental, although significant, ways, such as gathering for a drink to remember a deceased fellow or erecting an individual gravestone.

---

⁹⁴ Dionysos devotees: *AGRW* 31 = *GRA* I 57 = *IG* VII 686; archers: *GRA* I 59 = *SEG* 26:614; cf. *SEG* 32:487. Butchers: Marchand (2015: 258, no. 5; new reading of *IG* VII 687). See *AGRW* 31, Marchand (2015), and Roesch (1982: 119–202), on associations in Tanagra and Boiotia.
⁹⁵ On this brother language, see Harland (2009: 63–81).
⁹⁶ See ibid. (2014: 410–17).
⁹⁷ *ICiliciaBM* II 190–202; *TAM* II 223. See the comments on *GRA* I 150. For Rhodian territories, see Fraser (1977: 58–70), van Nijf (1997: 48–9). For Kos, see the plots belonging to Hermaists (*IKosS* EF 78), Apolloniasts (*IKosS* EF 201, 214), Anubiasts (*IKosS* EF 458), Bacchiasts (*IKosM* 492), Athenaiasts (*IKosS* EF 399–400), Homonoists (*IKosB* 285), Isiasts (*IKosM* 493) (cf. *IG* XII,2 271, for fullers on Mytilene).
⁹⁸ Kontorini (1989: 73–85, no. 10) = *SEG* 39:737. Cf. Gabrielsen (2001: 229–30), Faraguna (2012: 144).
⁹⁹ Cf. Fraser (1977: 60–1).

Judeans settled in Egypt

Literature from the Hellenistic or Roman eras provides a window into elite Judean perspectives on giving to 'the poor, the widow and the orphan' to some degree, but this is not much help in assessing actual practices of mutual aid within group settings in the diaspora.[100] In the story about Tobit's time in Assyria, for instance, Tobit's advice to his son includes the following:

> For all those who practice righteousness, practice pity (*eleēmosynēn*) from your possessions and do not let your eye hold a grudge when you practice pity. Do not turn your face away from anyone who is poor, and the face of God will not be turned away from you. If you have many possessions, practice pity from them in proportion. If you have few, do not be afraid to practice this in relation to the little you have. For you will be storing up a good deposit for yourself for an urgent day. For pity saves you from death and prevents you from going into the darkness. For pity is a good gift for all who practice it in front of the most high.
>
> Tobit 4:7–16, translated by Harland

The scrolls found at Qumran likewise give somewhat extensive glimpses into attitudes towards wealth and principles of mutual aid pertaining to a somewhat peculiar Judean group in the homeland itself. Some scholars helpfully explore issues of wealth in the Dead Sea scrolls and others engage in careful comparative studies that bring in the evidence of associations with respect to communal regulation.[101] But, once again, our focus in this study is on practices within Judean associations alongside others in the diaspora, not the homeland. In the previous chapter, we have already surveyed some evidence for mutual aid in connection with the poor as reflected in rabbinic literature, looking at two different practices that may have been practised in the diaspora.

For Egypt, in particular, so far there is virtually *no epigraphic evidence* for mutual material aid among members of Judean groups, at least based on our survey of William Horbury and David Noy's *Jewish Inscriptions of Graeco-Roman Egypt*.[102] So we have to rely on papyri or other sources of information to see how members in these diaspora groups accessed such resources through internal social connections. A further implication for studying non-Judean associations is that a lack of *inscriptional* references to such issues should not be taken as an indication that socioeconomic assistance was not important within a particular set of groups. Our sources are often very specific and simply do not provide a balanced view of the moving picture that is social life.

Evidence for Judeans in Egypt providing loans to other Judeans comes from the district of Arsinoites beginning in the Ptolemaic era. Three papyri indicate mutual

---

[100] Cf. Tobit 4:7–16; 12:8–10; Josephus, *Against Apion* 2.207, 211–14, 283. On Josephus' and Philo's views on wealth and giving, see Peterman (1997: 42–9), Schmidt (1983), Downing (1985).

[101] See, for example, the discussions and bibliographies of Murphy (2002, on wealth) and Gillihan (2012, on comparison with associations). Cf. Weinfeld (1986).

[102] Horbury and Noy (1992).

material support among members of an association in the likely event that the Judean creditor and the Judean debtor in each case attended the same Judean prayer-house or belonged to the same ethnic association or 'corporate body' (*politeuma*) of Judeans (*CPJ* I 20, 23, 24). It is important to note that we have yet to find reference to such a 'corporate body' of Judeans or a 'prayer-house' (*proseuchē*) at Tebtynis specifically. Nonetheless, an inscription and several papyri spanning our period do show the existence of such meeting places for Judean groups elsewhere in the district of Arsinoites. Also, it was common for those in the military or descendants of soldiers to form associations based on common ethnicity in various parts of this district.[103] So it is reasonable to propose that there would be an association of Judeans at Tebtynis or at Krokodilopolis, and that the Judeans attested in the three documents below may have interacted with one another as ongoing participants in gatherings of the ethnic association.

Although we cannot be certain that the following loan agreements always entailed members of the same association, then, this papyrological evidence is suggestive of such. If not, then it at least attests to those of a common ethnic identification financially supporting one another. Some of this is also roughly contemporary with the Demotic association regulations and Greek papyri from Egypt that involved adherents of an association financially assisting or providing loans to assist members.

To our knowledge, the earliest Judean case is from Tebtynis. This documents in just a few sentences a loan between Mousaios son of Simon, who is identified as a Judean descending from military settlers, and Lasaites, who is likewise identified in this way (*CPJ* I 20 = *PTebt* III 815; 228–221 BCE). The amount is 108 bronze drachmas at an interest rate of 2 drachmas per month (i.e. the typical 24 per cent). The Pentateuch's prohibitions regarding interest on loans were evidently either unnoticed or interpreted as irrelevant in this context (see Ex 22:24; Lev 25:35–7; Deut 23:20–1; cf. Josephus, *Against Apion* 2.208).

Another more extensive record of a loan is made between Judean descendants of military settlers, in this case at Krokodilopolis, also in the Arsinoites district (*CPJ* I 23 = *PTebt* 817; 182 BCE). We know that settlers engaged in the military (or descendants of such) did form 'corporate bodies' (*politeumata*) at this locale, too (e.g. Cilicians in *IFayum* 15 = *SB* IV 7270; 125–100 BCE), and it would not be a far stretch to imagine Judeans here belonging to a similar group. This time, the deed of loan goes into details regarding Sostratos' offer of his house as security to borrow the sum of two talents and 3,000 bronze drachmas (= 15,000 bronze drachmas total), 'including interest' (if *atokos* is to be interpreted as 'including interest' in papyri, rather than 'interest-free' as the editors of *CPJ* had assumed).[104] This was about the equivalent of 250 silver drachmas at the ratio of 60:1, and the amount was to be paid within the year. Otherwise the creditor, Apollonios, would be entitled to seize the property offered as security.

---

[103] E.g. *IJudEgypt* 117 = *CPJ* III 1532A (246–221 BCE); *CPJ* I 129.5–6 (218 BCE); *CPJ* I 134.29 (c. 100 BCE); *CPJ* I 432.58 (113 CE). A corporate body of Cretans is attested at Tebtynis (*PTebt* I 32), a similar group of Idumeans at Memphis (*OGIS* 737), and another of Cilicians at Krokodilopolis (*IFayum* 15 = *SB* IV 7270). Cf. *PTebt* III 700, lines 38–40 on *politeumata* generally.

[104] On this terminology of interest, see Pestman (1971).

A third document, which is pictured in Figure 8.2, has Judeans at Tebtynis both as creditor and debtor, but, in this case, it seems clear that the two men were also business partners involved in the same occupation. Yet no merchant guild or Judean gathering is mentioned. The witnesses to the contract are also identified as Judeans, potentially belonging to the same group devoted to the Israelite god at a village called Trikomia. Judas son of Josepos, a descendant of military settlers, arranged a loan for Agathokles son of Ptolemy, a Judean belonging to a detachment of the Ptolemaic army (*CPJ* I 24 = *PTebt* III 818; 174 BCE).[105] The contract clarifies that Agathokles had previously received a loan of 5 talents (= 30,000 bronze drachmas) from Judas 'as an advance towards a retail trade business in partnership (*eis probolēn koinēs ergasias meatbolikēs*)' (lines 17–18). This amounts to about 250 silver drachmas at the 120:1 ratio common in this era. It seems that only 17,500 bronze drachmas had actually been used, and so the remaining 12,500 was to be returned to Judas. The new contract arranged to give Agathokles an additional year to repay the 2 talents (= 12,000 bronze drachmas) and 500 bronze drachmas at the standard 24 per cent interest rate. The debt would be increased by half if not paid within the year, again typical for this part of Egypt. Although these were by no means interest-free loans, these three cases nonetheless point to members of the same ethnic group gaining access to material resources from other adherents of the Israelite god and, potentially, affiliates of the same prayer-houses or gatherings.

The instances of mutual aid we have observed among Egyptian associations and the Hellenistic practice of gathering together a friendly loan shed light on some cases of manumission that involve associations of those devoted to the Israelite god.[106] It is important at least to note imperial rulings summarized in the *Digest* which presume that a partnership (*corpus*) or association (*collegium*), like a city, could corporately own and manumit enslaved persons, at least by the time of Ulpian (*c*. 170–223 CE; *AGRW* L49 = *Digest* 2.4.10.4). This presumes that manumission by an association was quite common, and we have already seen instances from Attica in an earlier era. There is, in fact, at least one very clear (although late) instance of enslaved Judeans being manumitted using resources from the common fund of a Judean 'gathering' (*synagōgē*). This late-third-century CE papyrus comes from Oxyrhynchos, south of the Arsinoites district (*GRA* III 276 = *POxy* IX 1205 = *CPJ* III 473; 291 CE). Although the deed is quite heavily damaged on the left side, some important features of the legal action are discernible: two siblings (belonging to a family of Aurelii), who were related to a village official (*exēgētēs*) and are *not* identified as Judeans, manumit (*eleutherōsis*) and release (*apolysis*) their house-born enslaved person (*oikogenē doulēn*), who was named Paramone (literally, 'Possessed'), as well as her two (or three) young children (ages 4 and 10). Most importantly for us here, the apparently large amount for the manumission of these three enslaved persons – 14 talents (= 84,000 drachmas), perhaps at a time of fivefold inflation – was paid 'by the gathering of the Judeans' (*para tēs syna[g]ōgēs tōn*

---

[105] Cf. Modrzejewski (1997: 115–20).
[106] Harrill (1998).

Figure 8.2 Loan agreement involving Josepos and Agathokles (*PTebt* III 818). Courtesy of the Center for the Tebtunis Papyri, University of California, Berkeley.

Ioudaiōn, line 7).[107] It is not clear whether these communal funds were drawn from the normal resources in the group's treasury or whether a special collection or friendly loan was raised for the occasion, as in some cases of manumission in Attica.

Unlike this Oxyrhynchos case, none of the Judean manumission inscriptions from the Bosporan region (southern Russia) directly refers to the use of communal funds to

---

[107] Alfred Wassink's (1991) evaluation of inflation and prices in the third century proposes a fivefold decrease in the value of the denarius from 215–293 CE, which, if correct, would explain this large figure. For somewhat different evaluations of inflation, see Rathbone et al. (2009: 323), Scheidel (2010: 428), Jones (1953). On Judeans at Oxyrhynchos, see also *POxy* II 335.

pay for manumission. But there the Judeans were the enslavers, not the enslaved (see *GRA* II 95 for a full discussion). It may well be that raising a fund to assist friends or fellow immigrants in gaining manumission was more widely practised by Judean associations, but our sources do not allow us to be confident in this regard. Generally speaking, as far as we have been able to determine, the surviving materials for Judean or other immigrant associations do not happen to supply further glimpses into this or other practices of mutual material assistance, beyond provisions associated with burial.

Groups of Jesus adherents

Recognizable evidence for groups dedicated to both the Israelite god and Jesus in the first two centuries is almost entirely literary. So we have virtually no distinguishable epigraphic, papyrological or archaeological sources pertaining to social activities and mutual assistance among members of these groups for the first two centuries. To put it another way, if material evidence was all we had, we would have to admit that there was far more evidence for mutual aid (or 'charity' if you prefer) among some 'pagan' associations than there was for groups focused on Jesus. Yet we do have literary evidence, evidence of a kind that is almost entirely absent for other types of associations. For instance, *letters* by leaders of an association to its members are few and far between in the first two centuries beyond groups of philosophers and associations devoted to the Israelite god or Jesus.[108]

There are significant references to mutual assistance in the literary sources, including assistance that overlaps with some of the practices we have witnessed within other associations.[109] Unfortunately for the social historian interested in cultural practices and social interactions, this literary evidence is prescriptive or reactionary, coming from the perspective of a particular literate individual, rather than the group as whole (unlike collectively established association regulations). This literature is *prescriptive* in advocating certain behaviours among adherents. Yet, unlike the prescriptive association regulations that specify fines and take a sort of legal force within the group, for instance, it is difficult to assess how important or how well implemented such prescriptions by a literate individual were in social interactions. Or the literature is *reactionary* in defending adherents of Jesus against the negative perceptions or accusations of 'crimes' by some outsiders – accusations of human sacrifice, cannibalism and incest among the more dramatic ones. Neither type of source is particularly helpful for the historian who aims to reconstruct a likely scenario regarding social practices among participants in the groups in question. Although the negative stereotypes that draw on ethnographic discourses are likely based on ignorance (rather than misunderstanding, as previously

---

[108] Do, however, see *AGRW* 289 = *PMich* IX 575, from Karanis in Egypt (see Chapter 5) and *GRA* III 215 = *PLips* II 131, from first-century Tebtynis (letter opening only).

[109] The focus here is on practices rather than ideological explanations or justifications offered by ancient authors regarding such behaviours. For recent studies of ideological factors surrounding Judean concepts of 'almsgiving' or 'charity', see, among others, Garrison (1993), Meeks (1993), Finn (2006), Hays (2009), Downs (2011), Gray (2011).

believed), the characterizations show that devotees of Jesus, like some Judeans, could be viewed as morally base and uncivilized in their practices, rather than as paragons of virtue or mutualism.[110] The retorsion argument of many apologetic writers was precisely to turn these accusations on the accusers, with those outside the group being portrayed in similarly negative terms (e.g. Minucius Felix, *Octavius*). Similarly, those with one style of following Jesus could sling accusations of unethical or abhorrent behaviours against those with another style. Yet the social historian needs to refrain both from taking sides in rhetorical battles and from uncritically adopting the moralizing perspectives of our historical subjects.

Having made these preliminary comments, we can move on to the point that both prescriptive and apologetic literary sources by educated followers of Jesus in the first two centuries clearly present the *ideal* of mutual aid as central to group self-understanding. It is difficult to measure the degree to which this ideal was reflected in social practice, however, and repetition of the prescriptions suggests that behaviours did not line up with the ideal. The author of *2 Clement*, for instance, worries about perceptions by outsiders: 'When they see that we not only do not love those who hate us, but do not even love those who love us, they mock us and the name ["Christian"] is slandered' (*2 Clement* 13.4).

Still, there are numerous positive calls for mutual aid of various sorts in these literary sources. Building on teachings attributed to Jesus – which themselves were based upon Israelite and second temple Judean tradition (see especially, Ex 22:20-36) – these literate authors sought, in part, to encourage people to help fellow adherents in material ways. These teachings included the call to 'love your neighbour as yourself' (Matt 22:39 // Leviticus 19:18); to 'give to every one who begs from you' (Lk 6:30 // Tobit 4:7, 16; 12:8-10); to 'love your enemies, do good, and lend, expecting nothing in return' (Lk 6:35 // Ex 22:24; Lev 25:35-7; Deut 23:20-1); and, to feed the hungry and visit the imprisoned (Matt 25:34-6). In some early ethical teaching (and contemporary Judean parenesis), the concern of the Pentateuch, Israelite prophets and writings (as well as Ancient Near Eastern literature, generally) for 'the widow', 'the orphan' and 'the poor' are echoed as well.[111] This particular emphasis on these three subgroups as worthy of special assistance is, then, specific to some Israelite or Judean cultural traditions and these traditions were inherited by certain followers of Jesus. Orphans and widows do not appear as a focus of attention in any sources relating to non-Judean associations, but nor do they appear as a focus of attention in the authentic letters of Paul, for instance.

It should be clarified that this chapter is *not* concentrated on rhetorical tendencies, attitudes or ideologies about 'the poor' or about wealth, which have been the focus of many useful studies.[112] The focus here is rather on signs that members of a group engaged in *practices and behaviours* to materially support other participants in the same group, including but not limited to poor members. Here we can only be selective

---

[110] On the ethnographic cultural context of such accusations, see Harland (2009: 161-81).
[111] On the relation between prescriptions and social practice among the Israelites or Judeans, see Sneed (1999), Schmidt (1983), Downing (1985), Peterman (1997: 42-9). Cf. *Sirach* 35.14-26.
[112] E.g. González (1990), Holman (2008), Longenecker and Liebengood (2009), Rhee (2012).

in sketching out some examples of calls to mutual aid with material implications, observing the difficulties in moving from rhetoric to social interactions.

The letters of Paul are, of course, filled with moral exhortations aimed at promoting certain behaviours among members of these groups, and there are clear signs that mutual assistance plays a role. Building on Denise Kimber Buell's study, Ryan Schellenberg's recent work helpfully engages the question of whether Paul's admonitions to materially help others are aimed primarily at wealthier members who are to help less well-off members in the form of 'charity' or 'almsgiving' (as Longenecker tends to assume) or whether Paul anticipates those with lesser means sharing with one another.[113] Schellenberg stresses mutualism or sharing among those of somewhat equal means as the principal focus of the exhortations. In the previous chapter, we have already explored the collection of money in Pauline assemblies to send to 'the poor' in Jerusalem, which may or may not be a reference to those who were literally poor in a material sense. Paul gives the impression of success in actually raising the funds for this collection among assemblies in at least Macedonia and Attica.

As to the question of whether adherents addressed by the letters actually engaged in the other mutually supportive behaviours Paul advocates, it is difficult to determine. For there are both signs of divergence from Paul's way (as with contingents at Corinth) and apparently enthusiastic adoption of his advice on certain issues (as at Thessalonica and Philippi). Paul's characterization of the situation at Corinth leaves the impression that mutual enmity and rivalries were at times more prevalent than mutual support in some circles, particularly among some of the 'noble' (*eugenēs*) adherents at Corinth.[114] Paul raises concerns about his recipients taking disputes to civic authorities in Corinth. He advises that disagreements among members should be handled internally, which is a concern we have witnessed in connection with other associations (1 Cor 6:1–11). The communal meals at Corinth are, in Paul's view, another place where divisions rather than mutuality prevails, as 'each of you goes ahead with your own supper, and one goes hungry and another becomes drunk' (1 Cor 11:21). This rings of concerns over taking one another's place and engaging in disputes at banquets of other associations as witnessed in regulations.

Other Pauline letters give the impression that some adherents were more in line with Paul's advice about how to assist and treat one another. Paul's moral exhortations in what is likely his earliest letter (*c.* 50 CE) are focused, as often, on sexual restraint (1 Thess 4:1–8). But there is the call to continue to 'love one another' (4:9) and the frequent use of fictive familial language ('brothers') seemingly to underline that point. There is a lack of any clear prescriptions pertaining to material assistance among members at Thessalonica (based on 1 Thess), however. Paul's letter to the group at Philippi centres on praising the recipients as a concrete model of material aid in financially supporting Paul's own teaching activities, providing gifts or benefactions on several occasions. Yet, here, very little is said regarding similar practices between members. Finally, Paul's letter to Rome once again elicits the metaphor of the body to express the mutuality that

---

[113] Schellenberg (2018). Cf. Buell (2008).
[114] See, for instance, Marshall (1987), Chow (1992), Clarke (1993).

he hoped would exist, although with few specific instructions, perhaps due in part to the fact that Paul did not know this group as well as others (Rom 12:4–5; cf. 1 Cor 12:12–31). So Paul's letters do provide a window into both the ideal (Paul's promotion of what he considered mutual support) and the real (certain contingents at odds with one another or at odds with Paul himself) within groups in the mid-first century.

Since we have often been dealing with regulations, it might be appropriate to turn to signs of mutual material assistance within our earliest surviving regulation used by Jesus adherents, the *Didache* or *Teaching of the Twelve Apostles*. This writing, which likely dates to the first half of the second century and originates in Syria, begins by echoing back precisely such prescriptive teachings attributed to Jesus as those mentioned earlier (those presented in some of the biographies or 'gospels' of Jesus). In particular, the regulation emphasizes the need to give without expecting in return, but also adds a warning against any member receiving when not in need (*Didache* 1.1–6; cf. 15.4). The author (or authors) returns again to the issue of giving to other adherents or partners (*koinōnoi*), stating that: 'you shall not turn away from someone in need, but shall share everything with your brother, and not claim that anything is your own' (*Didache* 4.8).[115] Buell's study of this and other similar passages draws attention to the fact that this is not necessarily envisioned as a case of 'charity' in the sense of a wealthier person helping a poorer member, but rather a case of mutual support among those in less secure material circumstances. She thinks this is focused on those 'at or near subsistence'.[116] In particular, the broader context of the *Didache* passage suggests it is those engaged in manual labour – those who acquire resources through working with their hands (*dia tōn cheirōn*) – that are the target of the prescription (*Didache* 4.5–6). Similarly, the *Shepherd of Hermas* (*Similitudes* 5.3.6) pictures a scenario in which a follower of Jesus engaged in fasting (on bread and water) would save the money usually used for other food in that same period in order to offer it to a widow, orphan or someone else who was 'falling behind' in material needs. This, too, implies that the giver would not usually have excess funds to support other members and would only possess modest material means.

There is a counterbalance to the *Didache*'s call to give, however, in the warning about adherents from elsewhere who accept material assistance while travelling: 'If the one who comes is merely passing through, assist him as much as you can. But he must not stay with you for more than two or, if necessary, three days. However, if he wishes to settle among you and is a craftsman, let him work for his living' (*Didache* 12.1–3; cf. *Didascalia Apostolorum* 17). So there are limits attached to the call for socioeconomic aid in some cases.

In this regulation, there are no references to the group's potential role in burial. Nor are there any references to loaning practices (interest-free or interest-bearing) among members which, potentially, could have been founded upon sayings attributed to Jesus mentioned earlier (e.g. Lk 6:32–5), if known to the author of the *Didache*.[117] While the *Didache* does not deal with helping those in prison, the later *Didascalia* (third century CE),

---

[115] Cf. *Epistle of Barnabas* 19.9–12; *2 Clement* 16.1–4; *Sirach* 4.31; Downs (2011).
[116] Buell (2008). Cf. Schellenberg (2018).
[117] Later guilds consisting of Christians continued to offer members loans: e.g. *PStrass* IV 287, from the sixth century CE. Cf. Fikhman (1994: 37).

which builds on the *Didache* in other respects and also pertains to Syria, does provide instructions to leaders (overseers) to assist members who were imprisoned unjustly (*Didascalia apostolorum* 19). There are also guidelines for helping widows and orphans in that later work (*Didascalia apostolorum* 17–18). In both of these regulatory documents, the calls for action are aimed at assisting the poor and others within the group, not outsiders.

Similar to Paul in certain respects, Ignatius of Antioch's letters (written around 110 CE) are filled with the call to harmony among members of the groups he addresses. But this is harmony of a particular sort under the authority of a threefold hierarchical structure of 'overseer' (bishop), 'elders' (presbyters) and 'servants' (deacons). Furthermore, this is concord united against certain alternate or 'evil' teachings, particularly teachings among those who adopt a certain approach to Judean scriptures (at Philadelphia) and those who say that Jesus only *appeared* to suffer or have a full fleshly existence (at Smyrna). In fact, there are very few passages in Ignatius' letters to the assemblies in Asia aimed at advocating material support among members. This may be due, in part, to the fact that Ignatius is far more concerned that his recipients reject those who espouse 'evil' teachings and accompanying practices.

Among his complaints about those who hold alternate opinions (*hoi heterodoxountoi*) – probably those who downplay Jesus' fleshly existence and suffering, in this case – is that such people do not engage in mutual assistance of fellow members. Ignatius (knowingly or unknowingly) echoes the Israelite prophetic tradition: 'They have no concern for love, none for the widow, none for the orphan, none for the oppressed, none for the prisoner or the one released, none for the hungry or thirsty' (*Smyrna* 6.2).[118] Here, Ignatius is listing what he does expect of his recipients, and it is worth noticing that practical help (or 'love', to use his terms) for those who had been imprisoned is included. This practice of accusing alternative groups devoted to Jesus with failure to engage in ethical behaviour, particularly mutual aid, becomes somewhat standard in the literature and, of course, cannot be taken at face value.[119] With respect to Ignatius' reference to captives, we have seen that regulations of associations in Egypt in particular emphasize the need to help fellow members imprisoned due to debt or other issues, and at least one inscription from Attica echoed such expectations.

Among the purposes of friendly loans in Attica and at Delphi was to raise funds to assist an enslaved person seeking manumission. We have seen similar collective action by a Judean association at Oxyrhynchos. Ignatius' letter to Polycarp, the overseer of a group at Smyrna, is among the earliest pieces of evidence that deal directly with the issue of using *communal funds* to support certain members of groups devoted to Jesus. The focus in this passage is on widows, on the one hand, and enslaved persons seeking manumission, on the other (*Polycarp* 4.1, 3):

---

[118] Cf. *Polycarp* 4.1, on widows; 1 John 3:17; *Shepherd of Hermas* 38.10.
[119] See Harland (2009: 178–9). Cf. Epiphanius, *Panarion* 26.3–5; *Gospel of Judas* 39.12–23.

Do not let the widows be neglected. After the Lord, you be their guardian. Let nothing happen without your decree ... Do not treat slaves, whether male or female, arrogantly, but neither let them be full of themselves. Instead, let them serve even more for the glory of god, that they may obtain from god a better freedom. *They should not desire to be set free using the common fund*, so that they may not be discovered to be slaves of desire (*mē eratōsan apo tou koinou eleutherousthai, hina mē douloi eurethōsin epithymias*).

This passage has been explored at length in an insightful study by Albert Harrill, which need not be rehearsed here, except to address some relevant issues.[120]

We have already explained the importance of the friendly loan or collection raised by an association, sometimes to help someone in dire straits. In certain cases, the funds gathered in such a financial collection could be used to manumit someone who was enslaved. Regardless of the reasons for Ignatius doing so (some of which Harrill attempts to reconstruct), what is clear is that Ignatius is here *forbidding* the use of communal money to sponsor the manumission of enslaved persons who were participants in the group. In this sense, it seems he is going against the grain of expectations of mutual aid by members in some other associations and within assemblies devoted to Jesus at Smyrna. Still, in Ignatius' view, such communal funds *were* supposed to be used to support widows, a view shared by the author of the Pastoral epistles in cases where a 'real' widow did not have family members to financially support her (1 Tim 5:3-16); however, like Ignatius' concern that communal funds not be 'misused', the author of 1 Timothy stresses the primary importance of family members (5:8, 16) in financially supporting (at least younger) widows so that they would not be a financial burden on the assembly.[121] So there are restrictions on the use of communal funds to assist participants in both cases. Ignatius himself denies one form of socioeconomic assistance while affirming another, but the reasons for this variation are less than clear, in our view.

Nonetheless, the fact that Ignatius speaks directly against a specific practice implies that, on some occasions and in some groups devoted to Jesus, resources from the common fund or a specific collection were, in fact, being used for this purpose in keeping with local cultural custom. With respect to enslaved people in such groups of Jesus adherents, more commonly attested than this practice of manumission is the call for the enslavers 'to persuade [slaves] to become Christians, and when they have done so to call them "brothers" without distinction', as in Aristides' *Apology* (15, echoing Paul's letter to Philemon in some respects).

The apologetic literature provides further references to the sorts of social capital that was accessible to members of these associations devoted to Jesus. Petitions (real or fictive) to emperors by authors such as Aristides (c. 117–138 CE) and Justin Martyr (c. 155 CE) were often concerned to refute rumours of improper behaviours among adherents, the most extreme ones being the accusations of human sacrifice, cannibalism and incest directly addressed by Justin (cf. *Letter of the Churches of Lyons*; Minucius

---

[120] Harrill (1993) = ibid. (1998).
[121] On which, see, most recently, LaFosse (2011).

Felix, *Octavius*). The response was to assert positive models of behaviour as the norm, with the implication being that outsiders would see such behaviour as in some sense positive or at least *normal* on local Greek standards (cf. 1 Peter 2:11–3:22). Both Aristides and Justin echo passages in the Judean scriptures in claiming that groups devoted to Jesus would regularly offer financial aid to certain adherents, including widows, orphans, the poor and 'strangers' from other communities (Aristides, *Apology* 15; Justin, *First Apology* 67). Both also suggest that captives or the imprisoned would likewise receive help (cf. *1 Clement* 55:2).

Justin clarifies what he sees as the common procedure for raising funds to support these people in difficult circumstances. On the main day of meeting, Sunday,

> those who are well to do, and willing, give what each thinks appropriate. What is collected is deposited with the president (*to syllegomenon para tō proestōti apotithetai*). He supports the orphans and widows; those who, through sickness or any other cause, are in need; those who are in bonds; and, the foreigners travelling among us. In general, he takes care of all who are in need.
>
> *First Apology* 67.6–7

This pictures members regularly – weekly – engaging in collections with the money being deposited in a common fund or treasury maintained by a functionary, who was responsible for redistribution to members in need. Although expressing the ideal in grander terms, it is also worth mentioning that the author of Luke-Acts claims that the earliest followers of Jesus in Jerusalem formed a common fund which was used to support any who had need (see also Chapter 3). Yet this is portrayed as a pooling of resources and possessions in a context where everything 'was held in common' (Acts 4:32–5).[122]

For associations in Egypt, we have seen that there was a concern to assist members who had been imprisoned. As Carolyn Osiek's study shows, the call for adherents of Jesus to rescue or give aid to captives or prisoners, in particular, is commonly attested in the literature.[123] This call may, at times, be closely connected to Israelite traditions on the positive treatment of captives and the enslaved (Lev 25:42, 55; Deut 15:15). There is some confirmation that the moral exhortations were, at times, heeded. Paul's more incidental references to receiving assistance to meet his needs while in prison are suggestive (e.g. Phil 3:19–30).

Yet, perhaps the most solid evidence in confirming actual practice among Jesus adherents in helping those captive or imprisoned comes from an outsider, Lucian of Samosata (*Peregrinus* 11–13). Lucian's satire has the Cynic philosopher Peregrinus, during his time as prophet and leader of the 'Christians', being helped while in prison. The adherents are pictured leaving 'nothing undone in the effort to rescue him'. According to Lucian, adherents brought meals to him in prison and others came to him from cities of Asia with expenses drawn 'from the common fund' (*apo tou koinou*) of their society. Supplying meals was among the expectations of associates assisting others in prison in the Demotic regulations discussed earlier.

---

[122] On the relation between this rhetoric and reality, see Sterling (1994; contrast Bartchy, 1991).
[123] Osiek (1981). E.g. Matthew 25:36, 39, 43; Hebrews 13:3 and 10:34; *1 Clement* 55.2 and 59.4; Ignatius, *Smyrnaeans* 6.2; *Shepherd of Hermas* 8.10.

Defenders of those devoted to Jesus, such as Aristides and Tertullian, also claim that these groups provided burial for those who could not readily pay for a proper funeral. Aristides writes that: 'whenever one of their poor passes from the world, each one of them according to his ability gives heed to him and carefully sees to his burial' (*Apology* 15; cf. Tertullian, *Scapula* 4). When arguing that the Christian association (*secta, factio*) should be considered legitimate and, in fact, beneficial rather than harmful, Tertullian points out that this association had a 'treasury' (*arca*). This was a treasury where monthly – rather than weekly, as in Justin's scenario – voluntary donations were gathered as 'deposits of piety' (*Apology* 39.5–6; trans. LCL):

> Even if there is a treasury (*arcae*) of some sort, it does not collect money paid in entrance fees (*honoraria*), as if conscientiousness (*religio*) could be bought. Once a month, everyone brings some modest amount – or whenever he wants, and only if he wants and if he is able. For nobody is forced to do this, and it is voluntary. You might call them the deposits of piety. In fact, these funds are not spent on banquets, drinking, or unpleasant taverns, but on feeding and burying the poor, on boys and girls who do not have parents, on aged domestic slaves, on shipwrecked persons, and on any who are in the mines, on islands, or in prisons, provided that they are in such places for the sake of god's sect (*secta*).

The description here makes it very clear that this is indeed a picture of mutual aid *among fellow adherents* ('brothers', as Tertullian goes on to say). This is not a vision of adherents helping outsiders, it should be clarified.

Burying the poor was an important part of this situation. Our earliest examples of memorial tombs for followers of Jesus suggest that, like other associations, the common funds of assemblies could at times be used to pay for a memorial or casket for a member or leader. One of the earliest tombs identifiable as belonging to a Jesus adherent, dating to about 200–210 CE, comes from Temenothyrai in Lydia. This involves the use of 'the Lord's fund' (*ek tou kyriakou*) to supply a well-decorated memorial for an overseer (*episkopos*), although we could suppose that, in theory, he may have been a 'poor' one.[124] In many other cases, adherents of these groups, like others in the ancient Mediterranean, followed the pattern of burial by family rather than by association. Nonetheless, associates in many groups could still offer moral support by attending the funeral, by holding a feast in the deceased's honour, or by coming to the site on subsequent occasions to remember the dead and care for the grave.

Conclusion

As with many things in ancient history, we only have partial access to practices of mutual material assistance within some associations, Judean gatherings and groups devoted to Jesus. Certain types of evidence, such as the papyri, provide more detailed information for certain associations, while epigraphy supplements the picture for

---

[124] Tabbernee (1997: no. 3).

places outside of Egypt. For those groups devoted to the Israelite god, we often need to rely largely on literary exhortations or on representations of ideal behaviours, although these sources, too, provide insight into the possibilities. While the papyri sometimes shed light on socioeconomic interactions among members of Egyptian associations, it is difficult to evaluate the relation between prescriptive exhortations or reactive apologetics in literature, on the one hand, and day-to-day social conditions, on the other. And yet the momentary glimpses into social life these limited materials offer do begin to indicate that mutual assistance was an important principle at work within a significant number of groups, whether devoted to the Israelite god or not.

There were three types of activities pertaining to socioeconomic assistance that we first witnessed in the Demotic regulations of Ptolemaic Egypt: providing funds or loans to fellow adherents in need; coming to a member's aid when that member faced legal or other difficult situations, including imprisonment; and, attending or ensuring an appropriate funeral or burial after death. These three echoed back in materials from subsequent centuries and from other parts of the Greek-speaking eastern Mediterranean, even though the evidence is, unfortunately, partial. These three areas of mutual assistance show how closely knit social ties could provide access to social capital in the ancient context, contributing to the longevity of certain associations.

Conclusion

This bird's eye perspective on local social life by way of associations in the eastern Mediterranean amply shows that group survival was by no means guaranteed. The survival of a given group was, of course, dependent upon local social, political and economic circumstances at a particular time, and these circumstances could differ from one group to another and from one city or region to the next. Despite the diversity, there were recurrent patterns that we observed for many different types of associations. In the struggle for survival, collective agency was central as groups with varying means were often primarily sustained by participants within the group by means of communal procedures. Sometimes substantial contributions from benefactors did play a more important role for certain groups, particularly extended family associations. Overall, though, group cohesion and material sustainability were intimately connected. Any decline in membership could be a potential threat to the well-being of an association, particularly an association that functioned at or near the material means of its members, like the Tebtynis associations that we highlighted.

Correspondingly, the degree to which members were tied to one another, and to the group as a whole, could closely correspond to a group's level of success and potential longevity. Associations relied on the ongoing commitment and material contributions of their members. In return, such members received a number of benefits beyond the most obvious social attachments the group offered. Communal collections aimed at honouring deities and other purposes illustrate well the collective action and material procedures that were the lifeblood of many associations of various types, immigrant associations included. The fact that associations could themselves be a magnification of commonly accepted principles of reciprocity and mutual aid within society is, therefore, closely linked to material circumstances and survival. As a local, more or less tightly knit social network, an ongoing association provided participants access to social capital in the form of resources of various kinds, both material and non-material.

Associations devoted to the Israelite god, like other ethnic or minority associations, were among these unofficial groups that needed to develop strategies for addressing local circumstances, managing material resources and meeting members' needs in order to survive. These groups – despite being minorities with respect to their devotion to a foreign god – were by no means alone in offering participants socioeconomic assistance in difficult circumstances during life and at death. Approaching group sustainability from the perspective of nitty-gritty material circumstances has allowed us to observe how gatherings of Judeans and assemblies of Jesus adherents, like other associations, could in many important respects be woven within the everyday social fabric of local communities in the ancient Mediterranean world.

APPENDIX

Women Participating in Associations, 1st Century BCE–2nd Century CE

Source	List type	Region	Group	Total size	Women
First century BCE					
IThraceL 212	Members	Maroneia, Thrace	'Servants' of Isis and Sarapis (*therapeutists*)	63	1
IG V,1 209 = AGRW 29	Members	Sparta, Peloponnesos	Banqueters (*sitēthentes*)	33	3
IChiosMcCabe 82	Contributors	Chios, Aegean	Devotees led by 'servants'	13+	13+
IG VII 3224	Members	Orchomenos, Boiotia	Friends to the gods	21	0
IG II² 2360	Members	Athens, Attica	Fellow sacrificers (*synthytai*)	84	0
SEG 54: 235 = GRA I 47	Members	Epano Liosa, Attica	Contributors (*eranistai*)	130	34
IMilet 798	Members	Miletus, Ionia	Sanctuary devotees (*temenitai*)	20	0
SEG 43:59	Members	Rhamnous, Attica	Contributors (*eranistai*)	11+	0
IG V,1 210	Members	Sparta, Peloponnesos	Poseidon devotees (*Tainarioi*)	56	1
IG V,1 211	Members	Sparta, Peloponnesos	Poseidon devotees	52	0
IG V,1 212	Members	Sparta, Peloponnesos	Poseidon devotees	55	1(?)
IKyme 37 = GRA II 105	Contributors	Kyme, Aiolis	Partners (*metechontes*)	50+	27
IG VII 33	Members	Megara, Central Greece	Sacrificing associates (*orgeōnes*)	4	0
First century CE					
PMich V 247	Members	Tebtynis, Egypt	Unknown	16	0
PMich V 248	Members	Tebtynis, Egypt	Unknown	9	0
IG X,2.1 259 = GRA I 76	Members	Thessalonica, Macedonia	Initiates (*mystai*)	17	0

Source	List type	Region	Group	Total size	Women
First century BCE					
PMich V 243 = AGRW 300	Members	Tebtynis, Egypt	Livestock dealers (?)	16	0
PMich V 244 = AGRW 301	Members	Tebtynis, Egypt	Exempted ones (hoi apolysimoi)	24	0
PMich V 246	Members	Tebtynis, Egypt	Synod (synodos)	15	0
TAM Suppl III 201	Members	Direvli, Western Rough Cilicia	Stonemasons	10	0
SEG 46: 744 = GRA I 65	Members	Edessa, Macedonia	Associates (synētheis)	13	1
IEph I 20 = GRA II 127	Contributors	Ephesos, Ionia	Fishermen	98	7
ISmyrna 731–2 = AGRW 190	Members	Smyrna	Synod (synodos)	18+	0
CIRB 76	Members	Pantikapaion, Bosporan region	Society members (thiasitai)	19	0
IG X,2.1 68 = AGRW 51	Members	Thessalonica, Macedonia	Fellow banqueters (synklitai)	38	0
Second–third centuries CE					
IG X,2.1 58 = AGRW 47	Members	Thessalonica, Macedonia	Sacred object-bearers (hieraphoroi) and fellow banqueters (synklitai)	14	0
CIL III 633 II–IV = GRA I 68	Members	Philippi, Macedonia	Soldiers (sodales)	71 (II) 23 (III) 10 (IV)	0
Robert 1937, 513–15	Members	Hyllarima, Caria	Contributors (eranistai)	11	0
IPrusaOlymp 52	Members	Bithynia	Initiates (mystai)	44+	0
IEph 1602	Members	Ephesos, Ionia	Initiates	100+	0
IBosp 1262	Members	Tanais, Bosporan region	Society members (thiasitai)	30	0
CIL XI 6310	Members	Pisaurum, Umbria	Devotees (cultores) of Iovis Latium	27	3 + 1 patron
CIL III 5196	Members	Celeia, Noricum	Devotees (cultores) of Mercurius Augustus	20	0
IBosp 1054	Members	Hermonassa, Bosporan region	Synod (synodos)	11	0
CIL XIV 246	Members	Ostia, Latium	Ferry workers (corpus traiectus Luculli)	192	0
ILLPN 610	Members	Noricum	Builders (collegium subaedianorum)	57	22
IG X,2.1 244	Members	Thessalonica, Macedonia	Unknown	20	0

Appendix: Women Participating in Associations 191

Source	List type	Region	Group	Total size	Women
First century BCE					
IGUR 160 = *AGRW* 330	Contributors	Terre Nova, Sicily	Initiates (*mystai*) of Dionysos	402	110
CIL XIV 250 = *AGRW* 314a	Members	Ostia, Latium	Sailors and accountants	128	0
IEph 1600	Membership	Ephesos, Ionia	Initiates of Dionysus	c. 51	0
IBosp 1134 = *GRA* II 93	Members	Gorgippia, Bosporan region	Society (*thiasos*)	44+	0
IBosp 1277 = *AGRW* 91	Members	Tanais, Bosporan region	Synod (*synodos*)	37+	0
AÉ 1994, no. 1334	Contributors/ Members	Virunum, Noricum	Devotees of Mithras (*cultores dei invicti Mithrae*)	98 (including 25+ contributors)	0
CIL XIV 251 = *AGRW* 314b	Members	Ostia, Italy	Sailors and accountants	272	0
ITomis 83	Members	Tomis, Moesia	Tree-bearers devoted to Cybele	38	2
CIL III 5191	Members	Celeia, Noricum	Devotees (*cultores*) of Iovis Optimus Maximus	20	0
CIL III 11699	Members	Celeia, Noricum	Devotees (*cultores*) of Volkanus Augustus	72	0
CIL XIV 252	Members	Ostia, Italy	Boat owners	16	0
IThraceD, letter O (p. 316)	Members	Serdica, Thrace	Devotees of Hypsistos	17+	0
IG II² 2361 = *GRA* I 52	Members and contributors	Piraeus, Attica	Sacrificing associates (*orgeōnes*) devoted to goddess Belala	24 (members) 17 (contributors)	1 (member); 17 (contributors)
ZPE 188 (2014), 277	Members	Ulpiana, Dalmatia	Women (*mulieres*)	12	12 (and 1 mother)
CIL III 6150	Members	Nicropolis by Istrum, Moesia Inferior	Devotees of Dionysos (*collegium Bacchii vernaculorum*)	77	3
CIL III 870	Members	Napoca, Dacia	'Asians' (*collegium Asianorum*)	43	17 (and 1 mother)
CIL II 5812	Members	Segisamum, Hisp. Tar.	Unknown	21	6
AE 1977, no. 265b	Members	Classis (Ravenna) Italy	Unknown	62	7 (and 5 mothers)
IG II² 4817	Members	Athens, Attica	Devotees of Artemis Kolainis	19	6
GRA I 84	Members	Augusta Traiana, Thrace	'Company' (*speira*)	4	0
IGBulg 1626 = *GRA* I 85	Members	Augusta Traiana, Thrace	Fellow banqueters (*symposiasts*) of Asklepios	12	0

Source	List type	Region	Group	Total size	Women
First century BCE					
Piccottini 1993, 119	Members	Virunum	Builders (*collegium sub(a)edianorum*)	52	19
SEG 46: 800 = GRA I 72	Members	Pydna, Macedon	Devotees of Zeus Hypsistos (*thrēskeutai*)	34	3

Bibliography

Book series and other periodical abbreviations follow:

Patrick H. Alexander et al. (eds), *The SBL Handbook of Style* (Atlanta, GA: Society of Biblical Literature, 2014), available at: http://www.jstor.org/stable/j.ctt14bs6ct.

In addition:

AM   *Mitteilungen des Deutschen archäologischen Instituts, Athenische Abteilung.*
IM   *Mitteilungen des Deutschen archäologischen Instituts, Istanbuler Abteilung.*

Adams, C. (2007) *Land Transport in Roman Egypt: A Study of Economics and Administration in a Roman Province*, Oxford: Oxford University Press.
Adams, E. (2013) *The Earliest Christian Meeting Places: Almost Exclusively Houses?*, London: T&T Clark.
Adler, P. S. and S.-W. Kwon (2002) 'Social capital: Prospects for a new concept', *Academy of Management Review*, 27: 17–40.
Alföldy, G. (1985) *The Social History of Rome*, translated by David Braund and Frank Pollock, London: Croom Helm.
Allen, R. C. (2009) 'How prosperous were the Romans? Evidence from Diocletian's Price Edict (AD301)', in A. Bowman and A. Wilson (eds), *Quantifying the Roman Economy*, Oxford: Oxford University Press, pp. 327–45.
Alston, R. (2002) *City in Roman and Byzantine Egypt*, London: Routledge.
Ameling, W. (1990) 'Koinon TΩN ΣΙΔ ΩΝΙΩΝ', *ZPE*, 81: 189–99.
Anderson, R. T. (1971) 'Voluntary associations in history', *American Anthropologist*, 73: 209–22.
Arnal, W. E., R. S. Ascough, R. A. Derrenbacker and P. A. Harland (eds) (2016) *Scribal Practices and Social Structures among Jesus Adherents: Essays in Honour of John S. Kloppenborg*, BETL, 285, Leuven: Peeters.
Arnal, W. E. and R. T. McCutcheon (2013) *The Sacred is the Profane: The Political Nature of 'Religion'*, New York: Oxford University Press.
Arnaoutoglou, I. (2003) *Thusias heneka kai sunousias: Private Religious Associations in Hellenistic Athens*, Athens: Academy of Athens.
Arnaoutoglou, I. (2007) 'Group and individuals in IRhamnous 59 (SEG 49.161)', in J.-C. Couvenhes and S. Milanezi (eds), *Individus, groupes et politique à Athènes de Solon à Mithridate*, Perspectives Historiques, Tours: Presses Universitaires François-Rabelais, pp. 315–37.
Arnaoutoglou, I. (2012) 'Cultural transfer and law in Hellenistic Lycia: The case of Symmasis' foundation', in Bernard Legras (ed.), *Transferts culturels et droits dans le monde grec et hellénistique*, Paris: Publications de la Sorbonne, pp. 205–24.
Arnaoutoglou, I. (2015) 'Cult associations and politics: Worshipping Bendis in classical and Hellenistic Athens', in V. Gabrielsen and C. A. Thomsen (eds), *Private Associations*

and the Public Sphere: Proceedings of a Symposium Held at the Royal Danish Academy of Sciences and Letters, 9–11 September 2010, Copenhagen: Det Kongelige Danske Videnskabernes Selskab, pp. 25–56.

Asad, T. (2003) *Formations of the Secular: Christianity, Islam, Modernity*, Cultural Memory in the Present, Stanford, CA: Stanford University Press.

Ascough, R. S. (1996) 'The completion of a religious duty: The background of 2 Cor 8.1–15', *NTS*, 42: 584–99.

Ascough, R. S. (1998) *What Are They Saying about the Formation of Pauline Churches?*, New York: Paulist Press.

Ascough, R. S. (2000) 'The Thessalonian Christian community as a professional voluntary association', *JBL*, 119: 311–28.

Ascough, R. S. (2003) *Paul's Macedonian Associations: The Social Context of Philippians and 1 Thessalonians*, WUNT 161, Tübingen: Mohr Siebeck.

Ascough, R. S. (2007) '"A place to stand, a place to grow": Architectural and epigraphic evidence for expansion in Greco-Roman associations', in Z. A. Crook and P. A. Harland (eds), *Identity and Interaction in the Ancient Mediterranean: Jews, Christians and Others. Essays in Honour of Stephen G. Wilson*, Sheffield: Sheffield Phoenix Press, pp. 76–98.

Ascough, R. S. (2016) 'Reimagining the size of Pauline Christ groups', in W. E. Arnal, R. S. Ascough, R. A. Derrenbacker and P. A. Harland (eds), *Scribal Practices and Social Structures among Jesus Adherents: Essays in Honour of John S. Kloppenborg*, BETL, 285. Leuven: Peeters, pp. 547–66.

Ascough, R. S., P. A. Harland and J. S. Kloppenborg (eds) (2012) *Associations in the Greco-Roman World: A Sourcebook*, Waco, TX: Baylor University Press.

Audin, A. (1986) *Gens de Lugdunum*, Collection Latomus, 190, Bruxelles: Latomus: Revue d'études latines.

Ausbüttel, F. M. (1982) *Untersuchungen zu den Vereinen im Westen des römischen Reiches*, Frankfurter Althistorische Studien, 11, Kallmünz: Verlag Michael Lassleben.

Balch, D. L. (2004) 'Rich Pompeiian houses, shops for rent, and the huge apartment building in Herculaneum as typical spaces for Pauline house churches', *JSNT*, 27: 27–46.

Balch, D. L. and C. Osiek (eds) (2003) *Early Christian Families in Context: An Interdisciplinary Dialogue*, Grand Rapids, MI: Eerdmans.

Banks, R. J. (1980) *Paul's Idea of Community: The Early House Churches in Their Cultural Setting*, Grand Rapids, MI: Eerdmans.

Barclay, J. M. G. (1996) *Jews in the Mediterranean Diaspora from Alexander to Trajan (323 BCE–117 CE)*, Edinburgh: T&T Clark.

Barclay, J. M. G. (2004) 'Poverty in Pauline Studies: A response to Steven Friesen', *JSNT*, 26: 363–6.

Barclay, J. M. G. (2006) 'Money and meetings: Group formation among Diaspora Jews and Early Christians', in A. Gutsfeld and D.-A. Koch (eds), *Vereine, Synagogen und Gemeinden im kaiserzeitlichen Kleinasien*, STAC, 25, Tübingen: Mohr Siebeck, pp. 113–27.

Bartchy, S. S. (1991) 'Community of goods in Acts : Idealization or social reality?', in B. A. Pearson, A. T. Kraabel, G. W. E. Nickelsburg and N. R. Petersen (eds), *The Future of Early Christianity: Essays in Honor of Helmut Koester*, Minneapolis, MN: Fortress Press, pp. 309–18.

Barton, S. C. and G. H. R. Horsley (1981) 'A Hellenistic cult group and the New Testament churches', *JAC*, 24: 7–41.

Baslez, M.-F. (2006) 'Entraide et mutualisme dans les associations des cités grecques à l'époque hellénistique', in Michel Molin (ed.), *Les régulations sociales dans l'antiquité*, Histoire, Rennes: Presses Universitaires de Rennes, pp. 157–68.

Baugh, S. M. (1990) *Paul and Ephesus: The Apostle among His Contemporaries*, University of California.
Bauschatz, J. (2007) 'Ptolemaic prisons reconsidered', *Classical Bulletin*, 83: 3-48.
Beard, M., J. North and S. Price (1998) *Religions of Rome*, Cambridge: Cambridge University Press.
Beck, R. (1998) '"Qui mortalitatis causa convenerunt": The meeting of the Virunum Mithraists on June 26, A. D. 184', *Phoenix*, 52: 335-44.
Beek, B. van (2013) 'Kronion Son of Apion, Head of the *grapheion* of Tebtynis', *Leuven Homepage of Papyrus Collections*, available at: https://www.trismegistos.org/arch/archives/pdf/93.pdf.
Bendlin, A. (2011) 'Associations, funerals, sociality, and Roman law: The *collegium* of Diana and Antinous in Lanuvium (CIL 14.2112) reconsidered', in Markus Öhler (ed.), *Aposteldekret und antikes Vereinswesen: Gemeinschaft und ihre Ordnung*, WUNT, 280, Tübingen: Mohr Siebeck, pp. 207-96.
Bendlin, A. (2016) '"Sodalician associations"? *Digests* 47.22.1 *pr.* and Imperial Government', in W. E. Arnal, R. S. Ascough, R. A. Derrenbacker and P. A. Harland (eds), *Scribal Practices and Social Structures among Jesus Adherents: Essays in Honour of John S. Kloppenborg*, BETL, 285, Leuven: Peeters, pp. 435-63.
Bérard, F. (2012) 'Les corporations de transport fluvial à Lyon à l'époque romaine', in N. Tran and M. Dondin-Payre (eds), *Collegia: Le phénomène associatif dans l'Occident romain*, Scripta Antiqua, 41, Bordeaux: Ausonius Éditions, pp. 135-54.
Berranger, D. (2000) *Paros II: Prosopographie générale et étude historique du début de la période classique jusqu'à la fin de la période*, CRCA, Aubière: Presses Universitaires Blaise Pascal.
Bertrand-Dagenbach, C. (ed.) (1999) *Carcer: Prison et privation de liberté dans l'Antiquité classique*, Paris: de Boccard.
Billings, B. S. (2011) 'From house church to tenement church: Domestic space and the development of early urban Christianity – The example of Ephesos', *JTS*, 62: 541-69.
Binder, D. (1999) *Into the Temple Courts: The Place of the Synagogues in the Second Temple Period*, SBLDS, 169, Atlanta: Society of Biblical Literature.
Biscardi, A. (1983) 'Le régime de la pluralité hypothécaire en droit grec et romain', *JJP*, 19: 41-59.
Blyth, P. H. (1999) 'The consumption and cost of fuel in hypocaust baths', in J. DeLaine and D. E. Johnston (eds), *Roman Baths and Bathing: Proceedings of the First International Conference on Roman Baths Held at Bath, England, 30 March-4 April 1992, Journal of Roman Archaeology*, 37: 87-98, Portsmouth, RI: Journal of Roman Archaeology.
Boak, A. E. R. (1923) 'The anagraphai of the Grapheion of Tebtunis and Kerkesouchon Oros Pap. Michigan 622', *JEA*, 9: 164-7.
Boak, A. E. R. (1937) 'The organization of gilds in Greco-Roman Egypt', *TPAPA*, 68: 221-30.
Bolkestein, H. (1939) *Wohltätigkeit und Armenpflege im vorchristlichen Altertum*, Utrecht: A. Oosthoek Verlag.
Bollmann, B. (1998) *Römische Vereinshäuser: Untersuchungen zu den Scholae der römischen Berufs-, Kult- und Augustalen-Kollegien in Italien*, Mainz: Von Zabern.
Bonnell, V. E. and L. Hunt (eds) (1999) *Beyond the Cultural Turn: New Directions in the Study of Society and Culture*, New Directions in the Study of Society and Culture, Berkeley, CA: University of California Press.
Bosanquet, R. C. (1898) 'Excavations of the British School at Melos. The Hall of the Mystae', *JHS*, 18: 60-80.

Boulay, T. (2012) 'Les "groupes de référence" au sein du corps civique de Téos', in P. Fröhlich and P. Hamon (eds), *Groupes et associations dans les cités grecques, IIIe siècle av. J.-C.-IIe siècle apr. J.-C.*, Hautes études du monde gréco-romain, 49, Genève: Droz, pp. 251–75.

Bowman, A. and A. Wilson (eds) (2009) *Quantifying the Roman Economy: Methods and Problems*, Oxford Studies on the Roman Economy, Oxford: Oxford University Press.

Bowman, A. K. and J. D. Thomas (1984) *Vindolanda: The Latin Writing-Tablets*, Britannia, 4, London: Society for the Promotion of Roman Studies.

Brashear, W. M. (1993) *Vereine im griechisch-römischen Ägypten*, Xenia: Konstanzer althistorische Vorträge und Forschungen, 34, Konstanz: Universitätsverlag Konstanz.

Broekaert, W. (2011) 'Partners in business: Roman merchants and the potential advantages of being a *Collegiatus*', *AncSoc*, 41: 221–56.

Bruneau, P. (1970) *Recherches sur les cultes de Délos a l'époque hellénistique et a l'époque impériale*, Bibliothèque des École française d'Athènes et de Rome, 270, Paris: de Boccard.

Bruneau, P. (1982) '"Les Israélites de Délos" et la juiverie Délienne', *BCH*, 106: 465–504.

Bruneau, P. D. (1983) *Guide de Délos*, Paris: de Boccard.

Buell, D. K. (2008) '"Be not one who stretches out hands to receive but shuts them when it comes to giving": Envisioning Christian charity when both donors and recipients are poor', in *Wealth and Poverty in Early Church and Society*, Grand Rapids, MI: Baker, pp. 37–47.

Burkett, J. P. (2006) *Microeconomics: Optimization, Experiments, and Behavior*, Oxford: Oxford University Press.

Burton, G. P. (1975) 'Proconsuls, assizes and the administration of justice under the empire', *JRS*, 65: 92–106.

Burton, G. P. (1993) 'Provincial procurators and the public provinces', *Chiron*, 23: 13–28.

Calhoun, G. M. (1913) *Athenian Clubs in Politics and Litigation*, Austin, TX: University of Texas Bulletin.

Carbon, J.-M. and V. Pirenne-Delforge (2013) 'Priests and cult personnel in three Hellenistic families', in M. Horster and A. Klöckner (eds), *Cities and Priests, Cult Personnel in Asia Minor and the Aegean Islands from the Hellenistic to the Imperial Period*, Berlin: De Gruyter, pp. 65–119.

Carney, T. F. (1975) *The Shape of the Past: Models and Antiquity*, Lawrence, KA: Coronado Press.

Carolsfeld, L. S. von (1969 [1933]) *Geschichte der juristischen Person*, Aalen: Scientia Verlag.

Cavendish, J. C., M. R. Welch and D. C. Leege (1998) 'Social network theory and predictors of religiosity for black and white Catholics: Evidence of a Black Sacred Cosmos?', *JSSR*, 37: 397–410.

Cenival, F. de (1972) *Les associations religieuses en Egypte d'après les documents démotiques*, Publications de l'Institut français d'archéologie orientale du Caire, Bibliothèque d'étude, 46, Cairo: Institut français d'archéologie orientale.

Chaniotis, A. (2002) 'The Jews of Aphrodisias: New evidence and old problems', *Scripta Classica Israelica*, 21: 209–42.

Chow, J. K. (1992) *Patronage and Power: A Study of Social Networks in Corinth*, JSNTSup, 75, Sheffield: JSOT Press.

Clarke, A. D. (1993) *Secular and Christian Leadership in Corinth: A Socio-Historical and Exegetical Study of 1 Corinthians 1–6*, Leiden: Brill.

Clarysse, W. (2010) 'Egyptian temples and priests: Graeco-Roman', in A. B. Lloyd (ed.), *A Companion to Ancient Egypt*, Malden, MA: Wiley-Blackwell, pp. 274–90.

Clarysse, W. and D. J. Thompson (2004) *Counting the People in Hellenistic Egypt*, 2 vols, Cambridge Classical Studies, Cambridge: Cambridge University Press.
Clemente, G. (1972) 'Il patronato nei collegia dell'imperio romano', *Studi Classici e Orientali*, 21: 142–229.
Clerc, M. (1885) 'Inscription de Nysa', *BCH*, 9: 124–31.
Cole, S. G. (1984) *Theoi Megaloi: The Cult of the Great Gods at Samothrace*, EPRO, 96, Leiden: Brill.
Couch, H. N. (1929) *The Treasuries of the Greeks and Romans*, Manasha, WI: George Banta Publishing Company.
Crook, Z. A. (2004) *Reconceptualising Conversion: Patronage, Loyalty, and Conversion in the Religions of the Ancient Mediterranean*, Berlin: De Gruyter.
Crosby, M. and J. Young (1941) 'Greek inscriptions', *Hesperia*, 10: 14–30.
Daux, G. (1972) 'Trois inscriptions de la Grèce du Nord', *CRAI*, 116: 478–93.
De Robertis, F. M. (1938) *Il diritto associativo romano dai collegi della Repubblica alle corporazioni del Basso Impero*, Bari: Laterza.
De Robertis, F. M. (1955) *Il fenomeno associativo nel mondo romano*, Neapal.
De Robertis, F. M. (1971) *Storia delle corporazioni e del regime associativo nel mondo romano*, Bari: Adriatica Editrice.
Deissmann, A. (1922 [1909]) *Light from the Ancient East: The New Testament Illustrated by Recently Discovered Texts of the Graeco-Roman World*, translated by Lionel R. M. Strachan, Peabody: Hendrickson.
Dickey, S. (1928) 'Some economic and social conditions of Asia Minor affecting the expansion of Christianity', in S. Jackson Case (ed.), *Studies in Early Christianity*, New York: Century Co., pp. 393–416.
Dmitriev, S. (2005) *City Government in Hellenistic and Roman Asia Minor*, Oxford: Oxford University Press.
Dodds, E. R. (1965) *Pagan and Christian in an Age of Anxiety: Some Aspects of Religious Experience from Marcus Aurelius to Constantine*, Cambridge: Cambridge University Press.
Donaldson, T. L. (2007) *Judaism and the Gentiles: Jewish Patterns of Universalism (to 135 CE)*, Waco, TX: Baylor University Press.
Dörpfeld, W. (1884) 'Ein antikes Bauwerk im Piräus', *AM*, 9: 279–87.
Dörpfeld, W. (1894) 'Die Ausgrabungen an der Enneakrunos. II', *AM*, 19: 143–51.
Downing, F. G. (1985) 'Philo on wealth and the rights of the poor', *JSNT*, 24: 116–18.
Downs, D. J. (2006) 'Paul's collection and the Book of Acts revisited', *NTS*, 52: 50–70.
Downs, D. J. (2008) *The Offering of the Gentiles: Paul's Collection for Jerusalem in its Chronological, Cultural, and Cultic Contexts*, Tübingen: Mohr Siebeck.
Downs, D. J. (2011) 'Redemptive almsgiving and economic stratification in 2 Clement', *JECS*, 19: 493–517.
Ebel, E. (2004) *Die Attraktivität früher christlicher Gemeinden: Die Gemeinde von Korinth im Spiegel griechisch-römischer Vereine*, WUNT, 178, Tübingen: Mohr Siebeck.
Ecker, A. and B. Eckhardt (2018) 'The Koinon of Kosadar in Maresha: A Hellenistic private association in the Levant', *IEJ*, 68: 192–207.
Eckhardt, B. (2016a) 'The eighteen associations of Corinth', *GRBS*, 56: 646–62.
Eckhardt, B. (2016b) 'Romanization and isomorphic change in Phrygia: The case of private associations', *JRS*, 106: 147–71.
Eckhardt, B. (2017a) 'Craft guilds as synagogues? Further thoughts on "Private Judean-Deity Associations"', *JSJ*, 48: 246–60.
Eckhardt, B. (2017b) 'Temple ideology and Hellenistic private associations', *DSD*, 24: 407–23.

Eckhardt, B. (2017c) 'Vereins- und Stadtkult im Heiligtum der Artemis Kalliste in Athen', *Athenaeum*: 31–42.
Eckhardt, B. (2018) 'Heritage societies? Private associations in Roman Greece', in T. M. Dijkstra, I. N. I. Kuin, M. Moser and D. Weidgenannt (eds), *Strategies of Remembering in Greece Under Rome (100 BC – 100 AD)*, Publications of the Netherlands Institute at Athens, Leiden: Sidestone Press, pp. 71–81.
Eckhardt, B. and A. Lepke (2018) 'Mystai und Mysteria im kaiserzeitlichen Westkleinasien', in M. Blömer and B. Eckhardt (eds), *Transformationen paganer Religion in der römischen Kaiserzeit, Rahmenbedingungen und Konzepte*, RVV 72, Berlin: De Gruyter, pp. 39–80.
Edson, C. (1948) 'Cults of Thessalonica (Macedonia III)', *HTR*, 41: 153–204.
Elliott, J. H. (1990 [1981]) *A Home for the Homeless: A Social-Scientific Criticism of I Peter, Its Situation and Strategy*, Minneapolis, MN: Fortress Press.
Ellis-Evans, A. (2012) 'The ideology of public subscriptions', in P. Martzavou and N. Papazarkadas (eds), *Epigraphical Approaches to the Post-classical Polis*, Oxford: Oxford University Press, pp. 107–22.
Engelmann, H. (1975) *The Delian Aretalogy of Sarapis*, EPRO, 44, Leiden: Brill.
Erichsen, W. (1959) *Die Satzungen einer ägyptischen Kultgenossenschaft aus der Ptolemäerzeit nach einem demotischen Papyrus in Prag*, Historisk-filosofiske Skrifter udgivet af det Kongelige Danske Videnskabernes Selskab, 4.1, Copenhagen: Ejnar Munksgaard.
Faraguna, M. (2012) 'Diritto, economia, società: Riflessioni su eranos tra età omerica e mondo ellenistico', in B. Legras (ed.), *Transferts culturels et droits dans le monde grec et hellénistique*, Paris: Publications de la Sorbonne, pp. 129–53.
Faucher, T. and C. Lorber (2010) 'Bronze coinage of Ptolemaic Egypt in the second century BC', *American Journal of Numismatics*, 22: 35–80.
Fee, G. D. (1987) *The First Epistle to the Corinthians*, NICNT, Grand Rapids, MI: Eerdmans Publishing.
Ferguson, W. S. (1944) 'The Attic Orgeones', *HTR*, 37: 61–140.
Fikhman, I. F. (1994) 'Sur quelques aspects socio-économiques de l'activité des corporations professionnelles de l'Égypte byzantine', *ZPE*, 103: 19–40.
Filson, F. V. (1939) 'The significance of the early house churches', *JBL*, 58: 109–12.
Fine, J. V. A. (1951) *Horoi: Studies in Mortgage, Real Security and Land Tenure in Ancient Athens*, HesperiaSup, 13 9, Baltimore, MD: American School of Classical Studies at Athens.
Finley, M. I. (1951) *Studies in Land and Credit in Ancient Athens, 500–200 BC: The 'Horos'-Inscriptions*, New Brunswick, NJ: Rutgers University Press.
Finley, M. I. (1973) *The Ancient Economy*, Berkeley, CA: University of California Press.
Finn, R. (2006) *Almsgiving in the Later Roman Empire: Christian Promotion and Practice 313–450*, Oxford Classical Monographs, Oxford: Oxford University Press.
Fischer-Bovet, C. (2014) *Army and Society in Ptolemaic Egypt*, Armies of the Ancient World, Cambridge: Cambridge University Press.
Foucart, P. (1873) *Des associations religieuses chez les Grecs: Thiases, éranes, orgéons, avec le texte des inscriptions relatives à ces associations*, Paris: Klincksieck.
Fraser, P. M. (1977) *Rhodian Funerary Monuments*, Oxford: Clarendon Press.
Friesen, S. J. (2004) 'Poverty in Pauline studies: Beyond the so-called new consensus', *JSNT*, 26: 323–61.
Friesen, S. J. (2010) 'Paul and economics: The Jerusalem collection as an alternative to patronage', in M. D. Given (ed.), *Paul Unbound: Other Perspectives on the Apostle*, Peabody, MA: Hendrickson, pp. 27–54.

Gabrielsen, V. (1993) 'The status of "Rhodioi" in Hellenistic Rhodes', *Classica et Mediaevalia*, 43: 43–69.
Gabrielsen, V. (1994) 'The Rhodian associations honouring Dionysodoros from Alexandria', *Classica et Mediaevalia*, 45: 137–60.
Gabrielsen, V. (1997) *The Naval Aristocracy of Hellenistic Rhodes*, Studies in Hellenistic Civilization, Aarhus: Aarhus University Press.
Gabrielsen, V. (2001) 'The Rhodian associations and economic activity', in Z. Archibald (ed.), *Hellenistic Economies*, London: Routledge, pp. 215–44.
Gabrielsen, V. and C. A. Thomsen (eds) (2015) *Private Associations and the Public Sphere: Proceedings of a Symposium Held at the Royal Danish Academy of Sciences and Letters, 9-11 September 2010*, Copenhagen: Det Kongelige Danske Videnskabernes Selskab.
Gager, J. G. (1975) *Kingdom and Community: The Social World of Early Christianity*, New Jersey: Prentice-Hall.
Gambetti, S. (2009) *The Alexandrian Riots of 38 C.E. and the Persecution of the Jews: A Historical Reconstruction*, JSJSup, 135, Leiden: Brill.
Gardner, G. E. (2009) 'Giving to the poor in Early Rabbinic Judaism', PhD thesis, Princeton University, New Jersey.
Gardner, G. E. (2015) *The Origins of Organized Charity in Rabbinic Judaism*, Cambridge: Cambridge University Press.
Garnsey, P. and R. P. Saller (1987) *The Roman Empire: Economy, Society and Culture*, London: Duckworth.
Garrison, R. (1993) *Redemptive Almsgiving in Early Christianity*, Sheffield: T&T Clark.
Geertz, C. (1962) 'The Rotating credit association: A middle rung in development', *Economic Development and Cultural Change*, 10: 241–63.
Gehring, R. W. (2009) *House Church and Mission: The Importance of Household Structures in Early Christianity*, Grand Rapids, MI: Baker Academic.
Georgi, D. (1992 [1965]) *Remembering the Poor: The History of Paul's Collection for Jerusalem*, Nashville, TN: Abingdon Press.
Gerlach, L. P. H. and V. Hine (1970) *People, Power, Change: Movements of Social Transformation*, Indianapolis, IN: Bobbs-Merrill.
Gibbs, M. (2011) 'Trade associations in Roman Egypt: Their raison d'être', *AncSoc*, 41: 291–315.
Gilliam, J. F. (1976) 'Invitations to the kline of Sarapis', in A. Ellis Hanson (ed.), *Collectanea Papyrologica: Texts Published in Honor of H.C. Youtie*, Papyrologische Texte und Abhandlungen, 19, Bonn: Rudolf Habelt, pp. 315–24.
Gillihan, Y. M. (2012) *Civic Ideology, Organization, and Law in the Rule Scrolls: A Comparative Study of the Covenanters' Sect and Contemporary Voluntary Associations in Political Context*, STDJ, 97, Leiden: Brill.
González, J. L. (1990) *Faith and Wealth: A History of Early Christian Ideas on the Origin, Significance, and Use of Money*, San Francisco, CA: Harper & Row.
Gordon, R. (1996) 'Two Mithraic albums from Virunum, Noricum – Gernot Piccottini, *Mithrastempel in Virunum* (aus Forschung und Kunst 28, Verlag des Geschichtsvereins für Kärnten, Klagenfurt 1994)', *JRA*, 9: 424–6.
Gray, A. M. (2011) 'Redemptive almsgiving and the rabbis of late antiquity', *Jewish Studies Quarterly*, 18: 144–84.
Gruen, E. S. (2016) 'Synagogues and voluntary associations as institutional models: A response to Richard Ascough and Ralph Korner', *JJMJS*, 3: 125–31.
Hands, A. R. (1968) *Charities and Social Aid in Greece and Rome*, Aspects of Greek and Roman Life, London: Thames & Hudson.

Hanges, J. C. (2012) *Paul, Founder of Churches: A Study in Light of the Evidence for the Role of 'Founder-Figures' in the Hellenistic-Roman Period*, WUNT, 292, Tübingen: Mohr Siebeck.
Hardy, E. G. (1906) *Studies in Roman History*, London: Swan Sonnenschein & Co.
Harland, P. A. (1999) 'Claiming a place in polis and empire: The significance of imperial cults and connections among associations, synagogues, and Christian groups in Roman Asia (c. 27 BCE–138 CE)', Toronto: University of Toronto.
Harland, P. A. (2003) *Associations, Synagogues, and Congregations: Claiming a Place in Ancient Mediterranean Society*, Minneapolis, MN: Fortress Press.
Harland, P. A. (2005a) 'Spheres of contention, claims of preeminence: Rivalries among associations in Sardis and Smyrna', in R. S. Ascough (ed.), *Religious Rivalries and the Struggle for Success in Sardis and Smyrna*, 14: 53–63, Studies in Christianity and Judaism. Waterloo: Wilfrid Laurier University Press.
Harland, P. A. (2005b) 'Familial dimensions of group identity: "Brothers" (ἀδελφοί) in associations of the Greek East', *JBL*, 124: 491–513.
Harland, P. A. (2006) 'Acculturation and identity in the diaspora: A Jewish family and "pagan" guilds at Hierapolis', *Journal of Jewish Studies*, 57: 222–44.
Harland, P. A. (2007) 'Familial dimensions of group identity (II): "Mothers" and "fathers" in associations and synagogues of the Greek world', *JSJ*, 38: 57–79.
Harland, P. A. (2009) *Dynamics of Identity in the World of the Early Christians: Associations, Judeans, and Cultural Minorities*, New York: Continuum / T&T Clark.
Harland, P. A. (2012) 'Banqueting values in the associations: Rhetoric and reality', in D. E. Smith and H. Taussig (eds), *Meals in the Early Christian World: Social Formation, Experimentation, and Conflict at the Table*, Houndmills, Basingstoke: Palgrave, pp. 73–86.
Harland, P. A. (2013) *Associations, Synagogues, and Congregations: Claiming a Place in Ancient Mediterranean Society*, 2nd revd edn, Kitchener: Philip A. Harland. Available at: http://philipharland.com/publications/Harland 2013 Associations-Synagogues-Congregations.pdf.
Harland, P. A. (2014) *Greco-Roman Associations: Texts, Translations, and Commentary. II. North Coast of the Black Sea, Asia Minor*, BZNW, 204, Berlin: De Gruyter.
Harland, P. A. (2015) 'Associations and the economics of group life: A preliminary case study of Asia Minor and the Aegean Islands', *Svensk Exegetisk Årsbok*, 80: 1–37.
Harland, P. A. (2016) 'Fund-raising and group values in the associations', in W. E. Arnal, R. S. Ascough, R. A. Derrenbacker and P. A. Harland (eds), *Scribal Practices and Social Structures among Jesus Adherents: Essays in Honour of John S. Kloppenborg*, BETL, 285, Leuven: Peeters, 2016, pp. 465–82.
Harland, P. A. (2018) 'Die wirtschaftlichen Dimensionen des Vereinslebens', in B. Eckhardt and C. Leonhard (eds), *Juden, Christen und Vereine im Römischen Reich*, RVV 75, Berlin: De Gruyter.
Harland, P. A. (2019, 7: 207–232) '"The most sacred society (*thiasos*) of the Pythagoreans": Philosophers forming associations', *Journal of Ancient History*.
Harnack, A. (1905) *The Expansion of Christianity in the First Three Centuries*, London: Williams and Norgate.
Harrill, J. A. (1993) 'Ignatius, Ad Polycarp. 4.3 and the corporate manumission of Christian slaves', *JECS*, 1: 107–42.
Harrill, J. A. (1998) *The Manumission of Slaves in Early Christianity*, Tübingen: Mohr Siebeck.
Harrill, J. A. (2011) 'Divine judgment against Ananias and Sapphira (Acts 5:1–11): A stock scene of perjury and death', *JBL*, 130: 351–69.

Harris, E. M. (1988) 'When is a sale not a sale? The riddle of Athenian terminology for real security revisited', *CQ*, 38: 351–81.
Harris, E. M. (1992) 'Women and lending in Athenian society: A "horos" re-examined', *Phoenix*, 46: 309–21.
Harris, E. M. (1993) 'Apotimema: Athenian terminology for real security in leases and dowry agreements', *CQ*, 43: 73–95.
Harris, E. M. and K. Tuite (2000) 'Notes on a "horos" from the Athenian Agora', *ZPE*, 131: 101–5.
Hatch, E. (1881) *The Organization of the Early Christian Churches: Eight Lectures Delivered before the University of Oxford, in the Year 1880*, London: Longmans, Green and Co.
Hatzfeld, J. (1912) 'Les Italiens résidant à Délos mentionnés dans les inscriptions de l'île', *BCH*, 36: 5–218.
Hays, C. M. (2009) 'By almsgiving and faith sins are purged? The theological underpinnings of Early Christian care for the poor', in B. W. Longenecker and K. D. Liebengood (eds), *Engaging Economics: New Testament Scenarios and Early Christian Reception*, Grand Rapids, MI: Eerdmans, pp. 260–80.
Hellerman, J. H. (2001) *The Ancient Church as Family*, Minneapolis, MN: Fortress Press.
Hemelrijk, E. A. (2008) 'Patronesses and "mothers" of Roman collegia', *Classical Antiquity*, 27: 115–62.
Hemelrijk, E. A. (2015) *Hidden Lives, Public Personae: Women and Civic Life in the Roman West*, Oxford: Oxford University Press.
Hill, C. (1972) *The World Turned Upside Down: Radical Ideas During the English Revolution*, London: Temple Smith.
Hiller von Gaertringen, F. and S. Saridakis (1900) 'Inschriften aus Rhodos', *AM*, 25: 107–10.
Hirschmann, V. (2004) 'Methodische Überlegungen zu Frauen in antiken Vereinen', in L. de Ligt, E. A. Hemelrijk and H. W. Singor (eds), *Roman Rule and Civic Life: Local and Regional Perspectives*, Amsterdam: J. C. Gieben, pp. 401–15.
Hobsbawm, E. J. (1959) *Primitive Rebels: Studies in Archaic Forms of Social Movements in the 19th and 20th Centuries*, Manchester: Manchester University Press.
Hock, R. (1979) 'The workshop as a social setting for Paul's missionary preaching', *CBQ*, 41: 438–50.
Hock, R. (1980) *The Social Context of Paul's Ministry: Tentmaking and Apostleship*, Philadelphia, PA: Fortress Press.
Holman, S. R. (ed.) (2008) *Wealth and Poverty in Early Church and Society*, Grand Rapids, MI: Baker Academic.
Holmberg, B. (1990) *Sociology and the New Testament: An Appraisal*, Minneapolis, MN: Fortress Press.
Hopkins, K. (1983) *Death and Renewal: Sociological Studies in Roman History*, Cambridge: Cambridge University Press.
Horbury, W. (1984) 'The Temple tax', in B. Bammel and C. F. D. Moule (eds), *Jesus and the Politics of His Day*, Cambridge: Cambridge University Press, pp. 265–86.
Horbury, W. and D. Noy (1992) *Jewish Inscriptions of Graeco-Roman Egypt*, Cambridge: Cambridge University Press.
Horrell, D. G. (2004) 'Domestic space and Christian meetings at Corinth: Imagining new contexts and the buildings east of the theatre', *NTS*, 50: 349–69.
Hurtado, L. W. (1979) 'The Jerusalem collection and the book of Galatians', *JSNT*, 5: 46–62.
Husselman, E. M. (1970) 'Procedures of the Record Office of Tebtunis in the first century A.D.', in *Proceedings of the Twelfth International Congress of Papyrology*, Toronto: Hakkert, pp. 223–38.

Ismard, P. (2010) *La cité des réseaux: Athènes et ses associations, VIe–Ier siècle av. J.-C.*, Paris: Publications de la Sorbonne.
Jakobsen, J. R. and A. Pellegrini (eds) (2008) *Secularisms*, Durham: Duke University Press.
Jones, A. H. M. (1953) 'Inflation under the Roman empire', *Economic History Review*, 5: 293–318.
Jones, C. P. (1983) 'A deed of foundation from the territory of Ephesos', *JRS*, 73: 116–25.
Jones, C. P. (2008) 'A Hellenistic cult-association', *Chiron*, 38: 195–204.
Jones, N. F. (1987) *Public Organization in Ancient Greece: A Documentary Study*, Memoirs of the American Philosophical Society, 176, Philadelphia, PA: American Philosophical Society.
Jones, N. F. (1999) *The Associations of Classical Athens: The Response to Democracy*, Oxford: Oxford University Press.
Jongman, W. M. (1988) *The Economy and Society of Pompeii*, Amsterdam: J.C. Gieben.
Jongman, W. M. (2007) 'The Early Roman empire: Consumption', in W. Scheidel, I. Morris and R. P. Saller (eds), *The Cambridge Economic History of the Greco-Roman World*, Cambridge: Cambridge University Press, pp. 592–618.
Joubert, S. J. (2000) *Paul as Benefactor: Reciprocity, Strategy and Theological Reflection in Paul's Collection*, Tübingen: Mohr Siebeck.
Joubert, S. J. (2001) 'One form of social exchange or two? "Euergetism," Patronage, and Testament Studies', *BTB*, 31: 17–25.
Judge, E. A. (1960) *The Social Pattern of the Christian Groups in the First Century*, London: Tyndale Press.
Kamen, D. (2014) 'Sale for the purpose of freedom: Slave-prostitutes and manumission in ancient Greece', *CJ*, 109: 281–307.
Kaminski, G. (1991) 'Thesauros: Untersuchungen zum antiken Opferstock', *JDAI*, 106: 63–181.
Keil, J. (1930) 'XV. Vorläufiger Bericht über die Ausgrabungen in Ephesos', *JÖAI*, 26: 5–66.
Kelly, B. (2011) *Petitions, Litigation, and Social Control in Roman Egypt*, Oxford Studies in Ancient Documents, Oxford: Oxford University Press.
Kerri, J. N. (1976) 'Studying voluntary associations as adaptive mechanisms: A review of anthropological perspectives', *Current Anthropology*, 17: 23–47.
Klauck, H.-J. (1981) *Hausgemeinde und Hauskirche im frühen Christentum*, Stuttgarter Bibelstudien, 103, Stuttgart: Verlag Katholisches Bibelwerk.
Kloppenborg, J. S. (1996) 'Collegia and thiasoi: Issues in function, taxonomy and membership', in J. S. Kloppenborg and S. G. Wilson (eds), *Voluntary Associations in the Graeco-Roman World*, London: Routledge, pp. 16–30.
Kloppenborg, J. S. (2006) *The Tenants in the Vineyard: Ideology, Economics, and Agrarian Conflict in Jewish Palestine*, WUNT, 195, Tübingen: Mohr Siebeck.
Kloppenborg, J. S. (2011) '"Disaffiliation in associations and the ἀποσυναγωγός of John', *HvTSt*, 67: 1–16.
Kloppenborg, J. S. (2013) 'Membership practices in Pauline Christ groups', *Early Christianity*, 4: 183–215.
Kloppenborg, J. S. (2016) 'Precedence at the Communal Meal in Corinth', *NovT*, 58: 167–203.
Kloppenborg, J. S. (2017) 'Fiscal aspects of Paul's collection for Jerusalem', *Early Christianity*: 153–98.
Kloppenborg, J. S. (ed.) (2019) *Greco-Roman Associations: Texts, Translations, and Commentary. III. Egypt*, Berlin: De Gruyter.
Kloppenborg, J. S. and R. S. Ascough (2011) *Greco-Roman Associations: Texts, Translations, and Commentary. I. Attica, Central Greece, Macedonia, Thrace*, Berlin: De Gruyter.

Kloppenborg, J. S. and S. G. Wilson (eds) (1996) *Voluntary Associations in the Graeco-Roman World*, London: Routledge.
Kontorini, V. (1989) *Anekdotes epigraphes Rodou*, Athens: Institouto Tou Bibliou M. Kardamitsa.
Körte, A. (1896) 'Die Ausgrabungen am Westabhange der Akropolis IV. Das Heiligtum des Amynos', *AM*, 21: 287–332.
Köse, O. and R. Tekoğlu (2007) 'Money lending in Hellenistic Lycia: The Union of Copper Money', *Adalya*, 10: 63–79.
Kotrosits, M. (2015) *Rethinking Early Christian Identity: Affect, Violence, and Belonging*, Minneapolis, MN: Fortress Press.
Koukouvou, A. (2012) 'The Sarapieion. The sanctuary of the Egyptian gods rises from the city's ashes', in P. Adam-Veleni and A. Koukouvou (eds), *Archeology Behind Battle Lines in Thessaloniki of the Turbulent Years 1912-1922*, Archaeological Museum of Thessaloniki, 19. Thessaloniki: Ministry of Education and Religious Affairs, Culture and Sport, pp. 104–11.
Krause, J.-U. (1996) *Gefängnisse im Römischen Reich*, Heidelberger Althistorische Beiträge und Epigraphische Studien, 23, Stuttgart: Franz Steiner Verlag.
Krysan, M. and W. d'Antonio (1992) 'Voluntary associations', in E. F. Borgatta and M. L. Borgatta (eds), *Encyclopedia of Sociology*, 4, Basingstoke: MacMillan, pp. 2231–4.
Kubińska, J. (2001) 'Tiberius Claudius Lycus de Thessalonique et son thiase', *ZPE*, 137: 153–60.
LaFosse, M. T. (2011) 'Age matters: Age, aging and intergenerational relationships in Early Christian communities, with a focus on 1 Timothy 5', PhD thesis, University of Toronto.
Lambert, S. D. (1996) 'Notes on Two Attic "Horoi": And some corrigenda to "The Phratries of Attica"', *ZPE*, 110: 77–83.
Lambert, S. D. (2017) 'Two inscribed documents of the Athenian empire: The Chalkis Decree and the Tribute Reassessment Decree', *Attic Inscriptions Online*, 8: 1–43.
Langellotti, M. (2015) 'Sales in Early Roman Tebtunis: The case of the Grapheion Archive of Kronion', in E. Jakab (ed.), *Sale and Community Documents from the Ancient World*, Legal Documents in Ancient Societies, 5, Trieste: Edizioni Università di Trieste, 117–32.
Langellotti, M. (2016) 'Professional associations and the state in Roman Egypt: The case of first-century Tebtunis', *Chronique d'Egypte*, 91 (181): 111–34.
Lassère, J.-M. (2005) *Manuel d'épigraphie romaine*, Paris: Picard.
Last, R. (2013) 'Money, meals, and honour: The economic and honorific organization of the Corinthian Ekklesia', PhD thesis, University of Toronto.
Last, R. (2016a) *The Pauline Church and the Corinthian Ekklēsia: Greco-Roman Associations in Comparative Context*, SNTS, 164, Cambridge: Cambridge University Press.
Last, R. (2016b) 'The neighborhood (*vicus*) of the Corinthian *ekklēsia*: Beyond family-based descriptions of the first urban Christ-believers', *JSNT*, 38: 399–425.
Last, R. (2016c) 'The myth of free membership in Pauline Christ groups', in W. E. Arnal, R. S. Ascough, R. A. Derrenbacker and P. A. Harland (eds), *Scribal Practices and Social Structures among Jesus Adherents: Essays in Honour of John S. Kloppenborg*, BETL, 285, Leuven: Peeters, pp. 495–516.
Last, R. and S. E. Rollens (2014) 'Accounting practices in P.Tebt iii/2 894 and Pauline groups', *Early Christianity*, 5: 441–74.
Laum, B. (1964 [1914]) *Stiftungen in der griechischen und römischen Antike: ein Beitrag zur antiken Kulturgeschichte*, Aalen: Scientia Verlag.

Le Guen, B. (2007) 'Kraton, Son of Zotichos: Artists associations and monarchic power in the Hellenistic period', in Peter Wilson (ed.), *The Greek Theatre and Festivals: Documentary Studies*, Oxford: Oxford University Press, pp. 246–78.
Lendon, J. E. (1997) *Empire of Honour: The Art of Government in the Roman World*, Oxford: Oxford University Press.
Levine, L. I. (2000) *The Ancient Synagogue: The First Thousand Years*, New Haven, CT: Yale University Press.
Liebenam, W. (1890) *Zur Geschichte und Organisation des römischen Vereinswesens*, Leipzig: B.G. Teubner.
Lieu, J. (2004) *Christian Identity in the Jewish and Graeco-Roman World*, Oxford, UK: Oxford University Press.
Little, K. (1957) 'The role of voluntary associations in West African urbanization', *American Anthropologist*, 59: 579–96.
Liu, J. (2008) 'The economy of endowments: The case of Roman associations', in K. Verboven, K. Vandorpe and V. Chankowski (eds), *Pistoi dia tèn technèn: Bankers, Loans, and Archives in the Ancient World: Studies in Honour of Raymond Bogaert*, Studia Hellenistica, 44, Leuven: Peeters, pp. 231–56.
Liu, J. (2009) *'Collegia Centonariorum': The Guilds of Textile Dealers in the Roman West*, Columbia Studies in the Classical Tradition, 34, Leiden: Brill.
Liu, J. (2016) 'Group Membership, Trust Networks, and Social Capital: A Critical Analysis', in *Work, Labour, and Professions in the Roman World*, edited by Koenraad Verboven and Christian Laes, 203–226. Impact of Empire 23. Leiden: Brill.
Liu, J. (2017) 'Urban poverty in the Roman empire: Material conditions', in T. R. Blanton and R. Pickett (eds), *Paul and Economics: A Handbook*, Minneapolis, MN: Fortress Press, pp. 23–56.
Llewelyn, S. R. (2001) 'The use of Sunday for meetings of believers in the New Testament', *NovT*, 43: 205–23.
Lofland, J. and R. Stark (1965) 'Becoming a world-saver: A theory of conversion to a deviant perspective', *American Sociological Review*, 30: 862–75.
Longenecker, B. W. (2009a) 'Exposing the economic middle: A revised economy scale for the study of early urban Christianity', *JSNT*, 31: 243–78.
Longenecker, B. W. (2009b) 'Socio-economic profiling of the first urban Christians', in *After the First Urban Christians: The Social-Scientific Study of Pauline Christianity Twenty-Five Years Later*, London: T&T Clark, pp. 36–59.
Longenecker, B. W. (2010) *Remember the Poor: Paul, Poverty, and the Greco-Roman World*, Grand Rapids, MI: Eerdmans.
Longenecker, B. W. and K. D. Liebengood (eds) (2009) *Engaging Economics: New Testament Scenarios and Early Christian Reception*, Grand Rapids, MI: Eerdmans.
Longenecker, R. N. (1990) *Galatians*, WBC 41, Waco, TX: Zondervan.
Lupu, E. (2005) *Greek Sacred Law. A Collection of New Documents*, RGRW, 152, Leiden: Brill.
Lytle, E. (2012a) 'A customs house of our own: Infrastructure, duties and a joint association of fishermen and fishmongers (IK, 11.1a-Ephesos, 20)', in V. Chankowski and P. Karonis (eds), *Tout vendre, tout acheter: Structures et équipements des marchés antiques. Actes du colloque international, Athènes, École française d'Athènes, 16–19 juin 2009*, Bourdieux: Ausonius, pp. 213–24.
Lytle, E. (2012b) 'ἡ θάλασσα κοινή: Fishermen, the sea, and the limits of ancient Greek regulatory reach', *Classical Antiquity*, 31: 1–55.
Maass, E. (1893) 'Zur Hetäreninschrift von Paros', *AM*, 18: 21–6.

MacGillivray, E. D. (2009) 'Re-evaluating patronage and reciprocity in antiquity and New Testament Studies', *Journal of Greco-Roman Christianity and Judaism*, 6: 37–81.
MacMullen, R. (1966) *Enemies of the Roman Order: Treason, Unrest, and Alienation in the Empire*, Cambridge, MA: Harvard University Press.
MacMullen, R. (1974) *Roman Social Relations 50 B.C. to A.D. 284*, New Haven, CT: Yale University Press.
Macridy, T. (1904) 'A travers les nécropoles sidoniennes', *RB*, 13: 547–72.
Maehler, H. (1966) 'Zwei neue Bremer Papyri', *Chronique d'Egypte*, 41 (82): 342–53.
Maier, G. (1969) 'Eranos als Kreditinstitut', PhD thesis, Erlangen-Nürnberg.
Maillot, S. (2015) 'Foreigners' associations and the Rhodian state', in V. Gabrielsen and C. A. Thomsen (eds), *Private Associations and the Public Sphere: Proceedings of a Symposium Held at the Royal Danish Academy of Sciences and Letters, 9–11 September 2010*, Copenhagen: Det Kongelige Danske Videnskabernes Selskab, pp. 92–121.
Malherbe, A. J. (1983 [1977]) *Social Aspects of Early Christianity*, Philadelphia, PA: Fortress Press.
Malherbe, A. J. (2012) 'Ethics in context: The Thessalonians and their neighbours', *HvTSt*, 68: 1–10.
Mandell, S. (1984) 'Who paid the Temple tax when the Jews were under Roman rule', *HTR*, 77: 223–32.
Marchand, F. (2015) 'The associations of Tanagra: Epigraphic practice and regional context', *Chiron*, 45: 239–66.
Maresch, K. (1996) *Bronze und Silber: Papyrologische Beiträge zur Geschichte der Währung im ptolemäischen und römischen Ägypten bis zum 2. Jahrhundert n. Chr.*, Papyrologica Coloniensia, 25, Wiesbaden: Springer.
Marshall, P. (1987) *Enmity in Corinth: Social Conventions in Paul's Relations with the Corinthians*, WUNT, 23, Tübingen: Mohr Siebeck.
Martin, R. (1940) 'Un nouveau règlement de culte thasien', *BCH*, 64: 163–200.
Martinez, D. and M. Williams (1997) 'Records of loan receipts from a guild association', *ZPE*, 118: 259–63.
Meeks, W. A. (1983) *The First Urban Christians: The Social World of the Apostle Paul*, London: Yale University Press.
Meeks, W. A. (1993) *The Origins of Christian Morality: The First Two Centuries*, New Haven, CT: Yale University Press.
Meggitt, J. J. (1998) *Paul, Poverty, and Survival*, Studies of the New Testament and its World, Edinburgh: T&T Clark.
Meiggs, R. (1960) *Roman Ostia*, Oxford: Clarendon Press.
Melfi, M. (1998) 'Il vano del *thesaurós* nel santuario di Asclepio a Lebena', *ASAA*, 76–8: 282–314.
Meyer, E. A. (2004) *Legitimacy and Law in the Roman World: Tabulae in Roman Belief and Practice*, Cambridge: Cambridge University Press.
Meyer, E. A. (2009) *Metics and the Athenian Phialai-Inscriptions: A Study in Athenian Epigraphy and Law*, Historia Einzelschriften, 208, Wiesbaden: Franz Steiner Verlag.
Michels, C. (2011) 'Dionysos Kathegemon und der attalidische Herrscherkult: Überlegungen zur Herrschaftsrepräsentation der Könige von Pergamon', in L.-M. Günther and S. Plischke (eds), *Studien zum vorhellenistischen und hellenistischen Herrscherkult*, Berlin: Verlag Antike, pp. 114–40.
Mietz, M. (2016) 'The fuel economy of public bathhouses in the Roman empire', MA thesis, University of Gent.

Mikalson, J. D. (1998) *Religion in Hellenistic Athens*, Berkeley, CA: University of California Press.
Mikalson, J. D. (2016) *New Aspects of Religion in Ancient Athens*, RGRW, 183, Leiden: Brill.
Millett, P. (1991) *Lending and Borrowing in Ancient Athens*, Cambridge: Cambridge University Press.
Mishnun, F. (1950) 'Voluntary associations', *Encyclopaedia of the Social Sciences*, 15: 283–7.
Mitrofan, D. (2014) 'The Antonine Plague in Dacia and Moesia Inferior', *Journal of Ancient History and Archaeology*, 1: 9–13, available at: doi:10.14795/j.v1i2.53.
Modrzejewski, J. (1997) *The Jews of Egypt: From Rameses II to Emperor Hadrian*, Princeton, NJ: Princeton University Press.
Mommsen, T. (1843) *De collegiis et sodaliciis romanorum. Accedit inscriptio Lanuvina*, Kiliae: Libraaria Schwersiana.
Monson, A. (2006) 'The ethics and economics of Ptolemaic religious associations', *AncSoc*, 36: 221–38.
Monson, A. (2007a) 'Private associations in the Ptolemaic Fayyum: The evidence of Demotic accounts', in M. Capasso and P. Davoli (eds), *New Archaeological and Papyrological Researches on the Fayyum*, Papyrologica Lupiensia, 14, Lecce: Congedo Editore, 181–96.
Monson, A. (2007b) 'Religious associations and temples in Ptolemaic Tebtunis', in J. Frösén, T. Purola and E. Salmenkivi (eds), *Proceedings of the 24th International Congress of Papyrology, Helsinki, 1st–7th of August 2004*, Helsinki: Societas Scientiarum Fennica, pp. 769–79.
Monson, A. (2013) 'Rules of an association of Soknebtunis', in R. Ast, H. Cuvigny, T. M. Hickey and J. Lougovaya (eds), *Papyrological Texts in Honor of Roger S. Bagnall*, American Studies in Papyrology, 43. Oxford: American Society of Papyrologists, pp. 209–14.
Monson, A. and C. Arlt (2010) 'Rules of an Egyptian religious association from the early second century BCE', in H. Knuf, C. Leitz and D. von Recklinghausen (eds), *Honi soit qui mal y pense. Studien zum pharaonischen, griechisch-römischen und spätantiken Ägypten zu Ehren von Heinz-Josef Thissen*, Orientalia Lovaniensia Analecta, 194, Leuven: Peeters, pp. 113–22.
Mordtmann, J. H. (1885) 'Zur Epigraphik von Kyzikos', *AM*, 10: 200–11.
Mortensen, E. (2015) 'Ktistes: Mythical founder hero and honorary title for new heroes', in J. Fejfer, M. Moltesen and A. Rathje (eds), *Tradition: Transmission of Culture in the Ancient World*, Acta Hyperborea, 14, Copenhagen: Museum Tusculanum Press, pp. 213–38.
Moya, J. C. (2005) 'Immigrants and associations: A global and historical perspective', *Journal of Ethnic and Migration Studies*, 31: 833–64.
Moyer, I. S. (2008) 'Notes on re-reading the Delian aretalogy of Sarapis (IG XI.4 1299)', *ZPE*, 166: 101–7.
Munck, J. (1959) *Paul and the Salvation of Mankind*, London: SCM Press.
Murphy, C. M. (2002) *Wealth in the Dead Sea Scrolls and in the Qumran Community*, STDJ, 40, Leiden: Brill.
Nahapiet, J. and S. Ghoshal (1998) 'Social capital, intellectual capital, and the organizational advantage', *Academy of Management Review*, 23: 242–66.
Nielsen, I. (2014) *Housing the Chosen: The Architectural Context of Mystery Groups and Religious Associations in the Ancient World*, Turnhout: Brepols.
Nielsen, T. H., L. Bjertrup, M. H. Hansen, L. Rubinstein and T. Vestergaard (1989) 'Athenian grave monuments and social class', *GRBS*, 30: 411–20.

Nilsson, M. P. (1957) *The Dionysiac Mysteries of the Hellenistic and Roman Age*, Lund: C.W.K. Gleerup.
Nilsson, M. P. (1961) *Geschichte der griechischen Religion*, Munich: C.H. Beck'sche Verlagsbuchhandlung.
Nock, A. D. (1933) *Conversion: The Old and New in Religion from Alexander the Great to Augustine of Hippo*, Oxford: Oxford University Press.
Nolan, B. T. (1981) 'Inscribing costs at Athens in the fourth century B.C.', PhD thesis, Ohio State University.
Nongbri, B. (2008) 'Dislodging "embedded" religion: A brief note on a scholarly trope', *Numen*, 55: 440–60.
Nongbri, B. (2013) *Before Religion: A History of a Modern Concept*, New Haven, CT: Yale University Press.
Oakes, P. (2004) 'Constructing poverty scales for Graeco-Roman society: A response to Steven Friesen's "Poverty in Pauline Studies"', *JSNT*, 26: 367–71.
Oakes, P. (2009a) 'Methological issues in using economic evidence in interpretation of Early Christian texts', in B. W. Longenecker and K. D. Liebengood (eds), *Engaging Economics: New Testament Scenarios and Early Christian Reception*, Grand Rapids, MI: Eerdmans, pp. 9–35.
Oakes, P. (2009b) *Reading Romans in Pompeii: Paul's Letter at Ground Level*, Minneapolis, MN: Fortress Press.
Ogereau, J. M. (2012) 'The Jerusalem collection as κοινωνία: Paul's global politics of socio-economic equality and solidarity', *NTS*, 58: 360–78.
Öhler, M. (2005) 'Die Jerusalemer Urgemeinde im Spiegel des antiken Vereinswesens', *NTS*, 51: 393–415.
Öhler, M. (2011a) 'Ethnos und Identität: Landsmannschaftliche Vereinigungen, Synagogen und christliche Gemeinden', in A. Lykke and F. Schipper (eds), *Kult und Macht: Religion und Herrschaft im syro-palästinensischen Raum*, WUNT, 319, Tübingen: Mohr Siebeck, pp. 221–48.
Öhler, M. (ed.) (2011b) *Aposteldekret und antikes Vereinswesen: Gemeinschaft und ihre Ordnung*, WUNT, 280, Tübingen: Mohr Siebeck.
Öhler, M. (2014) 'Cultic meals in associations and the Early Christian Eucharist', *Early Christianity*, 5: 475–502.
Öhler, M. (2015) 'Gründer und ihre Gründung: Antike Vereinigungen und die paulinische Gemeinde in Philippi', in B. Schließer, J. Frey and V. Niederhofer (eds), *Der Philipperbrief des Paulus in der hellenistisch-römischen Welt*, WUNT, 353, Tübingen: Mohr Siebeck, pp. 121–51.
Öhler, M. and N. Zimmermann (2017) 'Domestic religion in Greco-Roman antiquity and Early Christianity', *Archiv für Religionsgeschichte*, 18–19 1: 3–6.
Oliver, J. H. (1989) *Greek Constitutions of Early Roman Emperors from Inscriptions and Papyri*, Memoirs of the American Philosophical Society, 178, Philadelphia: American Philosophical Society.
Osborne, M. J. (2004) 'Five Hellenistic decrees of the Salaminian Thiasotai of Bendis', *ΗΟΡΟΣ*, 17–21: 657–72.
Osborne, R. (1988) 'Social and economic implications of the leasing of land and property in classical and Hellenistic Greece', *Chiron*, 18: 279–323.
Osiek, C. (1981) 'The ransom of captives: Evolution of a tradition', *HTR*, 74: 365–86.
Papazarkadas, N. (2011) *Sacred and Public Land in Ancient Athens*, Oxford: Oxford University Press.
Parker, R. (2010) 'A funerary foundation from Hellenistic Lycia', *Chiron*, 40: 103–20.

Parkin, A. (2006) '"You do him no service": An exploration of pagan almsgiving', in M. Atkins and R. Osborne (eds), *Poverty in the Roman World*, Cambridge: Cambridge University Press, pp. 60–82.
Patterson, J. R. (1992) 'Patronage, collegia and burial in Imperial Rome', in S. Bassett (ed.), *Death in Towns: Urban Responses to the Dying and the Dead, 100–1600*, Leicester: Leicester University Press, pp. 15–27.
Patterson, J. R. (1994) 'The collegia and the transformation of the towns of Italy in the second century AD', in *L'Italie d'Auguste Dioclétien*, Collection de L'École Française de Rome, 198, Rome: École Française de Rome, pp. 227–38.
Patterson, J. R. (2006) *Landscapes and Cities: Rural Settlement and Civic Transformation in Early Imperial Italy*, Oxford: Oxford University Press.
Paula Fredriksen, Paul: The Pagans' Apostle. New Haven, CN: Yale University Press, 2017.
Pelletier, A. (1982) *Vienne antique: De la conquête romaine aux invasions alamaniques*, Roanne: Horvath.
Perry, J. S. (2006) *The Roman Collegia: The Modern Evolution of an Ancient Concept*, Leiden: Brill.
Perry, J. S. (2011) 'Organized societies: Collegia', in M. Peachin (ed.), *The Oxford Handbook of Social Relations in the Roman World*, Oxford: Oxford University Press, pp. 499–515.
Perry, J. S. (2015) '"L'état intervint peu à peu": State intervention in the Ephesian bakers' strike', in V. Gabrielsen and C. A. Thomsen (eds), *Private Associations and the Public Sphere: Proceedings of a Symposium Held at the Royal Danish Academy of Sciences and Letters, 9–11 September 2010*, Copenhagen: Det Kongelige Danske Videnskabernes Selskab, pp. 183–205.
Pestman, P. W. (1971) 'Loans bearing no interest?', *JJP*, 16–17: 7–29.
Peterman, G. W. (1997) *Paul's Gift from Philippi: Conventions of Gift-Exchange and Christian Giving*, SNTS, 92, Cambridge: Cambridge University Press.
Petzl, G. (2009) 'Bedrohter Kultvollzug: Hilfe von höherer Stelle', in Á. Martínez Fernández (ed.), *Estudios de epigrafía griega*, San Cristóbal de La Laguna: Universidad de La Laguna, pp. 377–86.
Piccottini, G. (1993) 'Ein römerzeitliches Handwerkerkollegium aus Virunum', *Tyche*, 8: 111–23.
Piccottini, G. (1994) *Mithrastempel in Virunum*, Aus Forschung und Kunst, 28, Klagenfurt: Verlag des Geschichtsvereines für Kärnten.
Planeaux, C. (2000) 'The date of Bendis' entry into Attica', *CJ*, 96: 165–92.
Pleket, H. W. (1973) 'Some aspects of the history of athletic guilds', *ZPE*, 10: 197–227.
Pleket, H. W. (1983) 'Urban elites and business in the Greek part of the Roman empire', in P. Garnsey, K. Hopkins and C. R. Whittaker (eds), *Urban Elites and Business in the Greek Part of the Roman Empire*, Berkeley, CA: University of California Press, 131–44.
Pleket, H. W. (1984) 'Urban elites and the economy in the Greek cities of the Roman empire', *MBAH*, 3: 3–36.
Poland, F. (1909) *Geschichte des griechischen Vereinswesens*, Leipzig: Teubner.
Polanyi, K. (1968) *Primitive, Archaic and Modern Economies: Essays of Karl Polanyi*, Garden City, NY: Anchor.
Pomeroy, S. B. (1975) *Goddesses, Whores, Wives, and Slaves: Women in Classical Antiquity*, New York: Shocken Books.
Préaux, C. (1948) 'A propos des associations dans l'Egypte gréco-romaine', *RIDA*, 1: 189–98.
Pugliese Carratelli, G. (1939) 'Per la storia delle associazioni in rodi antica', *ASAA*, 1–2: 147–200.
Radin, M. (1910) *Legislation of the Greeks and Romans on Corporations*, [New York]: Columbia University, Morehouse and Taylor Press.

Radt, W. (1988) *Pergamon: Geschichte und Bauten, Funde und Erforschung einer antiken Metropole*, Köln: DuMont Buchverlag.
Rajak, T. (1984) 'Was there a Roman charter for the Jews?', *JRS*, 74: 107-23.
Rajak, T. and D. Noy (1993) '*Archisynagogoi*: Office, title and social status in the Greco-Jewish synagogue', *JRS*, 83: 75-93.
Ramsay, W. M. (1889) 'Inscriptions d'Asie Mineure', *REG*, 2: 17-37.
Rapske, B. (1994) *The Book of Acts and Paul in Roman Custody*, The Book of Acts in its First Century Setting, 3, Grand Rapids, MI: Eerdmans.
Rathbone, D., A. K. Bowman and A. Wilson (2009) 'Earnings and costs: Living standards and the Roman economy', in *Quantifying the Roman Economy*, Oxford: Oxford University Press, pp. 299-326.
Raubitschek, A. E. (1981) 'A New Attic Club (ERANOS)', *J. Paul Getty Museum Journal*, 9: 93-8.
Rauh, N. K. (1993) *The Sacred Bonds of Commerce: Religion, Economy, and Trade Society at Hellenistic Roman Delos, 166-87 BCE*. Amsterdam: J.C. Gieben.
Reden, S. von (2007) *Money in Ptolemaic Egypt: From the Macedonian Conquest to the End of the Third Century BC*. Cambridge: Cambridge University Press.
Reden, S. von (2010) *Money in Classical Antiquity*, Key Themes in Ancient History, Cambridge: Cambridge University Press.
Reden, S. von (2016) 'Money and prices in the Papyri, Ptolemaic period', *Oxford Handbook Online*, available at: http://www.oxfordhandbooks.com/view/10.1093/oxfordhb/9780199935390.001.0001/oxfordhb-9780199935390-e-71.
Reekmans, T. (1948) 'Monetary history and the dating of Ptolemaic papyri', *Studia Hellenistica*, 5: 15-43.
Reynolds, J. (1977) 'Inscriptions', in J. A. Lloyd (ed.), *Excavations at Sidi Khrebish Benghazi (Berenice), Volume I: Buildings, Coins, Inscriptions, Architectural Decoration*, Supplements to Libya Antiqua, 5, Libya: Department of Antiquities, Ministry of Teaching and Education, People's Socialist Libyan Arab Jamahiriya, pp. 233-54.
Reynolds, J. and R. Tannenbaum (1987) *Jews and God-Fearers at Aphrodisias: Greek Inscriptions with Commentary*, CambPhSocSup, 12, Cambridge: Cambridge Philological Society.
Rhee, H. (2012) *Loving the Poor, Saving the Rich: Wealth, Poverty, and Early Christian Formation*, Grand Rapids, MI: Baker Books.
Richardson, P. (1996) 'Early synagogues as collegia in the diaspora and Palestine', in *Voluntary Associations in the Graeco-Roman World*, J. S. Kloppenborg and S. G. Wilson (eds), London: Routledge, pp. 90-109.
Richardson, P. (2004) *Building Jewish in the Roman East*, Waco, TX: Baylor University Press.
Rider, B. C. (1916) *The Greek House*, Cambridge: Cambridge University Press.
Rigsby, K. J. (1996) 'Craton's legacy', *EA*, 26: 137-9.
Robert, L. (1937) *Étude anatoliennes: Recherches sur les inscriptions grecques de l'Asie Mineure*, Études orientales publiées par l'Institut français d'archéologie de Stamboul, 5, Paris: de Boccard.
Robert, L. (1960) 'Inscriptions d'Asie Mineure au Musée de Leyde', *Hellenica*, 11-12: 214-62.
Roesch, P. (1982) *Études béotiennes*, Paris: de Boccard.
Roussel, P. (1916) *Les cultes égyptiens à Délos du IIIe au Ier siècle av. J.-C.*, Annales de l'Est, Paris: Berger-Levrault, pp. 29-30.
Royden, H. L. (1988) *The Magistrates of the Roman Professional Collegia in Italy from the First to the Third Century A.D.* Biblioteca di Studi Antichi, 61, Pisa: Giardini Editori e Stampatori.

Rudolf, H. (1899) *Koische Forschungen und Funde*, Leipzig: Dieterich'sche Verlags-Buchhandlung.
Runesson, A. (2001) *The Origins of the Synagogue: A Socio-Historical Study*, ConBNT, 37, Stockholm: Almqvist & Wiskell International.
Rüpke, J. (2007) *A Companion to Roman Religion*, Malden, MA: Blackwell Publishing.
Rüpke, J. (2014) *From Jupiter to Christ: On the History of Religion in the Roman Imperial Period*, Oxford: Oxford University Press.
Rüpke, J. (2016) *On Roman Religion: Lived Religion and the Individual in Ancient Rome*, Cornell Studies in Classical Philology, Ithaca, NY: Cornell University Press.
Saavedra Guerrero, M. D. (1991) 'La mujer y las asociaciones en el imperio romano', PhD thesis, Universidad de Cantabria.
San Nicolò, M. (1913) *Ägyptisches Vereinswesen zur Zeit der Ptolemäer und Römer*, 2 vols, Munich: C.H. Beck'sche Verlagsbuchhandlung.
Schäfer, A. (2002) 'Raumnutzung und Raumwahrnehmung im Vereinslokal der Iobakchen von Athen', in U. Egelhaaf-Gaiser and A. Schäfer (eds), *Religiöse Vereine in der römischen Antike. Untersuchungen zu Organisation, Ritual und Raumordnung*, STAC, 13, Tübingen: Mohr Siebeck, pp. 173–207.
Scheidel, W. (2010) 'Real wages in early economies: Evidence for living standards from 1800 BCE to 1300 CE', *Journal of the Economic and Social History of the Orient*, 53: 425–62.
Scheidel, W. (ed.) (2012) *The Cambridge Companion to the Roman Economy*, Cambridge Companions to the Ancient World, Cambridge: Cambridge University Press.
Scheidel, W. and S. J. Friesen (2009) 'The size of the economy and the distribution of income in the Roman empire', *JRS*, 99: 61–91.
Scheidel, W., I. Morris and R. P. Saller (eds) (2007) *The Cambridge Economic History of the Greco-Roman World*, Cambridge: Cambridge University Press.
Schellenberg, R. S. (2018) 'Subsistence, swapping, and Paul's rhetoric of generosity', *JBL*, 137: 215–34.
Schiess, T. (1888) *Die römischen Collegia Funeraticia nach den Inschriften*, Munich: Ackermann.
Schmeller, T. (1995) *Hierarchie und Egalität: Eine sozialgeschichtliche Untersuchung paulinischer Gemeinden und griechisch-römischer Vereine*, Stuttgarter Bibelstudien, 162, Stuttgart: Verlag Katholisches Bibelwerk.
Schmidt, T. E. (1983) 'Hostility to wealth in Philo of Alexandria', *JSNT*, 19: 85–97.
Schnöckel, K. H. (2006 [1956]) *Ägyptische Vereine in der frühen Prinzipatszeit: eine Studie über sechs Vereinssatzungen (Papyri Michigan 243–248)*, UVK, Universitätsverlag.
Schräder, H. (1896) 'Die Ausgrabungen am Westabhange der Akropolis, III: Funde im Gebiete des Dionysion', *AM*, 21: 265–86.
Schulz-Falkenthal, H. (1965) 'Zur Frage der Entstehung der römischen Handwerkerkollegien', *WZHalle*, 14 (2): 55–64.
Schulz-Falkenthal, H. (1966) 'Zur Lage der römischen Berufskollegien zu Beginn des 3. Jhs. u.Z. (die Privilegien der centonarii in Solva nach einem Reskript des Septimius Severus und Caracalla)', *WZHalle*, 15: 285–94.
Schwarzer, H. (1999) 'Untersuchungen zum hellenistischen Herrscherkult in Pergamon', *IM*, 49: 249–300.
Schwarzer, H. (2002) 'Vereinslokale im hellenistischen und römischen Pergamon', in U. Egelhaff-Gaiser and A. Schäfer (eds), *Religiöse Vereine in der römischen Antike: Untersuchungen zu Organisation, Ritual, und Raumordnung*, Tübingen: Mohr Siebeck, pp. 221–60.

Schwarzer, H. (2006) 'Die Bukoloi in Pergamon: Ein dionysischer Kultverein im Spiegel der archäologischen und epigraphischen Zeugnisse', *Hephaistos*, 24: 153–67.
Schwarzer, H. (2008) *Das Gebäude mit dem Podiensaal in der Stadtgrabung von Pergamon: Studien zu sakralen Banketträumen mit Liegepodien in der Antike*, Altertümer von Pergamon, 15.4, Berlin: De Gruyter.
Sewell, W. H. (1997) 'Geertz, cultural systems, and history: From synchrony to transformation', *Representations*, 59: 35–55.
Sewell, W. H. (1999) 'Concept(s) of culture', in V. E. Bonnell and L. Hunt (eds), *Beyond the Cultural Turn: New Directions in the Study of Society and Culture*, New Directions in the Study of Society and Culture, Berkeley, CA: University of California Press, pp. 35–61.
Siebert, G. (1968) 'Sur l'histoire du sanctuaire des dieux syriens à Délos', *BCH*, 92: 359–74.
Skarsaune, O. (2007) 'The Ebionites', in O. Skarsaune and R. Hvalvik (eds), *Jewish Believers in Jesus: The Early Centuries*, Peabody: Hendrickson, pp. 419–62.
Smith, J. Z. (1982) 'In comparison a magic dwells', in *Imagining Religion: From Babylon to Jonestown*, Chicago Studies in the History of Judaism, Chicago, IL: University of Chicago Press, pp. 19–35.
Smith, J. Z. (1990) *Drudgery Divine: On the Comparison of Early Christianities and the Religions of Late Antiquity*, Chicago Studies in the History of Judaism, Chicago, IL: University of Chicago Press.
Sneed, M. (1999) 'Israelite concern for the alien, orphan, and widow: Altruism or ideology?', *ZAW*, 111: 498–507.
Sokolowski, F. (1955) *Lois sacrées de l'Asie Mineure*. École française d'Athènes, Travaux et mémoires des anciens membre étrangers de l'école et de divers savants, 9, Paris: de Boccard.
Sokolowski, F. (1969) *Lois sacrées des cités grecques*, École française d'Athènes, Travaux et mémoires des anciens membres étrangers de l'école et de divers savants, 10, Paris: de Boccard.
Sosin, J. D. (1999) 'Tyrian stationarii at Puteoli', *Tyche*, 14: 275–84.
Sosin, J. D. (2000) 'Perpetual endowments in the Hellenistic world: A case-study in economic rationalism', PhD thesis, Duke University.
Sosin, J. D. (2001) 'Accounting and endowments', *Tyche*, 16: 161–75.
Spiegelberg, W. (1908) *Die demotischen Papyrus*, Catalogue général des antiquités égyptiennes du Musée du Caire, 2, Strassburg: Dumont-Schauberg.
Stang, J. R. (2007) 'The city of Dionysos: A social and historical study of the Ionian city of Teos', PhD thesis, State University of New York at Buffalo.
Stark, R. B. and W. S. Bainbridge (1985) *The Future of Religion: Secularization, Revival and Cult Formation*, Berkeley, CA: University of California Press.
Stavrianopoulou, E. (2006) *'Gruppenbild mit Dame': Untersuchungen zur rechtlichen und sozialen Stellung der Frau auf den Kykladen im Hellenismus und in der römischen Kaiserzeit*, Stuttgart: Franz Steiner Verlag.
Sterling, G. E. (1994) '"Athletes of Virtue": An analysis of the Summaries in Acts (2:41–7; 4:32–5; 5:12–16)', *JBL*, 113: 679–96.
Tabbernee, W. (1997) *Montanist Inscriptions and Testimonia: Epigraphic Sources Illustrating the History of Montanism*, Patristic Monograph Series, 16, Macon, GA: Mercer University Press.
Taylor, C. (2011) 'Women's social networks and female friendship in the ancient Greek city', *Gender and History*, 23: 703–20.
Teixidor, J. (1980) 'L'assemblée législative en Phénicie d'après les inscriptions', *Syria*, 57: 453–64.

Temin, P. (2013) *The Roman Market Economy*, Princeton, NJ: Princeton University Press.
Terpstra, T. T. (2013) *Trading Communities in the Roman World: A Micro-Economic and Institutional Perspective*, Leiden: Brill.
Theissen, G. (1982 [1974]) *The Social Setting of Pauline Christianity: Essays on Corinth*, edited by John H. Schütz, Philadelphia, PA: Fortress Press.
Thompson, D. J. (1984) 'The Idumeans of Memphis and the Ptolemaic *politeumata*', in *Atti Del XVII Congresso internazionale di papirologia*, Naples: Centro Internazionale per lo Studio dei Papiri Ercolanesi, pp. 1069–75.
Thompson, D. J. (1988) *Memphis under the Ptolemies*, Princeton, NJ: Princeton University Press.
Thompson, E. P. (1964) *The Making of the English Working Class*, New York: Pantheon Books.
Thompson Crawford, D. J. (1984) 'The Idumeans of Memphis and the Ptolemaic Politeumata', in *Atti del XVII Congresso Internazionale di Papirologia*, Naples: Centro internazionale per lo studio dei papiri ercolanesi, pp. 1069–75.
Thomsen, C. A. (2015) 'The *Eranistai* of classical Athens', *GRBS*, 55: 154–75.
Thomson, R. J. A. (1980) 'Respecifying the effects of voluntary association on individuals in a traditional society', *International Journal of Comparative Sociology*, 21: 288–301.
Tod, M. N. (1906) 'A statute of an Attic thiasos', *ABSA*, 13: 328–38.
Tod, M. N. (1932) 'Clubs and societies in the greek world', in *Sidelights on Greek History*, Oxford: Basil Blackwell, pp. 71–96.
Touna, V. (2017) *Fabrications of the Greek Past: Religion, Tradition, and the Making of Modern Identities*, SMTSR, 9, Leiden: Brill.
Tran, N. (2006) *Les membres des associations romaines : Le rang social des collegiati en Italie et en Gaules, sous le Haut-Empire*, Collection de l'École française de Rome, Rome: Publications de l'École française de Rome.
Tran, N. (2011) 'Les collèges professionnels romains: "clubs" ou "corporations"? L'exemple de la vallée du Rhône et de *CIL* XII 1797 (Tournon-sur-Rhône, Ardèche)', *AncSoc*: 197–219.
Tran, N. (2016) 'The social organization of commerce and crafts in ancient Arles: Heterogeneity, hierarchy, and patronage', in M. Flohr and A. Wilson (eds), *Urban Craftsmen and Traders in the Roman World*, Oxford Studies on the Roman Economy. Oxford: Oxford University Press, pp. 254–77.
Trebilco, P. R. (1991) *Jewish Communities in Asia Minor*, Cambridge: Cambridge University Press.
Trevett, C. (1996) *Montanism: Gender, Authority, and the New Prophecy*, Cambridge: Cambridge University Press.
Trümper, M. (2002) 'Das Sanktuarium des "Établissement des Poseidoniastes de Bérytos" in Delos. Zur Baugeschichte eines griechischen Vereinsheiligtums', *BCH*: 265–330.
Trümper, M. (2004) 'The oldest original synagogue building in the Diaspora: The Delos Synagogue reconsidered', *Hesperia*, 73: 513–98.
Trümper, M. (2005) 'Modest housing in Late Hellenistic Delos', in B. A. Ault and L. C. Nevett (eds), *Ancient Greek Houses and Households: Chronological, Regional, and Social Diversity*, Philadelphia, PA: University of Pennsylvania Press, pp. 119–39.
Trümper, M. (2006) 'Negotiating religious and ethnic identity: The case of clubhouses in Late Hellenistic Delos', *Hephaistos*, 24: 113–40.
Tsirigoti-Drakotou, I. (2006) 'Τιμητικό ψήφισμα από την Ιερά οδό', in N. C. Stampolides (ed.), *Γενέθλιον. Ἵδρυμα Ν. Π. Γουλάνδρη Μουσείο Κυκλαδικής Τέχνης*, Athens: Goulandris Museum of Cycladic Art, 285–94.
Turner, E. G. and O. Neugebauer (1949) 'Gymnasium debts and new moons', *BJRL*, 32: 80–96.

Ustinova, Y. (2005) 'Lege et consuetudine: Voluntary cult associations in the Greek law', in V. Dasen and M. Piérart (eds), *Idia kai dèmosia : Les cadres 'privés' et 'publics' de la religion grecque antique*, Kernos supplements, 15, Liège: Presses Universitaires de Liège, pp. 177–90.
van der Horst, P. W. (2003) *Philo's Flaccus: The First Pogrom*, Leiden: Brill.
van der Horst, P. W. (2016) 'Organized charity in the ancient world: Pagan, Jewish, Christian', in *Jewish and Christian Communal Identities in the Roman World*, Ancient Judaism and Early Christianity, 94, Leiden: Brill, pp. 116–33.
van Minnen, P. (1987) 'Urban craftsmen in Roman Egypt', *MBAH*, 6: 31–88.
van Nijf, O. (1997) *The Civic World of Professional Associations in the Roman East*, Dutch Monographs on Ancient History and Archaeology, 17, Amsterdam: J.C. Gieben.
van Nijf, O. (2002) 'Collegia and civic guards. Two chapters in the history of sociability', in W. Jongman and M. Kleijwegt (eds), *After the Past: Essays in Ancient History in Honour of H. W. Pleket*, Mnemosyne Supplements, 233, Leiden: Brill, pp. 305–40.
Venticinque, P. F. (2009) 'Common causes: Guilds, craftsmen and merchants in the economy and society of Roman and Late Roman Egypt', PhD thesis, University of Chicago.
Venticinque, P. F. (2010) 'Family affairs: Guild regulations and family relationships in Roman Egypt', *GRBS*, 50: 273–94.
Verboven, K. (2007) 'The Associative Order: Status and ethos among Roman businessmen in Late Republic and Early Empire', *Athenaeum*, 95: 861–93.
Verboven, K. (2009) 'Magistrates, patrons and benefactors of voluntary associations: Status building and Romanisation in the Spanish, Gallic and German provinces of the Roman empire', in B. Antela-Bernárdez and T. Ñaco dei Hoyo (eds), *Transforming Historical Landscapes in the Ancient Empires*, BAR International Series, 1986, Oxford: British Archaeological Reports, pp. 159–67.
Verboven, K. (2011a) 'Professional *collegia*: Guilds or social clubs?', *AncSoc*, 41: 187–95.
Verboven, K. (2011b) 'Resident aliens and translocal merchant collegia in the Roman empire', in O. Hekster and T. Kaiser (eds), *Frontiers in the Roman World*, Leiden: Brill, pp. 335–48.
Verboven, K. (2012) 'City and reciprocity: The role of cultural beliefs in the Roman economy', *Annales (English edition)*, 67: 599–627.
Verboven, K. (2015) 'The knights who say NIE: Can neo-institutional economics live up to its expectation in ancient history research?', in *Structure and Performance in the Roman Economy: Models, Methods and Case Studies*, 350, Collection Latomus, Brussels: Latomus, pp. 33–57.
Verboven, K. (2016) 'Guilds and the organisation of urban populations during the Principate', in K. Verboven and C. Laes (eds), *Work, Labour, and Professions in the Roman World*, Impact of Empire, Leiden: Brill, pp. 173–202.
Verreth, H. (2009) *The Provenance of Egyptian Documents from the 8th Century BC till the 8th Century AD*, Trismegistos Online Publications, 3, Leuven: Trismegistos, available at: http://www.trismegistos.org/dl.php?id=7.
Veyne, P. (1990) *Bread and Circuses: Historical Sociology and Political Pluralism*, translated by Brian Pearce, London: Allen Lane.
Vondeling, J. (1961) *Eranos*, Groningen: J.B. Wolters.
Voutiras, E. (2005) 'Sanctuaire privé – culte public?: Le cas du Sarapieion de Thessalonique', in V. Dasen and M. Piérart (eds), *Idia kai dèmosia: Les cadres 'privés' et 'publics' de la religion grecque antique*, Kernos supplements, Liège: Presses Universitaires de Liège, 273–8.
Wallace-Hadrill, A. (1994) *Houses and Society in Pompeii and Herculaneum*, Princeton, NJ: Princeton University Press.

Waltzing, J.-P. (1891) 'Review of: *Zur Geschichte und Organisation des römischen Vereinswesens. Drei Untersuchungen* von W. Liebenam. Leipzig, Teubner, 1890', *Revue de l'instruction publique en Belgique*, 34: 161–76.
Waltzing, J.-P. (1895) 'The Roman guilds and charity', *Charities Review*, 4: 345–62.
Waltzing, J.-P. (1895–1900) *Étude historique sur les corporations professionnelles chez les Romains depuis les origines jusqu'à la chute de l'Empire d'Occident*, Mémoires couronnés et autres mémoires publiée par l'Académie royale des sciences, des lettres et des beaux-arts de Belgique, 50, Brussels: F. Hayez.
Waltzing, J.-P. (1898) 'Les collèges funéraires chez les romains [I]', *Le musée belge. Revue de philologie classique*, 2: 281–94.
Waltzing, J.-P. (1899) 'Les collèges funéraires chez les romains [II]', *Le musée belge. Revue de philologie classique*, 3: 130–57.
Wanamaker, C. A. (1990) *The Epistles to the Thessalonians: A Commentary on the Greek Text*, NIGTC, Grand Rapids, MI: William B. Eerdmans Publishing.
Wassink, A. (1991) 'Inflation and financial policy under the Roman empire to the Price Edict of 301 A.D.', *Historia*, 40: 465–93.
Wedderburn, A. J. M. (2002) 'Paul's collection: Chronology and history', *NTS*, 48: 95–110.
Weinfeld, M. (1986) *The Organizational Pattern and the Penal Code of the Qumran Sect: A Comparison with Guilds and Religious Associations of the Hellenistic-Roman Period*, Freibourg: Editions Universitaires.
Welch, K. W. (1981) 'An interpersonal influence model of traditional religious commitment', *Sociological Quarterly*, 22: 81–92.
Wendt, H. (2014) 'James C. Hanges, *Paul, Founder of Churches: A Study in Light of the Evidence for the Role of "Founder-Figures" in the Hellenistic-Roman Period*. A review essay', *Religion and Theology*, 20: 292–302.
West, W. C. (1990) 'M. Oulpios Domestikos and the Athletic Synod at Ephesus', *Ancient History Bulletin*, 4: 84–9.
Westermann, W. L. (1932) 'Entertainment in the villages of Graeco-Roman Egypt', *JEA*, 18: 16–27.
White, L. M. (1997) *The Social Origins of Christian Architecture*, HTS, 42, Valley Forge, PA: Trinity Press.
Wilhelm, A. (1898) 'Die sogenannte Hetäreninschrift aus Paros', *AM*, 23: 409–40.
Will, E. and M. Schmid (1985) *Le sanctuaire de la déesse syrienne*, Exploration archéologique de Délos, 35, Paris: de Boccard.
Williams, M. H. (1992) 'The Jews and Godfearers inscription from Aphrodisias: A case of patriarchal interference in early 3rd century Caria?', *Historia*, 41: 297–310.
Wittenburg, A. (1990) *Il testamento di Epikteta*. Università delgi Studi di Trieste 4, Trieste: Giulio Bernardi Editore.
Wycherley, R. E. (1970) 'Minor shrines in ancient Athens', *Phoenix*, 24: 283–95.
Young, N. H. (2003) '"The use of Sunday for meetings of believers in the New Testament": A response', *NovT*, 45: 111–22.
Youtie, H. C. (1948) 'The *kline* of Sarapis', *HTR*, 41: 9–29.
Ziebarth, E. (1896) *Das griechische Vereinswesen*, Stuttgart: S. Hirzel.
Zoumbaki, S. (2005) 'The collective definition of slaves and the limits to their activities', in Vasilis I. Anastasiadēs (ed.), *Esclavage antique et discriminations socio-culturelles*, Panagiōtēs Doukellēs, and Panepistēmio Aigaiou, Bern: P. Lang, 217–32.
Zuiderhoek, A. (2009) *The Politics of Munificence in the Roman Empire: Citizens, Elites and Benefactors in Asia Minor*, Cambridge: Cambridge University Press.

Index of Inscriptions and Papyri

Agora		98	101	221	56
16:161	96, 106, 169	101	93	222a	124
		102	93	223	81, 90, 103, 117
AGRW		105	101		
1	165	111	116	224	84, 95, 103, 117
2	117	112	116		
5	102, 117	115	101	225	95
6	117	116	41	229	53, 55, 84, 88, 121
7	94, 114, 117, 163	117	96, 112		
		118	117	234	82
9	105, 110, 114	121	55, 77, 112, 163	243	68, 96
				244	55
10	81	124	117	247	64
11	105, 114	144	116	249	65
14	101	145	85, 101	250	102
16	155	151	116	255	49, 66, 92
18	55, 81	152	77, 109	256	92
21	54, 55	154	109	257	67, 172
22	54, 115	155	109	258	85
22b	124	158	109	271–4	172
29	189	160	102	276	82
30	115	161	109	277	82
31	173	162	129	281	165
37	94, 110	174	108	287	83, 155
42	77	175	108, 116	289	111, 178
43–54	10	176	115	293	36
46	77	179	64	295	96, 163
47	78, 190	181	155	298	155
48	78	184	101	299	94, 157, 162
50	78, 105	186	102	300–3	162
54	94	188	101	300	113, 159, 190, 163
55	94	189–95	53		
56	94	190	112, 190	301	114, 164, 190
58	105, 109	191	117		
60	82	194	102	302	96, 97, 114, 133
69	34	201	94		
72	82	202	55	305–7	49
73	126	203	108	304	161
79	64	213	55, 110	305	155
88	173	214	94	306	41, 155
97	101	215	36, 94	310	46, 96, 118

Index of Inscriptions and Papyri

314a	191	XIV 246	190	I 35	91, 154, 156
314b	191	XIV 250	191	I 36	49, 54, 55,
317	35, 77, 96	XIV 251	191		156
330	77, 191	XIV 252	191	I 37	127
B1–B28	85	XIV 2112	4, 46, 96,	I 39	156
B2	86		158	I 42	54
B6	88	XIV 2120	25	I 43	170, 171
B7	56, 86			I 47	170, 189
B8	88	*CJZC*		I 48	51, 65, 66,
L13	55, 110	70–2	140		156
L16	97			I 49	53, 66
L39	41	*CPJ*		I 50	47, 110,
L40	41, 171	I 20	175		116, 127,
L43	41, 118	I 23	175		170, 171
L49	176	I 24	175, 176	I 51	47, 86
L53	40, 118	I 129	175	I 52	191
L54	41	I 134	175	I 53	54, 115
		I 432	175	I 57	173
BGU		II 153	38	I 59	173
1216	85	III 473	176	I 61	115
IV 1137	165	III 1532A	175	I 64	94
				I 65	190
CIG		*GIBM*		I 68	190
3068	155	IV 896	51, 55	I 69	77
3069	155			I 71	25
3070	155	*GRA*		I 72	192
3071	155	I 4	105, 114	I 73	156
3082	64, 66	I 6	49, 92	I 76	105, 189
3540	123	I 7	104	I 77	56
		I 8	44, 166,	I 83	82, 156
CIJ			167, 172	I 84	191
722–3	54	I 11	155, 156	I 85	191
		I 13	84, 127, 156	I 134	155
CIL		I 14	96, 169	I 150	173
II 5812	191	I 15	49, 156, 172	II 93	191
III 63	190	I 17	36, 48, 166,	II 95	178
III 870	191		172	II 99	25, 141
III 5191	191	I 18	84	II 105	59, 127,
III 5196	190	I 19	168, 170		189
III 6150	191	I 21	101	II 110	49
III 11699	191	I 23	55	II 111	96, 112
VI 786	49	I 24	156	II 115	49
VI 9398	25	I 25	103, 156	II 116	49, 77
VI 10109	24	I 27	83	II 117	25, 55, 77,
VI 30983	25	I 28	101		112, 163
VI 33885	96	I 31	36	II 123	49
VI 34004	25	I 32	84, 156	II 127	129, 190
XI 6310	190	I 33	49, 66, 84,	II 128	49, 139
XII 1898	23		91, 156	II 129	49

Index of Inscriptions and Papyri

II 137	49, 53	*IAph*		2225	53, 121
II 139	102	11.55	142	2575	123
II 141	155	12.27	66		
II 143	25, 55, 56			*IDelta*	
II 147	72	*IBerenike*		I 2	36
II 149	108	17	155	I 446	83, 155
II 150	172	18	155		
II 152	55, 112			*IEph*	
II 191	94, 162	*IBeroia*		14	91
II 214	96	371	64, 94	20	81, 102, 123, 129, 190
III 154	54	372	94, 110		
III 160	83, 155				
III 163	53	*IBosp*		22	101
III 168	165	78–108	94	213	53, 102
III 170	36	104	173	215	133
III 188	160	987	64	1503	131
III 189	36	1134	191	1595	53
III 190	36	1259–86	94	1600	191
III 193	78	1262	190	1687	91
III 194	43, 46, 78, 96	1277	191	2212	109
				2213	94, 173
III 195	28, 76	*ICariaR*		2304	108, 116
III 202	82	162	97	2603	190
III 205	165			3214	68
III 206	113, 159, 163	*ICiliciaBM*		3334	68
		II 190–202	173	3801	102
III 208	105			4337	53
III 210	96	*IDacia*			
III 212	164	I 31	34	*IErythrai*	
III 215	178			122	91
III 216	90	*IDelos*			
III 220	96	372A	122	*IFayum*	
III 221	82	442A	122	15	175
III 229	82	460T	122	73	82
III 235	163	1417	60, 122, 123	205	82
III 238	111			II 109	82
III 240	110	1519	81, 103, 84, 95, 99, 103	II 122	82
III 247	82	1520		II 134	82
III 248	161				
III 269	111	1521	66	*IG*	
III 271	83	1522	66	I³ 369	106
III 276	176	1713	82	II² 337	81
III 286	160	1731	123	II² 343	92
III 287	36	1737	82	II² 999	86, 92
III 290	96	1772–96	49	II² 1012	54, 102
		1783	95	II² 1252	86, 92
IApamBith		1898	123	II² 1253	86
35	24, 35, 141	2220–304	121	II² 1259	86
		2224	121, 122	II² 1261	101

II² 1265	169	V,1	189	I 1095	53
II² 1271	84, 127	V,2	25		
II² 1273	84	VII 33	189	IGUR	
II² 1275	44, 163, 166, 172	VII 235	123	160	77, 191
		VII 686	173	235	41
II² 1277	172	VII 687	25, 173	236	41
II² 1278	47, 166, 172	VII 2850	83	237–38	41
		VII 3224	189		
II² 1282	84	VII 3376	168	IHerakleiaPont	
II² 1283	55, 81	IX,1²	115	2	66
II² 1289	35	IX,2	66, 123		
II² 1291	170	X,2	78, 94, 105, 109, 189, 190	IHierapJ	
II² 1292	25			133	109
II² 1293	66, 100			195	109
II² 1298	99, 170	XI,4	25, 53, 56, 59, 60, 75, 86, 90, 119, 120, 122, 145	227	109
II² 1301	103			234	109
II² 1314	101				
II² 1316	53			IHistria	
II² 1317	101			167	82
II² 1317b	101	XII,1	37, 49, 61, 64, 66, 67, 68, 83, 92, 105, 123, 170, 173		
II² 1322	84			IHyllarimaMcCabe	
II² 1323	172			18	170
II² 1324	84				
II² 1325	66, 84, 91			IJO	
II² 1326	54, 55			I Ach 58–9	54
II² 1327	91, 154	XII,127	67	I Ach 66	124
II² 1329	127	XII,2	123, 173	I Ach 67	124
II² 1339	114	XII,3	55, 65, 68, 70, 85, 96, 108, 123	I Mac1	77
II² 1343	51, 65			II 26	85
II² 1361	105, 114			II 32	108
II² 1366	54, 115	XII,4	68, 90	II 36	101
II² 1368	86, 94, 114, 158, 163	XII,5	110, 125	II 168	85, 101
		XII,7	169	II 196	110
		XII,8	107, 108	II 206	116
II² 1369	53, 66	XIV 830	33, 35, 77, 96	II 223	94
II² 1553–778	168				
II² 2336	124	XIV 1054	41	IJudEgypt	
II² 2354	25	XIV 1055	41	22	54
II² 2360	76, 189	XIV 1109	41	117	175
II² 2361	191	XIV 1110	41		
II² 2499	104			IKallatis	
II² 2501	104	IGBulg		35	126
II² 2701	107	674	95	36	108
II² 2720	107	1401	95	45	64
II² 2721	169	1626	191	46	82
II² 2935	169	I 77	64	80	82
II² 2940	169	IGLAM			
II² 2946	84	106	92	IKamiros	
II² 4817	191	IGR		84	64

Index of Inscriptions and Papyri

IKilikiaBM		285	123	*IRhamnous*	
II 190–202	94	394	65	II 59	83
II 201	36	*ILydiaHM*		*IRhodB*	
IKios		96	68, 155	12	170
22	101	*ILydiaM*		155	170
IKos		145	93	*IRhodM*	
155–9	94	*IMagnMai*		44	64
IKosB		117	108, 117	46	92
274	64	215	25, 55	*IRhodPC*	
275	64	*IMilet*		5	67, 105
285	173	360	139	18	81, 173
287	64	798	189	*IRhodPer*	
IKosM		935	64	87	123
466	95	939	155	115	123
492	173	*IMT*		501	125
493	173	1539	95	556	123
IKosPH		1801	116	*ISamos*	
382	55, 90	1937	116	10	114
IKosS		*IOlbiaD*		*ISelge*	
ED		88	124	T48	94
89	123	*IPergamon*		*ISmyrna*	
EF		161a	123	218	94, 173
78	173	255	123	639	53
201	173	374	96, 112	653	101
214	173	485	101	654	97
399–400	173	*IPerinthos*		697	102
458	173	59	95	706	112
460	64	*IPhilippiP*		712	133
EV		II 029/G215	77	721	102
278	170	II 133/G441	77	731	112, 190
IKyme		*IPriene*		732	190
13	91	108	91	753	125
37	59, 127, 189	111	91	*IStrat*	
ILLRP		195	123	149	25
511	165	*IPrusaOlymp*		174	25
ILS		52	190	352	25
3840	25	159	93	666	25
7342	25	1028	101	*ITomis*	
ILindos		1036	93	83	191
251	65			132	95
252	102				

Index of Inscriptions and Papyri

IThraceL
18   82
212   189

ITlos
28   72

LSAM
72   68
73   123

LSCG
143   125
155   123

MAMA
I 437   116
IV 230   64

NewDocs
I 1   110
V 5   129, 131

NGSL
5   114

OGIS
51   155
325   53, 155
326   155
737   85, 155, 175

P. Chicago Field Mus. dem.
31321   30

P. L. Bat.
XXII 5 dem   30

P. Turin dem. Suppl.
6086   30

PAthen
41   96, 125

PCairDem
30606   94

PCairo
II 30605   151, 157, 158, 159, 161
II 30606   157, 158, 162
II 30618   158
II 30619   158, 159, 160
II 31179   157, 158, 160

PEnteuxis
20   36
21   36

PGrenf
I 31   161

PHamb
I 34   163

PHamburgDemotic
1   157

Philippi
II 340/L58   25

PKöln
57   55, 110

PLilleDemotic
29   160
98   25

PLips
II 131   178

PLond
VI 1912   38
VII 2193   96, 158, 163

PMich
II 121   96
II 123   90, 91, 163
II 124   90
V 313   105
V 243   113, 158, 159, 162, 163, 164, 190
V 244   114, 162, 165, 190
V 246   162, 190
V 247   162, 189
V 248   162, 189
V 322b   96
V 245   96, 97, 114, 133, 162
VIII 511   110
IX 575   111, 179

PMilanVoglDemotic
Inv. 77–8   157

POslo
III 143   90

POxy
I 110   110
II 335   177
III 523   110
VIII 128   79
IX 1205   176
XII 1484   110
XIV 1639   30
XIV 1755   110
XXXI 2592   110
LII 3693   110
LXII 4339   110

PPetr
III 136   96

PPetrie
III 39   158

PPrague
   159, 160, 161

PRyl
II 94   165
IV 580   36
IV 586   161
IV 589   161

PStanfordGreenDemotic
21   157, 158, 159

PStrass
IV 287   181

PTebt		204/0216	102	41:182	122
I 32	175	308/0301	101	41:683	122
I 33	158			41:1638	82
I 109	29, 30	*RIG*		42:17	140
I 110	29, 30	1225	95	43:26	145
I 112	29, 30			43:59	189
I 116	29, 30	*SB*		44:60	101
I 118	28, 43, 76, 96	I 681	85	45:902	108
		I 4549	111	46:744	190
I 117	29, 30	III 6184	82	46:800	192
I 120	29, 30	III 6254	82	46:1524	117
I 121	29, 30	III 6319	97	49:222	122
I 208	29, 30	III 7182	78, 96	49:1683	93
I 224	29, 30	IV 7270	175	52:872	122
II 401	96	IV 7290	83	53:822	126
III 700	42, 175	V 8929	85, 155	54:235	170, 189
III 815	175	X 10278	78	54:794	53, 82
III 817	175			54:1628	82
III 818	176, 177	*SEG*		55:1654	82
III 894	43, 46, 78, 96, 125	3:587	124	55:2071	122
		3:674	81, 173	56:203	103, 154
		4:418	101	57:198	122
PTebtunisSuppl		12:100	106	57:777	64
1578	158	17:503	115	58:1640	72, 108
		18:33	66, 100	59:152	101
PTexas		24:203	104	60:665	94
Inv. 8	160	26:614	173		
		29:36	169	*SGDI*	
RICIS		29:1195	93	1804	168
101/0424	60	31:122	116, 127, 158, 171	1878	168
112/0502	123			2317	168
112/0703	66	31:983	97		
113/0538	78	32:453	76	*TAM*	
202/0101	56, 57, 122	32:454	76	II 223	173
202/0103	122	32:487	173	IV 22	82
202/0106	122	32:1149	91	V 91	97
202/0109	122	32:1982	168	V 536	147
202/0114	60	33:145	85	V 537	147
202/0115	60, 122	33:147	96	V 1148	116
202/0121	59, 122	34:1266	97	V 1539	25, 55, 77, 112, 163
202/0124	59, 120, 122	39:737	64, 126, 173		
202/0194	53, 55, 84, 88	39:1211	132	*TAM Suppl*	
202/0801	110	41:171	169	III 201	190

Index of Ancient Literary Sources

Acts
2   63
4   63, 184
18 79
19 133
20 145
28 79

Aelius Aristides, *Orations*
45   55, 110

Aristides, *Apology*
15   152, 183, 184, 185

Aristotle, *Nichomachean Ethics*
1160a   169

Aristotle, *On Sterility*
511b   145

1 Clement
55   184
59   184

2 Clement
13   179
16   181

Colossians
4   79

Deuteronomy
15   184
23   175, 179

Didache
1   181
4   181
12 181
14 145
15 181

Didascalia apostolorum
17   181, 182
18   182
19   182

Digest
2   176
3   41, 118
47 4, 40, 41, 118

Dio Cassius, *Roman History*
63   145

Ephesians
5   39

Epiphanius, *Panarion*
26   182

Epistle of Barnabas
19   182

Exodus
20   137
22   175, 179

Gospel of Judas
39   182

Gospel of Peter
35   145

Hebrews
10   184
13   184

Hesiod, *Works and Days*
722–3   167

Homer, *Odyssey*
1   167
11   167

Ignatius, *Magnesians*
4   39
7   39
9   145

Ignatius, *Philadelphians*
4   39

Ignatius, *Polycarp*
4   182

Ignatius, *Smyrneans*
4   39
6   182, 184
8   39

Ignatius, *Trallians*
7   39

1 John
1–3   39
2   33
3   182
4   39

2 John		6	163,	4	79,		
7–11	39		180		147,		
		9	148,		180		
3 John			149				
9–10	39	11	180	1 Peter			
		12	181	2:11–3:22	184		
Josephus, *Against Apion*		16	79,				
2	174,		124,	Philo, *Embassy to Gaius*			
	175		135,	132–4	39		
			143,	311–15	140		
Josephus, *Antiquities*			144,				
14	137,		145,	Philo, *For Flaccus*			
	138,		146	28	138		
	139			53–7	39		
16	140	Paul, 2 Corinthians		86–91	38		
		8	143,	136–40	38		
Justin Martyr, *First Apology*			147,				
67	184		148	Philo, *Special Laws*			
		9	143,	1	137,		
Leviticus			147,		140		
25	175,		148				
	179,	10–13	143,	Plato, *Laws*			
	184		148,	11	167,		
			149		168		
Lucian, *The Dance*							
15	97	Paul, Galatians		Pliny, *Letters*			
79	97	1	143,	10	41,		
			149		171,		
Lucian, *Peregrinus*		2	142,		172		
11–13	184		143				
				Pliny the Elder, *Natural*			
Luke		Paul, Philemon			*History*		
6	179,	2	79	2	36		
	181						
		Paul, Philippians		Revelation			
Matthew		1	147	1	146		
17	137	3	184				
22	179	4	148,	Shepherd of Hermas			
25	179,		149	5	181		
	184			8	184		
		Paul, Romans		38	182		
Minucius Felix, *Octavius*		15	142,				
	179		143,	Sirach			
			148	4	31		
Mishnah Peah		16	79	35	179		
8	142						
		Paul, 1 Thessalonians		Strabo, *Geography*			
Paul, 1 Corinthians		1	51, 79	12	36		
1–4	39	2	79, 147	14	131		

Tacitus, *Annals*		1 Timothy		*Tosefta Peah*	
2	36	5	183	4	141,
14	41	16	183		142
Tertullian, *Apology*					
39	118	Tobit			
Tertullian, *Scapula*		4	174	*Tosefta Shabbat*	
4	185	12	179	16	142

Index of Modern Scholars

Adams, Edward 80
Alföldy, Géza 5, 20
Arnaoutoglou, Ilias 35, 80, 168

Barclay, John M. G. 7, 20, 138
Baslez, Marie-François 153
Baugh, Steven 129
Bauschatz, John 159
Billings, Bradly S. 80
Broekaert, Wim 165
Bruneau, Philippe 124
Buell, Denise Kimber 181

Calhoun, George Miller 166
Carney, T. F. 8

Deissmann, Adolf 19
Downs, David J. 145–6, 148

Ecker, Avner 115
Eckhardt, Benedikt 12n47, 115
Elliott, John H. 19–20
Ellis-Evans, Aneurin 134
Engelmann, Helmut 58

Finley, Moses 132–3, 168
Foucart, Paul 92
Friesen, Steven 7–8, 18–21, 26–7, 31

Gabrielsen, Vincent 6, 32, 64, 92
Gager, John 19
Gardner, Gregg Elliot 141–1
Gibbs, Matthew 5, 133

Hanges, James 56
Harrill, Albert 183
Hatsfeld, Jean 123
Hemelrijk, Emily 24–6
Horbury, William 174
Horrell, David 80

Horsley, G. H. R. 129–2
Horst, Pieter van der 6, 152

Kaminski, Gabriele 122–4
Kloppenborg, John S. 7, 133–4

Lambert, Stephen 107
Langellotti, Micela 123
Lieu, Judith 6, 152
Liu, Jinyu 6, 20, 34, 109
Llewelyn, S. R. 145
Longenecker, Bruce W. 7, 20–1, 31, 52, 55, 152, 180
Lytle, Ephraim 128–32

MacMullen, Ramsay 5, 22–4, 27
Malherbe, Abraham 19
Mandell, Sara 137
Meggitt, Justin J. 6, 19–20, 31, 152
Melfi, Milena 122
Meeks, Wayne 19–20, 22
Millett, Paul 167–8
Mommsen, Theodor 4, 17, 21, 151–2
Monson, Andrew 6, 153, 157

Nijf, Onno van 5, 17, 132–3
Nilsson, M. P. 58

Oakes, Peter 8, 80, 85
Osiek, Carolyn 184

Parker, Robert 73–4
Poland, Franz 4, 55, 65
Polanyi, Karl 8
Patterson, John 16–18, 21
Perry, Jonathan 4, 165
Pleket, H. W. 132–3

Rajak, Tessa 139
Raubitschek, Antony E. 171

Reden, Sitta von 29–30
Rüpke, Jörg 11, 23, 53

Scheidel, Walter 8, 18, 20, 26–7, 31
Schellenberg, Ryan 180
Schwarzer, Holger 88

Theissen, Gerd 19
Thompson Crawford, Dorothy J. 85
Thomsen, Christian 168–70
Tilly, Charles 157

Touna, Vaia 10–11
Trümper, Monika 88

Venticinque, Philip F. 6, 153
Verboven, Koenraad 5, 133
Verreth, Herbert 156–7

Young, Norman H. 146

Ziebarth, Erich 53

Subject Index

almsgiving (*see* mutual aid or support)
association, definition of 9–13

burial (*see* funerary practices)

charity (*see* mutual aid or support)
Christians (*see* Jesus adherents)
class (*see* status)
collegia funeraticia, problems with category of 4–5, 10, 17–21, 46
collegia tenuiorum (*see collegia funeraticia*)

decline, precarity, and disbandment 1–2, 33–42, 75–6, 108–12
diplomacy with civic or imperial institutions 81, 102–13, 139

earthquakes 36–8, 173
economy, definition of 8–9
ethnic or immigrant associations and networks
    Berytians 49, 84–5, 88–9, 95, 99, 103
    Egyptians 49, 56–62, 81
    Idumeans 85
    Israelites 88, 124–5, 135–42
    Judeans 1–4, 6–7, 38–9, 49, 54–5, 63, 77, 83, 85, 88–9, 94, 100–2, 108–9, 120–1, 135–42, 174–8
    Kitians 81
    Romans or Italians (settlers) 95, 122, 123
    Sidonians 84, 92
    Syrians 84–6, 121–2
    Thracians 55, 81
    Tyrians 33, 35, 77, 81, 90 n.54
ethnic conflict 38–9

family and household networks 1, 55, 58, 67, 68–74, 77, 79, 94, 108, 112, 126, 152, 161–2, 167, 173, 183, 185, 187

financial practices, concepts, and expenses
    benefaction 91–3, 99–104
    bronze drachmas, value of 29–30
    collection 3, 37, 39, 54, 55, 59, 63, 66, 84, 92, 93, 119–50, 152, 155, 167–73, 176–7, 180, 183–4
    'collectors' (*praktores*) 127–8
    contributions or 'fees' for membership 30–1, 43–4, 46, 94, 96, 109–17, 144–5, 59–60
    'contribution-society', 'contributors' (*eranos, eranistai*) 53–4, 66–7, 81, 92, 107, 126, 167–73, 189–90
    fees (*see* contributions)
    fines 35, 45–7, 61, 71, 74, 94, 109–17, 158–60, 163
    funerary contribution or expense 36, 46–7, 93–4, 149–50
    loan (including *eranos*-loan) 43–4, 48, 66–7, 70, 73, 80, 100, 106–9, 157, 160–2, 165–70, 174–8, 181–3
    monumentalizing expenses 91–3
    mortgage, mortgage or security stone (*horos*) 35, 105, 168–70
    renting or leasing 33–5, 48, 58–9, 77–81, 101, 104–9
    sale or purchase 42, 45, 57–9, 62, 73, 81–3, 89, 93, 131
    treasurer (*tamias*) 36n8, 48, 66–7, 83, 90, 91, 95–6, 101, 107, 110 n.35, 114, 117, 128, 145, 154–5, 161–5, 170–2
    treasury, common fund, or collection receptacle (*thēsauros*) 117–18, 119–25, 144–5
    writing and archiving expenses 89–91
founder 3, 49, 52–74, 112
fishermen and fish-dealers at Ephesos 128–33

funerary practices including burial 4–5, 10, 17–21, 36–7, 46, 70, 77, 80, 81, 82, 93–4, 109, 125–6, 151–2, 161–2, 172–3, 181, 185

household (*see* family and household networks)

Jesus adherents 1–4, 6–8, 18–22, 34, 39–40, 52, 55, 62–3, 79–80, 116, 117, 120–1, 124, 128, 135, 142–9, 151–3, 178–86
Jews (*see* ethnic or immigrant associations, Judeans)

meeting places or buildings 36–42, 49, 54–5, 59, 71–2, 76–89, 123, 125, 126, 128–9, 141, 155, 175

mutual aid or support 3–4, 6, 106, 108, 114, 141, 151–86

plagues 34–8

'religion', problems with category of 11–12, 53 n.6
riots or civic disturbances 38–9, 41–2

social capital 6, 153–4
status, socioeconomic 15–32

temple contributions or temple tax 136–40

women in associations 23–6, 36, 100–1, 106, 125, 128, 141, 144, 189–92

www.ingramcontent.com/pod-product-compliance
Lightning Source LLC
Chambersburg PA
CBHW072107010526
44111CB00037B/2025